GCE

A2 Level for **OCR**

Health & Social Care

Series editor: Neil Moonie

www.heinemann.co.uk

✓ Free online support
✓ Useful weblinks
✓ 24 hour online ordering

01865 888058

Heinemann

Inspiring generations

Heinemann Educational Publishers
Halley Court, Jordan Hill, Oxford OX2 8EJ
Part of Harcourt Education

Heinemann is the registered trademark of Harcourt Education Limited

Text © Neil Moonie, Sylvia Aslangul, Carol Blackmore, Dee Spencer-Perkins,
Beryl Stretch, 2006

First published 2006

10 09 08 07 06
10 9 8 7 6 5 4 3

British Library Cataloguing in Publication Data is available
from the British Library on request.

10-digit ISBN: 0 435352 93 8
13-digit ISBN: 978 0 435352 93 6

Contents

Introduction

This book has been written to support students who are studying for the GCE A2 OCR award. The book is designed to support the A2 Units of the award listed below:

Unit 10	Care practice and provision (internally assessed)
Unit 11	Understanding human behaviour (externally assessed)
Unit 12	Anatomy and physiology in practice (externally assessed)
Unit 13	Child development (internally assessed)
Unit 15	Social trends (externally assessed)
Unit 16	Research methods in health and social care (internally assessed)

This book has been organised to cover each of these units in detail. Headings are designed to make it easy to follow the content of each unit and to find the information needed to support achievement. As well as providing information each unit is designed to stimulate the development of the thinking skills needed to achieve an advanced award.

Assessment

Each unit will be assessed by coursework or by an external assessment designed and marked by OCR. Detailed guidance for coursework assessment and external test requirements can be found in the unit specifications. Further guidance and specimen assessment materials may be found at OCR's web site: www.ocr.org.uk. This book has been designed to support students to achieve high grades as set out in OCR's guidance available during 2005.

Special features of this book

Throughout the text there are a number of features that are designed to encourage reflection and to help students make links between theory and practice. In particular this book has been designed to encourage a depth of learning and understanding and to encourage students to go beyond a surface level of understanding characterised by a reliance on memorising and describing issues. The special features of this book include:

What if?
Thought provoking questions or dilemmas are presented in order to encourage reflective thinking. Sometimes these questions might provide a basis for reflection involving discussion with others.

Think it over
Questions and points for reflection are presented following the presentation of important information.

Did you know?

Interesting facts or snippets of information are included to encourage reflective thinking.

Try it out

Practical activities or tasks that might be undertaken by individuals or groups are suggested. These activities may encourage a deeper level of exploration and understanding.

Scenario

We have used this term in place of the more traditional term 'case study' because the idea of people being perceived as 'cases' does not fit easily with the notion of empowerment – a key value highlighted by government policy. Scenarios are presented throughout the units to help explain the significance of theoretical ideas to Health, Social Care and Early Years settings.

Consider this

The 'consider this' feature is used at the end of each section in order to present a brief scenario followed by a series of questions. These questions are designed to encourage reflection on and analysis of the issues covered within the section.

Key concept

Because the authors believe that the development of analytic and evaluative skills requires the ability to use concepts, the authors have identified key concepts and offered a brief explanation of how these terms might be used.

Section summary

Schematic diagrams, tables or other systems for providing an overview of theoretical content are used at the end of sections in order to help clarify the theory in each section.

Assessment guidance

At the end of each unit there is a 'how you will be assessed' section that provides either sample test material for externally assessed units or outline guidance and ideas designed to help students achieve high grades when preparing internally assessed coursework. Please note that the assessment questions are designed to contribute towards practice for the candidates' assessment but are not written to mirror OCR's A2 Level questions.

Glossary

This book contains a useful glossary to provide fast reference for key terms and concepts used within the units.

References

There is a full list of references used within each unit together with useful websites at the end of each unit.

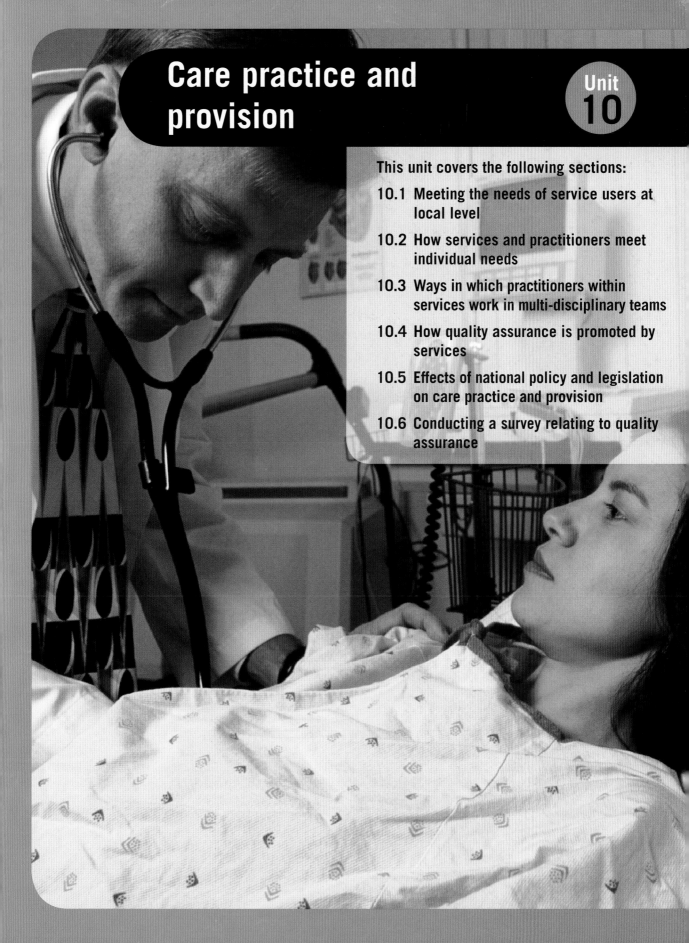

Care practice and provision

This unit covers the following sections:

10.1 Meeting the needs of service users at local level

10.2 How services and practitioners meet individual needs

10.3 Ways in which practitioners within services work in multi-disciplinary teams

10.4 How quality assurance is promoted by services

10.5 Effects of national policy and legislation on care practice and provision

10.6 Conducting a survey relating to quality assurance

Everyone who works in health, social care and early years services must understand their role in meeting service users' individual needs. However, most practitioners do not work alone, and it is important to understand the benefits of working in multi-disciplinary teams and to be aware of the significance of quality assurance in raising standards of care provided. An understanding of how national policy and legislation affect local services is also necessary.

How you will be assessed

This unit is assessed through a portfolio of work. The mark for that assessment will be the mark for this unit. You will need to undertake an investigation to show how demographic factors influence the organisation and provision of health, social care and early years services in your local area and show how two different local services meet the needs of one service user. Your evidence will include:

* information about how two demographic characteristics influence the provision of services in the area

* how, from two different services, practitioners work in multi-disciplinary teams to identify and meet the needs of one service user

* research and analysis of quality assurance methods used by the two services for the service user

* an evaluation of the effects of one national policy or one piece of legislation on care practice and how this has affected the service user.

While you are working through this unit it may be helpful to build up a resource file of materials from your local area or from national websites. Examples of material that could be useful include:

* articles in the local paper about health and social care provision

* booklets from local trusts that explain the services they provide

* leaflets from local social services that describe who has access to services and how services are organised

* news items in national papers such as *The Guardian* (which has a regular section on health and social care matters on Wednesdays, and more detailed information on a related website)

* articles from *Community Care* – this magazine often explains how national policy is being organised and has a useful website.

A list of relevant websites is provided at the end of this unit.

Section 1: Meeting the needs of service users at local level

Care practice and provision is complex and ever-changing. You need to understand the concepts of 'needs' at a local and individual level, and how effective care practice and provision aims to respond to changing needs and priorities.

Services work together to identify and meet local needs. You need to understand how local planning is influenced by a variety of factors, including local demographic characteristics and trends and national targets and priorities.

Health and social services have been traditionally provided by three sectors, but informal care is also essential to the provision of care, so there are four sectors providing care.

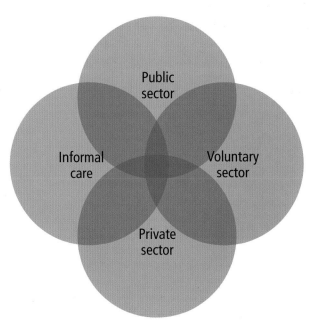

FIGURE 10.1 *The four sectors providing health and social care*

The public or statutory sector

This sector includes the NHS (National Health Service), which provides services in hospitals and in the community, and local social services organised by local councils.

Statutory services are funded by central and local government through taxation and national insurance contributions, and are not organised on the basis of profit.

Private services

Private health and social care organisations are run to make a profit, and provide a range of services, including private hospitals, private residential homes, and private nurseries.

Voluntary services

These services are provided by voluntary (or non-profit making) organisations. They are usually registered as charities and may provide services to particular client groups. For example, Age Concern provides day centres for older people, Mencap provides a range of services for clients with learning difficulties, and the National Children's Home (NCH) provides support for children and families.

Informal services

These services are provided outside the other three sectors and are usually unpaid. Examples of informal care could be a local church lunch club, a baby sitting group or family members caring for older relatives. All four sectors work together at a local level.

Mixed economy of care

The provision of health and social care services by a combination of these sectors is often referred to as a 'mixed economy of care'.

> **Key concept**
>
> *Mixed economy of care:* this term refers to the provision of care from a range of service providers.

The Conservative government of the 1980s felt that introducing competition between service providers would result in cost-effective, high-quality services. For example, instead of most services being provided by the local social services, these services would be commissioned from the private or voluntary sector, and social services would concentrate on providing services to clients who had complex needs. This approach is still the basis of health and social care policy today, with more and more services being provided by the private or voluntary sectors.

Organisation of the provision and commissioning of services may be changed in the future. In 2005 the role of PCTs as commissioners and providers was being scrutinised by the Department of Health.

With the NHS and Community Care Act (1990) hospital trusts were able to arrange contracts with private agencies, particularly for catering and cleaning, instead of employing people directly to do this work.

Since 1990 there has been a great deal of legislation affecting the provision of health and social care services, these are covered in Section 5.

Local demographic characteristics and trends

Services need to identify the population they serve in terms of numbers and age range. Services use census figures for much of the information, but will also use birth rates,

Mixed Economy of Care

A local Primary Care Trust (PCT) and local council work together to identify the characteristics of the population, and develop a plan to meet local needs. Social care and health care services are developing 'joint working' through partnership, and each body will take the lead for certain aspects of the plan.

The PCT takes the lead for health and it will do this through improving local health services and reducing health inequalities. The council may take the lead in housing and the provision of social care services in the community. Both agencies would work together on child protection issues.

The role of the voluntary sector is being increasingly developed through agreements called 'compacts' with the local PCTs and the local councils. These agreements ensure that the voluntary sector is involved in planning and delivering services. In addition to the development of 'compacts', partnership agreements are the basis for agreeing local plans for health and social care services. Local partnership agreements are required by government. The voluntary sector is seen as having a good understanding of local issues and can often relate to 'hard to reach' groups that may be overlooked by mainstream services. Many excluded people feel more comfortable contacting a voluntary organisation than contacting social services. Voluntary organisations also offer 'best value' service, as their costs can be reduced through the use of volunteers, but they also employ project workers and other paid staff to negotiate contracts with the council or the health trusts.

death rates and other data to identify trends. Some councils do their own research. In one area, a survey was conducted by the local council to establish the need for housing and whether people were content with their current housing. Housing is a key issue for all councils. In areas where there is a high proportion of older people, the council may need to increase the availability of sheltered housing. There are also implications for the council if there are a large proportion of older home owners who live alone and cannot afford to maintain their properties. For example, one council operates a programme called 'Staying Put' where older people are encouraged to remain safely in their own homes (if that is their wish) by offering grants or loans to help them maintain their property. The birth rate is also significant when planning service provision for children. For example, if the birth rate continues to fall, fewer places will be needed in nursery and primary schools.

National standards, targets and objectives

Many national policy initiatives have influenced the provision of health care, and this is discussed in more detail in Section 5. An example that has affected all sectors of health and social care provision is the National Service Framework (NSF) for Older People. This requires health and social care statutory services to reach targets on certain aspects of care for older people. The NSF for Older People has eight Standards, which can be found on the Department of Health website.

The NSF is a ten-year programme (started in 2001) that covers all older people whether they are in hospital, in residential care or living in their own homes. It is monitored by the Healthcare Commission. Standard 5 of the NSF relates to stroke and has the targets that must be reached. By April 2002, every general hospital caring for people with stroke should have had plans to develop a specialist stroke unit to be in place by April 2004.

Think it over

Does your local hospital have a specialist stroke unit with a stroke specialist in charge? Some hospitals have nurses who are stroke consultants who work on these specialist wards. In a stroke unit there should be a multi-disciplinary team that includes speech therapists, physiotherapists, dieticians and clinicians.

NHS targets that have an impact on local services include the requirement for people to be able to see a GP within 48 hours of contacting the surgery, and the target of four hours for patients to be seen in hospital A&E departments. These targets all impact on the provision of services and the organisation of health and social care staff. The extent to which these targets are met will be discussed in the annual reports of hospital trusts and PCTs so that information on progress is publicly available.

The influences of local demography on service planning

The health needs of the local population

The local PCT is responsible for identifying the health needs in their area. The Director of Health in the PCT produces an annual report in which the health needs of the population are clearly stated and the health plan to meet these needs is produced.

Demographic influences on planning could include:

* the proportion of disabled people in the area
* the age profile of the local population
* unemployment levels
* the number of single-parent families
* the number of older people in the population.

Communities are assessed using information in each of the following domains:

* income
* employment
* health and disability

* education, skills, training
* barriers to housing and services
* crime
* living environment.

This information contributes to an overall score for each community. The lower the score, the higher the level of deprivation.

The characteristics of the most deprived wards in England include:

* income deprivation
* unemployment
* children living in poverty
* older people living in poverty
* a high proportion of black and minority ethnic groups
* poor accessibility to housing and services
* a higher proportion of lone parents
* a higher proportion of people with no car
* high crime rates
* poor health including long-term illness and disability.

* high teenage pregnancy rates
* low birth weights of babies
* unemployment or unskilled work leading to low incomes in many households
* high smoking rates among deprived groups including pregnant women
* increasing obesity
* many groups are socially excluded.

Key concept

Deprivation index: the Indices of Multiple Deprivation 2004 were produced by the Office of the Deputy Prime Minister (ODPM) and are used as a basis to explore community disadvantage.

What if?

If you were the Director of Public Health of this PCT, what measures would you put in place to support people who are affected by these problems?

SCENARIO

PCT annual health report

'The PCT is responsible for the people in the area and this includes people who are not registered with a doctor. The population includes people who are homeless, refugees and asylum seekers as well as those who live in long-term care.'   [Extract]

The report goes on to identify the key problems in the area. Many of these problems arise from socio-economic factors, and a deprivation index is used to identify those areas locally which are most at risk from poor health.

In the PCT report the following issues are seen as a problem locally:

* high infant mortality rate in babies born to mothers under 20 years of age

The Director of Public Health of this PCT recommended the following actions:

* to reduce inequalities in determinants of health by increasing access to services and increasing local provision of services to hard to reach groups – e.g. drop-in clinics for refugees and older people
* to develop and implement a tobacco control policy
* to develop and implement a childhood obesity strategy
* to develop an annual programme identifying local health needs
* to lead local action to reduce unemployment and to improve the retention of employees.

In a Sure Start Centre in the area, the team is trying to address some of these issues in various ways.

FIGURE 10.2 *Services offered at a Sure Start Centre*

How local plans are developed and produced

Local delivery plans (LDPs)

Councils and health trusts must be able to estimate how many people may need their services. Demographic data, including the age and disability structure of the local population, is reviewed by the local council and the PCT. The two organisations work together to produce a Local Delivery Plan which identifies local needs and plans the provision of suitable services to meet them. A strategy group (usually of senior managers) monitors the LDP and reviews and reports its progress to the PCT and to the local council.

Try it out

In your local area there should be a similar Partnership Board. They will have their own website – usually via the website of the local council. Look up the website and see what the priorities are for your local area.

Key concept

Stakeholders: a broad term used to describe everyone who has an interest in the development of policies and services in a local area.

We could say that all the members of the partnership group are stakeholders, but not all stakeholders have an equal amount of influence on the decisions made. Stakeholders have an important role in raising issues and voicing the concerns of certain groups in the area.

Producing plans for delivering local health and social care services

Most plans cover a period of five years. As Table 10.1 shows, the action required and the lead organisation responsible are identified, and the aims and the timescale are clearly stated. Plans are the result of detailed consultation with stakeholders who report to a steering committee which then decides upon the action required. This is then agreed with the board.

Partnerships	Wellwood Locality Committee, Public Health Working Group, Wellwood Borough Council
Existing Plans	Wellwood Locality Business Plan, Health Inequalities Report, Wellwood Borough Council Corporate Action Plan, Local Development Plan for the Wellwood PCT: Supporting People Strategy.

COMMUNITY STRATEGY PRIORITY	COMMUNITY STRATEGY ACTION	PARTNERS (LEAD PARTNER IN BOLD TEXT)	TARGET	TIMESCALE
Address Health Inequalities	Address health inequalities in mainstream policy and area-based initiatives	**Public Health Working Group** The Wellwood Partnership PCT	Identify 2–3 cross-cutting priorities with sign-up from all organisations to reduce health inequalities	March 2006
	Target interventions at vulnerable groups at greater risk of inequalities	**Public Health Working Group** PCT Mental Health Partnership Board LBS Voluntary Sector	Identify one vulnerable group and devise and implement an action plan to improve their health	March 2006
Develop Preventative Health	**Proposed Target** To improve the health of children and young people by increasing the number participating in physical activity	**PCT** Wellwood Borough Council Learning for Life CEI	The number of 5–16 year-olds participating in an average of 2 hours of high quality P.E. and school sport a week within and outside of the curriculum during one complete school year	N/A
Integration and modernisation of health and social care	Integration of Health and Social Care for older people's services and children and young people's services	**Wellwood Borough Council** Voluntary Sector PCT	Integration of services to be significantly established	April 2006
	Develop a jointly agreed model of community-based care to support the work of developing Local Care Hospitals	**Wellwood Borough Council** Voluntary Sector PCT	Agree model Implementation of community model Full model	October 2005 2008 2010

TABLE 10.1 *A partnership plan to improve health and well-being*

SCENARIO

Ashley Spa

Ashley Spa is an urban area in the West Midlands. 375,000 people live in this area. The data shows the following profile:

* a high rate of teenage pregnancies – the rate of pregnancies in young women aged 16–17 years is 78 per 1,000

* most hospital admissions relate to chronic conditions such as respiratory and cardiac (heart) problems

* there is a high proportion of older people living on their own

* there is a large ethnic minority population, mainly of Bangladeshi and Pakistani origin

* there are 3,000 people registered as disabled

* unemployment has increased recently with the closure of a large manufacturing firm.

The local partnership board is meeting to discuss the key issues in the area and the aims for future service planning. This stakeholder group consists of 34 representatives from social services, local health services (hospital and community), the council, voluntary sector, youth groups, faith and belief groups, the police, schools, businesses, leisure, and the residents' association. The group meets to discuss the partnership plans five times a year and progress is covered in an annual report.

The commissioning of services

Health and social care services develop a commissioning strategy for all the services they provide, you may be able to access an example from your local council. Like most plans for health and social care, these strategies have a five-year programme. The service providers (the health and social care providers) will consult with professionals, users and voluntary organisations before developing a commissioning strategy, which stakeholders will be asked to comment on.

SCENARIO

'Seamless' service

A local council has decided to develop a strategy for commissioning services for older people, as part of the integration of health and social care services so that a 'seamless' service can be developed that will be more effective for both the service user and the provider. Many government policies influence the development of local plans and have a focus on promoting independence for older people. In developing the strategy the council went through the following stages:

* they identified key aspects of the population, related to age, ethnic background, health needs, and the number of people identified as carers

* they consulted with key stakeholders including service providers, professional groups, users and carers, and collected responses from these groups

* they predicted possible trends in the demand for services between 2007 and 2012

* they mapped current service provision, identifying the organisations that were providing the service and the client group being supported

* they reviewed current transport provision.

From this data, the strategic group was able to make a prediction about future demand for services and resources, including both the finances needed and staff required.

The report concluded that the commissioning service will take into account:

* the need to promote independence of older people and maintain them in their own homes

* the need to develop a range and choice of services that are person-centred and reflect the needs of individuals

continued on next page

* the use of direct payments when possible to encourage people to choose the services they use

* the importance of quality issues alongside the need for cost-effective services

* the services would be commissioned from a range of providers, including the private sector as well as the voluntary and statutory sector.

Key concept

Direct payment system: a system by which payments can be made directly to the service user in order for them to purchase care.

The process of monitoring and evaluating service provision

Monitoring and evaluating service provision is discussed in more detail in Section 4. Apart from outside bodies such as the Health Care Commission and the Commission for Social Care Inspection, all organisations have monitoring and review built into their annual review of services, including voluntary organisations.

SCENARIO

Age concern branch

A local Age Concern offers a range of services, shown in Figure 10.3. Each project, or service, offered has a project manager who runs the service and provides regular reports to the trustees on progress. This report includes the numbers of people using the service and satisfaction surveys that have been done with clients. One of the projects is an advocacy service for older people. In the most recent report, the number of people using the service has reduced, although those who have used the service were happy with the help they received.

continued on next page

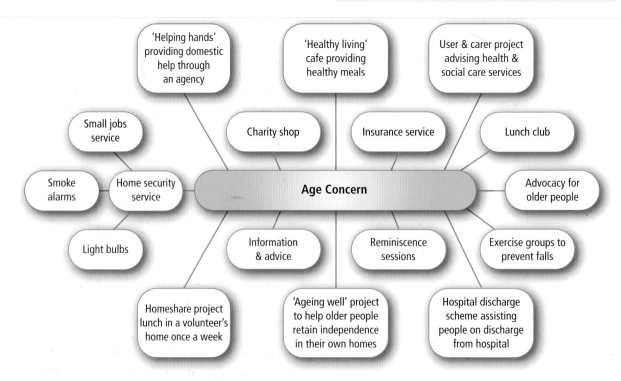

FIGURE 10.3 *The range of services offered by an Age Concern branch*

As a result of monitoring the performance of the project, it was decided to advertise the scheme more widely locally, and that leaflets about the service should be given to health and social care workers to raise awareness. The project leader visited some sheltered housing complexes and local clubs to tell people about the service. As a result, the numbers using the service increased.

Developing services

When developing any planned service provision, you need to ask the following questions.

* Is there a need for the service?

* How will the service be publicised?

* How will it be monitored and reviewed?

* Who will deliver the service?

* Where will the service take place?

SCENARIO

Retinal screening service

A PCT planned and set up a retinal screening service for people with diabetes so that any visual problems could be identified quickly. In the initial monthly figures it was noted that many people who had been sent appointments did not attend. People who had not attended were contacted and asked why they had not come to the centre. The results showed that transport was a problem as the centre was not easily accessible by public transport. By working with volunteer drivers, this problem was resolved.

Monitoring and reviewing services can help to ensure that any service meets the needs of the community it serves, but it is difficult to identify all possible problems that may occur. The retinal service was needed in the area, but the location caused access problems for patients. This problem was identified through the monitoring process.

Examples of NHS services provided locally

Although health and social care services are working more closely together there are still certain services that are provided by the NHS.

Secondary health services are based in hospitals and provide medical and surgical care, as well as A&E departments.

Primary health services are based in the community and provided by members of the primary health care team from GP practices. Members of the primary health care team include GPs, practice nurses, district nurses, health visitors, and community midwives. The reorganisation of primary care is taking place and PCTs are now also responsible for providing dental and pharmacy services. Community podiatrists, physiotherapists, speech and language therapists and occupational therapists also work in the community and are employed by the PCT.

Community care

This is provided by a range of providers. People can either be looked after in their own homes (domiciliary care), in residential care, or in intermediate care.

Key concept

Intermediate care: services designed to assist the patient in their discharge from hospital towards independence, or to prevent admission to hospital. These services can be provided locally in rehabilitation beds in a range of settings, including private nursing homes, or in the patient's own home.

A mix of practitioners from health and social care provide support in the community, as the following scenario shows.

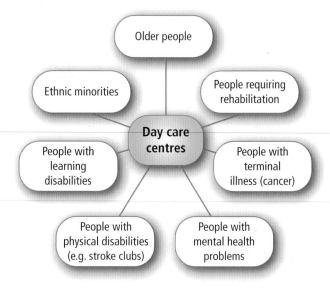

FIGURE 10.4 *The client groups who may attend day care centres*

Day care centres

Day care centres provide for a number of client groups, as shown in Figure 10.4.

Some centres are provided by the NHS – for example, day hospitals attached to mental health units, and some are provided by social services – for example, day centres for people with learning disabilities who also receive some vocational training.

Many centres are provided by voluntary organisations – such as the Stroke Association or Age Concern. Services at these centres may include hairdressing, bathing, chiropody, physiotherapy, and speech therapy. Apart from the service provided, day care services provide social support for people who could be isolated in the community.

Pre-schools and nurseries

Government policy has focused on the need to increase the provision of child care and pre-school places in the community. The range of providers of pre-school care includes private nurseries, as well as nurseries attached to infant schools and crèches attached to work places. Child care providers, including childminders, must be registered with The Office for Standards in Education (OFSTED) and are inspected regularly.

Summary

In this section we have looked at factors that affect the provision of health and social care in local areas. These factors include the population profile of an area, and the range of needs of different groups. We have discussed how services are planned, commissioned and evaluated.

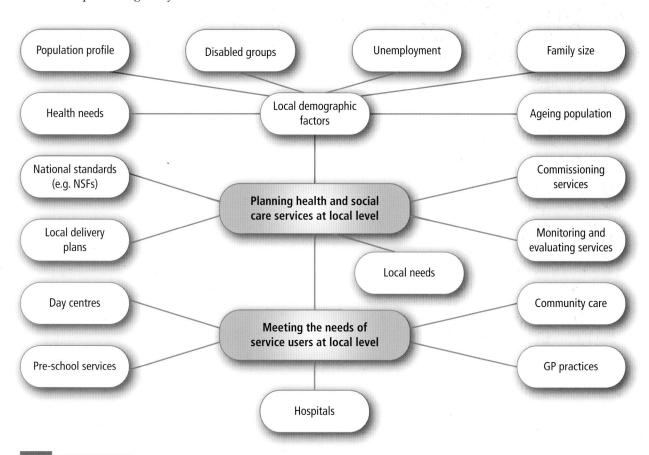

Consider this

A network of Healthy Living Centres (HLCs) is being developed in the UK. The aim is to promote health by helping people of all ages to maximise their health and well-being. HLCs involve a range of partnerships at local level.

An HLC has been set up in a deprived area in South London. A steering group has been formed to plan and provide a range of activities.

Membership of the steering group includes:

* members of the local council

* members of the local church

* a worker from the local Health Promotion Unit

* local residents

* representatives of the voluntary sector

* a community nurse.

This HLC is partly funded by the national lottery and partly by the local council.

continued on next page

Certain activities were identified as meeting the needs of the community and the current programme includes provision for the children, parents and older people. These include:

* a toy library
* a play centre
* a mother and toddler group
* numeracy and literacy workshops for adults
* parenting skills courses
* behaviour management sessions for parents with very active children

* healthy eating courses
* exercise classes for older people.

Criticisms of this approach have been that it is 'top down', rather than 'bottom up'.

1. How could the steering group ensure that marginalised groups are included and that all members of the community have their say?

2. What sort of evidence would you use to evaluate the success of the HLC?

Section 2: How services and practitioners meet individual needs

Individual service users have a range of needs which must be met, including physical, intellectual, emotional and social needs. In a care assessment the nurse or care worker identifies the client's range of needs and develops a plan to meet these needs. Care assessments are covered in detail in Section 3. This section covers a range of approaches used in health and social care to help services and practitioners meet the needs of individuals.

Preventative and treatment approach

The saying 'prevention is better than cure' certainly applies to modern approaches to health and social care. For example, preventing disease through immunisation has had a dramatic effect on the level of childhood illnesses.

Treatment of diseases at an early stage can reduce death rates and improve outcomes. Although prevention and treatment of disease is an important aspect of modern medicine, this medical approach may raise possible difficulties.

Disabled people, older people and those on low incomes may have difficulty accessing healthy diets including fresh fruit and vegetables. Studies of young mothers who continue to smoke, indicate that smoking helps them cope with their problems. Anxieties about the possible harmful

Anxieties about immunisation may affect take-up of preventative treatments

> ### Key concepts
>
> *Primary prevention:* changing lifestyle or taking other actions to make diseases less likely. Stopping smoking and eating a healthy diet fits this model. Although immunisation isn't a lifestyle change, it is also primary prevention.
>
> *Secondary prevention:* identifying disease at an early stage through screening, such as for cancer.

effects of immunisation may affect the take-up of 'jabs'. The social and psychological needs of individuals may conflict with the possible benefits of primary prevention approaches.

In secondary prevention, many patients find screening procedures, such as cervical smear tests and breast screening, uncomfortable and painful. Preventative programmes may increase levels of anxiety about possible cancer, so although they may identify physical or medical needs, they may not support the patient's emotional and intellectual needs. Many treatments for cancer have unpleasant side effects and the patient may prefer to have a better quality of life and forego the treatment.

Health and social care workers should be aware that service users have social, intellectual and emotional needs and they should be supported to make an informed choice about any treatment offered.

The holistic approach

The holistic approach takes account of the whole person and does not just focus on their disease. If someone has diabetes, this can be made worse by stress and other factors in their life, and so taking a holistic approach can help ensure that these factors are considered and addressed as well as the physical symptoms of diabetes.

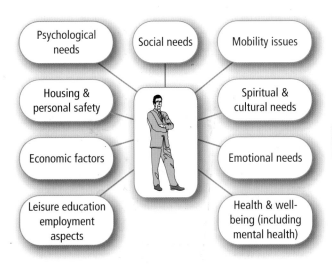

FIGURE 10.5 The holistic approach to assessing individual needs

This approach covers all aspects of a person; social, mental, emotional, spiritual and physical.

In traditional medicine, people were seen in terms of their diagnosis; e.g. 'the appendix in bed number 12'. In training health and care workers nowadays a person is always considered as an individual rather than a diagnosis. When someone enters hospital or is referred to a care service, a detailed assessment is made of their physical, intellectual, emotional and social needs (see the FACS approach, page 21).

The empowerment approach

Empowerment means giving people the opportunity to make decisions and not treating them as passive receivers of health and social care services, but helping them become active participants in the care planning process and in decision-making. Patients and clients need to be given access to information so that they can make an informed choice. Service users, carers and service providers can all benefit from the empowerment approach.

Advocacy

Advocacy is an important aspect of empowerment. It developed as a result of changes in policy – particularly related to the closure of long-stay hospitals in the 1980s when people with learning disabilities were discharged into the community. These people needed access to advocates who could support them and help them get the services they needed. Closure of large mental hospitals was another factor as advocates for this group were also needed. Recently, advocacy has become a more generalised approach covering a range of issues and client groups.

> **Key concept**
>
> *Advocacy:* supporting people to speak for themselves and:
>
> * being on the person's side when they want to say something
>
> * helping people to understand their rights and making sure these are respected
>
> * providing information and support so choices can be made and problems resolved, e.g. so that a person is able to give informed consent to an operation.

SCENARIO
Advocacy partners

Advocacy Partners is a registered charity based in the south of Britain. It provides advocacy to people with learning and physical disabilities as well as older people. The charity, set up in 1981, was the first independent advocacy scheme in Britain.

In the annual report the director writes about how the organisation supports people to make the changes they want by:

* making time – getting to know the person's preferences, views and needs

* listening closely to what the person is saying

* taking the person's side

* being person-centred – concentrating on the person as an individual

* being clear about what they can do – there are some things that cannot be changed or cannot be achieved and it is important that the client isn't given false hope or promises.

A range of short- or long-term advocacy approaches are available.

Here are some examples of the work this organisation has done recently.

SCENARIO 1
Edwina

Edwina (aged 80) could no longer use her bathroom due to the effects of severe arthritis. Social services felt unable to make the necessary changes, but instead offered to provide staff to take her to have a bath at a day centre. Edwina valued her independence and privacy. Her advocate helped her to challenge the decision and she now has a new 'wet room' in her home. Edwina is really pleased and feels safe and independent. Social services have also been saved the continued cost of a support service.

SCENARIO 2
Alex

Alex (aged 45) has severe learning disabilities and he was recently diagnosed with a life-threatening illness. His consultant concluded that Alex should not have the necessary surgery, as his quality of life would remain poor due to his disability. Shona, Alex's advocate, worked closely with his support staff and the consultant. Eventually she was able to persuade the consultant that if Alex was able to express himself he would explain the many things he enjoyed and that made his life pleasurable despite his illness. Surgery was carried out and Alex has made a full recovery.

Think it over

Look at the examples and think about the implications for both the service user and the service provider.

The behavioural approach

In this approach health practitioners try to influence the health of the patient or client by encouraging them to modify their behaviour. This approach would include campaigns and other tactics to encourage people to adopt healthy behaviours, such as:

* stop smoking campaigns

* encouraging people to do more exercise

* increasing awareness about factors that affect health.

Try it out

In your local Health Promotion Unit you will find many examples of leaflets encouraging people to adopt healthy lifestyles. The staff from the unit visit schools, colleges and clubs to encourage people in this way. Perhaps you could mount your own display in your college and ask people if what they see would affect their behaviour. Changing behaviour is very difficult, as we have seen with the failure of stop smoking and safe sex campaigns.

are ways of identifying the physical, intellectual, emotional and social needs of service users. We have looked at how prevention can reduce illness and accidents, and how different approaches or models of health and care can be used to help meet the individual needs of service users.

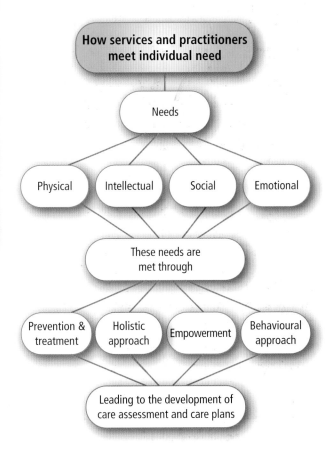

Summary

In this section we have seen that the needs of individual service users must be recognised and assessed to provide appropriate services. Users and carers must be actively involved in the care-planning process. Individual care plans

continued on next page

3. Jatinder Khan takes her six-month-old son Jamil to the GP as he has a skin rash around his neck and face. The GP diagnoses eczema and gives Jatinder a steroid cream to put on. He doesn't ask her about Jamal's lifestyle or diet. He seems anxious to finish surgery as he is running late.

4. Margaret is in her 60s. She has arthritis in her knee which is getting progressively worse. Sometimes it is so bad she cannot walk down the road. She takes painkillers but they don't have much effect. The GP explains she could refer Margaret to the hospital for an opinion from the orthopaedic surgeon. Recent X-rays show that the arthritis has become much worse and a total knee replacement may be needed in the future, so that Margaret can be more active. Margaret is very anxious about a possible operation. The GP gives her a leaflet about joint replacement and arranges for her to have physiotherapy to strengthen her muscles. The GP suggest that she comes back to the surgery once she has completed the physiotherapy and they can discuss what may be the best way forward. The GP tells Margaret she does not have to have the operation if she doesn't want to.

5. Sam and Dom are both 19 and really enjoy going out on a Friday night with their mates. They drink about nine pints of lager each. Sam's mother is a nurse and she is concerned about her son's drinking. She gets him some leaflets about the dangers of drinking alcohol and tells him how she has seen patients with severe liver damage because of their drinking.

Look again at the different models and list the advantages and disadvantages of each, for both service user and service provider. For example, treatment can have a rapid result but the patient may feel they have been pushed into a particular course of action without really understanding why.

Section 3: Ways in which practitioners within services work in multi-disciplinary teams

This section discusses how the roles of practitioners in health, social care and early years have changed in recent years, including the increasing use of multi-disciplinary teams working together to identify and meet the needs of service users.

Key concept

Multi-disciplinary teams (MD teams): teams of workers from different specialist professions who provide care for patients or clients. Multi-disciplinary teams work in the community or in the hospital. They can work with a particular client group, such as children or people with mental health problems.

SCENARIO

Multi-disciplinary working

In a Sure Start Circle there is a central office where all the team work together to support children and families in the area.

Referrals to the team may come from school nurses, voluntary groups or GPs, or families can self-refer. Sara is the team leader. She is a social worker and the nominated Child Protection Officer for the centre. She organises team meetings to discuss particular concerns. Members of the team have regular training, as child protection issues are constantly developing. The midwife on the team advises pregnant women and encourages them to stop smoking. The health visitor visits families and records any issues of concern. The family support worker visits families at home and offers advice. She also runs parenting groups, and gives advice on benefits. There are several Tamil families on the estate so the team runs a drop-in coffee morning to advise families on health and other issues. An interpreter attends these sessions.

continued on next page

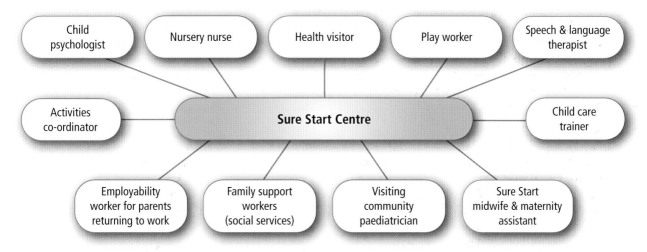

FIGURE 10.6 *The members of the Sure Start team*

Sara feels that Sure Start multi-disciplinary teams are making a great difference to the lives of families and children in deprived areas. Families know where to turn to for help, rather than being confused about which agency to contact. This kind of teamwork reduces bureaucracy for service users and for the team, as service users have to supply information only once and it is centrally stored. Team-working also means service users get quicker access to a wider range of services. Working in a team has benefits for the staff as well, as they can discuss problems with colleagues and refer clients quickly to receive the support they need.

Recent changes in practitioner roles

Until recently, health and social care workers worked in isolation from each other and there seemed to be a clash of cultures between health and social care. Health professionals addressed clinical needs and social care workers tended to look at social needs, including offering advice on managing incomes and applying for benefits.

With the development of the single assessment process, both health and social care workers have been trained to assess clinical and social needs, although there is often a separate financial assessment by a finance officer from the council. Single assessments are being developed for other

Key concept

The single assessment process: a key health or social care worker assesses all the needs of the service user. This may be undertaken in one session, depending on the health of the client.

groups, including children through the Common Assessment Framework (CAF) for children (see page 20).

The following needs are assessed:

* health and well-being (including mental health)
* personal and domestic care routines
* housing and personal safety
* spiritual and cultural needs
* social support and relationships
* finance
* leisure, education and employment
* transport.

If there is a recognised unpaid carer, their needs are also assessed.

Other changes to practitioner roles

Health care assistants are taking on many of the roles associated with registered nurses – such as running blood pressure clinics – although they are still supervised. Nursery nurses perform some developmental checks previously undertaken by health visitors. These changes are a result of a shortage of certain trained staff, increased technology, and policy requirements. GPs are increasingly performing minor surgery and developing their skills in specialist areas such as dermatology (skin problems) and musculo-skeletal problems so patients can be treated locally and need not travel to hospital.

Multi-disciplinary therapy teams in the community

There have been examples of changes in the organisation of therapy services such as physiotherapy, occupational therapy, speech and language therapy. In the past, therapists visited a range of clients; for example, a stroke patient, a child, and someone recovering from an accident. In order to use therapists more effectively they will be grouped into teams, with each team focussed on a particular client group such as children, rehabilitation, or intermediate care. Teams will consist of a therapist from each discipline. The therapy multi-disciplinary team assesses the patient and draws up a care plan. A key worker (now called the lead professional) who is responsible for delivering and monitoring the care plan is identified.

Children's issues related to assessment in the community

Services for children in health and social care are often managed differently, because they are seen as particularly vulnerable and their needs may change rapidly. Child protection issues are a key concern and form the rationale for how services are organised. With increased integration between health and social care services and education, multi-agency working is more likely. A child will be assigned a lead professional who could be from health, social services or education.

The Common Assessment Framework (CAF) for Children

This is a standardised approach to assessing the needs of babies, children and young people. It was developed in 2005 from the Green Paper *Every Child Matters* (2003). Copies of the framework are on the website (www.everychildmatters.gov.uk/key-documents). The professional uses a checklist

> **Stage 1**
> **Preparation**
> *Talk to child/young person and their parent(s). A pre-assessment checklist may be used. You may decide a fuller assessment is not needed at this time, but if you decide it is appropriate you seek the agreement of the child/young person. You may talk to colleagues.*

> **Stage 2**
> **Discussion**
> *Complete the assessment with child, parent(s), or family. Use information from all sources. You agree the actions that the service and the family will deliver. You record this.*

> **Stage 3**
> **Service delivery**
> *You deliver on your actions. You refer to other services, depending on the needs of the child. You monitor progress. If a range of agencies are used, you identify a lead professional who is the contact at all times.*

FIGURE 10.7 *The stages of the common assessment framework*

to decide whether a common assessment is needed. The parents are involved throughout the process.

The CAF is a useful way of developing closer collaboration between health, education and social services. As with other multi-disciplinary teams working with one client, there will be a lead professional who will:

* be a single point of contact for everyone involved

* develop a care plan

* take responsibility for ensuring that appropriate services are delivered

* review progress

* reduce overlap from other practitioners.

All multi-disciplinary teams work to improve the service for the client by team work and good communication. Team members also feel supported by the team.

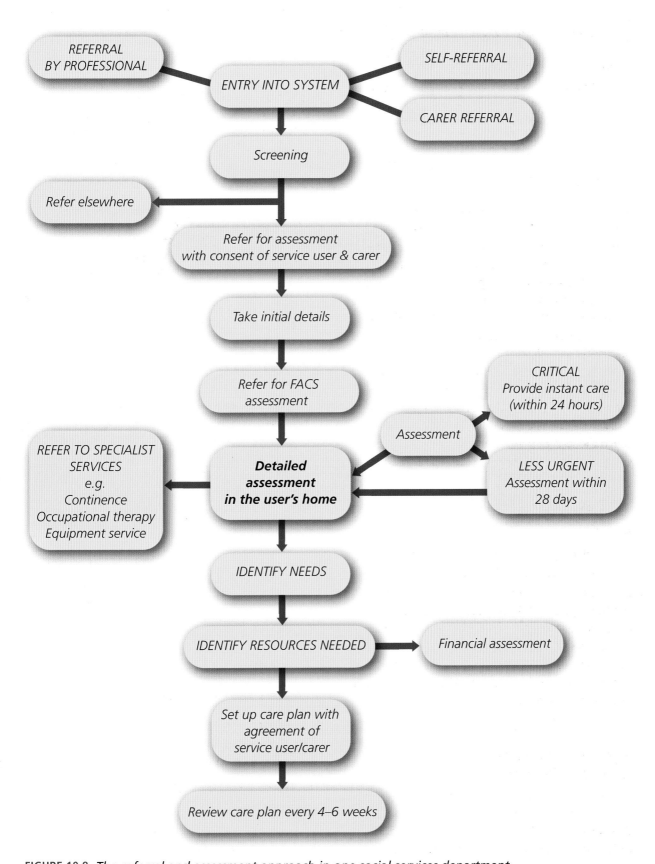

FIGURE 10.8 *The referral and assessment approach in one social services department*

Assessment of need and the care-management cycle

In all multi-disciplinary teams, assessment forms part of the care-management cycle.

The initial assessment of needs and the care-management cycle in health and social care in the community

Providers of health and social care services have to organise services to meet each individual's unique needs. This involves three important aspects:

✱ the initial assessment of needs

✱ the care plan

✱ assessment of service provision – monitoring and reviewing of care plans.

It is crucial to involve service users and carers in this process. Care planning should be needs-led and benefit the service user's health and well-being. If there is a carer, their needs should be included in the care planning.

The process of care planning in the community

With the development of closer working between health and social care in the community, care planning has become more streamlined. With the development of IT systems, many care assessments are emailed to practitioners involved in the person's care. Previously, service users were often asked the same questions by different professionals as part of the care-planning process. Multi-disciplinary working should help prevent this.

Care planning based on the needs of the individual was seen as a cornerstone of the NHS and Community Care Act (1990). However, with increasing demands on the service (partly caused by the increasing numbers of older people in the population) social services have had to develop criteria which determine who will receive care services and how these will be delivered. In 2003, the Department of Health produced a document called *Fair Access to Care Services: Guidance on Eligibility Criteria for Adult Social Care*. Fair Access to Care Services is often abbreviated to FACS. Under FACS guidance, councils should assess an individual's presenting needs and prioritise them. An assessment of the risks that may occur if care is not provided will be made. Councils should focus on those in greatest immediate- or longer-term need. The guidance should provide a more consistent approach to needs assessment in all parts of England and Wales.

Referral for assessment of need

In social services there has been an increase in joint-working with the local PCT; a person coming for assessment may be referred to the PCT for health services. In most areas, a single phone number is given as the initial contact number and the caller (whether a health or social care professional, a service user or a carer) will be referred to the appropriate service.

FIGURE 10.9 *The care-management cycle*

Assessment of need

With more joined-up working between health and social care, the lead professional could either be a health worker or a social worker. They assess the needs of the user, normally visiting them at their home, in hospital if they are about to be discharged, or in a rehabilitation unit. Although the guidance focuses on the user, carers should also be involved in the assessment process.

Under FACS, eligibility criteria for service are graded into four bands, which describe the seriousness of the risk if needs are not addressed.

The bands are as follows:

* *Critical:* this includes situations when life is or will be threatened, serious abuse or neglect has occurred or may occur, or serious health problems have developed.

* *Substantial:* this covers less critical factors, but there is still a substantial risk to the person if care is not delivered.

* *Moderate* and *Low:* bands which have a lower level of risk.

The full details of FACS are available on the Department of Health website (www.dh.gov.uk/seg/facs).

When FACS was first introduced, councils had to consult carers and users and ask for comments on the proposed bands. Many carers felt that reducing the services available to people in the lower bands would increase the strain on carers. The condition of clients could therefore deteriorate so that they would move to the substantial and critical bands and the demand for services could increase still further.

The rest of the care-management cycle

Once the assessment has been carried out, the process continues:

* *Deciding eligibility for service:* do service users fit criteria used by social services?

Q	No need	Critical		Substantial		Moderate		Low	
1	☐	Life is/will be threatened.	☐						
2	☐	Significant health problems have/will develop.	☐						
3	☐	There is/will be immediate little choice about vital aspects of the immediate environment.	☐	Is/will be only partial choice and control over the immediate environment.	☐				
4	☐	Serious abuse/neglect has/will occur.	☐	Abuse or neglect has occurred/will occurred.	☐				
5	☐	Is/will be an inability to carry out vital personal care or domestic routines.	☐	Is/will be an inability to carry out the majority of personal care and domestic routines.	☐	Is/will be an inability to carry out several personal care or domestic routines.	☐	Is/will be an inability to carry out one or two personal care or domestic tasks.	☐
6	☐	Vital involvement in work, education or learning will not be sustained.	☐	Involvement in many aspects of work education or learning cannot/will not be sustained.	☐	Involvement in several aspects of work, education or learning cannot/will not be sustained.	☐	Involvement in one or two aspects of work, education or learning cannot/will not be sustained.	☐
7	☐	Vital social support systems and relationships cannot/will not be sustained.	☐	The majority of social support systems and relationships cannot/will not be sustained.	☐	Several social support systems and relationships cannot/will not be sustained.	☐	One or two social support systems and relationships cannot/will not be sustained.	☐
8	☐	Vital family and other social roles and responsibilities cannot/will not be undertaken.	☐	The majority of family and other social roles and responsibilities cannot/will not be undertaken.	☐	Several family and other social roles and relationships cannot/will not be undertaken.	☐	One or two family and other social roles and responsibilities cannot/will not be sustained.	☐

FIGURE 10.10 *Areas covered in a FACS assessment*

* *Drawing up a care plan:* who will do what and when. This may include targets such as the date by which a person may achieve a particular activity, e.g. dressing themselves independently.

* *Identifying services to be provided:* the person and/or their carer should have contact details of everyone involved in their care.

* *Review of the care plan and service provision:* may take place three months after the start of the plan, or less frequently depending on the situation. A sudden change in the health or mobility of the person may increase frequency.

* *Equipment acquired for a service user:* should be reviewed on an annual basis.

Figure 10.11 is an example of a care plan for a patient who has been discharged home after a knee replacement.

A recent development in health and social care has been the organisation of Integrated Community Equipment Services (ICES), when the local PCT and the council jointly organise the provision of equipment that is easily accessible in the community.

The role of service users and carers

In all stages of care planning, service users and carers should participate: the patient or client is central to the care-planning process. In some cases the client may not understand the process and may need assistance from an advocate.

Effective care planning should assist both the client and the carer. The client should feel that their needs have been carefully assessed and the care will help them lead a fulfilling and healthy life as far as is possible. The carer should feel part of the process and that their contribution is valued and recognised.

Care planning must take account of the individual's culture, language, intellectual ability, and mobility. Councils must be aware of the rights of service users and comply with the Sex Discrimination Act (1975) the Disability Discrimination Act (1995) the Human Rights Act (1998) and the Race Relations (Amendment) Act (2000).

Different kinds of assessment

Assessment is a term used in many contexts in health and social care, some common terms used follow.

Name: Florence Ashley				
D.O.B: 1.1.22				
Date of Assessment: 13.6.06				
Targets	**How can targets be met**	**Action to be taken**	**Whose commitment**	**Review date**
To improve mobility	Attend weekly physio at local hospital. Review equipment provision in home and order additional aids if needed	Arrange transport and book appointment O.T. to visit home	Debbie Smith community physio (lead professional) Mary Jones O.T. assistant	13.7.06 13.7.06
To maintain wound care	Home visit by district nurse to monitor wound	Co-ordinate DNi visits	Debbie Smith lead professional Sara Barker DN	20.6.06
To maintain good circulation	To encourage mobility. to change compression stockings	Visits by H.C.A 4 times a week	Pam Ball H.C.A.	20.6.06

FIGURE 10.11 *Example of a care plan*

Financial assessment

Most social services departments make a charge for services provided following a care assessment, but this is subject to a financial assessment (or means test). The charging policy is set locally and will vary according to region. However, with FACS it is hoped that national guidelines will soon be in place so that people will be assessed in a similar way, no matter where they live. The person being assessed for care must complete a financial assessment to determine the contribution they will make.

Carers' assessment (Carers and Disabled Children's Act, 2000)

Carers who provide a substantial amount of care now have a right to a needs assessment themselves. Social services may provide a break for the carer, or respite care for the person they care for.

CPA assessment (care programme approach)

Under the NSF (National Service Framework) for Mental Health, people with mental illness are now assessed using the CPA approach. This includes assessing the carer's needs. The assessment should be reviewed at least once a year.

Family assessment (Children Act, 1989)

In the case of a child with special needs, the assessment should look at the whole family when considering the provision of appropriate services.

Young carers' assessment

Under the terms of the Carers and Disabled Children's Act (1990) and the Carers Recognition and Services Act (1995), young people under 18 who provide care to adult family members are also entitled to an assessment of their needs. The assessment of a young carer would include support that they may need at school and could include arranging a holiday or break from caring.

Occupational therapy (OT) assessment

This looks at the physical needs of a person and how to support them in their own home so that they can retain their independence (see Figure 10.12).

Stairs	Yes	No	Describe, listing any concerns
None			
Into Home			
To Bathroom			
To Toilet			
To Bedroom			
To Kitchen			
Stair Rails			
Garden to Pavement			
Heating			
Central Heating			
Gas Fires			
Solid Fuel			
Able to Use Safely			
Adequate			
No Heating			
Eligible for Grant			
Do fires need checking?			
Toilet/Bathroom			
Upstairs Toilet			
Downstairs Toilet			
Outside Toilet			
Commode			
Bathroom			
Bath Aids			
General			
Can manage oven			
Can manage microwave			
Does oven need checking?			
Are there smoke alarms?			

FIGURE 10.12 *An OT assessment*

Risk assessment

All service providers – such as social services, a home care agency or a voluntary organisation – have a legal responsibility to undertake a risk assessment before they provide services, in order to protect the health and safety of their staff.

If services are to be provided in a client's own home certain things covered in a risk assessment, include:

* layout and location of the home

* any overprotective dogs

* any risks associated with having to move the person who has care needs.

Carers and the service manager will discuss possible risks and how to deal with them. Risks can include safety issues for the client, or for other people. For example, a risk assessment of someone with a mental health problem will assess the level of risk the person poses to themselves (for example, self-harm) or to others. In a care assessment for someone with dementia, it may be decided that the risks of the person remaining in their own home are too high and they will need residential care.

In an organisation, risk assessments may include health and safety issues in the workplace, and also financial risk. Many

private care homes have been closed as the fees charged are higher than the local social services will pay for, and relatives cannot pay the additional cost.

Further issues related to care planning

Direct payments

In the FACS document the government urges councils to encourage the use of direct payments whenever possible. In this scheme, the council decides what services are required and how much they will cost. This sum will be made available to the client, who can purchase services from private agencies or individuals.

Advantages of direct payments

The client decides what services they will have and when. For example, they could ask a care worker to come at particular times of the day, rather than not knowing when a council care worker will come to their house. Direct payments are seen to empower the client.

Disadvantages of direct payments

Some clients would not want to take responsibility for organising their care and paying for it; some would not understand the process. Until now, younger adults have mostly tended to use direct payments.

Resource issues

Although the NHS and Community Care Act (1990) advocates a needs-based approach, with the increased demand for services (partly because of the increasing life expectancy of clients) there is pressure on resources. Resources include staff as well as equipment and other therapies (e.g. speech therapy, physiotherapy). The FACS approach limits resources by categorising clients into levels of support needed. Sometimes age may be used as a means of identifying resource provision. In one London area, children over seven are not referred for speech therapy because of the shortage of speech therapists in the area. In one Mental Health Trust there is a shortage of child psychiatrists and psychologists so children are not referred to the local CAMHT (Child and Adolescent Mental Health team) unless they are suicidal. Resource allocation is part of the assessment process. The concept of 'best value' or 'cost-effectiveness' is linked to the effective use of scarce resources. Local councils have to undertake a regular 'best value' review of their services to see if costs can be reduced but quality maintained. Critics of the 'best value' approach argue that cutting costs must lead to a reduction in the quality of services.

Demand for resources within the NHS may limit the availability of services, such as physiotherapy

Confidentiality issues

Confidentiality refers to the privacy of information provided by the client in the course of treatment or in the provision of service. With the development of email systems transferring personal data about clients between health and social care services, confidentiality has become a key issue. Care workers insert a special code to access data, but concerns have been raised by patients' groups about confidentiality. In some cases a client may not wish her family to know her personal

details – and this could include her main carer, so it is important that care workers respect the wishes of their clients.

The Data Protection Act (1984) protects information held on computer-based records; all data should be:

* accurate and up to date

* obtained fairly and lawfully

* used only for specified lawful purposes

* kept confidential.

In this section we have seen examples of practitioners working in multi-disciplinary teams. By having one lead professional responsible for co-ordinating care, communication problems should be reduced and the service user knows which worker to contact if there is a problem. However, some professionals may have a problem adapting to working with colleagues with a different background and training from their own.

When interagency working goes wrong

There have been examples of poor interagency working that have resulted in the abuse of young children going undetected. Nowadays, children's services work in partnership with schools, health teams and the police. Many of the cases reported in the press have resulted in lengthy inquiries and recommendations for future practice. Child protection issues are seen as a key issue for all partners in child care. Partnership boards are responsible for developing services for children across all areas of health, social care and education in the local area. Parents and other voluntary groups are also represented. It is hoped that by developing closer working relationships across all agencies, families and children will be supported and problems identified at an early stage.

This section has discussed how multi-disciplinary teams work together to provide services in health and social care. Health care is not just about physical health, but also about supporting mental and emotional well-being. Therefore, a multi-disciplinary approach helps ensure that all an individual's needs are met. The drawing-up of a detailed assessment and care plan is an important part of multi-disciplinary working.

Working in a multi-disciplinary team should ensure an integrated approach to the provision of services, and also benefit team members. With vulnerable client groups such as older people, people with learning disabilities or mental health problems, and children, early intervention is essential before serious problems develop. The role of the lead professional is vital in the co-ordination of services. Although service provision is in response to the needs of clients, resources available in health and social care are limited. We have seen examples of effective use of resources when teams are grouped together to support particular client groups. Cost-effectiveness is linked to the concept of 'best value' as part of service reviews. However many critics of this approach are concerned that 'best value' services may lead to a reduction in quality provision.

Summary

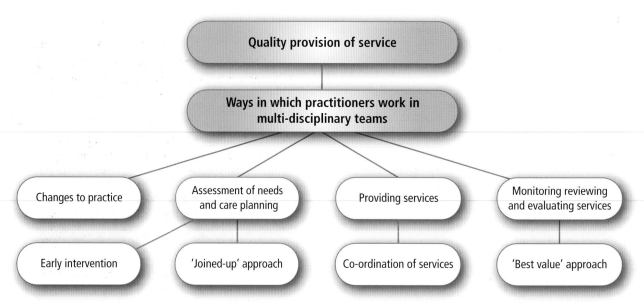

Quality provision of service

Ways in which practitioners work in multi-disciplinary teams

Changes to practice | Assessment of needs and care planning | Providing services | Monitoring reviewing and evaluating services

Early intervention | 'Joined-up' approach | Co-ordination of services | 'Best value' approach

Consider this

1. Tim is 35. He is a milkman. He is a diabetic but he doesn't bother too much with his diet. He is married with two young children and he is very active. He often forgets to check his blood sugar levels. One Monday morning he lost consciousness and woke up in A&E. He was told he had suffered a stroke. He was admitted to the specialist stroke unit, where the stroke nurse consultant assessed him and found he had the following problems:

   * loss of speech

   * weakness down the left side of his body

   * problems with swallowing.

   Identify which practitioners would be part of the multi-disciplinary team to help him with these problems. Are there any voluntary organisations which may help him now and in the future?

2. Ann, the School Nurse, visited the local primary school and assessed Maggie (aged 5) as part of her initial school assessment. The teacher had already expressed concern about Maggie as she felt her speech was delayed although her hearing appeared normal. Her behaviour in the classroom was erratic and she had attacked other children on occasions, biting and scratching them. She sometimes wets herself during the day and at night. Maggie's mother said all these problems started when her baby sister was born four months earlier.

continued on next page

Can you identify health and care professionals who may help Maggie?

3. Beatrice is 90. She lives on her own. She has severe arthritis and diabetes. She had a fall recently and broke her hip. After a successful operation and a period in intermediate care she is being discharged.

   Can you identify members of the health and social care team who may help her at home? Are there any voluntary groups who may also help her?

   All Beatrice wants to do is live at home and be left in peace.

4. Georgie (aged 14) is the youngest of three sisters. Her mother has noticed that she never seems to eat at meal times. She wears baggy clothes and seems to feel the cold. She is always weighing herself. She stays in her room all the time and never goes out with her friends from school. Her mother is anxious she may be developing anorexia like her older sister Natasha, who was ill for a long time but has now recovered.

   Can you identify which health and social care professionals may help this family?

Section 4: How quality assurance is promoted by services

In this section you need to learn what is meant by quality assurance and how services implement quality-assurance procedures, including those which have been introduced by central government. This section needs to be read in conjunction with Section 5, as many of the systems have been set up under legislation and through the development of national monitoring bodies.

The terms **standards**, **governance** and **quality control** are now commonplace in health and social care services. Organisations in health and social care must be accountable. Press reports of poor provision, unfair treatment and neglect of vulnerable groups have led to improved services.

Standards in health and social care

Standards related to services are increasingly being developed through NSFs for different aspects of health provision, including NSFs for older people and for coronary heart disease (CHD). As part of these NSFs, PCTs often work with social services and NHS hospital trusts and they must meet certain standards of service within a set time limit. Targets, such as those related to waiting times in A&E departments, are set nationally but local statutory agencies may agree targets to address issues of concern in the local area. For example, one PCT is working with colleagues in social care to

Key concepts

Standards: relate to the level of service required. Standards are increasingly being developed; e.g. NSFs (National Service Frameworks). National targets are being set by government for health and social care.

Governance: the organisation and delivery of services so that they meet the standards required by the inspection bodies.

Quality control: the systems put in place by health and social care organisations to ensure that services are of a high quality.

reduce the level of teenage pregnancies, as the local rate is much higher than the national UK rate.

Aspects of quality assurance

Quality-assurance mechanisms used by services take many forms.

Improving information and consultation with service users

Many changes in the involvement of patients and the public in health services took place because of the NHS Plan (2000) and the Health and Social Care Act (2001). Section 11 of this act places a duty on NHS organisations to have arrangements for involving patients and the public in how services are organised. The NHS, as well as local councils and social service departments, now involve users in the development of services, and provide information about services offered in various ways including leaflets and websites.

Involving service users in the NHS and social care

Section 11 of the Health and Social Care Act (2001) places a duty on NHS trusts to involve and consult with patients and the public in service planning, operation, and proposals for change. Previously trusts involved the public only when there was a planned change to service provision, such as the closure of a hospital or specialist unit. Local councils also have a duty to consult the public. Examples of consultation include sending questionnaires to all households in the area, asking them to comment on the community services available (e.g. transport and housing).

PALS (patients' advice and liaison services)

All NHS trusts have to have a PALS service which offers advice to patients. In a hospital the PALS office is usually near the main reception, and all patients using the trust should be advised of its existence. PALS tries to resolve problems on the spot – this could be dealing with a complaint about cleaning on a ward, or the quality of the food. PALS gives information to patients, their carers, and their families about local health services and puts people in touch with local support groups. They direct people to ICAS (Independent Complaints and Advocacy Service) or the trust's own complaints service. They may refer issues to the hospital management and the patients' forums. PALS produce a leaflet about their services which is freely available from the NHS Trust.

Patients' Forums (Patient and Public Involvement Forums)

All NHS trusts have a PPI Forum, these were set up in 2003. They are statutory bodies of voluntary patients and others living in the community, appointed by the Commission for Patient and Public Involvement in Health (CPPIH). PPI Forums have powers to inspect all premises used by NHS patients, including private hospitals. They monitor the quality of services from the patient's perspective, and contribute evidence to other monitoring bodies, such as the Overview and Scrutiny Committees set up by local councils to monitor NHS services in the area. Representatives from the forums also sit on NHS committees and represent the interests of patients. PPI Forums hold several meetings a year in public, and these are advertised in the local press.

Patient Choice

The Patient Choice initiative is an example of how patients are being involved in making decisions about their own care. The initiative was developed because of problems with long waiting times for some operations, and also high levels of patients not attending outpatient clinics or cancelling admission to hospital. Patient Choice means that patients can select the hospital they go to for an operation, as in some areas waiting lists are shorter than others. The complete implementation of this plan depended on operating national IT systems. These are still undergoing development, so the Patient Choice initiative has been delayed. GPs are concerned that some groups of patients may have difficulty making an informed choice. Waiting lists have reduced for some operations, but this has been due to the NHS use of private hospitals and new specialist centres rather than through Patient Choice.

Patients' Charters

In January 2001 the Patients' Charter was replaced by the new NHS Charter, *Your Guide to the NHS*. It is designed to give patients a clear guide to their rights and responsibilities, and to the standards and services they can expect under the NHS Plan. The guide gives information about where to get the most appropriate treatment. It also explains how patients can make a complaint.

Key points include:

* *Responsible use of the NHS:* keeping appointments, returning equipment when it is no longer needed, paying any charges promptly and treating NHS staff with respect.

* *Easier access to information:* users of the guide are encouraged to access the most appropriate health services. For example, they could contact NHS Direct, their local pharmacist, a walk-in centre, or see a nurse. Responsible use of services is encouraged. In the past many

people used A&E for problems that could be dealt with elsewhere, and this meant delays for people with urgent conditions.

* *Targets for hospital treatment:* patients should expect to wait no more than 17 weeks for an outpatient appointment, and no more than nine months for in-patient care. People with suspected cancer should be seen within two weeks of being referred to a specialist.

* *Cancelled operations:* if an operation is cancelled on the day of surgery, the hospital should offer another date within 28 days or pay for an operation at the time and hospital of the patient's choice.

* *A&E waiting times:* no one should wait more than four hours in an A&E department from arrival to admission, transfer or discharge.

* *Right to complain:* any patient complaint must be handled sensitively, effectively and without delay.

Patients can contact their local pharmacy for advice

Implementing quality

Service standards in the NHS and social care

As a result of numerous policies and legislation, standards in the NHS and social care are being developed in a range of areas. NSFs are one way of developing standards which are monitored by the trust and social services working in partnership.

In the NSF for Older People there are eight standards that must be achieved within ten years. In one area in South London, there has been a local implementation group set up to monitor the development of the NSF for Older People. The membership includes professionals from the local council, the hospital trust, the PCT, the voluntary sector, and older people. Progress made on the NSF is monitored and discussed at meetings and action plans are drawn up so that targets set by government will be met.

In a recent meeting, Standard 8 was discussed. This relates to the promotion of health and active life in older age. The PCT has developed an exercise programme for older people in partnership with Age Concern, and flu immunisations are being offered to all people over 65 in the area. However, some older people do not want to take part in exercise programmes and others are nervous about having flu injections. Standards can only be achieved with the co-operation of service users, and they should have choice.

Using performance measures in the NHS

In April 2004 the Commission for Health Care Audit and Inspection (CHAI) was set up. This took over the work of the Commission for Health Improvement (CHI) and the Mental Health Commission (MHAC). It also took over the work of the Audit Commission looking at the cost-effectiveness of the NHS, and the work of the National Care Standards Commission (NCSC) that dealt with independent (usually private) health care. However the name caused confusion and CHAI is now known as the Healthcare Commission.

League tables for hospitals were launched in 2002 to try to improve standards, but many areas rated do not cover direct patient care but are focussed on meeting waiting list targets, out-patient waiting times, and the time patients wait in A&E. Acute hospitals are rated in 44 areas ranging from cancelled operations to cleanliness and staff morale. Trusts were awarded stars for performance but critics complain that this system is not a true reflection of quality.

In 2006, the Healthcare Commission will take over monitoring performance in the NHS and will assess standards by looking at how far hospitals have met government targets. Self-assessment will be done by trusts, there will be fewer inspection visits and star ratings will be abolished.

The Health and Social Care Act (2003) gives the Healthcare Commission the overall function of encouraging improvement in public health and health care in England and Wales.

The key aims of the Healthcare Commission are to monitor:

* the availability of, access to, quality and effectiveness of health care

* the economy and efficiency of provision of health care

* the availability and quality of information to the public about health care

* the need to safeguard and promote the rights and welfare of children and the effectiveness of measures to do so.

The main statutory functions of the commission include:

* carrying out reviews and investigations of the provision of health care and the arrangements to promote and protect public health, including studies aimed at improving economy, efficiency and effectiveness in the NHS

* promoting the co-ordination of reviews undertaken by other bodies

* publishing information about the state of health care across the NHS and the independent sector, including the results of national clinical audits

* reviewing the quality of data relating to health and health care.

Statutory functions in England only:

* reviewing the performance of each local NHS organisation and awarding an annual rating of performance

* regulating the independent health care sector through annual registration and inspection

* considering complaints about NHS bodies that have not been resolved through their own complaints procedures

* publishing surveys of the views of patients and staff.

This new body will cover a great deal to do with quality in the NHS and will work in partnership with the Audit Commission and the Commission for Social Care Inspection. In addition to these functions the Healthcare Commission must ensure that all NHS organisations comply with the Human Rights Act and the Race Relations (Amendment) Act. Look for details of the Healthcare Commission on its website (www.healthcarecommission.org.uk).

Using performance measures in social care

Quality in the social services

The Commission for Social Care Inspection (CSCI) was set up in April 2004 to replace the Social Services Inspectorate (SSI), the SSI and Audit Commission Joint Review Team and the social care functions of the National Care Standards Commission (NCSC).

CSCI is responsible for:

* inspections of all social care organisations (statutory, private and voluntary) against national standards, and publishing reports

* registering services that meet national minimum standards

* inspections of local social service authorities

* publishing an annual report to parliament on progress in social care and analysing expenditure

* publishing star ratings for local authorities.

The CSCI sets out regulations, standards and information about specific social care standards. These apply to Care Homes for Adults (18–65), Care Homes for Older People, Children's Homes, domiciliary care, fostering services, nurses' agencies and residential family centres.

These standards are a way of promoting good practice and identifying areas for improvement. There are supplementary standards for young people aged 16 and 17.

Young people at 16 to 17 years of age are moving into adulthood and therefore need to be supported in this process. Homes for these young people should take only 16 to 25 year olds, and their facilities and services should reflect the needs of this client group. Education, training and employment are very important and should be present in the care plan agreed with the young person and reviewed frequently. As many of these young people will be leaving the care of social services, they will need to have a Leaving Care Plan. This outlines the support and assistance a young person will receive to enable a successful transition to adulthood. The plan will include arrangements for:

* education, training and employment
* securing safe and secure accommodation
* support for disabled young people
* financial assistance to enable the young person to set up and maintain independent accommodation
* claiming welfare benefits where this is identified as a need
* general and specialised health education and health care and other specialist services such as counselling
* maintaining existing support networks as defined by the young person and creating new networks.

There are 41 regulations attached to care homes accommodating young people.

Standard 14: Leisure

14.1 Staff ensure that service users have access to, and choose from, a range of appropriate leisure activities.

14.7 Birthdays, name days, cultural and religious festivals are celebrated and service users participate in planning these events.

14.8 Activities provide a balance between free and controlled time, are experiential, and provide a mix of time with and without adults.

14.9 Service users under the age of 18 do not have access to, or watch, videos certified as suitable for over 18s, and systems and policies are in place to safeguard users when computer networking or on the Internet.

14.10 Leisure interests and areas in which a service user has talents or abilities are encouraged and financially supported.

Risks are part of life, and risk taking, whether it is in a care home, school or family life is part of developing an ability to make decisions. In care work there will be clients who need support in making decisions, and the care worker or advocate is responsible for enabling clients to make choices about what they do.

Improving registration and inspection procedures

Although the CSCI is currently responsible for inspecting children's social services, this role will be transferred to OFSTED in the future, as children's social services are merging with education departments to form children's trusts, while adult social services are working more closely with primary care and mental health trusts. There have been many changes in the regulation and inspection of service, and with health and social care services working more closely together in the future further changes are likely to occur.

Monitoring in the NHS

Overview and Scrutiny Committees (OSCs)

The Health and Social Care Act (2001) gave new powers to overview and scrutiny committees in local councils who have social service responsibilities. Since 2003, OSCs have had the authority to review and scrutinise all matters related to the planning, provision and operation of health services in the area covered by the council. OSCs have been established in accordance with the regulations, to consist of elected members (councillors) and representatives of voluntary organisations and PPI Forums. Their emphasis is on issues of health service changes, health inequalities and strategic direction. There is a close working relationship between the OSC and the PPI Forums, as forums can refer issues of concern to the OSC. OSCs meet in public but members of the public are not able to contribute to the meeting. However there are often interesting items on the agenda about services in the area which will help you understand how the local system operates.

Internal monitoring

Every NHS organisation has its own system for monitoring performance and service delivery. Every NHS trust reports annually on the quality of service provision and the arrangements to deal with complaints and risk management.

SCENARIO
Overview and scrutiny

In an acute hospital in South East England, concern was expressed by members of the public, the local press, the trusts, the PPI Forum and the local Overview and Scrutiny Committee about the high levels of MRSA in the hospital. The trust has a duty to provide information about the infection rates and as a result of the concern raised, an action plan was produced by the Infection Control Committee to show how they would improve the infection rates at the hospital. The infection control consultant came to meetings of the OSC and the PPI Forum to explain the action plan and monitoring of the plan will be done by the OSC and the PPI Forum.

Correct handwashing techniques will help to reduce the spread of MRSA in hospitals

What if?

The NHS and the services it provides are varied and complex. It is led by highly-trained professionals. Can you think of any problems that could arise for lay members on the OSC and the PPI Forum who do not have extensive medical knowledge?

Try it out

If you obtain the annual report from your local NHS hospital trust or PCT, it will include a section on performance monitoring. There are regular public meetings of the boards of the local trusts and if you attend one of these and look at the papers available at the meeting you will get a good idea of what the trust is doing to improve performance.

Registration and inspection in social care

Registration in social care

Registration is the process through which the CSCI assesses whether those who wish to offer care services for children and vulnerable adults are suitable, and whether these services will be operated safely and in accordance with the regulations and standards set by the government. The CSCI operates using three essential criteria to decide whether a person, an organisation, or a service is suitable. The following aspects are checked carefully:

* *fitness of premises:* the premises are fit for the purpose of the service

* *fitness of persons:* the people running and managing the service are fit to do so

* *fitness of services and facilities:* the services and facilities meet legal requirements, are suitable and safe, and meet the needs of the service users as interpreted through the National Minimum Standards.

Inspection visits help to maintain standards in residential homes

Anyone who wishes to open a residential home must apply for registration. The application is very detailed and the person who has overall responsibility for the service (known as the registered person) must give details of their qualifications and training. In many homes there is a manager who runs the home on a daily basis (known as the registered manager) and details about this person would also be included in the registration application. The service provided would also have to be described in detail. Services registered and inspected by the CSCI include:

* care homes providing personal and/or nursing care

* adult placement services

* children's homes

* schools accommodating one or more pupils for more than 295 days a year

* residential family centres

* domiciliary care agencies

* nurses agencies

* independent fostering agencies

* voluntary adoption agencies.

Apart from registering homes and services for a wide range of client groups, the CSCI also regulates services through a process of inspection. This inspection can include services that are not registered with the CSCI. These are:

* local council fostering services

* local council adoption services

* accommodation provided by Further Education Colleges, boarding schools, and residential special schools for students under 18. (Schools and colleges are registered with the Department for Education and Skills.)

Inspection in social care

Inspection is the main way in which CSCI assesses the quality of the service provided. The aim of inspection is to raise standards in care services to at least the national minimum standards set by the government.

What care homes should expect during an inspection visit

Inspectors will interview at least 10 per cent of service users. In homes where there are fewer than four residents, all service users will be asked to comment on the care they receive. Inspectors will also check care plans, staff records, accident books, fire books, the ways service users' finances are managed, medication records, and other health and safety aspects.

Many service users could be confused or have problems with communication, so it is important that they are encouraged to speak about their experiences. The inspectors will also observe how staff behave towards residents and they will probably visit a home for a day so they can see how meal times are managed.

The National Minimum Standards state that residential homes are the 'home' of the residents, who should be treated with respect and maintain their dignity. Living in a care home isn't just about being kept 'safe'. The principles applied when providing residential care focus on the importance of promoting the residents' independence, helping them make their own decisions, keeping their individuality, and keeping family and community contacts. Residents should have an opportunity to comment on the care they receive. Some homes have a comments book in which residents can write their views. Other homes have a residents' council to discuss issues with the staff.

Childcare inspection: OFSTED

OFSTED (the Office for Standards in Education) set up in 1993, is responsible for the quality of education in all maintained schools and nursery schools. It has developed its inspection role to cover childminding and out-of-school care for children up to the age of 8. It has four main functions to ensure that day-care providers and childminders meet the national standards.

1. *Registration:* childminders and day-care providers must be registered by OFSTED

2. *Inspection:* OFSTED inspects childcare providers every three years to judge the quality and standards of the childcare provided and the premises

3. *Investigation:* OFSTED investigates any complaints or concerns voiced by parents or members of the public, and issues raised in inspection reports

4. *Enforcement:* OFSTED can take action if there is a risk to children in the service provided, which may lead to the cancellation of the registration of the childminder or care provider.

For more details on OFSTED look at this website (www.ofsted.gov.uk).

Evaluating the quality of services experienced by users in the NHS

Hospital trusts administer the UK In-patient Survey to everyone who has been an in-patient for at least one night. The survey is part of the monitoring process and is required by the Healthcare Commission. It consists of 68 questions and covers seven key areas. These are:

* emergency and planned admissions

* the environment and facilities

* care and treatment, especially pain relief

* doctors and nurses

* adequacy of patient information

* discharge

* overall impression.

Here are some of the questions patients were asked.

1. After arriving at hospital, how long did you wait for admission to a room or a ward?

2. During your stay in hospital, did you ever share a room or bay with a member of the opposite sex?

3. How clean was the hospital room or ward that you were in?

4. How clean were the toilets and bathrooms that you used?

5. How would you rate the courtesy of the doctors?

In one trust the scores were good for emergency care, the numbers of nurses on duty and explanations of test results. However the trust scored badly on information and communication, food and the use of mixed-sex wards. As a result of this survey the trust has drawn up a plan to improve these areas.

Surveys like this are useful to identify areas of poor quality, but you have to be aware of the sample size and the scoring system. In this survey, 481 patients took part and there was a 61.6 per cent response rate. Patients' responses can be affected by a range of factors: different people have different ideas about what is a 'good meal', for example.

National Patients' Surveys take place every year. In 2004 a number of these surveys took place:

* children and young people survey

* ambulance trusts survey

* service users in mental health trusts survey.

The surveys are collated by the NHS survey advice centre and are used for the performance ratings of trusts.

Monitoring service users' views in social care

New ways of obtaining the views of service users have developed. Many people who receive care in their own homes, in sheltered housing or in residential accommodation are nervous about criticising the care they receive. In one London borough, volunteers from Age Concern interviewed older people about their experiences of the home care provided by a range of agencies commissioned by the local council. Older people feel more at ease talking about their experiences to another older person. The results of the interviews are reported back to the council and changes are made in response to issues raised. Although there are still problems of confidentiality as people are nervous about being identified, this has proved a useful way of getting people's views.

Rewarding good practice

The Charter Mark

The Charter Mark is the national standard for customer service excellence, as promoted by the Cabinet Office. Organisations can apply for formal assessment through one of four independently accredited assessment bodies. All public sector organisations can apply, and voluntary organisations that provide a public service are also eligible. Organisations are assessed on evidence submitted against the following six standard criteria.

> **The six criteria for achieving Charter Mark status**
> The organisation can:
>
> 1. set standards and perform well
>
> 2. actively engage with customers, partners and staff
>
> 3. be fair and accessible to everyone and promote choice
>
> 4. continuously develop and improve
>
> 5. use resources effectively and imaginatively
>
> 6. contribute to improving opportunities and quality of life in the communities it serves.

Successfully certificated Charter Mark organisations may display the Charter Mark logo on stationery and other publications. This may attract clients and commissioning agencies. Organisations not wishing to go through formal assessment are encouraged to use the Charter Mark self-assessment approach as part of the self-monitoring of services and to identify areas for improvement. You can find more information about the Charter Mark and the Self Assessment Tool at www.chartermark.gov.uk.

CUSTOMER SERVICE EXCELLENCE

FIGURE 10.13 *The Charter Mark*

Investors in People

Investors in People (IIP) is another type of award that rewards good practice in providing a service; it was set up in 1990. A detailed explanation of the award and how organisations apply for it is on the IIP website (www.investorsinpeople.co.uk). Public and private organisations can apply for the award. Social services departments, voluntary organisations and hospitals have all successfully applied. Examples of organisations that have achieved the IIP award include Great Ormond Street Hospital for Children, the Cambridge branch of the National Autistic Society, and Suffolk Social Care Services. An external assessor tests the agency against a set of standards, the assessment includes talking to staff, clients and managers. IIP stresses the importance of everyone in an organisation working together to provide a good service.

Developing procedures for complaints and providing opportunities for suggestions from service users and staff

In the NHS

In every NHS trust there is a designated manager responsible for dealing with complaints. Complaints are studied carefully, as they may indicate failure to provide an adequate service, or a need for staff training. Complaints in primary care are initially dealt with by the GP practice concerned. However if a complaint cannot be resolved it will be referred to the PCT.

In a hospital trust, complaints are dealt with by a designated officer, and records of complaints and their outcomes are kept. A quarterly report is provided to the board meeting. In most trusts there are opportunities for staff to raise issues about the services provided, either through their line manager or through their union representative. In some trusts monthly meetings of the Chief Executive and staff members discuss services.

Independent Complaints Advocacy Services (ICAS)

These were also established after the Health and Social Care Act 2001. They are independent bodies which help patients pursue a complaint about a particular NHS service. They also offer information and advice and will act as advocate for the patient (e.g. write letters, attend meetings and speak on their behalf). They also advise patients of the options available if they wish to complain. Citizens Advice Bureaux can tell people the location of their local ICAS.

In social services

All social services departments have a complaints policy for service users. Most complaints are about access to or charges for services. Service users are advised to contact advocates to help them with a complaint. Older people may use the support of a voluntary organisation, such as Age Concern. There are several stages in the complaints procedure and if the matter cannot be resolved locally through a complaints panel, the complaint can be taken to the Ombudsman. As with health trusts, a complaints manager monitors complaints and presents a regular report to the council. In all councils there are suggestion boxes and frequent departmental meetings to discuss how services may improve.

Raising the training levels within the sector

In social care

In order to have a competent workforce in social care, the Commission for Social Care Inspection

(CSCI) has issued guidance on the qualifications of managers and care staff in all aspects of care provision, including domiciliary care agencies and care homes for older people and children. The policy states the numbers of qualified staff that should be on duty. CSCI states that all care staff should have attained qualifications to the appropriate standard by December 2005. As part of their inspection visit, inspectors will look at training programmes and the qualifications of staff. The Health and Social Care NVQ Level 2 is seen as the qualification that should be obtained in older people's services. In children's homes 80 per cent of all care staff should have completed NVQ Level 3 in Caring for Children and Young People. All staff in social care should have an individual learning programme agreed with their manager to ensure that they have sufficient training to meet the needs of the client group and the inspection standards. Apart from the NVQ, most care providers have an ongoing training programme including manual handling (safe lifting), health and safety, and first aid courses.

In the NHS

In the NHS, ongoing training is seen as essential in maintaining standards. All NHS doctors and nurses have individual learning plans. Doctors have to be revalidated at regular intervals to ensure they are up to date with current practice. As part of the NHS modernisation programme, the skills of doctors and nurses are reviewed and training programmes for both groups are updated. Hospital trusts may decide on a range of training programmes.

The government's policy of 'Life-Long Learning' means that training is seen as an ongoing process in the NHS. NVQs in Health and Social Care are encouraged by the NHS. Health Care Assistants (HCAs) who have completed their NVQ courses do a range of tasks in the community and in hospital. For example, HCAs work in clinics advising people with hypertension and diabetes, but they are always supported by a registered nurse or doctor. Many RGNs (Registered

SCENARIO
Training day

Following discussions with patients and relatives, one hospital trust has developed a training day for staff to improve their skills in helping the dying and the bereaved. The Director of Nursing said: 'This is a difficult and emotional area requiring a high level of discretion, sensitivity and a different set of skills. This is why we started the new training programme.' The course includes:

* the meaning of death
* breaking the news to relatives and friends
* death of babies
* how to support other staff.

General Nurse) are undertaking further training so that they become Registered Nurse Practitioners. Registered Nurse Practitioners take responsibilities that were previously undertaken by doctors. These may include:

* running skin clinics
* performing minor surgery
* running asthma clinics.

Continued training is essential in heath and social care if the services are to meet the needs of the patients and clients.

Summary

In this section we have looked how standards are maintained in health and social care services through a range of approaches. The quality of services is monitored by outside agencies such as the Health Care Commission and the Commission for Social Care Inspection, and services are also monitored by the organisation itself.

How quality assurance is provided by services

- Managing complaints
- Staff training issues
- Patient surveys
- Rewarding good practice
- Star rating systems
- Consultation with service users
- Government guidelines
- National service frameworks
- Registration and inspection procedures

Section 5: Effects of national policy and legislation on care practice and provision

In this section we will consider some of the possible effects of national policies and legislation on care practice and provision. This includes the effects on service users, on services and on practitioners at both a national and a local level.

Key changes in policy and legislation

Since 1990 there has been a great deal of legislation affecting the provision of health and social care services. Some recent key changes are described below.

The New NHS: Modern Dependable (1997)

This White Paper set out the government's plans to modernise the NHS. GPs were organised into Primary Care Groups responsible to the local health authority, and local social services began to work more closely with their partners in health. The doctor–patient partnership was seen as an important way of building confidence in the health service.

The Health Act (1999)

This Act reformed primary care, allowing the creation of Primary Care Trusts, and requiring all Hospital Trusts to improve their services. The

Act also allowed the introduction of the following patient services:

* walk-in high street health centres

* increased use of day surgery in health centres

* health checks and advice sessions in new clinics

* one stop shops – varied health care services at one site

* wider health care partnerships, encouraging GPs to team up with pharmacists, counsellors and dentists to provide a range of services from one site.

The NHS Plan (2000)

The ten-year NHS Plan provides a vision of a health service designed around the patient. The targets include:

* 7,000 extra beds in hospitals and intermediate care

* over 100 new hospitals

* clean wards overseen by modern matrons

* better hospital food

* modern IT systems in every hospital and GP surgery

* 7,500 more consultants and 2,000 more GPs

* 20,000 more nurses and therapists

* childcare support for NHS staff with 100 on-site nurseries.

It is hoped that waiting times for treatment will be reduced and long waits in accident and emergency departments will be ended. For more details on the NHS Plan see the National Health Service website (www.nhs.uk/nhsplan). There is also an NHS Plan for Scotland (www.show.scot.uk/sehd/onh/onh-00.htm). The NHS Plan in Wales was published in 2001 (www.wales.gov.uk/healthplanonline).

The core principles on which the NHS Plan is based are:

1. The NHS will provide a universal service for all based on clinical need, not the ability to pay.

2. The NHS will provide a comprehensive range of services.

3. The NHS will organise its services around the needs and preferences of individual patients, their families and their carers.

4. The NHS will respond to the different needs of different populations.

5. The NHS will work continually to improve quality services and to minimise errors.

6. The NHS will support and value its staff.

7. Public funds for health care will be devoted solely to NHS patients.

8. The NHS will work together with others to provide a seamless service.

9. The NHS will help to keep people healthy and work to reduce inequalities.

10. The NHS will respect the confidentiality of individual patients and provide open access to information about services, treatment and performance.

Changes in social care

Changes in the NHS have impacted on services provided by social care agencies. Health and social care agencies work together to support patients discharged from hospital and also to prevent unnecessary hospital admissions. With the increase of partnership working and multi-disciplinary teams, this joint approach will increase. The main policy changes that have affected social services involve the provision of social services for children through the Children Act (2004). This Act builds on the previous Children Act of 1989 and sets out duties for local councils in England, which include these key duties:

* local councils must make arrangements to co-operate with education, the police, and other community organisations including the voluntary sector

* local councils must set up Local Safeguarding Children Boards

* local councils must set up databases containing details of children and young people in need, so that there is better sharing of information between agencies

* local councils must appoint a Director of Children's Services

* an integrated inspection framework of services for children set up by the council and its partners and Joint Area Reviews will assess

local social services progress in improving outcomes for children

* key agencies looking after children have a duty to safeguard and promote the welfare of children

* local councils must draw up a Children's and Young People's Plan to develop these services.

A National Children's Commissioner has been appointed by central government to champion the views and interests of children and young people.

The effects of national policy on service users

Legislation has had an effect on service users; patients and service users are more actively involved in health and social care services.

Rights and entitlement

With the Human Rights Act, the rights of patients and service users are paramount.

The Human Rights Act (1998)

The Human Rights Act (1998) has far-reaching implications for people working in health and social care. The Act makes it unlawful for a public authority (including the NHS and social services) to act in a way that is incompatible with any convention rights. The aim is to achieve a fair balance between the public interest and the individual's rights. The main Human Rights most relevant to health and social care are as follows:

* *Article 2:* Everyone's right to life shall be protected by law.

* *Article 3:* No one should be subjected to inhuman or degrading treatment or punishment.

* *Article 5:* Everyone has the right to liberty and security of person.

* *Article 6:* Everyone is entitled to a fair and public hearing in the determination of a person's civil rights and obligations, or of any criminal charge brought against him or her. Everyone is entitled to a fair and public hearing within a reasonable time by an independent and impartial Tribunal established by law.

* *Article 8:* Everyone has a right to respect for their private and family life, their home and their correspondence.

* *Article 9:* Everyone has the right of freedom of thought, conscience and religion.

* *Article 10:* Everyone has the right to freedom of expression.

* *Article 11:* Everyone has the right to freedom of peaceful assembly and to freedom of association with others, including the right to form and join Trade Unions for the protection of their interests.

* *Article 12:* Men and women of marriageable age have the right to marry and found a family according to the national laws governing the exercise of this right.

* *Article 14:* The enjoyment of the rights and freedoms set forth in this convention shall be secured without discrimination on any grounds such as sex, race, colour, language,

Think it over

Look at the following examples and decide which article of the Act is relevant.

1. mixed psychiatric wards

2. denial of fertility treatment to disabled women

3. placing of children of disabled parents in care instead of providing appropriate support

4. disabled people subjected to treatment without consent

5. refusal of treatment on grounds of life expectancy, impairment or quality of life

6. ECT and other psychiatric treatments

7. opening of service users' post, staff having keys to people's rooms, listening to residents' phone calls

8. denial of freedom to come and go from a residential home

9. denial of appropriate cultural facilities or food

10. denial of appropriate care/independent living support to disabled people

11. withdrawal of treatment to PVS patients (persistent vegetative state)

12. detentions under the Mental Health Act (especially if there are long delays before review tribunal)

13. sterilisation of people with learning disabilities

14. complaints procedures not easily accessible to clients

religion, political or other opinion, national or social origin, association with a national minority, property, birth or other status.

The Human Rights Act overlaps other legislation such as the Race Relations Act (1995) and the Disability Discrimination Act (1995). More detail on the Human Rights Act is available on the home office website (www.homeoffice.gov.uk).

Access

As a result of the Disability Discrimination Act (1995), all public agencies must ensure that there is access to the building and to information about procedures in various formats. One hospital trust has an access committee which monitors arrangements for staff and patients with disabilities. One area of concern has been the communication of laboratory results to patients who are blind or hearing impaired.

Consultation

In all public health and social care organisations, changes to how services are provided must be discussed with service users.

There are several questions that service users and carers ask about consultations like this.

✳ Do the views of service users and carers have an influence on the final outcome?

✳ Are trusts just going through the process because they must: i.e. without any real intention to act on the views of service users and carers?

One of the functions of the OSCs is to make sure that consultations involve all stakeholders and

that everyone's views are heard. If the committee finds that proper consultation on proposed changes has not taken place, it can refer the matter to the Secretary of State for Health.

The effects of national policy on services and practitioners

Government policy and legislation has had significant effects on health and care professionals who provide services. Some examples of changes of practice follow.

Roles and responsibilities

A good example of changing roles and responsibilities is in child protection. Because of the Children Acts of 1989 and 2004, child protection issues are a priority for all children's services. Every local authority area has a Children's and Families Director who oversees the service, and every organisation must have a named Child Protection Officer responsible for child protection issues.

Accountability

In the past it was often difficult to identify which professional was in charge of treatment or care planning. With the lead professional clearly identified on care plans in health and social care, accountability should be obvious.

Working collaboratively

Many examples of joint funding and collaborative working have developed as a result of policy. Sure Start Children's Centres, mentioned previously, are one good example; they involve detailed co-operation between health and social care practitioners. Another example is the collaboration between social services and hospital managers to improve discharge arrangements for patients in hospital.

Government policy has focused on the need to reduce length of stays in hospital. If social services cannot find a suitable placement for a patient being discharged, they are fined £120 for each night the patient remains in a hospital bed. Social services and hospital managers work together to improve discharge arrangements for patients. Patients not well enough to go home are discharged into **intermediate-care** beds in the community. Intermediate care is provided free of charge for six weeks; then the patient will be assessed. If social care is needed, patients may contribute to the cost. If continuing NHS care is required, it is provided free of charge. If the patient requires continuing care in their home, this will be provided by a multi-disciplinary team including workers from both health and social care services.

Being more responsive to the needs of service users

Walk-in Centres

The Health Act (1999) promoted a range of alternative to provide more flexible services. The development of Walk-in Centres in busy shopping areas or attached to acute hospitals has been one of these. They are open from 7 am to 11 pm, seven days a week and are available to everyone in the area, including homeless people. They give advice as well as treatment.

Health Action Zones

These were set up in 1998 to meet local population needs. They are usually in areas of poverty and deprivation. Examples of services provided include: diabetes clinics for Asian communities, accident prevention projects in the home, and sexual health services for young people. These are now the responsibility of PCTs but initial funding came from central government.

Changing existing provision

New technology in recent years has meant that patient stays in hospital have reduced and more surgical cases are undertaken as day cases. New technology is being tested to assist people to stay in their homes for longer,

SCENARIO

Example 1

In an area in Southern England, consultation is under way about the provision of a new hospital and the downgrading of the two acute hospitals currently in the area. The two old hospitals will become local out-patient clinics and will offer some therapy services and day surgery. This is part of the government's policy to centralise acute and specialist services in one hospital. Changes to service provision are always problematic, and concern has been expressed about access to one hospital for people who live on the edges of the district, as well as the environmental problems that will affect the area while the development takes place.

Example 2

A long-stay hospital for people with learning disabilities is being closed as a result of government policy. Many of the residents have lived in the hospital all their lives. There are 110 residents at the moment who will be transferred into community settings.

There are several problems with this policy. Relatives are concerned about where their family members will end up, and the level of care they will receive. Local people don't want care homes for these residents in their roads. Staff hope to be relocated with the patients they have looked after for many years. The changes have been presented by the PCT as an opportunity for residents to become integrated into the community and to develop their independence, but many residents are very disabled and most are of retirement age. Many policies may look good on paper, but the impact on local services and service users may cause problems.

through monitoring devices that can detect if the client is wandering, has fallen, or is taking their medication. Increasing provision will occur in the patient's home, with less care undertaken in hospital.

Joint funding

Partnership working between health and social care services has increased directly as a result of policy. One example is the development of Community Equipment Services.

The NHS Plan (2001) set targets for the integration of health and social services' community equipment services. Until these proposals, the supply of equipment was erratic. There were often problems deciding whether health or social services was responsible for providing equipment because it was unclear which agency was responsible for funding the services. With the new Integrated Community Equipment Service (or ICES) there is joint funding from social services and the local PCT and a management board decides how users and staff can get access to equipment easily.

EXAMPLES OF EQUIPMENT AVAILABLE THROUGH THE INTEGRATED COMMUNITY EQUIPMENT SERVICE	
Home-nursing equipment	→ Mattresses, beds, toilet seats, commodes
Minor adaptations	→ Grab rails, lever taps, improving lighting
Sensory equipment	→ Flashing doorbells, low vision optical aids, text phones
Mobility aids	→ Wheelchairs for short term use
Telecare equipment	→ Fall alarms, gas escape alarms, safe call
Children's equipment	→ Hoists, buggies, specialist toys, communication aids, specialist car seats

TABLE 10.2 *The range of equipment provided through the Integrated Community Equipment Service*

ICES fits into many policy initiatives such as promoting independence for older people, supporting intermediate care, reducing falls by older people, and giving support to carers. The ICES approach also fits into the NSF for Older People and the *Valuing People* White Paper that supports people with learning disabilities.

The effects of national policy on national and local care practice and provision

Improving quality

The development of NSFs for a range of services has improved quality in many aspects of health care. The NSFs include:

* NSF for Diabetes
* NSF for Children's Services
* NSFs for Renal Services
* NSF for CHD (Coronary Heart Disease)
* NSF for Mental Health.

All these NSFs set standards of care that affect the way health and social care services are provided for a range of client groups. Monitoring of health and care provision through a range of approaches has also improved the quality of service provision both nationally and locally.

Funding national priorities

The NHS budget is expected to reach £105.6 billion by 2007–08. The NHS Plan accounts for much of this extra investment to improve access and quality of services. Staffing and training costs are seen as priorities so that suitably trained staff will want to work in the service. Of the NHS budget, 75 per cent goes to PCTs who commission services from hospitals and elsewhere, but this may change in the future. The PCTs must manage their budgets and meet national targets. As you may have seen in the media, many trusts are in financial difficulties which will have a direct effect on the provision of services.

Summary

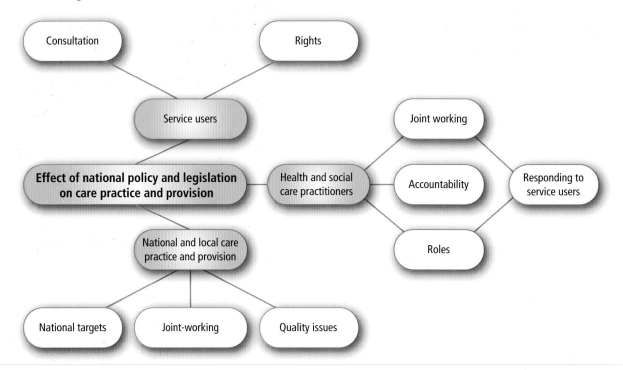

Consultation — Rights

Service users

Joint working

Effect of national policy and legislation on care practice and provision

Health and social care practitioners

Accountability

Responding to service users

National and local care practice and provision

Roles

National targets — Joint-working — Quality issues

Consider this

1. Sam (aged 45) has learning disabilities. He has lived all his life in a long-stay hospital. Now the hospital is being closed and he will be moved into a purpose-built home in the grounds of the hospital. He does not know who will be in the home with him.

   What legislation could be used to ensure his wishes are respected?

   How might advocacy help him?

2. Sheree went to a party on Friday night and had unprotected sex with someone she met for the first time. The doctors' surgery is closed until Monday.

   Where could Sheree get advice?

3. A new orthopaedic centre has opened for joint replacements. It is seen as a flagship for the NHS. The unit operates on a six day length of stay for patients who have surgery. Harry (aged 65) has had a hip replacement. He is concerned about how he will manage when he gets home.

   What community services may take over from the hospital care?

   What are the possible problems with discharging patients early?

Section 6: Conducting a survey relating to quality assurance

In this unit you need to conduct an investigation into the quality assurance mechanisms that are in place in two services used by a chosen service user. You need to prepare questions that will obtain the information you require. Jane's story (see page 47) may give you some ideas.

Your questions should cover the following areas:

* what systems are in place to implement and monitor quality assurance

* how data from quality assurance responses are used

* how quality assurance information is used to inform future practice.

In your investigation you could use a range of data from primary sources; including:

* an interview with a manager in the service
* questionnaires addressed to staff and patients or patients' representatives, such as the PPI Forum.

You will also need to use secondary sources. These could include:

* the annual report of the service
* the inspection report on the service
* various records, such as complaints and minutes of meetings as well as reports in your local newspaper on local services.

Units 15 and 16 give general guidance on how to do research.

If you decide to interview someone in a trust or social services, think about the questions you need to ask and note them down. It may be helpful if you send a copy of the questions you will ask to the person in advance so they can prepare their responses. You must tell the person the purpose of the interview and explain confidentiality issues. In your report, you should change the name of the service provider and the respondent so that they cannot be identified. Check through the questions you intend to ask and make sure they fit in with the information required for Section 6. You tutor may arrange a visit from a service manager.

SCENARIO

Jane

Jane is an A-Level student working on this unit. She decided to look at some information that would give her some details about the demographic factors that could influence the provision of services in her area. She looked at:

* the PCT Public Health Report that gave details of the health needs of the local population and the inequalities experienced by some groups
* the Local Delivery Plan – available from either the PCT or the local council
* the 2001 census figures for the area
* Jane had also collected press cuttings from her local paper about health and care issues. She visited her local library and asked for advice, and she used information from her college library about the local area.

From her investigations she found there was a high proportion of people over 75 living alone in the area.

Jane decided that she would look at the NSF for Older People as an example of current policy. This would give her a starting point for asking questions of health and social care service providers. She downloaded a summary of the NSF from the Department of Health website. Having looked at the eight standards she decided she couldn't cover all of them in her investigation, so she decided to focus on Standard 6, which was about Preventing Falls.

Jane had a neighbour, Mrs Brown (aged 80) who had had a fall in the last year and had been admitted to hospital with a broken hip. Mrs Brown lived on her own, and received services from Age Concern as well as social services. Jane decided to interview Mrs Brown about her experiences. Mrs Brown was quite a chatty woman who knew 'her rights'. She was a retired nurse and until her accident she had been very active in the community. Jane decided she would be a good person to interview. Before she interviewed her, Jane drew up a list of questions focusing on Mrs Brown's needs – physical, intellectual, emotional and social – and how social services and Age Concern identified her needs and whether the services they provided met her needs. She knew she had to be careful not to upset Mrs Brown by asking her personal questions. She decided she would ask Mrs Brown if she could interview her and she would assure her that the notes she took would be confidential and she would not use her real name. Jane wondered about tape recording

continued on next page

the interview – she decided she would ask Mrs Brown how she felt about that, too.

Jane had decided it would be interesting to compare how a statutory service worked compared with a voluntary organisation. Jane's tutor had invited a social worker to tell the students about her work. Many of the class had decided to investigate services provided by social services for their assignment, so this was an opportunity for students to find out about how the multi-disciplinary teams work in practice and what quality assurance systems were in place.

Finally, Jane had to think about how she could approach her local Age Concern. Mrs Brown had quite a lot of information about Age Concern as she attended exercise classes run by the local group. The local Age Concern had been closely involved with partners in health and social care in planning how to meet the targets of the NSF. The exercise class aimed to reduce falls in older people, but it also had a social function. Before she spoke to Mrs Brown, Jane hadn't thought that going to an exercise class could also help Mrs Brown in other ways. Mrs Brown told her that the classes were held in the hall of the Age Concern building. There was a snack bar which also provided lunches. There were between eight and ten regular attendees and Mrs Brown got to know them. There was a book club at the centre where she could borrow books. Jane realised that Mrs Brown's social, intellectual and emotional needs could also be met at the centre. Jane decided to contact the centre and interview the manager about the services provided to people like Mrs Brown, and how they identified the needs of clients who were referred to them. She had noticed an Investors in People certificate in the centre so, obviously, the organisation had some kind of quality assurance process in place. She decided she would ask about this as well. Jane wrote out a list of questions for Marian, the manager. She decided to give these to her before the interview.

At every stage in the assessment Jane found her tutor very helpful, but the work she did made her realise that the assessment needed a lot of careful thought and planning. She also found that the whole assessment took much longer than she had expected. She kept a work diary. In this she had written down what she needed to do for each stage of the assessment and she gave herself a target date by which to complete each task.

UNIT 10 ASSESSMENT

What you need to do

You need to produce an investigation to show how demographic factors influence the organisation and provision of health, social care and early years services in the local area, illustrating how two different local services meet the needs of one service user. The total number of marks allocated is 50.

Before you start

You need to think carefully about the two different services you want to use in the assessment and about the service user you will interview. Your tutor should be able to advise you.

Look at Jane's research process in the scenario above. What could you learn from her story? Careful planning would seem to be important, but you need to think about whom you will interview and what agencies you will approach quite early on in the course.

Good luck with your work!

Your evidence

You will need to produce evidence as set out in the assessment objectives (AOs). The number of marks allocated is shown in brackets.

AO1: information about how two different demographic characteristics influence the provision of services in the local area (10)

AO2: how, from two different services, practitioners work in multi-disciplinary teams to identify and meet the needs of one service user (10)

AO3: research and analysis of quality assurance methods used by the two services for the service user (15)

AO4: an evaluation of one national policy or one piece of legislation on care practice and provision and how this has affected the service user. (15)

AO1 students

In order to gain the highest marks you need to achieve the following:

❋ select two demographic factors which have influenced the organisation and provision of services

❋ produce a detailed explanation of all the stages in local planning

❋ use written expression with appropriate specialist vocabulary to explain how relevant demographic characteristics/trends are used to assess local needs and why it is important to involve local stakeholders in local planning.

At this level candidates give a comprehensive and in-depth account of how services are organised. Candidates also explain in detail how the local plan is monitored and reviewed and that there are no omissions or inaccuracies within the evidence.

AO2 students

In order to gain the highest marks you need to achieve the following:

❋ accurately and independently apply in-depth knowledge, understanding and skills to explain the approaches used by practitioners working in two different services

❋ analyse how practitioners meet the needs of the service user

❋ give an in-depth account, with detailed examples, of how practitioners work in multi-disciplinary teams

❋ apply in-depth knowledge, understanding and skills to analyse how working in multi-disciplinary teams benefits service users

❋ write in a manner which conveys appropriate meaning, using specialist vocabulary with accuracy making sure there are no errors/inaccuracies.

AO3 students

In order to gain the highest marks you need to achieve the following:

❋ select appropriate research techniques; reasons are given to justify the research techniques chosen

❋ use a range of primary and secondary information to comprehensively analyse the quality-assurance mechanisms used by the two services

❋ collect primary evidence through interviews, surveys or observation and secondary evidence via the Internet, organisational documents and publications

❋ no omissions or inaccuracies within the evidence.

References and further reading

Guide to the Social Services in 2005/06 (2005) London: Waterlow Publishing

Handy, C. (1993) *Understanding Organizations* Harmondsworth: Penguin

HM Government (1997) *The New NHS Modern Dependable* London: HMSO

HM Government (2000) *The NHS Plan* London: HMSO

HM Government (2003) Green Paper *Every Child Matters* London: HMSO

HM Government (2003) *Fair Access to Care Services* London: HMSO

HM Government (2004) White Paper *Every Child Matters: Next Steps* London: HMSO

HM Government (2005) Green Paper *Independence, well-being and choice* London: HMSO

Moonie, N. (2000) *Advanced Health and Social Care* Oxford: Heinemann

Moonie, N. (2004) *GCE AS Level in Health and Social Care* Oxford: Heinemann

Wellards NHS Handbook 2004–2005 (2004) Wadhurst East, Sussex: JMH Publishing Ltd.

Useful websites

Cabinet Office
www.cabinetoffice.gov.uk

Commission for Social Care Inspection
www.csci.org.uk

Community Care
www.communitycare.co.uk

Department of Health
www.dh.gov.uk

Healthcare Commission
www.healthcarecommission.org.uk

Home Office
www.homeoffice.gov.uk

Investors in People
www.investorsinpeople.co.uk

National Health Service
www.nhs.uk

NHS Plan for Scotland
www.show.scot.uk

NHS Plan for Wales
www.wales.gov.uk

Office for Standards in Education
www.ofsted.gov.uk

Understanding human behaviour

This unit covers the following sections:

11.1 Factors influencing human development

11.2 Theories of human development

11.3 Application of theories to aid the understanding of human behaviour of individuals in care settings

Each human being is unique. There is no one in the past, alive now, or in the future who will have exactly the same biology, life experience, environment, or thoughts as you. But what are the factors that result in the unique nature of each person?

This unit explores some of the influences that may impact on human development – including your own development. The second section of this unit looks at six broad psychological perspectives that have been used to try to understand human behaviour. The work of a range of famous psychological theorists is outlined. The final section of this unit focuses on examples of the role of theory in explaining behaviour in care settings.

How you will be assessed

This unit will be assessed by an external 90-minute test. The total number of marks allocated to the test is 100.

Questions may involve the use of illustrations, photographs, data and case studies or scenarios. All questions need to be answered.

Examples of questions are provided at the end of the unit, together with a reading list and a list of relevant websites.

Section 1: Factors influencing human development

Inherited influences

Each living cell in the human body has a nucleus containing 23 pairs of chromosomes. In each pair of chromosomes, one comes from the father and one from the mother. Each chromosome carries units of inheritance known as genes and the genes on each chromosome interact to create a new set of 'instructions' to make a new human being. Although half your chromosomes come from your mother and half from your father, your genetic pattern can be different from that of your mother or your father.

Think it over

Reece is 44 years old and seriously overweight. He is well-informed about the health risks associated with his weight, but he says that he can't do anything about it because his problem is genetic. Reece explains: 'You see I know people who are as thin as a rake and they don't eat any less than I do – I am meant to be this way, it runs in the family. I have tried but I just can't lose weight.'

Is Reece right – do inherited influences make us what we are?

Key concept

Genes: units that contain the information and instructions that control the development of living organisms. Genes influence individual differences, such as gender, hair and eye colour, height and skin colour.

An individual person results from the interaction of their genetic pattern and their environment. It has become fashionable for journalists to talk about 'genes for' criminal behaviour, or intelligence, or certain illnesses. It is extremely unlikely, however, that complex social behaviours can be explained purely in terms of the biochemical instructions for building cell structures.

As we learn more about genetics it is becoming widely accepted that genetic influences interact and are interlinked with environmental influences. So genetics may influence how we put on weight – but it is unlikely that genetics will be the only reason a person becomes overweight. It might be impossible to be overweight if there was little food available. Genetics may influence the development of our physiology, and in turn behaviour; however, our genetics do not directly control our actions.

Genetic influences

Some medical conditions, such as Tourette's syndrome, do 'run in families'. A person's genetic structure may cause the central nervous system to develop in a way that results in behaviour such as uncontrollable 'twitches', grunts or shouts. We do not know exactly how Tourette's syndrome is inherited. Many people with Tourette's syndrome can learn ways of managing and controlling the problem.

Did you know?

Tourette's syndrome

Tourette's syndrome is named after George Gilles de la Tourette, the doctor who first recognised the group of symptoms associated with the condition. Tourette's syndrome may involve uncontrollable facial twitches, blinks or jerks called 'tics'. In some people this progresses to making uncontrolled noises or shouting. People with Tourette's syndrome are at risk of being labelled and stereotyped as frightening or dangerous by members of the public who do not understand the condition.

Autism is another condition associated with the development of the nervous system that may be influenced by genetics. Once again, the causes of autism are not fully understood. Although an individual's genetics may play a role, autism is not necessarily inherited from a mother or father. People with autism may have difficulty interacting with other people and may have restricted language. Sometimes autism can result in very withdrawn behaviour. Autism is often diagnosed in the first 18 months of life. A less severe type of autism is known as Asperger's syndrome.

When trying to understand human behaviour it is very important not to ignore the impact of human physiology. A person's physiology will be influenced by their genetic inheritance. It would be a mistake to assume that people with Tourette's or Asperger's syndrome have simply learned to behave as they do.

It is important to recognise that in Reece's story, Reece may be correct – his physiology may be different from other peoples, and he may indeed find it harder to maintain a healthy body weight than some other people do. Even so, Reece's genetics do not directly create excessive body weight. If Reece had experienced different environmental and socio-economic influences, if he had developed a different self-concept – he might have found a way of managing his physiology and weight.

SCENARIO

Jack and Maxwell

Jack and Maxwell are brothers, both share a genetic tendency to become dependent on alcohol. Their parents rent accommodation in a deprived housing estate. Jack and Maxwell's parents split up and Jack goes to live with his grandmother.

Maxwell's story

Maxwell remains at home and his father re-marries. Maxwell does not get on with his stepmother and spends a lot of time playing with the children on the estate where he lives. Maxwell's friends hate school and are impressed by the status and wealth of the drug dealers who supply people in the neighbourhood. By the age of 11 Maxwell has tried a range of drugs including alcohol. His concentration at school is impaired through lack of motivation and the effects of substances he has tried. As Maxwell grows older he frequently drinks alcohol and finds that he 'needs to drink'. By 17 years of age he spends many evenings drinking and cannot manage to cope either with education or with the idea of getting a job. By early adulthood Maxwell is unemployed, has few friends, no qualifications and serious health problems.

Jack's story

Jack grows up with his grandmother who takes a close interest in his development. At school Jack mixes with friends who are interested in computers. Jack does not play out on the street but often goes to a friend of the family in the evening, where he can play on the computer. Jack is able to join a weekend project at school to develop IT skills. Jack imagines a future where he can have a career in information technology. He does not mix with people who drink alcohol or take drugs. At 16 years of age Jack believes that drinking is unhealthy and decides to avoid alcohol because he adopts the religious views of his grandparents. By early adulthood Jack has good educational qualifications and decides to study for a degree. He is in good health and has a range of supportive friends and relatives and believes he has few problems in life.

Genetic and socio-economic issues interact in these two case studies. Can you see how different socio-economic circumstances can alter the outcomes of a person's genetic inheritance?

Socio-economic influences

Family

Children are strongly influenced by the people who care for them. When children grow up within a family group, they will usually learn a wide range of ideas (or norms) about what is normal and how to behave. For instance, at mealtimes some families will have strict rules that everyone must sit down at the table and it is considered 'rude' if one person starts to eat before the others. Children learn to become social – they are socialised – by living with carers.

Children also learn ideas about what is right or wrong. They learn the customs of their culture and family, they learn to play gender and adult roles, and they learn what is expected of them and what they should expect from others. Socialisation teaches children ways of thinking, and these ways of thinking may stay with a person for life. Giddens (1997) explains that socialisation 'is the process whereby the helpless infant gradually becomes a self-aware, knowledgeable person, skilled in the ways of the culture into which he or she is born'. Socialisation involves learning the social norms of your culture.

It is important to distinguish between the concept of 'family' and the concept of 'household'. Household means a building, that could be a flat, a bungalow or a house, and who lives in the building. Households may include people who

FAMILY TYPE	DESCRIPTION
Extended families	Parents, children and grandparents and/or relatives live together and support each other
Nuclear families	Parents and their children live together and parents support the children
Lone-parent families	A lone or 'single' parent lives with and supports children
Reconstituted families	A parent and a step-parent who is not the biological mother or father of the children live with and support the children

TABLE 11.1 *Some types of family*

are not related, people who are friends, people who rent accommodation and so on. Family implies that people are related to each other.

Key concept

Family: a social group made up of people who are related to each other. Families provide a range of benefits for and influences on family members.

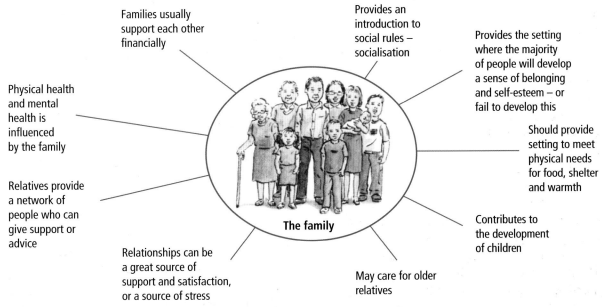

Families usually support each other financially

Provides an introduction to social rules – socialisation

Provides the setting where the majority of people will develop a sense of belonging and self-esteem – or fail to develop this

Physical health and mental health is influenced by the family

Should provide setting to meet physical needs for food, shelter and warmth

Relatives provide a network of people who can give support or advice

The family

Contributes to the development of children

Relationships can be a great source of support and satisfaction, or a source of stress

May care for older relatives

FIGURE 11.1 *Some ways in which families influence us*

The attitudes and beliefs that a person learns, for example beliefs about the importance of a healthy diet, or beliefs about the value of education, will be influenced by their early socialisation within a family.

Think it over

In the story of Maxwell and Jack above, family and socialisation have a major role in influencing what happens to them. Looking first at Maxwell and then at Jack, explain how the attitudes and social beliefs of the family they grew up with influenced the way they developed.

Income differences

The economic resources of an individual or family can make a major difference to a person's quality of life. The weekly income enables them to pay for their house or flat, and to buy food and clothes. Income mainly comes from:

* wages from employment
* profits from your business if you are self-employed
* benefits paid by the government
* money from invested wealth, such as interest on bank accounts or bonds
* money raised through the sale of property owned.

Income is not distributed equally in the UK. The top 20 per cent of households receive around 15 times more money each year than the poorest 20 per cent. Income is subject to taxation and other forms of redistribution; the highest earners pay tax on their income, whilst many poorer households receive benefits that increase income. After tax and benefits have been paid out, the richest 20 per cent are only four times better off than the poorest 20 per cent of households (National Statistics, 2004).

Did you know?

Approximately 10 per cent of the UK population has no savings or investments. Among the 20 to 34 age group, 20 per cent of people have no savings or investments and among young people aged 16 to 24, 56 per cent of people have no savings (Institute for Public Policy Research, 2004).

Nowadays households with an income lower than 60 per cent of **'median'** income in the UK are considered to be living in poverty. A median is the middle value in a range of numbers. So 'low income' means that you have an income that is only worth 60 per cent of the middle income level. This measure is used by the government's Social Exclusion Unit and also by the European Union for making comparisons between member countries. People with a very low level of income are poor relative to the expectations of most people.

Just over a sixth of Britain's population (17 per cent), was estimated by the Institute for Fiscal Studies to be living on a low income in the period 2001–02 (*Social Trends*, 2004). If a measure of income after housing costs is used then 22 per cent of households live in income poverty (Paxton and Dixon, 2004).

Key groups of people who have to live on very little money include:

* one-parent families
* unemployed people
* elderly people
* sick or disabled people
* unskilled couples (where only one person works in an unskilled job).

Social Trends (2004) estimates that around 30 per cent of children (3.8 million children) live in low income households (after housing costs). It states that 'children living in workless families or households have a much higher risk of low income than those in families with one or more adults in full-time work'. Around three-quarters of children living in 'workless' or lone-parent families live in low-income households (*Social Trends*, 2004).

The impact of low income

Paxton and Dixon (2004) quote research conclusions which show that: 'Children who grew up in poverty during the 1970s did worse at school, were six times less likely to enter higher education, and one-and-a-half times more likely to be unemployed – and earned 10 per cent less during their lifetimes than those who did not experience poverty as children.' They list three disadvantages of poverty.

* Poverty is associated with being a victim of crime: 4.8 per cent of people who earned under £5,000 a year were burgled in 2003–04 compared to only 2.7 per cent of people who earned over £30,000.

* Poorer communities are more likely to be in polluted areas. 'In 2003 there were five times as many industrial sites in the wards containing the most deprived 10 per cent of the population and seven times as many emission sources as in wards with the least deprived 10 per cent.'

* Low social class is associated with an increased risk of dying young. 'In 2003, children of fathers in the lower **social class** were twice as likely to die within one year of birth, five times more likely to die in a traffic accident and 15 times more likely to die in a house fire than those in the highest social class.'

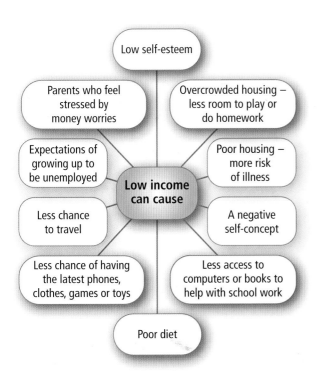

FIGURE 11.2 *Some problems a child belonging to a low-income family may face*

Education

Although everyone in the UK has the right to receive education, educational opportunities may not be exactly the same for everyone. In 1998 the Acheson report noted that schools in deprived neighbourhoods were likely to suffer more problems than schools in the more affluent areas. 'Schools in disadvantaged areas are likely to be restricted in space and have the environment degraded by litter, graffiti, and acts of vandalism. This contributes to more stressful working conditions for staff and pupils. Children coming to school hungry or stressed as a result of their social and economic environment will be unable to take full advantage of learning opportunities. Stress, depression and **social exclusion** may reduce parents' capacity to participate in their children's education.'

Education has a link with health in that low levels of educational achievement are associated with poor health in adult life (Acheson, 1998).

Paxton and Dixon (2004) discuss the links between low income and educational achievement. At primary school level they note 'between 1999 and 2002, pupils in schools where a lower proportion of the intake is eligible for free school meals made more progress at both Key Stage 2 (age 7 to 11) and Key Stage 3 (age 11 to 14) than those in schools where more were eligible for free school meals'. At secondary education level they reported that children from the higher social classes achieved more high-grade GCSEs than children from the lower social classes and lower-income families.

It is likely that the combined effects of poor resources, low expectations and the need to earn money often influence young people from low income families to give education a low priority.

Housing

People with high incomes often feel confident about their future and their ability to take out a mortgage to buy a home of their own. These people can also choose where and how they would like to live.

FIGURE 11.3 *Educational opportunities are not the same for all*

People on low incomes tend to have less choice. They may need to rent property in more densely populated housing areas. Wealthier people will often live in more spacious and less stressful conditions than low-income families.

According to the Acheson report, 'Poor quality housing is associated with poor health. Dampness is associated with increased prevalence of allergic and inflammatory lung diseases, such as asthma.' The Acheson report also noted, '40 per cent of all fatal accidents happen in the home. Almost half of all accidents to children are associated with architectural features in and around the home. Households in disadvantaged circumstances are likely to be the worst affected by such accidents.'

What if?

Look at the hazards listed in Figure 11.4. How do you think living in poor housing might influence a person's self-esteem?

Windows kept shut to conserve warmth – resulting in poor ventilation

Damp patch on wall from broken gutters outside – risk of infection from fungal spores

Door hinged outwards to create space (safety hazard)

Poor lighting

Overcrowded bedroom – helps spread droplet (airborne) infection, when combined with poor ventilation

Poor hygiene maintenance of bathroom facilities (lack of cleaning agents) – increased risk of skin and other contagious diseases

Portable radiant electric fire (safety hazard)

Poor maintenance of building – increased accident risk

Overcrowding may increase interpersonal stress, and coupled with other stressors may lead to poor mental health

FIGURE 11.4 *Poor housing may create a range of risks*

Many older people on low incomes worry about the cost of heating in their homes, as older properties are often less well insulated than modern properties. Older, poorly-maintained homes are likely to cost more to heat than recently built properties. For some people who live on a low income in high-density housing the problems shown in Figure 11.4 may create stress.

FIGURE 11.5 *The problems of low-income housing*

employers from starting businesses in these areas, which may help to cause unemployment. Unemployment may contribute to poor facilities because people have little money to spend. Growing up in a neighbourhood with widespread unemployment, crime and poor facilities may do little to motivate children to achieve a good education, so they may find it harder to get jobs. These problems 'feed off' each other, creating housing estates and areas where it is stressful to live. Neighbourhood may have a major impact on a person's chances of growing up to lead a fulfilled life.

FIGURE 11.6 *The neighbourhood you live in can affect your life chances*

Poor housing and low income may be part of a vicious circle

Growing up and living in the most deprived neighbourhoods may greatly restrict an individual's chance of developing their full intellectual, social or emotional potential. The problems of poor facilities and crime may stop

Culture

Culture refers to the traditions, beliefs, values and ideas that are passed on within a group of people. Culture is a major factor influencing the way a person develops their self-concept. Different geographical, ethnic, and religious groups may belong to different cultures. The way a person makes sense of life experience will be influenced by their socialisation into a system of assumptions, beliefs and values..

Key concept

Culture: the collection of values, norms, customs and behaviours that make one group of people distinct from others. A person's culture will influence the development of their self-concept.

Culture includes a very wide range of issues including religion, music, art, architecture, literature and language (including non-verbal language) as well as customs and beliefs.

Children are socialised into a culture. The customs and behaviours that you think of as being 'normal' will be strongly influenced by the culture that you have been socialised into. In the past many children were socialised into a culture shared by everyone in their neighbourhood. Everyone in the village, street or estate might share similar beliefs about religion, work and the importance or lack of importance of education. Parents would socialise children into the beliefs of a local culture and children would copy the behaviour of other people in the local community.

Nowadays culture is a more complex issue. People in the same neighbourhood may have very different assumptions about what is normal or acceptable behaviour. They may have very different beliefs about religion, may have different ethnic identities and different views about work and education. Many people identify with others over the Internet; to some extent people develop and design their own cultural assumptions. People may choose a culture to identify with – rather than just growing up as a member of a cultural tradition. In the UK the local neighbourhood does not necessarily influence people as much as it might have done a hundred years ago.

Access to health services

Areas with many low-income households may have poorer facilities than wealthier areas. Studies have shown that life expectancy is shorter in deprived areas compared to more affluent areas. Although the National Health Service (NHS) provides free health care for everyone, there are concerns that some groups of people may not receive the same access to GP services and preventative health measures as others. Deprived areas may have greater difficulty in recruiting GPs and nurses. The Acheson report in 1998 found that some health care premises in poorer areas were of lower quality than those in wealthier areas. This report also identified an 'inverse law' that meant that communities with the greatest need received the lowest level of service and resources, whilst those with the lowest need receive the highest level. The Acheson report stated: 'Communities most at risk of ill health tend to experience the least satisfactory access to the full range of preventive services, the so-called "inverse prevention law". Prevention services include cancer screening programmes, health promotion and immunisation. While differences are most noticeable amongst socio-economic groups it is likely that, for

In the past local community would often define cultural influences; today young people can interact with a very wide range of cultures

example amongst Bangladeshi women, additional inequalities in access are experienced. Lack of access to women practitioners can be a deterrent to Asian women taking up an invitation for cervical cancer screening. Local studies have shown that access to female practitioners is poorest in areas with high concentrations of Asian residents and that practices with a female doctor or nurse are more likely to reach the cervical cytology targets set out in the GP contract.'

The Acheson report also found that services for people with heart disease were worse for Asian people, despite higher mortality rates in this community.

The quality of health care services and active health promotion may be influenced by the socio-economic characteristics of a neighbourhood. The government now has targets to reduce the gap in life expectancy between health authority areas. There is an NHS Plan that is regularly updated to improve the quality of health services. Improved services for heart disease and cancer are a current priority.

Nutrition

The Acheson report (1998) noted that people in low socio-economic groups, 'spend more on foods richer in energy and high in fat and sugar, which are cheaper per unit of energy than foods rich in protective nutrients, such as fruit and vegetables'.

'People on low incomes eat less healthily partly because of cost, rather than lack of concern or information. Therefore increased availability of affordable 'healthy' food should lead to improved nutrition in the least well off.' The Acheson report found that:

* People in low socio-economic groups eat more processed foods containing high levels of salt, thus increasing the risk of cardiovascular disease.

* There is more obesity in low socio-economic groups than in higher groups – increasing the risk of ill-health for people in low socio-economic groups.

* Babies born to mothers in low socio-economic groups are more likely to have reduced birth weights than those in higher groups. Low birth weight is linked with the risk of cardiovascular disease in later life.

* Women in lower socio-economic groups are less likely to breast feed their babies. Breast feeding helps to protect infants from infection.

People with low incomes may find it harder to travel to supermarkets and stock up on cheaper food. Healthy food may cost more than processed food, which contains higher amounts of sugar and salt. A low income may push people to choose an unhealthy diet, because it can be harder and more expensive to choose a healthy one.

Many people do not follow government advice on diet. Government guidelines recommend that a healthy diet should include at least five portions of fruit and vegetables a day. A national diet and nutrition survey carried out between 2000 and 2001 found that only 13 per cent of men and 15 per cent of women follow this advice. No young men between 19 and 24 were following this advice. Some people may have been socialised into dietary and health habits that cause them to ignore government advice. People with a low income may have less choice when it comes to avoiding processed food.

Environmental influences

Pollution, which comes from a number of different sources, and stressful living conditions can influence people's health and well-being.

Air pollution

Air pollution is a potential cause of ill-health and premature death. It has been a major problem in cities and other urban areas for many years. The Acheson report (1998) quoted research that argued that particulate matter (small particles of soot that can affect human lungs) was responsible for over 8,000 deaths a year and over 10,000 hospital admissions.

Motor vehicles produce a range of pollutants, including carbon monoxide, nitrogen oxides, volatile organic compounds and particulate matter. People living near busy roads may be exposed to air pollution from motor vehicles. The positive news is that air pollution has been decreasing. Carbon monoxide emissions fell by 55 per cent between 1991 and 2002, nitrogen oxides fell by 40 per cent and particulate emissions by 48 per cent. Much of this improved air quality

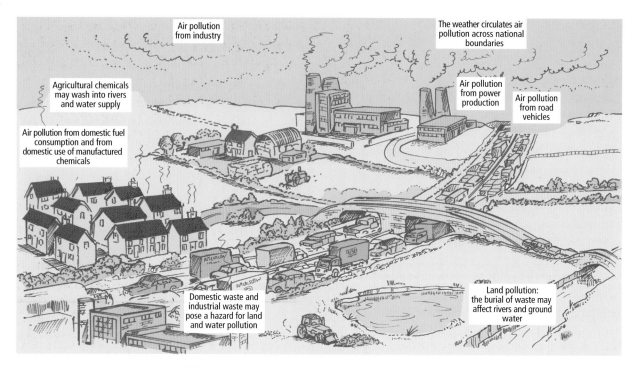

FIGURE 11.7 *There are many different sources of pollution*

may be due to improved vehicle technology and the use of catalytic converters on vehicle exhausts.

Less coal is now burned in power stations, and there have been improved pollution control measures in power generation. In part this may have contributed to a fall in sulphur dioxide emissions of 72 per cent between 1991 and 2002.

Noise pollution

Noise pollution may create stress and contribute to ill-health. A noisy home environment may prevent people from sleeping and may create a feeling of not being safe, secure and in control of your life. Noise pollution appears to be a growing problem – particularly in relation to 'noisy neighbours'. Details

FIGURE 11.8 *Despite improving air quality, air pollution is still an issue in urban settings*

NOISE COMPLAINTS ABOUT	1990–91	2002–03
Domestic premises (neighbours)	2,264	5,573
Commercial leisure or industrial activity	913	1,315
Aircraft	34	104
Road traffic	46	36

TABLE 11.2 *Noise complaints*
Source: adapted from Table 11.5 *Social Trends* (2005)

of noise complaints received by environmental health officers are shown in Table 11.2.

Water pollution

Social Trends (2005) reports that the quality of water in rivers and canals has improved over the last 15 years; this is due to the introduction of pollution control measures. Poor water quality can be caused by chemical pollution, including nitrates and lack of oxygen. In 2001 water in 66 per cent of rivers and canals was judged to be of good quality in England. This compares with only 43 per cent of rivers and canals in 1990. In 2003 only 1 per cent of rivers and canals in England were judged to be seriously polluted, with 6 per cent of rivers and canals judged to be of poor quality. In Wales in the same year 93 per cent of rivers and canals were judged to be of good quality compared with 86 per cent in 1990, and only 2 per cent were considered poor quality.

Psychological influences

Self-concept and concept of others

When we are born we do not understand anything about the world – we do not know that we are an individual person. The beginnings of self-awareness may start when an infant can recognise their own face in a mirror. This happens somewhere around 18 months to 2 years of age, when an infant begins to demonstrate that they are separate from other people.

From this point on, children begin to form ideas about themselves. Children are very influenced by the environment and culture they grow up in, and also by the relationships they have with family and friends. As a child's ability to use language develops this also affects how they can talk and explain things about themselves.

People develop an increasingly detailed understanding of 'self' as they grow older. Some ways in which people may describe their self-concept are explained in Table 11.3.

LIFE STAGE	SELF-CONCEPT
Childhood	At first children will only describe themselves in terms of categories such as being a boy or girl, their age and size. Later children use an increasing range of categories such as hair colour, details of address, activities that they like, factual details of parents or friends
Adolescence	Teenagers may start to explain themselves in terms of chosen beliefs, likes and dislikes, and relationships with other people
Adulthood	Many adults may be able to explain the quality of their lives and their thoughts about themselves in greater depth and detail than when they were younger
Old age	Some older adults may have more self-knowledge than they had when they were younger. Some older people may show wisdom in the way they talk about themselves.

TABLE 11.3 *Life stages and self-concept*

The self-concept which we imagine when we are very young is influenced by the family or carers that we grow up with. Primary school-age children are very influenced by the adults that they live with. As we grow older the friends we mix with gradually take over and influence what we think about or imagine ourselves to be like. Adolescents often develop the views and beliefs that their friends have, often compare themselves with others, and choose a particular set of friends to belong with.

Many people do not need to describe and explain a self-concept until they are ready to go out to work full-time or until they plan to leave home. It may be that many people can experiment with ideas of what they may be like and what they may be good at until they settle into adult commitments. For this reason some people may not be able to explain a clear self-concept until they are in their early twenties.

A clear sense of what you think your personality is like and what you think you are good at may be needed if you are to be happy, confident and successful at work and in love.

A positive self-concept involving self-esteem may help a person to:

* make effective social and emotional relationships with others

* make effective decisions at work

* have self-confidence when meeting new people

* cope with emotions and feelings when things go wrong

* feel confident when experiencing or learning new things.

Self-efficacy

General or 'global' self-concept may include our assessment of how good we are at things such as sport, academic writing or controlling our own habits. Our assessment of how good we are at something can be referred to as 'self-efficacy'. The psychologist Albert Bandura (1989) uses the term self-efficacy to include a person's ability to understand their capabilities, motivation, thought patterns and emotional reactions. Self-efficacy is how you estimate your abilities or what you

FIGURE 11.9 *The development of self-concept*

believe about yourself. It is learned from past experiences, from watching and thinking about what happens to others, from copying others and from feedback from other people. High self-efficacy means believing you will succeed at a task. Low self-efficacy means believing you will fail.

Once a person believes they are good at something, this belief will provide motivation to keep building on success. Of course, the opposite is also true. If you believe you are no good, then you will probably withdraw from the activity and avoid it.

Some people may learn to think of themselves as being able to control habits such as over-eating or taking drugs; other individuals may develop a low sense of self-efficacy and feel that they are unable to control their own lifestyle. People with low self-efficacy may experience their lives as a series of events that just 'happen to them'. Taking control of your own lifestyle may require a sense of confidence in your own emotional abilities. This sense of self-confidence might be learned in the company of family, friends and work colleagues.

Think it over

Reece has a serious weight problem and he has undertaken a program to help him to diet. At first he believed that the program would not work and that he could not lose weight. Reece did stick to the program and checked his weight every morning. After several weeks he began to notice that he was losing weight and he thought 'I can control my body weight.' Reece began to develop a sense of control. He describes this sense of control as: 'It's a bit like learning to float when you learn to swim – you have to learn the feeling.'

Reece now believes that he can choose to control his diet and his body weight. Reece has developed a sense of self-efficacy with respect to controlling his body – he not only believes he can do it – he can explain how it feels to be in control of his weight.

It is possible to have a positive general self-concept and yet have a low sense of self-efficacy with respect to specific skills or abilities. Reece may have had a positive self-concept and yet to begin with he did not believe he could control his weight. Reece had to experience success before he could develop the necessary sense of self-efficacy.

Do you think it is possible to develop a sense of self-efficacy without having practical experiences?

Do you think Reece could develop self-efficacy just by being told that he could control his weight?

Fear and anxiety

Self-efficacy will protect people from experiencing fear and anxiety. If you believe that you are good at something, and if you feel confident, then you are unlikely to become anxious or afraid. If you are good at mixing with other people, for example, then you are unlikely to become anxious when meeting new people.

Many people develop fears about aspects of daily life. Some people become afraid of encountering birds, spiders or animals. Other people are afraid of crowds. Some people do not like meeting new people. Some people are afraid of being on their own.

Key concept

Anxiety: involves experiencing a continuous high level of tension and worry. Anxiety can result in tension headaches, problems with sleeping, increased irritability and experience of aches and pains.

One explanation for the fears and anxieties people experience is that they feel out of control. If you do not feel confident that you know what to do, if you do not feel that you are the kind of person that is good at coping, then you may have a low sense of self-efficacy. The way that you think about yourself may result in anxiety

If you are not confident and cannot imagine how you will cope with a worrying situation you may feel a strong desire to withdraw from that situation. Many people restrict their lives by withdrawing from situations that they associate with low self-efficacy. For example if you do not think you are good at mixing with people then the easy solution is to withdraw from having to meet new people. But withdrawing from people limits the quality of life you will experience.

Concepts of other people

The development of self-concept involves using imagination to imagine who you are. But the question is – do we ever stop imagining? Although adults learn not to talk to people who are not 'real', perhaps the way we understand our friends and relatives is still a matter of imagination. In other words, we don't really know our friends – we only know our imagination of what they are like.

The way in which we understand our own self-concept and self-esteem will be influenced by our understanding of society and the people that we mix with. Other people influence our

Have you ever encountered a young friend or relative who has an imaginary friend?

Many 4- and 5-year-olds have an imaginary character, such as a friendly lion, who they talk to. Sometimes adults can get quite worried about this behaviour because in adult life talking to imaginary people is associated with mental health problems. The sociologist George Herbert Mead argued that children have to learn to make sense of people and that the way they do this is to use imagination. A young child is using their imagination to create characters and this helps them to understand how people function.

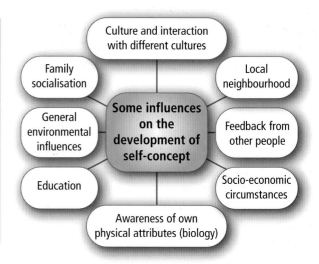

FIGURE 11.10 *Inherited, socio-economic and environmental influences interact with our understanding of self*

self-concept by the way they react to us. If people admire us and say nice things about us this may help to create a positive self-concept. If people treat us with abuse or neglect we may develop a negative self-concept. Historically some sociologists have thought that our self-concept is created by the people we mix with. It is as if we see reflections of our self in a mirror that other people hold up to us. This is only half the story though, because we use our own imagination to interpret the reflections of self that we receive from other people.

Summary

The interaction of influences

Human behaviour results from an interaction of human genetics, socio-economic influences,

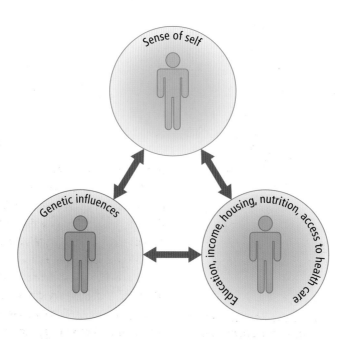

FIGURE 11.11 *We are influenced by the interaction of our genetics and our environment*

wider environmental influences and psychological factors including self-concept. One way to understand these interactions is to explore the interaction of our genetics and environment.

Our environment, social influences and genetics can explain a lot about our nature and behaviour. But people are not passive objects that are fixed and determined by environmental and socio-economic influences. Even an infant can influence their carers. Once a person develops a sense of self, that person will start to make choices and attempt to influence and control their environment. A person's understanding of their situation represents another area of influence on behaviour. People are capable of choices that can affect how socio-economic influences work, for example people have some choice over their diet and over the way they react to education. Many individuals have some choice about the environment they experience – it is possible for some people to move house. It may even become possible to avoid the consequences of our genetic structure by accessing modern scientific and medical treatments.

FIGURE 11.12 *The use of imagination may be the first step to breaking away from the consequences of inherited, environmental and socio-economic influences*

Consider this

Maisie is an 86-year-old member of a reminiscence group at a day centre. She is a happy person who feels in control of her life. During discussion Maisie talks about her life, explaining: 'Life was hard in them days, but everyone looked after everyone else, my family would go without things just so I could grow up fit and healthy. No one could want a better family, and all my life I've been lucky. I've never been rich but I always had enough to get by. Life is what you make it – I enjoy my life. I've got no time for people who moan and grumble – if something's not right in your life then do something about it – that's what I say.'

Maisie appears to have had positive family experiences but she grew up in a low-income family.

1. Can you identify some of the disadvantages that growing up on a low income may involve?

2. Can you identify some of the advantages that Maisie may have experienced growing up in a supportive family?

3. Can you explain how Maisie's self-concept may have contributed to a happy and successful life?

4. Can you describe how different types of influence can interact so that no one influence necessarily determines the quality of life that a person experiences?

Section 2: Theories of human development

Psychodynamic perspective

Sigmund Freud (1856–1939) developed a theory of the human mind that emphasised the interaction of biological drives and social environment. Freud's theory emphasises the power of early experience to influence adult personality.

Freud's theories are called **psychodynamic** theories. 'Psycho' means mind or spirit and 'dynamic' means energy or the expression of energy. Freud believed that people were born with a dynamic 'life energy' or 'libido' which initially motivates a baby to feed and grow and later motivates sexual reproduction. Freud's theory explains that people are born with biological instincts in much the same way as animals such as dogs or cats are. Our instincts exist in the unconscious mind – we don't usually understand our unconscious. As we grow we must learn to control our instincts to be accepted and fit in with other people. Society is only possible if people can 'control themselves'. If everybody did whatever they felt like, life would probably be short and violent, and civilisation would be impossible. Because people must learn to control their unconscious drives (or instincts), children go through stages of psychosexual development. These stages result in the development of a mature mind which contains the mechanisms that control adult personality and behaviour.

Freud's stages of psychosexual development

The oral stage

Drive energy motivates the infant to feed, and activities involving the lips, sucking and biting create pleasure for the baby. Weaning represents a difficult stage which may influence the future personality of the child.

The anal stage

Young children have to learn to control their muscles, and in particular the anal muscles. Toilet training represents the first time a child has to control their own body to meet the demands of society. The child's experiences during toilet training may influence later development.

The phallic stage

Freud shocked Europeans a century ago by insisting that children had sexual feelings toward their parents. Freud believed that girls were sexually attracted to their father and boys were sexually attracted to their mother. These attractions are called the Electra and Oedipus complexes, named after characters in ancient Greek mythology that experienced these attractions. As children develop they have to give up the opposite-sex parent as a 'love object' and learn to identify with the same-sex parent.

Children's experience of 'letting go' of their first love may have permanent effects on their later personality.

Latency

After the age of 5 or 6, most children have resolved the Electra and Oedipus complexes (Freud believed that this was usually stronger and more definite in boys, i.e. girls often continue with a sexual attachment to their father). Children are not yet biologically ready to reproduce so their sexuality is latent or waiting to express itself.

Genital

With the onset of puberty, adolescents become fully sexual and 'life drive' is focused on sexual activity.

> **What if?**
>
> Have you ever watched animals such as kittens develop? Freud's theories are often hard to accept in a society which is 'out of touch' with nature, but if you watch kittens they focus all their energy on getting milk from the mother cat – life energy seems almost visible. As kittens grow to young cats they will sometimes attempt to mate with parents. Freud's theories were based on the idea that people are animals – but animals that have to adapt their behaviour to the needs of society.
>
> How far do you think we forget or even deny our inner 'animal' drives?

Freud's mental mechanisms

Freud believed that we were born with an **'id'**. The 'id' is part of our unconscious mind hidden from conscious understanding. It is like a dynamo that generates mental energy which motivates human action and behaviour.

When a young child learns to control their own body during toilet training the **'ego'** develops. The 'ego' is a mental system which contains personal learning about physical and social reality. The 'ego' has the job of deciding how to channel drive energy from the unconscious into behaviour which will produce satisfactory outcomes in the real world. The 'ego' is both unconscious (unknown to self) and conscious (a person can understand some of their own actions and motivation).

The 'super ego' develops from the ego when the child gives up their opposite-sex parent as a 'love object'. The 'super ego' contains the social and moral values of the parent that has been 'lost' as a potential partner.

The essence of **psychodynamic** theory is that people are controlled by inner forces, but that people do not understand and cannot explain what is happening to them. For example, throughout adult life a person must find a way to release drive energy that is compatible with the demands of society and with the demands of the super ego. Sometimes people may feel sandwiched between the demands of their biology and social pressures. Typically, today's world often creates pressure to 'achieve a good career' and please parental values by 'doing well'. For some people the desire to enjoy their sexuality and perhaps have children may conflict with the pressure to achieve. The way people cope with these pressures will be strongly influenced by childhood experiences according to Freudian theory.

In order to understand an individual's behaviour, a therapist needs to understand what is happening in the individual's unconscious mind. Therapists and counsellors cannot begin to understand the unconscious mind by asking direct questions. To understand how early experience has influenced the unconscious mind therapists might explore an individual's dreams. Alternatively, a therapist might ask an individual to make up a story about a picture (the Thematic Apperception Test) or ask them what they see in an ink blot (the Rorschach test).

These indirect conversations are a way of learning about another person's unconscious mind. Freud originally used the method of 'free association' to access the unconscious mind of his patients. This 'talking cure' involves getting the patient or client to relax on a couch and just explain whatever comes into their mind in response to words that the psychoanalyst says.

Psychosexual stages of development and personality

Freud believed that a person's experiences in the first three stages would influence their adult personality. An infant whose feeding needs were always anticipated and met might grow up to be a rather passive person who allows others to make all the decisions. An infant whose need for milk was rarely met might also become fixated with the struggle for food. Ideally, infants should learn to communicate their needs but also learn that communication will result in a good response. Many people do not experience ideal conditions in early life so it is possible for life energy to become focused or fixated on the early stages of development.

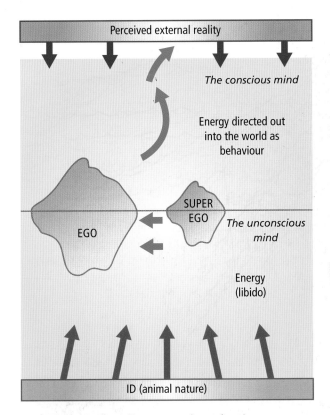

FIGURE 11.13 *Freudian mental mechanisms*

Key concept

Fixation: in Freudian theory, fixation is when life energy (called libido) remains attached to an early stage of development. Life energy can also become fixated on objects and people in a person's life. Most people will show signs of some fixation, but an excessive amount of fixation may result in extreme personality characteristics.

Personality characteristics associated with the oral stage

If life energy becomes fixated with the oral stage a person may tend to be passive, dependent on others and gullible. Such a person might also be attracted to oral pleasures such as eating, drinking or smoking. People who are extremely passive and perhaps manipulative might be understood as being fixated at the oral stage of development. Because of the way psychological defence mechanisms work, people with exactly the opposite personality, e.g. someone who is suspicious and avoids oral pleasure, might also be seen as reacting to an oral fixation. A well-adjusted adult will have a personality that lies between these extremes.

Personality characteristics associated with the anal stage

A fixation of life energy at this stage of development might result in characteristics of:

* hoarding, or being mean with money

* being stubborn

* being obsessed with tidiness and cleanliness.

The term anal–retentive is sometimes used to describe people who are obsessed with tidiness, cleanliness and controlling their money.

Once again, a person who is extremely generous, open to other people's suggestions and extremely untidy will be seen as reacting to a fixation with the anal stage. A well-adjusted adult will not be particularly mean or over-generous; not particularly stubborn or over-compliant; and not particularly tidy or untidy in their daily life.

Personality characteristics associated with the phallic stage

A fixation of life energy at this stage might result in extremes of personality involving:

* vanity and self-love

* recklessness

* obsession with sexual activity.

Again a person with exactly the opposite characteristics might be reacting to a

fixation at this stage. So a timid adult who avoids all reference to sexuality might also be fixated at the phallic stage. A well-adjusted adult will not display extreme personality characteristics.

People do not become fixated with the latency period, and the genital stage represents adulthood.

Regression

When people experience extreme emotional stress it may be hard for their ego to maintain 'normal' age-appropriate behaviour. A person may feel pulled by unconscious desires to return to a safer time in life. An adult or adolescent might, for example, have a childish temper tantrum involving shouting and screaming over some minor annoyance. This behaviour could be interpreted as a regression to the oral stage. The person is behaving like a young child again because the ego has lost control of the flow of life energy. Life energy has regressed to an earlier stage of development.

Most people will react with some degree of emotional regression if they are stressed, but excessive amounts of childish behaviour might suggest a fixation of life energy with the early stages of development that makes it difficult for the ego to manage daily living.

> **Key concept**
>
> *Regression*: in Freudian theory, regression is when a person's behaviour can be explained in terms of a return to behaviours associated with the first three psychosexual stages.

Fixation means that the person's personality is strongly influenced – perhaps unbalanced – by experiences in the first three life stages. Regression means that a person is reliving some emotional experience from one or more of the first three stages of life. Within Freudian theory, many people would be expected to experience some regression to and fixation with early development.

FIGURE 11.14 *An obsession with tidiness or untidy behaviour may both result from life energy regressing to the anal stage*

Defence mechanisms

The ego is the decision-making part of our mind. The ego has to work out how to get on with other people whilst also coping with our unconscious animal instincts and memories. The ego is under attack from the pressures of the real world and of the unconscious. If a person is to remain in good mental health, their ego must find a way of coping with all these pressures. Ego defences are ways in which people can make themselves feel safer and protect themselves from pressure.

Examples of defence mechanisms include:

* *denial:* blocking threatening information or thoughts from awareness

* *repression:* forcing memories from consciousness into the unconscious mind. Repression is a kind of motivated forgetting of unpleasant thoughts or memories

* *rationalisation:* reinterpreting events or memories to make them safer for the ego

* *displacement:* finding a different outlet for feelings, such as transferring anger towards a parent to an 'out-group'

* *projection:* projecting forbidden emotions onto others, i.e. what we see in others is sometimes in ourselves

* *sublimation:* a change of state in the way mental energy is directed, e.g. sexual drive is directed away from partners and into activities such as collecting things

* *reaction formation:* changing an emotion into its overemphasised opposite, e.g. changing love to hatred or hatred into aggressively expressed praise.

Key concept

Ego defence mechanisms: are ways in which people distort their understanding and memory in order to protect their ego.

What defence mechanisms might be involved in the behaviours described below?

1. Arnold lives alone in a three-bedroom house; he has filled all of the bedrooms, living rooms and corridor with old newspapers.
2. Arnold explains that he likes to collect newspapers because he is interested in recent history.
3. Andrea has chronic obstructive pulmonary disease which causes her distress and difficulty in breathing. She has a long medical history of illness. When asked about her health she claims that there is nothing wrong with her and that she is very well.
4. Andrea says that she has never experienced any serious illness in her life.
5. She says that her carers are 'angels sent from God – the most wonderful people in the world and the kindest, cleverest people she is ever met in her life'.
6. Andrea says that the manager of the home is trying to poison her, and she knows this is true because he does not like her.

Possible defence mechanisms at work:

1. Arnold may be using **sublimation** to redirect mental energy away from aspects of life that become threatening into a much safer activity of collecting things.
2. Arnold may be using **rationalisation** to avoid recognising the real reasons for collecting so many old newspapers.
3. Andrea may be using **denial** to block out awareness of the seriousness of her illness.
4. Andrea may be **repressing** memory of past ill-health in order to feel safer.
5. Andrea may feel distressed and angry about the situation and the care she is receiving, but she is using **reaction formation** in order to change her emotions into 'its overemphasised opposite'. Reaction formation prevents her from being fully aware of her situation and feelings.
6. Andrea may be **displacing** her anger and distress onto the manager and defending her ego against full awareness of her motivation for doing this by using the defence of projection to claim that he dislikes her – it's his fault, he started it!

Erikson's development of psychodynamic theory

Erik Erikson (1902–1994) based his theory on Freud's psychodynamic ideas. Erikson's first five stages of development are similar to Freud's and are developed from Freud's theory. The major difference between Freud's and Erikson's theory is that Erikson believed that people continue to develop and change throughout life. Freud only explained how early experience might influence adult life. Erikson believed that the events of adolescence and beyond were equally important in order to understand people's personality and behaviour.

Erikson originally stated that there were eight periods of developmental crisis an individual would pass through in life. These crises were linked to an unfolding maturational process and would be common to people of all cultures because they were 'psychosexual' in origin rather than linked to issues of lifestyle or culture.

How an individual succeeded or failed in adapting to each crisis would influence how their sense of self and personality developed. The early stages of development provide a foundation for later development. Each stage is described in terms of the positive or the negative outcomes that may happen following the developmental stage. Many people achieve an in-between outcome.

Basic trust versus mistrust

Birth to 18 months
Infants have to learn a sense of basic trust or learn to mistrust the world. If children receive good quality care this may help them to develop

	POTENTIAL POSITIVE OUTCOME	POTENTIAL NEGATIVE OUTCOME
1	Basic trust	Mistrust
2	Self-control	Shame and doubt
3	Initiative	Guilt
4	Competence	Inferiority
5	Identity	Role confusion
6	Intimacy	Isolation
7	Generativity	Stagnation
8	Ego-integrity	Despair

TABLE 11.4 *Erikson's eight life stages*

personalities which include a sense of hope and safety. If not, they may develop a personality dominated by a sense of insecurity and anxiety.

Self-control versus shame and doubt

From 18 months to 3 years
Children have to develop a sense of self-control or a sense of shame and doubt may predominate. They may develop a sense of willpower and control over their own bodies. If this sense of self-control does not develop, then children may feel that they cannot control events.

Initiative versus guilt

3 to 7 years
Children have to develop a sense of initiative which will provide a sense of purpose in life. A sense of guilt may otherwise dominate the individual's personality and lead to lack of self-worth.

Competence versus inferiority

Perhaps 6 to 15 years
The individual has to develop a sense of competence or risk the personality being dominated by feelings of inferiority and failure.

Identity versus role confusion

Perhaps 13 to 21 years
Adolescents or young adults need to develop a sense of personal identity or risk a sense of role confusion, with a fragmented or unclear sense of self.

Intimacy versus isolation

Perhaps 18 to 30 years
Young adults have to develop a capability for intimacy, love and the ability to share and commit their feelings to others. The alternative personality outcome is isolation and an inability to make close, meaningful friendships.

Generativity versus stagnation

Perhaps 30s to 60s or 70s
Mature adults have to develop a sense of being generative, leading to concern for others and for the future well-being of others. The alternative is to become inward-looking and self-indulgent.

Ego-integrity versus despair

Later life
Older adults have to develop a sense of wholeness or integrity within their understanding of themselves. This might lead to a sense of meaning to life or even to what could be called 'wisdom'. The alternative is a lack of meaning in life and a sense of despair.

Both Freud's and Erikson's views of human development are based on the notion that human biology creates a 'life trajectory' where stages of crises are inevitable. Both accept that individual social experiences will interact with biology to create an individual personality. The psychodynamic view of development emphasises the importance of individual experience and the interaction of biological stages and the environment. The relationship between children and parents is seen as a key influence on the development of personality. Personal development is understood in terms of definable stages.

The idea that human development fits eight stages (or five stages) of coping with crises or change does not make sense to everyone. Some psychologists claim that the theories are too rigid to provide a full understanding of human development. Some argue that human development does not involve a series of developmental crises or stages, and that people experience development as a sequence of gradual adjustment.

Psychodynamic theory provides an interesting way of interpreting past life experience – but it is possible to question whether people in the future will experience the biological pressures that Erikson originally identified in the middle of the twentieth century.

Castells (1997) argued that science now gives people the power to live longer, and also the power to delay reproduction and the effects of ageing. Sexuality can be decoupled from reproduction so that sexual behaviour becomes a form of recreational pastime rather than linked to a biological time clock for reproduction. As technology gives people the power to intervene in their own biological nature, notions of biologically controlled stages of development may become increasingly dated, at least with respect to adult life.

What if?

Think about your own development; did you experience times of crisis linked to issues like competence or inferiority in your own school life?

Do you think that your life will involve change through periods of crisis or more gradual and gentle change?

Freud's and Erikson's theories both emphasise the role of biological and sexual development in influencing the workings of our unconscious mind. But other psychodynamic theorists take a different view, and emphasise the role of relationships and attachment as the primary influences on the development of our unconscious mind. The psychodynamic perspective is broader than the work of Freud and Erikson.

The biological perspective

Human behaviour is undoubtedly influenced by brain and body chemistry. For example, some people become touchy or irritable when their blood sugar levels are low because they have not eaten. When people have a high body temperature they may become irrational.

Biological differences may explain why some people become aggressive or depressed, whereas other people in similar circumstances do not. **Trait** theorists assume that human personality is based on biological differences and that personality is relatively stable. We are born with different tendencies to react to the world in different ways. Two famous trait theories are summarised below.

Key concept

Traits: personality traits are inbuilt tendencies to react to people and events in certain generalised ways. A person's profile of traits will determine their personality.

Eysenck's theory

Eysenck's (1965) theory of personality involves three central traits which describe human personality.

Introversion/extroversion

An individual might be either hungry for experience and excitement, in which case they will be an extrovert; or eager to avoid excitement, in which case they will be an introvert. Most people are somewhere in between these extremes.

Stability/instability

Stability means a calm, confident and perhaps carefree approach to life. Instability means a moody, changeable and restless response to life events. Once again most people will fall somewhere in between these extremes.

Tough minded/tender minded

The tough-minded person might be careless of other people's feelings, rights or needs. Tender-minded individuals are likely to be concerned for individual feelings. Few people will demonstrate extreme tough- or tender-minded traits.

Eysenck's theory emphasised the biological basis for personality. He argued that criminal behaviour is particularly associated with high levels of extroversion and instability. He argued that people born with a high level of extroversion were less responsive to conditioned learning.

Cattell's theory

A second trait theory is based on the work of Cattell (1965), who argued that descriptions of human personality could be reduced to 16 basic traits. He invented a test called the 16 personality factor test or 16PF test. Test results and a profile are set out in Figure 11.15.

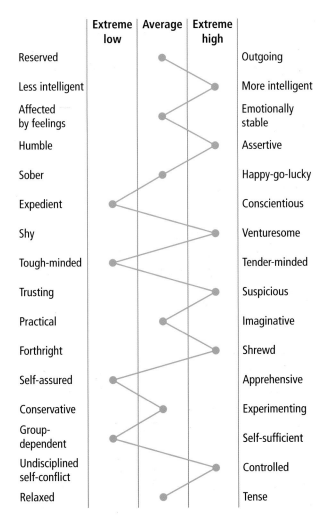

FIGURE 11.15 *A personality profile based on Cattell's 16 personality factors*

The assumption is that how reserved, tough-minded, or group-dependent a person is depends on their underlying biological nature.

A current trait theory

Some psychologists currently work with the idea that there are five main dimensions which summarise human personality. These five basic traits are listed in Table 11.5.

Extroversion Being talkative, energetic	v	Being quiet, reserved and shy
Agreeableness Being sympathetic, kind and affectionate	v	Being cold, quarrelsome and cruel
Conscientiousness Being organised, responsible	v	Being careless, frivolous and irresponsible
Emotional stability Being stable, calm and contented	v	Being anxious, unstable and 'temperamental'
Openness to experience Being creative, intellectual and open-minded	v	Being simple, shallow and unintelligent

TABLE 11.5 *Five basic personality traits, Zimbardo (1992)*

Humanist perspective

Humanistic theory stresses the importance of each individual person's subjective reality. It stresses the idea that each person experiences life differently. People are not seen as mechanisms that can be categorised, analysed and modified. There are no experts who can diagnose what is wrong with another person. Each person is the expert on themselves – and not on anyone else.

One of the major humanistic approaches was developed by Carl Rogers (1902–1987). Rogers' theory emphasises the importance of respect for the value of each individual person.

An overview of Rogers' theory

Every human being has an inbuilt tendency to explore, grow and develop to their full potential.

This inbuilt tendency is called the actualising tendency. In an ideal world people can draw on the inner strength of the actualising tendency to develop a positive and effective self-concept enabling them to live a secure and contented life. Unfortunately we live in a society full of power struggles. Children are taught that they must conform to other people's expectation if they are to be valued. Conditions of worth (see below) end up distorting many people's concepts of themselves. When people live with a distorted sense of who they are, they may cease to value themselves. In this state people are capable of harming themselves and others. People living with a distorted sense of self are likely to experience a wide range of psychological difficulties.

In Rogers' theory the actualising tendency is an inner biological need to grow and develop both physically and psychologically. The actualising tendency can give a person the power to develop, change and grow in order to direct their own life. Many people lose touch with their actualising tendency because social pressures result in a distorted and limiting self-concept.

> **Key concept**
>
> *Actualising tendency:* in Rogers' theory, this is an inner biological resource that can motivate a person to explore, change, cope and develop in life.

Conditions of worth

According to Rogers we are born with an inner tendency to grow and develop, but many people fail to develop self-esteem and to lead a happy, joyful life. A key problem is that our natural potential for growth and development is distorted by conditions of worth. Many children learn that they will only be valued by their family if they meet the conditions or demands that their family make of them. For example, some children are told that they will be rewarded – perhaps with a new bicycle – if they do well at school. Such children also get the message that if they don't do well they will be looked down on and perhaps experience emotional rejection. Many children grow up believing that they must fulfil their parents' expectations for them; for example, that they must follow the career that

their parents expect, or adopt the lifestyle – perhaps early marriage and children – that their parents expect. Children may come to believe that they will only be a worthwhile and valuable person if they are successful in becoming what is expected. This is called conditional positive regard.

Rogers argued that parents should show unconditional positive regard towards children. Unconditional positive regard does not mean that parents have to praise or tolerate everything their children do. It is important that parents are honest with their feelings. Unconditional positive regard simply means that the bond between parents and children is not conditional on the child fulfilling parental demands.

> **Key concepts**
>
> *Conditional positive regard:* the loving relationship is conditional on you doing and becoming what I want you to be. You will only be respected if you do what I expect and demand. If you fail to live up to my demands I will no longer respect or value you.
>
> *Unconditional positive regard:* the loving relationship is secure. I may argue with you, or even become angry with you, but I will always value you regardless of events.

> **SCENARIO**
>
> ### Jodie
>
> Jodie was born with potential athletic abilities. Jodie's inner tendency to self-actualise might have included a deep enjoyment of athletic activities such as running and body-building. Jodie's parents and friends saw these activities as inappropriate. So Jodie came to believe that she would be more popular and likeable if she dropped her interest in sport. Jodie decided to suppress her feelings in order to look good to others – she responded to conditional positive regard in order to please other people.
>
> What consequences might there be of living your life in order to please other people – and not responding to your own potential?

Rogers would have argued that is difficult to lead a fulfilled and happy life if you do not seek to develop your own personal interests and potential. Responding to conditional positive regard may block the development of your potential. A self-actualising person does not need to be what other people think they should be. The self-concept of a self-actualising person will fit their real experience of themselves and not be dependent on the wishes of other people.

Self-concept in Rogers' theory

During childhood we begin to form an idea of ourselves as an individual. We are powerfully influenced by family, friends and the community we live in. Our idea of self is constantly changing, and can be strongly influenced by conditions of worth. As well as a self-concept we may also have a 'self that I would like to be' – an 'ideal self' – that describes the person we would like to become. As long as our self-concept fits with our inner experience we will develop in a healthy way towards becoming a fully functioning person. For many people conditions of worth result in distorted beliefs about self – perhaps beliefs that we are what our families want us to be. These distorted beliefs can result in mental defences and in negative and destructive behaviours. Sometimes conditions of worth result in individuals developing low self-esteem when they fail to live up to other people's demands.

Rogers' theory is sometimes seen as being optimistic with respect to the potential for giving unconditional positive regard. Many people may continue to develop self-concepts which are dependent upon the conditional regard of others.

Abraham Maslow (1908–1970) developed a theory of self-actualisation which was similar to Rogers in some ways; but Maslow's theory accepts that many people will fail to self-actualise and live happy and fulfilled lives because their basic needs will not be met.

Maslow's theory of human need

Maslow originally identified five basic needs. In 1943 he wrote: 'There are at least five sets of goals, which we may call basic needs. These are briefly physiological, safety, love, esteem, and self-actualisation.' These five levels of need form the basis of Maslow's theory.

FIGURE 11.16 *Maslow's four deficit needs and the higher-level need to self-actualise*

* *Physiological needs:* food, warmth, shelter, sex, etc.
* *Safety needs:* physical and emotional freedom from threat.
* *A need to belong:* social inclusion and attachment to others.
* *Self-esteem needs:* respect and a secure sense of self/self-concept.

Maslow identified four basic needs that he called deficit needs. Deficit needs must be met before a person can fully develop their potential. He argued that most people in North American society spent their lives wrestling with deficit needs. Deficit needs limit and distort human development and the majority of people never achieve self-actualisation.

Maslow argued that if you are hungry, tired and threatened your whole attention will be focused on the struggle to survive. Other people spend much of their life looking for love or looking for a family or group that they can belong with. More fortunate people will seek achievements and career goals that will help meet their self-esteem needs. Only a few people – usually people who are middle-aged – are fully satisfied in terms of self-esteem, belonging, safety and physical needs.

Deficit needs

Michael is 22-years-old, homeless and drug dependent. He spends much of his time begging for money and his thoughts revolve around getting enough drugs to feel OK. Michael also thinks about food, warmth and having sex. Michael does not care about what other people think of him and he does not have a trusting relationship with any other person.

Emily is 22-years-old and has had many boyfriends although her relationships never work out. Emily says she intends to live alone when she can afford her own house.

Olara is 22-years-old and invests an immense amount of time and energy in physical training for sports competitions and in studying. She says 'I want people to look up to me – I've got to become the best – I want people to see me as a winner.'

Identify the main deficit needs that each of these three people are likely to be struggling with.

Maslow believed that there is a hierarchy with respect to the four deficit needs. This means that people will prioritise their survival and security before focusing attention on relationships. But physical, safety and belonging needs have to be at least partially met before people worry too much about what other people think of them. Concern about social status and self-esteem comes last among the deficit needs.

Self-actualisation

When a person has mostly met the deficit needs, they have the potential to become self-actualising. A person who is not worried about physical needs, a person who feels secure, a person who has experienced loving emotional attachments and a person who has enjoyed a high level of self-esteem is free to go beyond the normal pressures of life.

Self-actualisation involves 'becoming needs'. When people stop being controlled by deficit needs, they become free to explore their own creativity and potential – the person they might become.

Self-actualisation is at the top of the pyramid, but it is not just another deficit need. Self-actualising people are free. They are free from the deficit pressures that restrict the lives of most

FIGURE 11.17 *A self-actualised person goes beyond the deficit needs that rule most people's lives*

people in Western society. Maslow once suggested that perhaps as few as 2 per cent of people in North American society would achieve full self-actualisation in their lifetime.

People who achieve self-actualisation might have special qualities including:

* a more accurate perception of reality

* greater acceptance of self and others

* greater self-knowledge

* greater involvement with major projects in life

* greater independence

* creativity

* spiritual and artistic abilities.

So self-actualisation is the goal of living. People who self-actualise achieve a high degree of satisfaction from life. In a perfect world everyone would have the chance to self-actualise.

Maslow went on to develop his ideas about self-actualisation, and argued that many people experience becoming or 'growth' needs on the way to developing their full potential. These growth needs involve the need to understand and explore, and a need to explore artistic issues such as beauty. People may develop their potential in stages. Maslow also went on to identify a spiritual stage of development that went beyond the fulfilment of potential – he called this stage 'transcendence'. Some textbooks therefore show Maslow's hierarchy as involving seven stages. Some websites show Maslow's hierarchy as involving eight stages with the final stage of transcendence at the top.

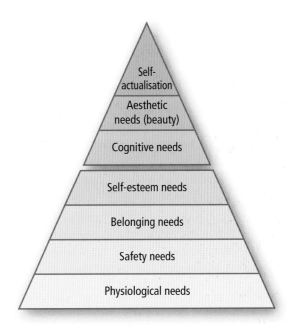

FIGURE 11.18 *Maslow's theory is sometimes explained as involving seven stages*

Maslow's hierarchy and human development

Maslow did not specify age ranges in relationship to his theory of needs, but he did suggest that very few people would achieve self-actualisation during adolescence or early maturity. It is also reasonable to assume that the physical safety and belonging deficit needs are key issues during infancy and childhood, whilst self-esteem needs are likely to be centrally important to teenagers and young adults who are developing their self-concept and identity.

FIGURE 11.19 *Some needs may be more important at different stages of development*

Constructivist perspective

Constructivism explains human development and behaviour in terms of the way an individual person builds an interpretation of the world. The things that we think and imagine are inventions of our mind; we construct our ideas of self and of other people. Our memories of events are often reconstructed and changed in our minds. Memories are rarely 100 per cent accurate representations of what might really have happened.

We use the cognitive abilities involved in perception, memory and thinking to construct our interpretation of what is real. Constructivism is usually understood as part of the cognitive perspective because it involves perception, memory and thinking. Two famous theorists who developed the constructivist approach are Jean Piaget (1896–1980) and Lev Vygotsky (1896–1934).

Piaget's theory of learning

Piaget believed that:

* Infants, children and adults actively seek to understand the world they live in. People build mental representations or theories of the world in their minds because it is human nature to do so.

* Children learn through experience. Teachers can only help or facilitate learning by helping to create useful experiences.

* As children grow older they develop increasingly complex ways of interpreting the world.

* Developing theories about the world involves processes called **accommodation** (fitting new information into existing schemas), **assimilation** (changing **schemas,** ideas and theories when new information is discovered), and **equilibration** (creating a balance between theory and experience in order to make sense of the world).

A simple explanation of Piaget's theory of learning might be based on a young child's experience of animals. Perhaps a child goes to a park and sees ducks for the first time. The child has already seen pictures of animals in books and has seen other animals in real life. The child will 'take in' or assimilate the idea of 'ducks' as a new category of animal. As the child experiences more

examples of ducks, the child will need to adapt their idea of what ducks can look like – this is called 'accommodation'. The child will now have a balanced theory of what ducks are, and will be able to identify them effectively.

First experience of ducks

Second experience of ducks

FIGURE 11.20 *Piaget's theory explains how children build their own understanding of the world*

As the child grows older they will lose their equilibration on this idea when they have to make sense of the idea that ducks are birds and not animals. Life involves constant development and changing of ideas.

In Piaget's theory, learning is a process which is constantly working to enable people to cope with or 'adapt to' their environment. Teachers should never try 'to put ideas into children'. Teachers are most successful when they create useful experiences which stimulate children to make sense, or make new sense, of their experience. Learning is about the changing of mental schemas – only the learner can change the way they think.

Children cannot learn skills before they are maturationally ready. Trying to teach abstract theories (such as psychodynamic theory) to 5-year-olds would never work – no matter what teaching skills a person had.

Piaget is also famous for his theory that there are stages of cognitive development. He developed his theory by observing and questioning young children, and believed that children progress through four stages of intellectual development.

Piaget's stages of cognitive development

The sensorimotor stage

* *birth to 1.5 or 2 years:* learning to use senses and muscles – thinking without language

The pre-operational stage

* *2 to 7 years*: pre-logical thinking – thinking in language but without understanding logic

The concrete operational stage

* *7 to 11 years:* logical thinking is limited to practical situations

The formal operational stage

* *from 11 years:* using logic and abstract thought processes – adult thinking.

Piaget believed that the four stages were caused by an inbuilt inherited pattern of development. Nowadays, research suggests that infants are more able to understand their world than Piaget thought. It also appears that most people take a lot longer than 11 years to become skilled at abstract logical thinking. The development of formal logical thought may also depend on the quality of education a person receives.

FIGURE 11.21 *A 5-year-old child is not ready to understand abstract concepts; but a 5-year-old may be able to understand the concrete (practical) experience of letting go of a balloon*

The sensorimotor stage

Piaget's observations led him to believe that infants were unable to make sense of what they saw. If a 6-month-old child was reaching for a rattle and the rattle was covered with a cloth then the child would act as if the rattle had now ceased to exist. Piaget believed that young infants had great difficulty in making sense of objects and that they were unable to use their imagination to remember objects. Towards the end of the **sensorimotor** period children would begin to internalise picture memories in their minds. Piaget noticed this in his daughter, Jacqueline, at 14 months of age. Jacqueline had seen an 18-month-old child stamping his feet and having a temper tantrum. The next day Jacqueline imitated this behaviour. Jacqueline must have been able to picture the behaviour in her mind to be able to copy it later.

The sensorimotor period ends when a child can understand that objects have a permanent existence – this is called **object permanence.** The child knows that objects still exist even if they are not looking at them. At the end of the sensorimotor period, children will know that their father and mother still exist even if they are not seen.

As the child loses a toy they will start to search for it, because it can be pictured and the child has learned how objects work. If an object can't be seen, it will have gone somewhere – it will not have just 'gone'. The end of the sensorimotor period is also a time when children are beginning to use one- and two-word utterances to recognise and describe things. Piaget believed that language was a powerful tool used to organise and construct our understanding of the world.

The pre-operational stage

Pre-operational means pre-logical; during this stage Piaget believed that children could not think logically. Children can use words to communicate, but they do not understand the logical implications involved in language. Piaget explained that pre-operational children cannot conserve number, mass and volume. For example conservation of number involves understanding that 10 buttons stretched out in a line involves the same number of buttons as 10 buttons in a pile. A young child might agree that there were 10 buttons in the line and in the pile, but then the child might say that there are more buttons in the line because it is longer! A child may be able to count to 10 but may not understand what the number 10 really means.

Try it out

Conservation of weight

Work with a 5-year-old child and ask the child to make two balls of plasticine that weigh exactly the same on scales. Check that the child agrees that the two balls are equal in weight. Then roll one ball out into a sausage shape. Ask the child if they think the two balls will still weigh the same. It may be that the child will focus on the way the plasticine looks and will say that one ball of plasticine now weighs more than the other.

The concrete operational stage

Children in the **concrete operational** stage can think logically provided they can see examples of the problem they are working with. For example suppose you ask the question: 'Samira is taller than Corrine, but Samira is smaller than Leslie,

FIGURE 11.22 *Understanding the concept of object permanence*

so who is the tallest?' You may find that the 7- or 8-year-old has difficulty in mentally imagining the information to enable them to answer the question. But if the child can see a picture of Samira, Corrine and Leslie they might quickly point out who is the tallest.

The formal operational stage

With formal logical reasoning (**formal operational** stage) an adult can solve complex problems mentally. For example, an adult can use formal logic to reason why a car won't start in the morning. Formal logic enables us to exchange complicated ideas without having to see the concrete and practical issues at first hand.

Whether or not Piaget was completely right about stages of development, his theory does serve to remind parents, teachers and care workers that children often think differently from adults. Children with pre-operational thinking may need to experience practical events to develop their understanding. Children with concrete logical thinking may need to see practical examples of issues described using language in order to understand them.

Vygotsky and social context

Vygotsky proposed a theory which emphasised the importance of a child's social context in influencing development. Vygotsky believed that thinking, memory and perception were strongly influenced by the culture a child lives in. A child's understanding of the world develops from their interaction with other people as well as 'the environment'.

Vygotsky's theories can be referred to as 'social constructivist' because of his emphasis on social interaction being the major influence on the way a child builds their understanding of the world.

Vygotsky argued that:

* culture and socialisation will greatly influence the nature and level of skills that a child will eventually develop

* the quality of parental communication and teaching will greatly influence the skills a child will develop

* the quality of conversation, play and instruction will influence how a child's language and intellectual skills develop.

'Internalisation' and 'the zone of proximal development'

Vygotsky offers two important concepts to help explain how children learn.

Internalisation

Vygotsky believed that successful cognitive development depended on a child building an internal 'understanding' of activities and skills. **Internalisation** might follow a process such as the example below.

A mother tries to encourage her son to complete a jigsaw puzzle. The mother explains how jigsaw puzzles work and demonstrates how to search for correct pieces and put them together. At this stage the child is socially involved with play and communication but the child does not understand how to do a jigsaw puzzle. The child will then attempt to find pieces of the puzzle, the mother will help him and repeat ideas to encourage him.

The child may begin to talk out loud to help him make sense of his actions. The child is beginning to learn, but has not yet internalised the skill of solving jigsaw puzzles. Finally, after lots of help, guidance and encouragement the child can work on the puzzle independently. He will be excited and will say how good he is at puzzles! At this stage the child has learned how to solve the puzzle – the child has internalised the external guidance and concepts his mother provided.

If you were teaching a child to read you might ask a child to read out loud. Reading out loud helps a child to practise skills, but 'Vygotskyans' might question whether the child was internalising anything. In other words is the child really learning when they read out loud? Vygotskyans might ask the child to explain the story they had read. By asking the child to explain, the teacher or parent is creating a social learning situation which requires the child to internalise ideas and concepts which they might otherwise only repeat without understanding.

Teachers who follow Vygotsky's views are likely to try to encourage a high level of **cognitive** performance from children – they will want children to internalise and understand rather than simply 'do' things.

The zone of proximal development

Vygotsky argued that teachers and parents should try to understand the level of thinking a child was working from and then try to move the child on to a deeper level, always staying within what was possible for a child to understand. The zone of proximal development is the range of a child's thinking and understanding that might realistically be developed in a given subject area.

SCENARIO

Fairness and the zone of proximal development

A father is talking to his 7-year-old daughter. The daughter might say that fairness is when 'everyone gets the same', e.g. when she and her younger sister both get the same size apple pie to eat. The father may have a much more complex understanding of equal opportunities based on ethical reasoning. The father will not be able to explain ethical philosophy to a 7-year-old, because such theories can't be assimilated or linked with the child's current understanding (they lie outside of the child's zone of proximal development). The father could try to move his daughter's thinking on by mentioning that the younger sister doesn't like apples – so giving everyone the same food isn't really fair. Fairness isn't having exactly the same treatment – it's having an 'equal feeling at the end', so the younger sister has to have something different for things to work out fairly. In this example the father is trying to encourage the daughter to develop a deeper understanding of equality and fairness working within issues that the daughter can understand. This is working within the zone of proximal development.

Constructivism and distorted thinking

Piaget and Vygotsky were early theorists who explained how we build or construct a mental interpretation of the outside world. Some people imagine that when they have a thought it must always be caused by real events in the outside world. For example, if you feel angry then perhaps somebody has made you have that feeling. Perhaps they should be punished for making you have the feeling? **Constructivism** would argue that the things that we think and the emotions that we experience are inventions of our own mind.

Some people have negative thoughts about themselves, thoughts that they might be unattractive, stupid or a failure. Some people react to these thoughts with the belief that 'if I think that and if I feel like that then it must be true!' A constructivist perspective would argue that we build our own inner world and that it is very important for adults to learn to question their own thoughts. Before becoming depressed because we have remembered some bad event, adults need to learn to challenge any negative thoughts or feelings that are not supported with evidence. Just because we can imagine something does not mean that it is real.

Behavioural perspective

Behaviourism explains human development in terms of how we learn from experience. Our learning from experience moulds and shapes our behaviour and personality. The Russian physiologist Ivan Pavlov (1849–1936), and American psychologists Edward Thorndike (1874–1949), John Watson (1878–1958) and Burrhus F. Skinner (1904–1990), all worked to develop behavioural theories of learning.

Edward Thorndike studied the way animals learn by observing their responses in controlled conditions. He noticed that animals would often learn by trial and error. For example, a hungry cat would experiment with ways of escaping from a cage to receive a reward of food. When the cat discovered actions that helped it escape, it would remember those actions. Thorndike believed any action that produced a good effect would be imprinted into the mind of the animal. In 1898, Thorndike wrote an article in which he explained 'the Law of Effect', which means that actions are governed by their consequences. Animals and humans will learn to repeat actions which produce good effects and avoid actions which have bad outcomes. This theory provided a foundation for the development of behaviourism. Behaviourists believed that theories of conditioning and reinforcement could explain all human behaviour.

Conditioning

In 1906, Pavlov published his work on **conditioned learning** in dogs. Pavlov had intended to study digestion in dogs, but his work ran into difficulties because his animals anticipated when their food was due.

Pavlov demonstrated that dogs would salivate (or dribble) whenever they heard a noise, such as a bell ringing, if the noise always came just before the food arrived. The dogs had learned to 'connect' or associate the sound of the bell with the presentation of food. It was as if the bell replaced the food; the dogs' mouths began to water to the sound of the bell. The dogs associated sounds with food. This learning by association was called conditioning.

The first time that Pavlov rang a bell, the stimulus of the bell would have been neutral. This means that the dogs had not learned to associate anything with it. Once the bell is associated with the arrival of food it has become a conditioned stimulus causing the conditioned response of dribbling.

In the first half of the twentieth century many people believed that all learned behaviour could be explained using the concept of conditioning.

Did you know?

When Pavlov's research was reported in Britain, Oscar Wilde (a famous author of the time) is reported to have said, 'Doesn't every intelligent dog owner know that?'

Some people develop anxiety states, or irrational fears, called **phobias.** To train people to control their behaviour, psychologists may use relaxation techniques. A person learns how to create a physical sensation of relaxation through deep breathing and muscle relaxing exercises. Once a person has learned this skill, they can condition the sensation to a word that they say to themselves. The person simply says 'relax' as they breathe out and the word 'relax' becomes a conditioned stimulus associated with the good feeling of relaxation. They can then use this learning to help them cope with fears. Someone who experiences fear and panic in crowds can say or even just think the word 'relax' and their conditioning will induce the relaxed feeling.

Conditioned learning can be used in a step-by-step way to help someone unlearn anxiety or fear. A person who is afraid of crowds might start by going out to slightly difficult settings to practise their conditioned relaxation skills. Following a step-by-step approach the person may be able to later face a really crowded situation. This approach is called systematic desensitisation.

Skinner's theories of conditioning

Like Thorndike, Skinner argued that learning is caused by the consequences of our actions. This means that people learn to associate actions with the pleasure or discomfort that follows. For example, if a child puts some yoghurt in their mouth and it tastes nice, they will associate the yoghurt with pleasure. In future they will repeat the action of eating yoghurt. On the other hand, if the yoghurt does not taste good they may avoid it in future. This principle is similar to the law of effect – behaviour is controlled by past results associated with actions.

Skinner developed new terminology to explain learning by association. Behaviour that operates on the environment to create pleasant outcomes is likely to strengthen or reinforce the occurrence of that behaviour. Behaviour operates on the world and so Skinner used the word 'operant' to describe behaviours which create learned outcomes. The term **'operant conditioning'** is used to describe learning through the consequences of action.

Classical conditioning (Pavlovian conditioning): learning to make association between different events. A stimulus results in a conditioned response.

Operant conditioning (Skinnerian conditioning): learning to repeat actions which have a reinforcing or strengthening outcome. In other words, people learn to repeat actions which have previously felt good or are associated with 'feeling better'.

Reinforcement

Skinner developed Thorndike's work on the 'law of effect' using the idea of reinforcement to explain how a behaviour is learned. *Reinforcement* means to make something stronger. For example, reinforced concrete is stronger than ordinary concrete. A reinforcer is anything that makes a behaviour stronger.

SCENARIO

Reinforcement at work

Amita is an infant who is eating while sitting in a highchair. Amita accidentally drops her spoon. She reacts with surprise that the spoon has gone. Her mother picks the spoon up and gives it back to Amita, smiling and making eye contact as she does so. This makes Amita feel good. Amita's mother goes back to her own dinner and stops looking at Amita. By accident, Amita drops the spoon again. Once again, mother gives Amita attention and the spoon is returned. Once again Amita feels good. Half-a-minute later, Amita drops the spoon on purpose – dropping the spoon has become reinforced. The consequences or outcomes of dropping the spoon feel nice – it is followed by attention.

Without understanding human behaviour parents might think that the child is being difficult, or that she is playing a game. What is happening is that Amita's behaviour of dropping the spoon is being 'reinforced' by her mother. Her mother is teaching her to drop the spoon although she doesn't realise what she is doing. Reinforcement is happening because Amita is getting a 'nice feeling' each time she drops the spoon and mother gives it back.

BEHAVIOUR	OUTCOME	CONSEQUENCES
Drop the spoon	Smiles, attention	Spoon dropping behaviour is reinforced and therefore becomes stronger and more frequent.

What if?

How could Amita's mother reinforce Amita not to drop the spoon?

It is important to remember that life experiences cause conditioning. Most conditioning happens without anyone planning or intending it. Reinforcement and punishment frequently take place in educational and social care settings. They happen whether anyone intended them to or not.

Positive and negative reinforcement

Both positive and negative reinforcement make behaviour stronger. Positive reinforcement identifies pleasurable outcomes for the individual who is reinforced. Negative reinforcement identifies a situation where something which is unpleasant ceases. For example, a child at school may be bored during their lesson. Poking the child next to them with a pencil may relieve the boredom. The child may receive negative reinforcement that makes them feel better, as a result of their disruptive behaviour. The reinforcement is 'negative' because an unpleasant state of boredom has ended. Negative reinforcement is very useful when explaining problems like phobias and anxiety states.

The opposite of reinforcement is punishment; punishment has the result of blocking behaviour whilst reinforcement always strengthens it.

The concepts of conditioning and reinforcement offer some useful tools for understanding the ways in which life experience can influence human behaviour, although they may not explain the whole complexity of human experience.

SCENARIO

Jason

Jason is a 23-year-old man with learning difficulties. He attends a day centre where he regularly lies across the main entrance to the centre. Staff become very concerned when Jason does this, and there is usually a lot of commotion involved in persuading Jason to stand up and leave the entrance.

Behaviourists would assume that Jason has learned this behaviour; the attention that he receives may be positively reinforcing his behaviour of lying in the doorway. Jason may also feel bored; lying in the doorway may relieve this boredom. Lying in the doorway may feel better than the alternatives – if this is the case, then his behaviour is being negatively reinforced.

In order to change Jason's behaviour, behaviourists would seek to reinforce an alternative behaviour. If Jason looked bored, staff might try to involve him in conversation. If Jason responds, staff might try to be particularly attentive and supportive. Staff attention might act

to reinforce conversational behaviour. Staff might try to gradually encourage Jason to talk to them rather than lie in the doorway. They might try to minimise the attention given when he lies in the doorway, but be very responsive and reinforcing towards communication.

Staff could not ignore lying in the doorway because it would be unsafe to do this. Staff would not punish Jason – this would be unethical – but it would also fail to encourage an alternative behaviour. If Jason does not lie in the doorway – perhaps he will set off the fire alarms instead. Behaviourism stresses the importance of reinforcing a new 'desirable' behaviour pattern to replace 'less desirable' behaviour.

Social learning perspective

The social learning perspective explains that behaviour is influenced by the social expectations of others. People change their behaviour depending on the social context in which they find themselves. A great deal of what people do is not consciously planned, and does not result either from conditioning or from unconscious dynamics. The social learning perspective argues that it is important to understand the role of group expectations or norms when trying to understand human behaviour.

Tajfel (1981) argued that social identity plays a significant role in influencing people's actions. Identity is learned through socialisation and subsequent life experience. A range of factors influence learning during socialisation, these may be seen as layers of influence that affect the development of identity (see Figure 11.23).

People categorise themselves in terms of the groups that they identify with. Gender, religion, race, class, age group and social roles, such as mother or sister, signify groups that we may identify with. If we belong to a particular age group for example, we may categorise ourselves as being like other people who are the same age. Older people may be seen as 'not like me'. It is possible to divide the world into people 'who are like me' and people 'who are not like me'. An 'in-group' is a group that you identify with – people 'who are like me'. An 'out-group' means people who are different.

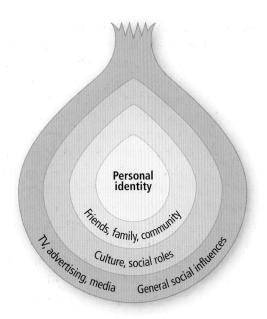

FIGURE 11.23 *Layers of influence – the onion theory*

Primary groups are small groups where you know each group member personally – such as your family. Secondary groups are large networks of people where you will not know everyone who belongs to the group – such as members of your gender or racial groups.

Tajfel argued that people develop social identities based on groups they identify with. In some situations, personal identity will give way to social identity. For example a thoughtful and caring individual may also be a football club supporter. When they join other supporters they may become abusive to rival supporters. Social identity takes over from the individual's 'personality' and behaviour conforms to the expectations of the group.

Social identity theory argues that much human behaviour can be understood as caused by an individual's conformity to the expectations of the social groups they identify with. Social identity theory would argue that it is wrong to try to explain everything in terms of individual personality.

Hedy Brown (1996) explained that individual judgement can be seriously affected by group membership. People's views can become more extreme or 'polarised' when they mix with other members of an in-group. Brown's research suggests that people trust ideas that come from people they see as being similar to themselves.

Latanè and social impact theory

Social impact theory suggests that many of our actions are influenced, or even caused, by the people that surround us. Put simply; humans often behave like sheep and copy others. Many actions are performed to conform to the expectation of others; people are great conformists. If you need an explanation for why people tell racist jokes or commit acts of vandalism, there is no need to look inside their heads. Instead of looking for inner attitudes or unconscious struggles inside the mind of the individual, we might be better off looking at the social context surrounding the person. For example, a person might vandalise a bus shelter because they are copying their friends. They may not be able to give a logical explanation for their actions.

Social impact theory developed from the work of Bibb Latanè and John Darley who investigated 'bystander apathy' in the late 1960s. Their research discovered that when people are alone they will often assist another person who has collapsed. When people are part of a group which generally ignores the person in need, individuals will follow the group and not provide assistance to a person who has fallen. The issue appears to be that most people are not directed by inner moral values, but take their cue from other people. It is all right to do things if everybody else is doing it; i.e. ignoring someone in need. We respond to the 'social impact' of the people that surround us. We go with the crowd and seek to fit in with the social norms of others.

Bandura and copying behaviours

Albert Bandura (born 1925) argued that people's behaviour is often copied from others; we imitate or copy others without any reinforcement or conditioned learning.

What if?

Suppose you had a friend who said he was very concerned about the welfare of homeless people. One day you both walked through a crowded underpass and everyone including your friend ignored a homeless person who was begging. When you asked your friend why he ignored the homeless person, he just looked embarrassed and couldn't explain.

How would social impact theory explain your friend's behaviour?

Bandura undertook a range of research to demonstrate that children would copy behaviours that they saw in adults. One experiment in 1963 involved children watching adults behaving aggressively towards an object called a 'bobo doll' (a 1960s toy consisting of an inflatable plastic skittle-shaped cylinder with sand at the bottom to make the skittle stand upright if it was hit or knocked over). The dolls usually had cartoon character faces. Children who watched adults behaving aggressively towards the doll were more likely to be aggressive toward the doll when they had a chance to play with it than children who had not seen the aggressive behaviour. This experiment confirmed that we are not just influenced by conditioning and reinforcement; we are also influenced by what we see happening to other people and also in the media.

It appears that people are more likely to imitate and copy another's behaviour if that person:

* is rewarded for their behaviour
* is perceived as being generally liked and respected
* is perceived to be similar to the observer and the person's behaviour:
  * 'stands out' and is very noticeable
  * can be copied by the observer without too much difficulty.

In a study in 1965, Bandura concluded that while children were more likely to imitate the behaviour

FIGURE 11.24 *People copy behaviours that are relevant to them*

of adults who had been rewarded, they learned and could copy any behaviour they had observed. There may be a difference between actually acting out what we see others doing and learning from observation. It may be enough to see aggressive behaviour for it to impact on us.

What if?

Suppose that some young children see early years care workers smoking outside a nursery building.

Children will not be able to obtain cigarettes in order to imitate the behaviour straight away, so does it make any difference to them if they watch an adult smoking?

Think it over

How might the following life experiences influence a person?

* Seeing an elder brother or sister praised for school achievement.

* Seeing a friend being praised and looked-up to because of violent behaviour.

* Seeing a neighbour do well from trading shares on the Internet.

* Seeing a person gain respect because they deal in drugs.

* Seeing a person being praised and thanked for caring for a relative.

Summary

AN OVERVIEW OF THE PERSPECTIVES			
Perspective	Famous theorists	Key features	Possible catch phrases
Psychodynamic	Freud, Erikson	Early experience has a major impact on the development of our conscious and unconscious mind. Adult personality and behaviour are governed by the unconscious as well as the conscious mind.	The human mind is like an angel (the conscious mind) riding a wild beast (the unconscious mind). The first few years of life are critical.
Biological Influences	Eysenck, Cattell	Genetics influence the biology of our nervous system. This influences our personality traits.	We are born with our personalities. You can't change your nature.
Humanistic	Rogers, Maslow	Neither the environment nor our early experience control our personality and behaviour. In Rogers' theory people have an inbuilt tendency to develop their potential – the actualising tendency. Problems with conditional regard (Rogers) or unmet deficit needs (Maslow) prevent people from fulfilling their potential.	The purpose of life is to develop your potential. Understanding, respect and value represent the key ways to help others.

continued on next page

Perspective	Famous theorists	Key features	Possible catch phrases
Constructivist (Cognitive)	Piaget, Vygotsky	This approach explores the processes involved in human thinking. The constructivist perspective explains how people build their own internal systems of thinking.	We are not controlled by the things that have happened to us; but we may be enslaved by our interpretation (or construction) of events.
Behaviourist	Pavlov, Skinner	Human behaviour and personality are learned through classical conditioning and reinforcement.	People are just complex machines. Behaviour can always be measured and controlled.
Social learning	Tajfel, Latanè	Human personality and behaviour are influenced by the social expectations of others. People conform to group expectations or norms. An individual's sense of self is strongly influenced by group values. People learn by imitating the behaviour of others.	If you want to understand a person's behaviour then look at their social context.

Consider this

Errol has diabetes and very high blood pressure; he has been advised that he must stop smoking if he wants to live. Errol cannot cope with the idea of giving up smoking. In discussion he says: 'You don't understand how it feels – I have to smoke, I get awful feelings if I can't get a smoke. Sometimes I wonder what's the point of it all anyway, I mean when your number's up, it's up, isn't it. We've all got to die – and what's the point of living – all the good times are gone. When you get older it's all downhill. Sometimes I think – yes, bring it on – there is nothing good in the future – I'm no use to anyone, so what!'

How might each of the perspectives above contribute toward understanding what is happening to Errol?

1) Psychodynamic: Can you explain how concepts such as regression, reaction formation and Erikson's stage of ego integrity versus despair might be relevant to explaining Errol's behaviour?

2) Constructivist: Can you identify how the beliefs about life and death that Errol has constructed may be influencing his decision to keep on smoking?

3) Humanistic: Can you explain how low self-esteem and a negative self-concept may have come about because of conditions of worth? What relevance might the concept of 'actualising tendency' have in understanding Errol's negative attitudes?

4) Behavioural: Can you explain how reinforcement might be maintaining Errol's behaviour?

5) Social learning: can you explain how imitation learning, the social impact of others or social identity issues could have influenced Errol to start smoking in the first place? Can you explain how Errol's current attitudes could be influenced by other people around him?

6) Biological perspective: can you identify how personality traits might be used to explain vulnerability to substance abuse?

Section 3: Application of theories to aid the understanding of human behaviour of individuals in care settings

Working with people involves managing your own emotions and feelings. Most people need to make sense of what is happening before they feel confident to cope with unexpected or challenging behaviours. Theories of human development are useful because they:

* can help to explain what is happening
* can help care workers to understand and manage their own emotions
* can suggest possible ideas for working with distressed or vulnerable service users.

Early years, pre-school care and education settings

SCENARIO

Abbie

Abbie is 3 years old and is looked after by a childminder during the working day. Abbie is one of five children the childminder cares for. Usually around midday Abbie becomes quite agitated and screams a lot. The screaming can last for 20 minutes to half an hour. She then becomes withdrawn and refuses to look at or talk with other children or the childminder.

Each of the six perspectives dealt with in the previous section raises questions that might help us to explore what might be happening.

The biological perspective

This might lead us to think about physical issues such as low blood sugar levels. Is Abbie hungry? Is she allergic to food additives? Alternatively, do her personality traits lead her to become inhibited and withdrawn?

Theories of human development may help us understand children's behaviour

The psychodynamic perspective

Freud's theory would remind us that Abbie's ego might not have found a way of coping with the strange situation she finds herself in – there may be a range of issues associated with the anal stage of development that Abbie may not yet have resolved.

The behaviourist perspective

Behaviourists would explore the possibility that Abbie's challenging behaviour has been reinforced in the past. Abbie may have learned to perform in this way because she has previously received attention for it.

The constructivist perspective

Constructivists might suggest that Abbie cannot understand her surroundings and what is happening – the challenging behaviour may be a reaction caused by an inability to understand the strange setting.

The humanistic perspective

There is the possibility of an unmet need – perhaps physical needs, perhaps emotional safety, perhaps love and belonging – Abbie is only three, and she may not feel safe without her mother.

The social learning perspective

Perhaps Abbie is copying behaviour of other children. Abbie's behaviour might involve a

Martha

Martha attends a day care centre. She often asks the people who bring her to the centre to check her house for spiders as she has a phobia (an irrational fear) of spiders. Martha will often talk about how terrified she has been because she has encountered a spider at home. Martha is also afraid of flies. Staff in the day centre do their best to help Martha to relax and make sure she does not encounter any insects.

Each of the perspectives offers a particular kind of explanation and approach to supporting someone with a phobia. For example, the behavioural explanation would explain that spiders behave in unusual ways – they walk on eight legs! Our attention is bound to be drawn to them. If we react with surprise when we encounter a spider it may create a very mild sense of tension. If we respond to that tension by withdrawing, we may experience a mild release of tension. That mild release of tension will create negative reinforcement. We feel better once we have got rid of the spider. If we keep withdrawing from encounters with spiders we will negatively reinforce ourselves until withdrawal becomes a learned reaction. At this point we will no longer be able to control our behaviour. Our conditioned reactions will force us to withdraw.

range of issues, and there could be some value in exploring all of the questions that the perspectives raise. It is not a matter of finding which perspective is true or correct, or which perspective has all the answers. Each of the perspectives may help us to think about important explanations.

Day care settings for older people

A general overview of possible reactions to Martha's phobia suggested by each of the perspectives is set out in Figure 11.25.

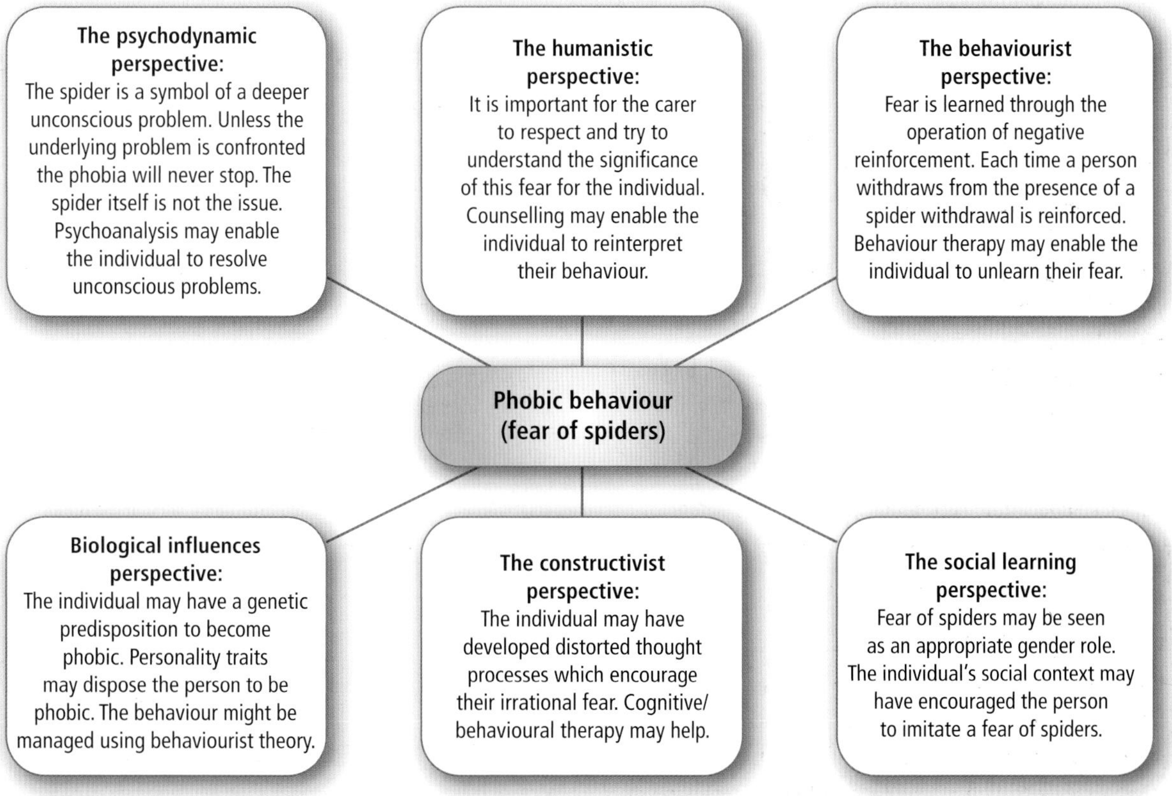

The psychodynamic perspective:
The spider is a symbol of a deeper unconscious problem. Unless the underlying problem is confronted the phobia will never stop. The spider itself is not the issue. Psychoanalysis may enable the individual to resolve unconscious problems.

The humanistic perspective:
It is important for the carer to respect and try to understand the significance of this fear for the individual. Counselling may enable the individual to reinterpret their behaviour.

The behaviourist perspective:
Fear is learned through the operation of negative reinforcement. Each time a person withdraws from the presence of a spider withdrawal is reinforced. Behaviour therapy may enable the individual to unlearn their fear.

Phobic behaviour (fear of spiders)

Biological influences perspective:
The individual may have a genetic predisposition to become phobic. Personality traits may dispose the person to be phobic. The behaviour might be managed using behaviourist theory.

The constructivist perspective:
The individual may have developed distorted thought processes which encourage their irrational fear. Cognitive/behavioural therapy may help.

The social learning perspective:
Fear of spiders may be seen as an appropriate gender role. The individual's social context may have encouraged the person to imitate a fear of spiders.

FIGURE 11.25 *Martha's reactions interpreted through the six theories*

Obsessive and compulsive behaviour

Many people have routines that they feel compelled to repeat. Some people may need to check their door locks repeatedly before going out or going to bed, some have an obsessive routine which involves checking that electrical or gas appliances are switched off. Individuals may develop an obsessive concern with food hygiene or hand washing, or invent routines such as tapping the ground with their foot ten times. This routine is then repeated, perhaps to the annoyance of other people nearby. Figure 11.26 summarises some different standpoints on obsessions.

Residential settings

George is an 84-year-old resident in a care home. He came into care because he has serious heart problems and couldn't cope alone. George becomes frustrated if he has to wait for anything, and can be verbally abusive; sometimes he threatens to hit people with his walking stick. Care workers say that these explosions of aggression just seem to happen; they do not do anything to provoke these outbursts. Figure 11.27 shows some of the different ways in which perspectives might explain aggressive behaviour.

The biological perspective

Biological explanations might focus on George's personality characteristics. George may not be sensitive to how his behaviour affects others. He might be 'tough-minded' while perhaps many of his carers are more sensitive and concerned about how they impact on other people. The tendency to behave without concern for other people might be inherited to some degree. In other words George's behaviour might not be consciously thought through or chosen, and it might not be learned through conditioning – it might just be the way he is. The biological perspective might also emphasise issues like low blood sugar, physical ill-health and the physiology of stress. Our biological condition will influence how we experience emotion and how we respond to other people.

The behavioural perspective

This perspective offers some straightforward ideas on understanding and managing aggressive behaviour using the concept of reinforcement. Aggression will become stronger if it leads to 'a good outcome'. So if George becomes aggressive; and then his needs are met; the aggressive behaviour may increase. When care workers use behaviourist theory they will try to reinforce calm

FIGURE 11.26 *Could there be some truth in all of these explanations?*

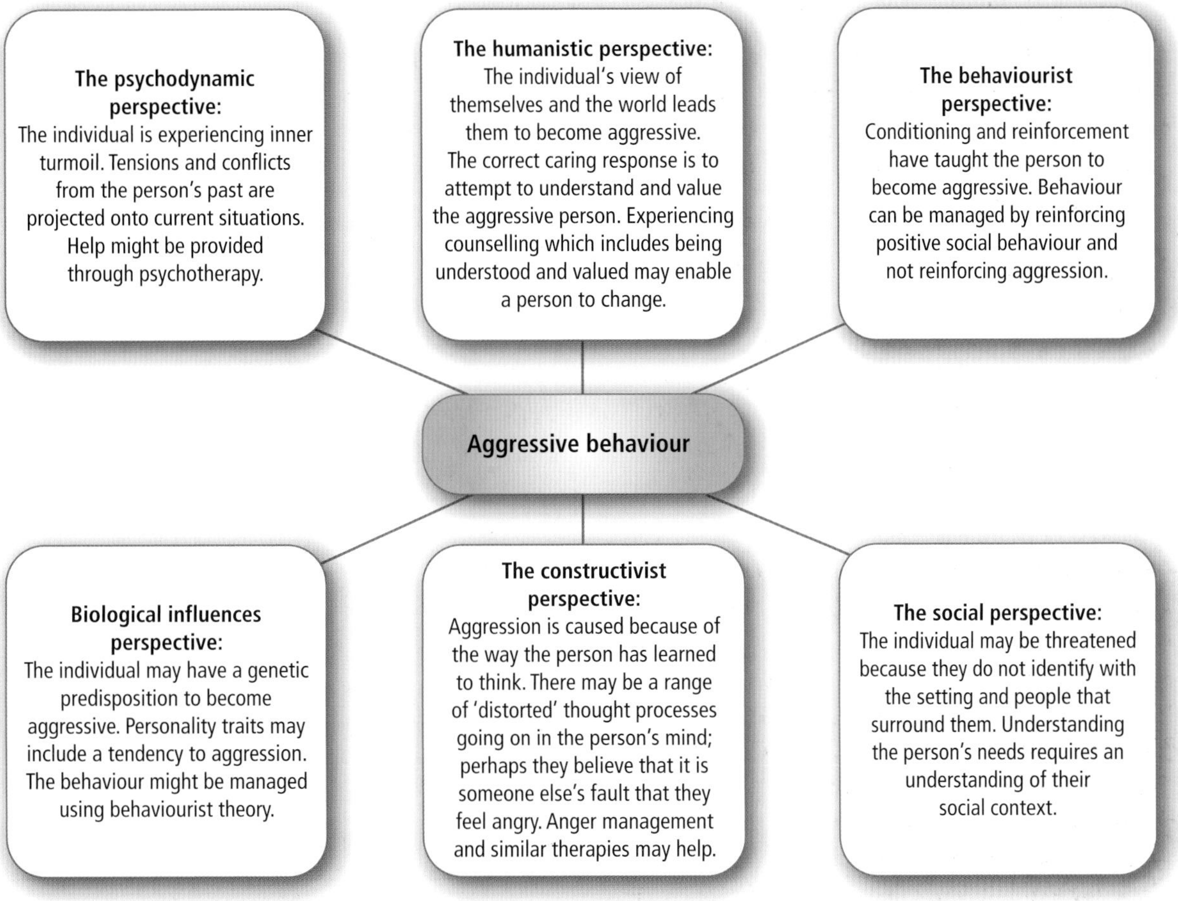

The psychodynamic perspective:
The individual is experiencing inner turmoil. Tensions and conflicts from the person's past are projected onto current situations. Help might be provided through psychotherapy.

The humanistic perspective:
The individual's view of themselves and the world leads them to become aggressive. The correct caring response is to attempt to understand and value the aggressive person. Experiencing counselling which includes being understood and valued may enable a person to change.

The behaviourist perspective:
Conditioning and reinforcement have taught the person to become aggressive. Behaviour can be managed by reinforcing positive social behaviour and not reinforcing aggression.

Aggressive behaviour

Biological influences perspective:
The individual may have a genetic predisposition to become aggressive. Personality traits may include a tendency to aggression. The behaviour might be managed using behaviourist theory.

The constructivist perspective:
Aggression is caused because of the way the person has learned to think. There may be a range of 'distorted' thought processes going on in the person's mind; perhaps they believe that it is someone else's fault that they feel angry. Anger management and similar therapies may help.

The social perspective:
The individual may be threatened because they do not identify with the setting and people that surround them. Understanding the person's needs requires an understanding of their social context.

FIGURE 11.27 *Perspectives to explain aggressive behaviour*

or co-operative behaviour. Perhaps a care worker will say: 'I am sorry that you are upset, would you be willing to talk to me.' The care worker might attempt to reinforce co-operation with thanks and non-verbal messages of gratitude, and not reinforce angry and aggressive behaviour. This might involve not showing an emotional reaction, such as anger or fear, in response to the George's behaviour. Instead the care worker might remain assertive and respond with statements such as 'I am sorry you feel that way, but please can we continue to talk.'

The care worker would be employing the concept of reinforcement to help manage the situation. If George experienced a good outcome when he talked to care staff, the tendency to talk might become stronger and aggressive behaviour might become less frequent.

The humanistic perspective

Humanistic theory would understand the situation very differently from behaviourism.

The idea of a managing another person's behaviour is contrary to the ideal of respecting and understanding another's sense of self. A care worker using humanistic approaches would not think 'how do I control this person's behaviour'. Instead they would attempt to build a deep understanding of George that would enable him to discuss his feelings and needs. Within this safe and supportive relationship, issues such as verbal abuse could be confronted in a caring way, which would meet the self-esteem needs of both George and his care worker.

The constructivist perspective

Constructivist theorists would be interested in the thought processes the aggressive individual was using. Perhaps the aggressive person attributes their feelings to the worker. George might think 'if I feel angry – it can only be because someone has made me feel this way – somebody must be treating me badly'. From this thought, the next step may be to decide 'Yes – it's my carer that makes me feel bad. They must be punished.' Many people allow their emotions and feelings to control what they think. Aggression and violence result directly from feelings of frustration or unhappiness. The individual may use 'distorted' cognitive processes to justify and guide their behaviour. Cognitive therapists might attempt to work with the individual's thought system.

The psychodynamic perspective

According to this view, we are all driven by unconscious struggles and issues which may go back to our early childhood. Early tensions that George experienced may still linger in his unconscious mind. The care worker's actions may be associated with tensions from his past. It could be that George is transferring the emotion he once felt towards his father to the care worker.

Put another way, the psychodynamic perspective would argue that aggressive behaviour cannot always be explained logically. Much human experience and action is bound up with unconscious motivations. It is a mistake to assume that human behaviour is, or should be, logical.

A detailed explanation for George's aggression could only be found during a process of psychoanalytic therapy. Psychoanalytic therapy would involve an attempt to explore the unconscious motivations which have come to exist within the individual's mind.

The social perspective

This perspective might alert us to the critically important issues associated with George's social identity. Gender, race and class (amongst other group membership variables) can have a major impact on how individuals understand themselves and their world. Social role or in-group–out-group conflict could be an issue to consider. George may have been socialised into believing that aggression is an acceptable or even desirable male characteristic. George may feel that his dignity and self-concept are threatened by being in a care home.

UNIT 11 ASSESSMENT

How you will be assessed

This unit will be assessed through a 90-minute written examination. Some questions relevant to this unit are set out below. Each question or part question displays in brackets the number of marks allocated. Please note that these assessment questions are designed to contribute towards practice for your candidates' assessment but are not written to mirror OCR's A2 Level questions.

Test questions

1. Piaget believed that intellectual development involved four stages. Write the names of his four stages by the age ranges below and briefly describe the key characteristics of each stage. (12)

Age range	Name of stage	Key characteristics
Birth to 1.5–2 years of age		
1.5–2 to 7 years of age		
7 to 11 years of age		
11 years and older		

2. Samuel is 7 years old and has difficulty making relationships with other people. He has been diagnosed to have Asperger's syndrome. It is likely that Asperger's syndrome is influenced by Samuel's genetics and biological makeup. Name three other types of influence that could affect Samuel's development. (3)

3. Shaheen lives with her mother and father in a large house that also accommodates her grandparents. Describe four positive or negative influences that Shaheen's family may have on her. (4)

4. Mitesh lives in a flat within a low-income housing estate. Olara lives in a detached house in a wealthy area. Describe three environmental or socio-economic factors that are likely to be different for Mitesh and Olara. (3)

5. Liam grew up on a low-income housing estate and for most of his childhood his parents were dependent on benefit. Liam did not do well at school and left with few qualifications. Recently Liam became interested in counselling through friends he met at work. He is now training to become a qualified counsellor and this involves exploring his own self-concept. Liam has a very positive attitude to life. Describe what is meant by self-concept. Explain why Liam might have a positive attitude to his life despite early socio-economic disadvantages. (6)

6. Explain what is meant by the terms id, ego and superego within Freudian theory. (6)

7. Explain what is meant by the stage of identity versus role confusion in Erikson's psychodynamic theory. (2)

8. Harriet has recently been diagnosed with a serious life-threatening illness. Harriet describes herself as being in good health and says that her diagnosis is nothing to worry about – everything will be fine. Identify a possible ego defence mechanism that Harriet may be using. Explain what is meant by ego defence mechanisms. (4)

9. Read the following statements made by Tom: 'I live for the day you know – I may be 75 but there are a lot of things I want to do with my life. I think that life is what you make it, isn't it? I learned to stop worrying about trivial things like money and jobs a long time ago. I enjoy my life and I think positively about every opportunity I get. I've always been a craftsperson, I make wooden furniture – it might not be your thing – but I get a nice feeling out of designing and creating things. Many years ago, I worked as a cabinet maker for a furniture company, in the end it got me down. I was told to do things cheaply rather than do them properly – so I left. I think if you're not enjoying your work then something is wrong. I was unemployed for a while but I didn't mind, I knew I would get by. What really matters in life is being able to look back on life and feel proud and pleased with what I've done. There is no one else I would have liked to have been. I've lived my life as I wanted.'

With reference to Maslow's theory explain what level of need Tom might be experiencing. Explain what is meant by 'deficit needs' and 'becoming needs.' (5)

Explain what is meant by the 'actualising tendency' in Carl Rogers' theory. Using Carl Rogers' theory explain what is meant by 'conditions of worth' and identify a reason to explain why Tom does not appear to be influenced by conditions of worth. (5)

10. Ross is a 5-year-old boy who has difficulty in attending to school work. Ross will often leave his seat to look for things on the floor or to talk to other children.

Explain how the theory of reinforcement might be used in order to explain why Ross often gets out of his seat. Explain how a classroom assistant might use the theory of reinforcement in order to encourage Ross to concentrate on his schoolwork. (6)

11. Sheveta is 8 years old and one day she asks her teacher in the playground: 'Why do people have wars?' Her teacher wants to reinforce curiosity and wants to give a reply. The teacher knows that the real answer is very complicated and abstract and will not be understood. Instead the teacher reminds Sheveta of an argument that she experienced a day or two earlier and explains that disagreements often lead to fighting between people.

Explain what is meant by 'concrete logical thinking' in Piaget's theory and how the teacher may have crafted his explanation to fit with Sheveta's stage of intellectual development. (4)

Explain what is meant by 'internalisation' in Vygotsky's theory and how discussing personal experience might assist Sheveta to internalise her understanding of people. (4)

Explain what is meant by the zone of proximal development. Explain why the teacher chose to talk about personal experience rather than complex theories of power and economics. (4)

12. Zoë always wants to take part in exciting and daring activities, whereas Poppy tries to avoid these activities and prefers watching TV. Explain what is meant by trait theory. How might Zoë's behaviour be explained using trait theory, and how might Poppy's behaviour be explained? (6)

13. Mark watches an aggressive argument between a male parent and a teacher in class. Later Mark acts out shouting and aggressive behaviour while playing with other children. Sarah also watched the argument but did not copy any of the behaviour. Explain Bandura's theory of imitation learning. Identify why Mark may have been aggressive using this theory. With reference to Bandura's research identify a reason why Sarah did not act out the aggression, yet Mark did. (6)

14. Joe attends a day centre and engages in obsessional checking of his wheelchair for much of the day. Outline how each of the following perspectives might contribute towards understanding Joe's obsessional behaviour: biological; behavioural; psychodynamic; humanistic; social learning. (20)

References and further reading

Acheson, D. (1998) *Independent Inquiry into Inequalities in Health* London: HMSO

Bandura, A., Ross, D., Ross, S. A. (1963) 'Imitation of film-mediated aggressive models', *Journal of Abnormal and Social Psychology*, 66, 3–11

Bandura, A. (1965) 'Influence of model's reinforcement contingencies on the acquisition of imitative responses', *Journal of Personality and Social Psychology*, 1, 589–95

Bandura, A. (1989) 'Perceived self-efficacy in the exercise of personal agency', *The Psychologist* 2 (10), 411–24.

Brown H. (1996) Classic studies of conformity. In Wetherell, M. *Identities, Groups and Social Issues* London: SAGE Publications

Castells, M. (1997) *The Rise of the Network Society* Oxford: Blackwell

Cattell R. B. (1965) *The Scientific Study of Personality* Harmondsworth: Penguin

Erikson, E. (1963) *Childhood and Society* New York: Norton

Eysenck, H. J. (1965) *Fact and Fiction in Psychology* Harmondsworth: Pelican

Giddens, A. (1997) *Sociology*, third ed. Cambridge: Polity Press

Maslow, A. H. (1943) A Theory of Human Motivation, *Psychological Review*, 50, 370–396

Paxton, W. Dixon, M, (2004) *The State of the Nation – an Audit of Injustice in the UK* London: Institute for Policy Research.

Social Exclusion Unit (1999) *Opportunity for All* London: HMSO

Social Trends, Vol. 34 (2004) London: HMSO

Social Trends, Vol. 35 (2005) London: HMSO

Tajfel, H. (ed.) (1978) *Differentiation Between Social Groups: Studies in the Social Psychology of Intergroup Relations* London: Academic Press

Tajfel, H. (1981) *Human Groups and Social Categories* Cambridge: Cambridge University Press

Zimbardo, P. G. et al. (1992) *Psychology and Life* London: HarperCollins

Zimbardo, P. G. et al. (1995) *Psychology: A European Text* London: HarperCollins

Useful websites

Institute for Public Policy Research
www.ippr.org
National Statistics
www.statistics.gov.uk

Anatomy and physiology in practice

This unit covers the following sections:

12.1 Respiratory system

12.2 Cardio-vascular system

12.3 Digestive system

12.4 Reproductive system

12.5 Renal system

12.6 Musculo-skeletal system

This unit develops your understanding of the structure and functions of the main body systems, so that you can explain the causes, symptoms and signs of a range of diseases and disorders. You will also learn about the importance of diagnostic testing and how the information obtained reveals vital details relevant to the disease and dysfunction. To complete your knowledge and understanding in this unit, you will investigate how the condition is treated and the care given to service users by health professionals.

How you will be assessed

This unit is externally assessed. The assessment consists of an examination lasting for 90 minutes. The total number of marks allocated to the paper is 100. The mark obtained on the examination will be the mark for the whole unit.

Questions may involve the use of illustrations, photographs and case studies or scenarios. All questions need to be answered.

Examples of questions are provided at the end of the unit, together with a reading list and a list of relevant websites.

Section 1: Respiratory system

The respiratory system comprises the anatomical structures and physiological processes that take vital oxygen from the air into the body and use the blood to transport oxygen to the body cells. Inside the body cells, internal respiration uses dissolved oxygen to release the energy from food.

Complex food molecules supply raw materials for growth, repair and essential maintenance of living cells. Energy resources are also chemically locked within food molecules. Respiration is the process that unlocks the energy and releases the components of the raw materials so that the heart can beat, muscles can contract, new cells can replace worn-out cells – in fact, it drives every chemical and physiological process in the human body. You could compare this to possessing a bag of coal that you are unable to set alight to get the heat and light that you want.

Respiration can be artificially subdivided into four sections to facilitate study, these are:

* breathing
* gaseous exchange
* blood transport
* internal or cell respiration.

Breathing

The thorax, or chest, is an airtight box containing the lungs, their associated tubes (the trachea, bronchi and bronchioles), and the heart.

The trachea, or windpipe, commences at the back of the throat, or pharynx, and divides into two main bronchi, each serving one lung on each side of the heart. The first part of the trachea is specially adapted to produce sound and is called the larynx, or voice box. It is protected by a moveable cartilage flap, the epiglottis, which prevents food entering during swallowing.

> **Did you know?**
>
> Metabolism is the total of all chemical processes occuring in the body. Some processes are involved in building up complex materials from simple molecules (anabolism) while others break down complex molecules, releasing energy and leaving simple molecules (catabolism).
>
> Metabolism = anabolism + catabolism

> **Did you know?**
>
> When any material, such as a crumb, manages to pass by the epiglottis, it invokes an intense bout of coughing by reflex action.

The trachea and the bronchi have rings of cartilage to prevent them collapsing; those in the

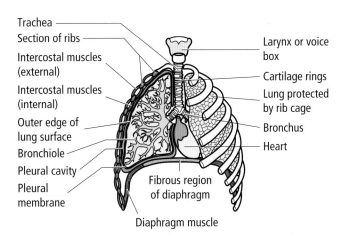

Trachea
Section of ribs
Intercostal muscles (external)
Intercostal muscles (internal)
Outer edge of lung surface
Bronchiole
Pleural cavity
Pleural membrane
Larynx or voice box
Cartilage rings
Lung protected by rib cage
Bronchus
Heart
Fibrous region of diaphragm
Diaphragm muscle

FIGURE 12.1 *Section through the thorax to display the respiratory organs*

trachea are c-shaped with the gap at the back against the main food tube, the oesophagus. This is because when food is chewed in the mouth, it is made into a ball shape (called a **bolus**) before swallowing. The bolus stretches the oesophagus as it passes down to the stomach, and whole rings of cartilage in the trachea would hamper its progress. The gap is filled with soft muscle tissue.

On entering the lung, each bronchus divides and subdivides repeatedly, spreading to each part of the lung. The tiniest subdivisions supplying air sacs in the lung are called bronchioles, and even these are held open by minute areas of cartilage.

The inner lining of the trachea and bronchi is composed of mucus-secreting and ciliated, columnar epithelium cells (Figure 12.2). Mucus is the sticky white gel which traps dust particles that may enter with the air, and cilia are microscopic filaments on the outer edges of cells. Cilia 'beat' towards the nearest external

orifice causing the flow of mucus (with its trapped dirt particles) to leave via the nose or the throat.

The lungs have a pink, spongy feel and are lined on the outside by a thin, moist membrane known as the **pleura.** The pleura continue around the inner thoracic cavity so that the two pleural layers slide over one another easily without friction. The surface tension of the thin film of moisture allows the two layers to slide, but not pull apart. This means that when the chest wall moves in breathing, the lungs move with it.

Forming the thoracic wall outside the pleura are the bones of the rib cage and two sets of oblique muscles joining them together. These are the external and internal intercostal muscles (*inter* means between and *costal* means ribs). The action of these muscles enables the rib cage to move upwards and outwards when you breathe in and vice versa when the air moves out of the chest.

A sheet of muscle called the diaphragm forms the floor and lower boundary of the thorax. The diaphragm is dome-shaped with the

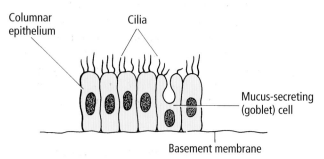

Columnar epithelium

Cilia

Mucus-secreting (goblet) cell

Basement membrane

FIGURE 12.2 *Mucus-secreting cells (**goblet cells**) and ciliated cells lining the trachea and bronchi*

highest, more fibrous, part in the centre and the muscular, fleshy fringes firmly attached to the lower ribs.

The only way that air can enter or leave the thorax is by the trachea, and the air-tight cavity of the thorax is vital for breathing. Rhythmic breathing is controlled by the respiratory centre in the brain. The process is shown in Figures 12.3 and 12.4.

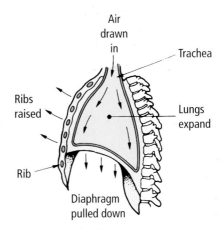

INHALATION

Air drawn in

Trachea

Ribs raised

Lungs expand

Rib

Diaphragm pulled down

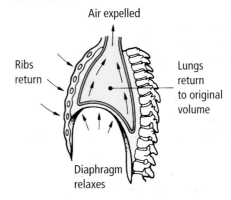

EXHALATION

Air expelled

Ribs return

Lungs return to original volume

Diaphragm relaxes

FIGURE 12.4 *Changes in the thorax during inspiration and expiration*

Nervous impulses from the brain cause the diaphragm and intercostal muscles to contract

Diaphragm flattens and the intercostal muscles cause the ribs to move upwards and outwards

Volume of the chest increases, so the pressure inside the chest must decrease

Surface tension between the pleura drags the lungs with the chest wall. As they expand, they fill with air

Air, containing oxygen, rushes down the trachea and bronchi to equalise the pressure with the external environment – **inhalation**

After a few seconds, the nervous impulses stop arriving and the elastic tissue in the lung causes recoil: the diaphragm rises and the ribs lower

The volume of the chest decreases, so pressure increases, causing air to rush out of the trachea – **exhalation**

The cycle repeats after a few minutes because the respiratory control centre becomes active again sending more nervous impulses

FIGURE 12.3 *The process of breathing*

What if?

Imagine a gunshot or stab wound enters the chest wall. Air can now enter through the wound more easily than through the trachea and the surface tension of the pleura is destroyed. The lung collapses to a much smaller size and is virtually useless. Individuals can live quite well with only one lung – but in this type of injury there is likely to be shock and loss of vital oxygen-carrying blood as well. The individual's life is threatened. First aid treatment would be to place a large pad over the wound as quickly as possible to prevent the lung collapsing and then send for an ambulance to get the individual to hospital quickly.

The composition of inspired (or inhaled) air, which is the air around us, and that of expired (or exhaled) air is shown in Table 12.1.

COMPONENT	INSPIRED AIR	EXPIRED AIR
Oxygen	20%	16%
Nitrogen	80%	80%
Carbon dioxide	Virtually 0% (0.04)%	4%
Water vapour	Depends on climate	Saturated

TABLE 12.1 *Composition of air*

Try it out

Study Table 12.1 and write down the differences between inspired and expired air that you can see. These are the changes that must have happened in the lungs by gaseous exchange.

Gaseous exchange

The bronchioles end in thousands of tiny air sacs, each of which contains a cluster of single-layered alveoli, rather like a bunch of grapes on a stem. The walls of the alveoli consist of very thin, flat simple squamous epithelium, and each alveolus is surrounded by the smallest blood vessels, known as capillaries. The walls of the capillaries are also composed of simple squamous epithelium, in a single layer. This means that the air entering the alveoli during breathing is separated from the blood by only two single-layered, very thin walls. There are elastic fibres round the alveoli enabling them to expand and recoil with inspiration and expiration respectively. A film of moisture lines the inside of each alveolus to enable the air gases to pass into solution. As the two layers of epithelium are so thin and semi-permeable, the dissolved gases can pass through easily and quickly. Although the largest component of air is nitrogen and this

Key concept

Diffusion: the passage of molecules from a high concentration of molecules to a low concentration of molecules.

too passes into solution, it takes no part in the process of respiration.

Diffusion occurs in liquids or gases because the molecules are in constant random motion, it is an overall 'equalling up' where a lot of molecules meet a few molecules. Diffusion will stop, in time, as the numbers of molecules become more evenly distributed. This is called equilibrium. (Note: this does not mean the molecules stop moving, only that there are equal numbers of molecules passing in both directions, so no overall gain or loss.)

In the human body, where diffusion is a common method of transport, a state of equilibrium is undesirable as it means overall transport would cease. To prevent equilibrium being attained, the high concentration must be continually kept high and the low concentration must also be maintained.

Breathing in fresh air replenishes the high concentration of dissolved oxygen molecules, while the removal of diffused oxygen by the bloodstream maintains the low concentration. With carbon dioxide, the situation is reversed – the high concentration is in the blood and the low concentration in the refreshed air, so diffusion removes dissolved carbon dioxide from the blood into the expired air from the lungs. Carbon dioxide and water are waste products from internal respiration in cells.

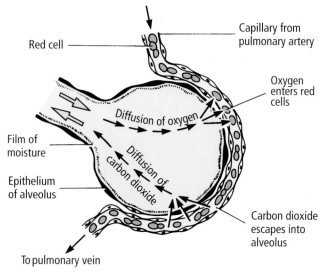

FIGURE 12.5 *Gaseous exchange in the alveoli*

The respiratory centres in the brain alternately excite and suppress the activity of the neurones supplying the the respiratory nerves (mainly the phrenic nerve to the diaphragm) causing inspiration and expiration. Nervous receptors, sensitive to chemicals dissolved in the blood (particularly oxygen, carbon dioxide and hydrogen ions) are located both centrally and peripherally in the body. These chemical receptors, or chemoreceptors, initiate reflexes when they are stimulated and send nerve impulses to the respiratory centre to change breathing activity and restore the concentrations of the chemicals. This is part of **homeostasis** in the body.

The main factors affecting breathing and respiration are:

* exercise
* emotion
* altitude
* release of **adrenaline**, such as in frightening circumstances.

All these increase the rate of ventilation or breathing to an appropriate level. When the stimulating factor is removed, ventilation returns to normal.

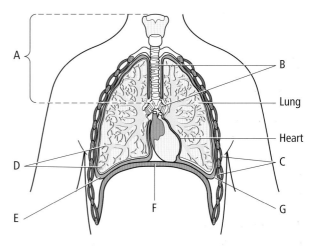

FIGURE 12.6 *Vertical section through the thorax*

Functions of the respiratory system

1. to provide a supply of oxygen for carriage by the blood to body cells
2. to remove waste products, carbon dioxide and water, from the blood to the exterior
3. to help maintain acid-base balance (hydrogen **ion** concentration) in body tissues
4. to assist in homeostasis.

Dysfunctions of the respiratory system

Asthma

This condition is more correctly termed bronchial asthma, to distinguish it from cardiac asthma, which is a condition associated with heart failure.

Bronchial asthma is characterised by recurring episodes of breathlessness, a feeling of tightness in the chest and wheezing. It can be mild, moderate or severe at different times of the day or night. Asthma commonly starts in childhood and often clears up in early adult life, although many adults also suffer from asthma and it can begin at any age. During a severe attack, there is distress, sweating and rapid heart rate, with the victim often unable to talk. Sometimes there is a bluish colour to the lips and face (where the skin is very thin) due to poor oxygenation of the blood.

Bronchitis

Inflammation of the bronchi produces a productive cough, yellow/green sputum or phlegm, raised temperature, wheezing and shortness of breath. It may be an acute infection coming on suddenly, or a chronic infection resulting in narrowing of the bronchi and bronchioles and accompanying destruction of the alveolar walls, known as emphysema. This is a very common condition in the UK, affecting more males than females.

Cystic fibrosis (CF)

This disorder is also known as mucoviscidosis for it is characterised by the production of very thick (viscid) mucus (muco-) which cannot flow easily to lubricate the intestines, nose, mouth, throat, bronchi and bronchioles. CF remains a serious disorder causing chronic lung infections and an impaired ability to absorb fats and other nutrients from food. People with CF are affected from birth, previously most sufferers died in childhood.

Some sufferers develop early symptoms, others may not show any symptoms for years. Typically, there are recurrent infections, particularly of the upper respiratory tract and chest, which can cause lung damage. Motions are often putty-coloured, greasy and 'smelly'. This is due to the sparsity of pancreatic enzymes. Sweat glands often do not function well and sweat is extra salty; this may give rise to heatstroke in hot weather.

Infertility can occur in both sexes and the condition may be diagnosed in adult life as a result of investigations by infertility clinics.

Children with CF may be classed as 'failing to thrive' and their growth may be impaired. The condition affects about 1 in 2,000 children and is more common in the white Caucasian population.

Causes of dysfunctions of the respiratory system

Asthma

No attributable cause for asthma can be found in some people, but others have an allergic reaction to an inhaled substance, known as an allergen. Common allergens include:

* pollens
* house dust and dust mites
* animal fur, feathers or skin flakes
* food or drugs.

Attacks can be triggered by stress, anxiety, exercise (particularly in winter), tobacco smoke or air pollutants.

Asthma is not directly inherited, but there is a strong tendency for the condition to run in families. Smoking during pregnancy exerts an influence and while there is no evidence that environmental pollution causes asthma, it can certainly worsen the condition. Approximately one child in ten in the UK has asthma.

Bronchitis

Acute bronchitis is often associated with a cold or influenza, but may also result from air pollution. Smoking tobacco products is the main cause of chronic bronchitis. Air pollution can be a major factor as well, resulting in more cases in industrial areas.

Cystic fibrosis

CF is caused by inheriting two recessive alleles for the condition, one from each parent. It is therefore a genetically inherited disorder.

Diagnostic techniques

Asthma

Asthma in children is usually diagnosed from a medical history. Although wheezing and breathlessness occur in other respiratory conditions, asthma is the only condition in which these vary so much from hour to hour or day to day.

The diagnosis can be confirmed by **peak-flow monitoring.** A peak-flow meter, often used to help diagnose asthma, measures the maximum speed at which air can flow out of the lungs. The narrowed air passages in asthma cause this rate to slow down. The meter consists of a hollow plastic tube with a gauge on the top. A disposable cardboard mouthpiece is inserted into one end of the tube, the patient takes a deep breath in and breathes out with maximum effort through the mouthpiece. The rate of flow registers on the gauge, enabling a reading to be taken. Patients are encouraged to take a peak-flow reading daily (see below) to monitor both their asthma and their medication. The readings are used in planning treatment.

Patient using a peak-flow meter

Bronchitis

Acute bronchitis is diagnosed from signs and symptoms and usually clears up after a few days. When bronchitis is caused by bacterial infection, antibiotics may be needed.

Chronic bronchitis will again be diagnosed from signs and symptoms, but chest X-rays, blood tests, sputum analysis and lung-function tests may be used to investigate the seriousness of the condition. Lung or pulmonary function tests may include the peak-flow monitoring described above and a measurement of lung volumes using a spirometer. Blood tests will involve measurement of blood gases, oxygen and carbon dioxide as well as haemoglobin and full blood count (in which all the different blood cell types are counted in a small sample) to eliminate other causes of breathlessness, cough and wheezing.

Cystic fibrosis

Cystic fibrosis is diagnosed on a medical history and a sweat test. Patients with cystic fibrosis produce sweat which has a higher salt content than average and this is used for confirming the diagnosis. X-rays of the chest monitor chest infections and lung damage and exclude other respiratory conditions.

Treatment: general principles

Asthma

Inhalers containing a fine aerosol spray of a drug (bronchodilator) which relaxes the muscle of the bronchi are used to treat asthma attacks. For chronic asthma, long-term treatment with corticosteroids may be needed. Corticosteroids are similar to a naturally-occurring group of hormones from the adrenal cortex. They are useful in treating inflammatory conditions where there is no obvious source of infection.

Asthma sufferers gradually learn by experience the main triggers for their attacks and try to avoid these where possible, such as animal hair, feathers, high pollen count days, smoky atmospheres, dust, etc. Avoidance of triggers will involve lifestyle changes for most asthmatic people.

Bronchitis

Inhalers similar to those used in asthma may relieve breathlessness, and oxygen therapy delivered through a mask and piped oxygen may be necessary. Antibiotics are used for infective bronchitis, and the service user should prevent further damage by not smoking and avoiding polluted areas.

Smoking is harmful to service users because:

* the bronchi are narrowed and this, rather like asthma, interferes with the air flowing into and out of the lungs

* less oxygen is available to the body cells because the carbon monoxide in cigarette smoke attaches firmly to the haemoglobin in the red blood cells, excluding oxygen

* cilia, responsible for the flow of mucus and the elimination of dirt and other particles from the respiratory tract, are destroyed

* gaseous exchange is less efficient

* increased mucus production, the accumulation of dust, and the destruction of cilia lead to 'smoker's cough'

* there is a greater risk of infection from accumulated debris and mucus

* elasticity of the lungs is reduced, leading to emphysema.

Cystic fibrosis

Physiotherapy to aid the flow of mucus in the chest, and appropriate antibiotic treatment to avoid further lung damage, are both important. Pancreatic enzymes are provided to aid food digestion. In some cases a heart-lung transplant may be considered, to replace damaged lungs.

Summary

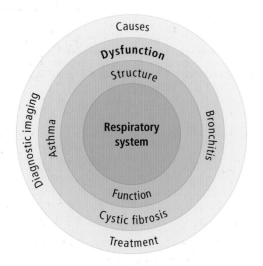

Consider this

Patrick was a coal miner for most of his life and his main leisure pursuit was going to the miner's welfare club after work for a smoke and a few pints of beer with his colleagues. He regularly smoked 50 hand-rolled cigarettes daily. Now retired, Patrick is not enjoying life as he expected to. He is confined to his home, cannot smoke, is reliant on oxygen for most of the day and cannot walk more than a few steps. His doctor has diagnosed chronic bronchitis and emphysema.

1. Can you identify the factors which have contributed to Patrick's illness?

2. Can you identify the structural and functional problems with his respiratory system?

3. Suggest how Patrick's lifestyle has influenced the development and progression of his condition.

4. Using the information given and your own knowledge of the respiratory system, evaluate Patrick's quality of life now.

Section 2: Cardio-vascular system

The cardio-vascular system is the main transport system of the body, carrying oxygen, carbon dioxide, nutrients such as amino acids, glucose and digested fats, hormones, antibodies and urea.

Structure of the cardio-vascular system

The heart

The heart is a muscular pump which forces blood around the body through a system of blood vessels; arteries, veins and capillaries. Blood carries dissolved oxygen to the body cells and at the same time removes the waste products of respiration: carbon dioxide and water. However, blood is also important in distributing heat around the body, as well as hormones, nutrients, salts, enzymes and urea.

The adult heart is the size of a closed fist. It is located in the thoracic cavity between the lungs, and protected by the rib cage. It is surrounded by a tough membrane, the pericardium, which contains a thin film of fluid to prevent friction.

The heart is a double pump, each side consisting of an upper chamber (the atrium) and lower chamber (the ventricle). The right side of the heart pumps deoxygenated blood from the veins to the lungs, where it is oxygenated. The left side pumps oxygenated blood from the lungs to the body. The two sides of the heart are completely separated by a septum. The blood passes twice through the heart in any one cycle, and this is often termed a double circulation.

A schematic diagram showing the double circulation with the heart artificially separated is shown in Figure 12.7.

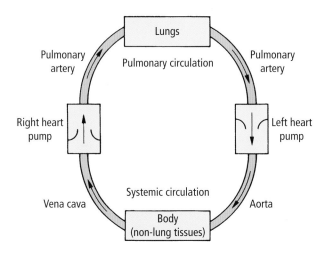

FIGURE 12.7 *Schematic diagram showing double circulation*

Each of the four heart chambers has a major blood vessel entering or leaving it. Veins enter the atria and arteries leave the ventricles.

Did you know?

It is useful to remember that atria have veins entering and ventricles have arteries leaving – in each case, A and V, never two As or two Vs.

The circulation to and from the lungs is known as the pulmonary circulation, and circulation around the body is called the systemic circulation. Arteries are blood vessels that leave the heart, while veins take blood towards the heart.

In pulmonary circulation, the pulmonary artery carrying deoxygenated blood leaves the right ventricle to go to the lungs. It divides fairly soon after leaving the heart, because there are two lungs to be supplied, into the right and left pulmonary arteries. The pulmonary veins (there are four of them), now carrying oxygenated blood, must enter the left atrium.

The main artery to the body leaving the left ventricle is the aorta and the main vein bringing blood back to the heart is the vena cava, which enters the right atrium. The vena cava has two branches, the superior vena cava returning blood from the head and neck and the inferior vena cava returning blood from the rest of the body. In many diagrams of the heart, these are treated as one vessel.

It is important that the blood flows in only one direction through the heart, so it is supplied with special valves to ensure that this happens. There are two sets of valves between the atria and the ventricles, one on each side. Sometimes these are called the right and left atrio-ventricular valves but older names are also used – the bicuspid (left side) and tricuspid valves. These names refer to the number of 'flaps' known as cusps that make up the valve, the bicuspid valve having two and the tricuspid having three cusps. Each cusp is fairly thin, so to prevent them turning inside out with the force of the blood flowing by, they have tendinous cords attached to their free ends. These are tethered to the heart muscles of the ventricles by small papillary muscles. The papillary muscles tense just before the full force of the muscle in the ventricles contracts, so the tendinous cords act like guy ropes holding the valves in place.

The two large arteries, the pulmonary and the aorta, also have exits guarded by valves called semi-lunar valves (so-called because the three cusps forming each valve are half-moon shaped). These valves are needed because when the blood has been forced into the arteries by the ventricular muscle contractions, the blood must not be allowed to fall back into the ventricles when they relax. These valves can also be called the pulmonary and aortic valves.

You should also understand that when you view a heart diagram or picture in front of you, you are looking at it the opposite way round, i.e. the right side of the heart diagram is on your left side and vice versa. If you get confused, pick up the diagram and place it over your heart facing outwards. Now it corresponds to your left and right hands.

Heart muscle is cardiac muscle, composed of partially striped, interlocking, branched cells. It is **myogenic**, which means capable of rhythmic contractions without a nerve supply. However, the atrial muscle beats at a different pace to the ventricular muscle so it needs a nerve supply to organise and co-ordinate the contractions so the heart is an efficient pump. The heart muscle has its own blood supply, the coronary arteries and veins.

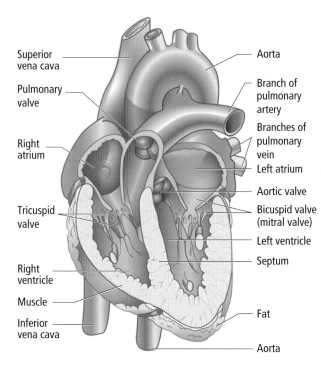

FIGURE 12.9 *Vertical section through the heart*

The muscular walls of the atria are much thinner than the ventricular walls, as the flow of blood from the atria is aided by gravity and the distance travelled by the blood here is very short – just from the atria to the ventricles. The ventricles are much thicker than the atria, but there are differences between the two ventricles. The right ventricle is about one-third the thickness of the left ventricle because the left ventricle has to drive oxygenated blood around the whole of the body, including the head and neck which involves pushing the blood upwards against the force of gravity.

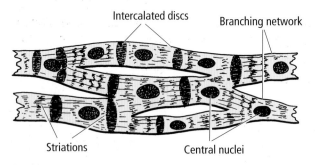

FIGURE 12.8 *Microscopic diagram of heart muscle*

Arteries and veins

Each type of blood vessel has structural and functional differences outlined in Table 12.2.

Each organ has arteries carrying oxygenated blood to it and veins draining deoxygenated blood away from it. The link vessels supplying the cells of the organ tissues are the capillaries. A protein-free plasma filtrate is driven out of the capillaries to supply the cells with oxygen and nutrients. Blood cells and **plasma proteins** in blood are too large to be forced out between the cells. A simple diagram of the blood circulation to the body organs is shown in Figure 12.11.

ARTERIES	VEINS	CAPILLARIES
Functional differences	**Functional differences**	**Functional differences**
Carry blood away from heart to organs	Carry blood to heart from the organs	Connects arteries to veins
Carry blood under high pressure	Carry blood under low pressure	Arterioles and capillaries cause greatest drop in pressure due to overcoming the friction of blood passing through small vessels
Usually contain blood high in oxygen, low in carbon dioxide and water *What are the exceptions?*	Usually contain blood low in oxygen, high in carbon dioxide and water *What are the exceptions?*	Delivers protein-free plasma filtrate high in oxygen to cells and collects up respiratory waste products of carbon dioxide and water
Large arteries close to the heart help the intermittent flow from the ventricles become a continuous flow through the circulation		

TABLE 12.2 *The differences in structure and function of blood vessels*

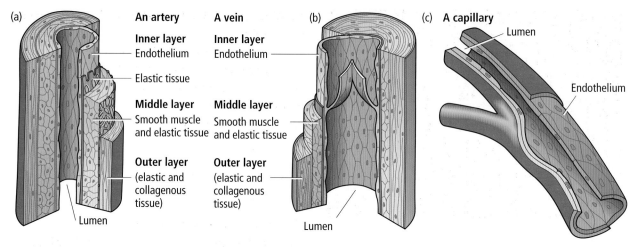

FIGURE 12.10 *Sections through blood vessels to show their structure*

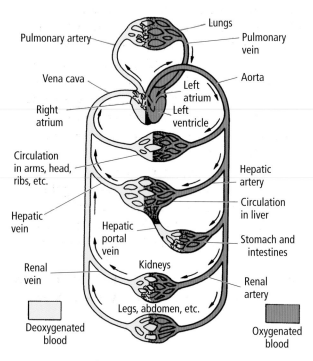

FIGURE 12.11 *The human circulatory system*

Blood and blood cells

Blood consists of straw-coloured plasma which carries several types of blood cells. Plasma is mainly water carrying dissolved gases (e.g. oxygen and carbon dioxide), nutrients (e.g. glucose and amino acids, salts, enzymes and hormones). A combination of important proteins, called the plasma proteins, are also present and have roles in blood clotting, transport, defence and osmotic regulation.

The most common cells in the plasma are red blood cells, or **erythrocytes.** These are very small cells with a bi-concave shape and elastic membrane. The elastic membrane is important as they must often distort to travel through the smallest capillaries. Erythrocytes have no nucleus in their mature state (the loss produces a depression in the top and bottom of the cell, hence their shape) to provide a larger surface area for exposure to oxygen. They are packed with **haemoglobin** which gives them a red colour – this is why blood is red. In oxygenated blood, the oxyhaemoglobin (in arterial blood) is bright red but, after the dissolved oxygen is delivered to body cells, the reduced haemoglobin (in venous blood) is dark-red in colour. Due to the absence of nuclei, erythrocytes cannot divide and have a limited lifespan of around 120 days.

White blood cells, or **leucocytes**, are larger, nucleated and less numerous. There are several types, but the most numerous are the **granulocytes** (also termed polymorphs, neutrophils and phagocytes). They are called granulocytes because they contain granules in their cytoplasm as well as lobed nuclei. They are capable of changing their shape and engulfing foreign material such as bacteria and carbon particles, a process known as phagocytosis. A granulocyte acts rather like an amoeba and is sometimes said to be amoeboid. Granulocytes, because of their ability to engulf microbes and

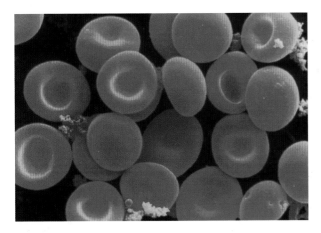

Human blood

foreign material, are very important in the defence of the body.

Smaller white blood cells, the **lymphocytes**, with round nuclei and clear cytoplasm assist in the production of **antibodies. Antigens** are found on the surface of disease-causing microbes or pathogens and act as identity markers for different types of pathogens (rather like name tags on school uniform). Antibodies neutralise antigens and prevent the microbes from multiplying. They can then be phagocytosed by granulocytes and monocytes. Antibodies are chemically globulins, types of plasma protein carried in the plasma.

In a completely different way from granulocytes, lymphocytes also contribute to the defence of the body because of their role in the production of antibodies.

Monocytes, another type of white blood cell, are larger than lymphocytes. They also have large round nuclei and clear cytoplasm. They are very efficient at phagocytosis of foreign material and, like granulocytes, can leave the circulatory blood vessels to travel to the site of an infection and begin phagocytosing pathogens very rapidly.

Thrombocytes are not true cells, but are usually classed with the white blood cells, and are more commonly called platelets. They are products of much larger cells which have broken up, and have an important role in blood clotting.

The function of the cardio-vascular system

The cardiac cycle comprises the events taking place in the heart during one heart beat. Taking the average number of beats in a minute (60 seconds) at rest to be 70, the time for one beat or one cardiac cycle is 70 divided by 60 seconds, or 0.8 seconds. This is based on an average resting heart rate. When the heart rate rises to, say, 120 beats during moderate activity, the cardiac cycle will reduce to 0.5 seconds. As we can see, the higher the heart rate, the shorter the cardiac cycle, until a limit is reached when the heart would not have time to fill between successive cycles.

Using the resting figures above, we can show the cycle in a series of boxes representing 0.1 second each to study the events occurring in the heart (Figure 12.12). The shaded boxes show when contraction is occurring, and relaxation time is left blank. The technical term for contraction is **systole** and for relaxation, **diastole.** The atria and ventricular activity is shown on separate lines.

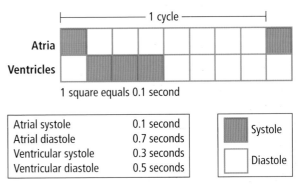

	0.1 second	
Atrial systole	0.1 second	Systole
Atrial diastole	0.7 seconds	
Ventricular systole	0.3 seconds	Diastole
Ventricular diastole	0.5 seconds	

FIGURE 12.12 *Timed events in the cardiac cycle; systole and diastole*

The events in the cardiac cycle can be described in stages as follows:

1. Both atria contract forcing blood under pressure into the ventricles.

2. Ventricles are bulging with blood and the increased pressure forces the atrio-ventricular valves shut (giving rise to the first heart sound – lubb).

3. Muscle in the ventricular walls begins to contract, pressure on blood inside rises and forces open the semi-lunar valves in the aorta and pulmonary artery.

4. Ventricular systole forces blood into the aorta (left side) and pulmonary artery (right side). These arteries have elastic walls and begin to expand.

5. As the blood leaves the ventricles, the muscle starts to relax. For a fraction of a second blood falls backwards, catching the pockets of the semi-lunar valves and making them close, which makes the second heart sound, dup.

6. With the ventricles in diastole, the atrio-ventricular valves are pushed open with the blood that has been filling the atria. When the ventricles are about 70 per cent full, the atria contract to push the remaining blood in rapidly and the next cycle has begun.

You can see that when the chambers are in diastole and relaxed, they are still filling. The cycle is continuous and with a high heart rate it is the filling time which has shortened.

The cardiac output is the quantity of blood expelled from the heart in one minute. To calculate this, you need to know the quantity of blood expelled from the left ventricle in one beat (known as the stroke volume) and the number of beats in one minute (or the heart rate). The average individual has a stroke volume of 70 cm^3 and a heart rate between 60 and 80 beats per minute. An individual who trains regularly might have a lower heart rate but a higher stroke volume.

Control of the cardiac cycle

The heart is controlled by the **autonomic nervous system**, which has two branches, the **sympathetic nervous system** and the **parasympathetic nervous system**. These two systems act rather like an accelerator and a brake on the heart. The sympathetic nervous system is active when the body is undergoing muscular work, fear or stress. It causes each heartbeat to increase in strength and heart rate to increase. The parasympathetic nervous system calms the heart output and is active during peace and contentment. The sympathetic nervous system is boosted by the hormone adrenaline during periods of fright, flight and fight.

Did you know?

Palpitations are forceful, often rapid heart beats that an individual becomes aware of – most commonly due to an active sympathetic nervous system together with adrenaline secretion as a consequence of fright, flight or fight.

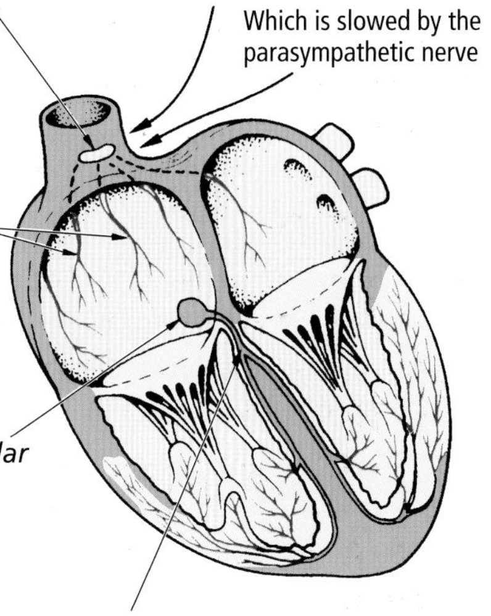

FIGURE 12.13 *Control of the cardiac cycle*

The sympathetic and parasympathetic nervous systems supply a special cluster of excitable cells in the upper part of the right atrium. This is called the sino-atrial node (S–A node) or in general terms 'the **pacemaker**'. An interplay of impulses from the sympathetic and parasympathetic nerves acting on the S–A node regulate the activity of the heart to suit circumstances from minute to minute, hour to hour and day to day.

Every few seconds, the S–A node sends out a cluster of nerve impulses across the branching network of atrial muscle fibres to cause contraction. The impulses are caught by another group of cells forming the atrio-ventricular node (A–V node) and relayed to a band of conducting tissue made of large, modified muscle cells called **Purkinje** fibres. The transmission of impulses is delayed slightly in the A–V node to enable the atria to complete their contractions and the atrio-ventricular valves to start to close.

Heart valves are located on a fibrous figure of eight between the atrial and ventricular muscle masses and the first part of the conducting tissue (the bundle of **His**) enables the excitatory impulses to cross to the ventricles. The bundle of

His then splits into right and left bundle branches which run down either side of the ventricular septum before spreading out into the ventricle muscle masses. Impulses now pass very rapidly so that the two ventricles contract together forcing blood around the body organs.

Did you know?

Any interference in the conducting system, possibly as a result of a blocked coronary artery causing tissue death, can result in a condition called heart block which can mean some parts of the heart beat at a different rhythm.

Dysfunction of the cardio-vascular system

Key concept

Dysfunction: an impairment of function – some parts are not working at maximum efficiency.

Changes in blood pressure

Blood pressure (BP) is the force exerted by the blood on the walls of the blood vessels. It is generated by the walls of the left ventricle during contraction. Although new units were devised some time ago to meaure BP in kPa (kiloPascals), most establishments in the UK still measure BP in millimetres of mercury, although mercury is no longer used in BP measuring equipment or sphygmomanometers. The units are mm Hg because Hg is the chemical symbol for mercury.

At first sight, BP recordings look like a fraction (e.g. 120/80 mm Hg, the so-called average BP for a young adult). However, this is only a way of displaying an upper systolic reading when the ventricles are contracting and a lower diastolic reading when they are relaxed.

The highest BP is found in large arteries close to the heart, such as the aorta, the carotid arteries and the arteries in the arms. There is a gradual drop in BP as the blood is forced through the medium and small arteries and the arterioles. The veins have little BP and blood has to be assisted back to the right atrium by skeletal muscle pressure in the limbs and the presence of valves to prevent backflow.

What if?

You are lying in bed – head, heart and legs are in the horizontal plane. Then the alarm clock rings. When you leap out of bed, your head is uppermost and your legs reach the floor – your BP has to adjust within a fraction of a second. What will happen if it takes longer?

Why are older people advised to sit up in bed slowly for a few minutes before swinging their legs to the floor?

Key concepts

Hypotension: the technical term for low BP with dizziness and fainting episodes. Many healthy people have a lower BP than average for people of their age and have no symptoms. Others may have some underlying disorder that causes hypotension. The most common type is postural hypotension caused by suddenly sitting or standing up.

Hypertension: characterised by an abnormally high BP at rest. The World Health Organization (WHO) defines hypertension as being consistently above 160/95 mm Hg, but many people are classed as mildly hypertensive if their BP is over 140–160/90–95 mm Hg.

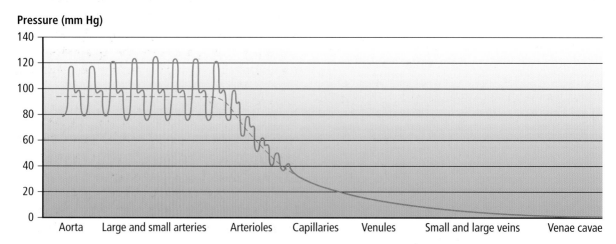

FIGURE 12.14 *Graph showing how BP varies in the circulation*

The condition affects between 10 and 20 per cent of people in the UK and is most common in middle-aged and elderly men. Many people, including younger adults, are unaware that they have hypertension and doctors advise that people should have their BP measured at regular intervals. Raised BP can lead to strokes and heart disease, both of which are life-threatening conditions.

Many people with hypertension have no identified underlying cause, and this is often known as essential hypertension. For some people a cause may be identified (see below).

Coronary artery disease

When the coronary arteries are narrowed or blocked, the heart muscle is starved of blood and this may cause chest pain, known as **angina pectoris.** This pain is commonly brought on by exertion and relieved by resting. The heart muscle demands more blood to compensate for the extra effort during the exertion and cannot receive it due to the narrowness of the vessels. The chest pain may be a dull ache or feeling of pressure spreading to the arms (particularly the left), neck or back. The arteries are narrowed due to the formation of fatty deposits or plaques on the arterial walls. These are termed atheromatous plaques and are commonly associated with hardening of the arterial walls (so-called **atherosclerosis**).

Heart attacks

Heart attack, coronary thrombosis (blood clots in the coronary arteries), or myocardial infarction (death of a wedge-shaped piece of cardiac muscle) tend to be synonymous. The narrowed coronary arteries have finally become blocked and the patient suffers chest pain, often severe. The pain is similar to angina but not relieved by resting. Atherosclerosis causes the inner lining of the arteries to become roughened, predisposing the blood to clot and finally close off the blood supply to the tissues after the blockage. If a major coronary artery or one of the larger branches is blocked, the patient may die. When a smaller branch is closed off, the patient may survive the heart attack with effective treatment.

Causes of dysfunction

When the causes of dysfunction can be identified, they usually fall into two broad categories: genetic disposition to hypertension or coronary heart disease, and lifestyle choices.

Diet

It has long been thought that diets rich in animal fats and dairy produce have been a major factor influencing both a raised cholesterol level and atherosclerosis. In turn, such a diet is also associated with obesity and being overweight – another factor influencing the development of heart disease and hypertension.

Alcohol

Long-term heavy drinking is associated with coronary heart disease, hypertension, heart failure and strokes. In addition, alcohol contains 'empty calories', calories which provide no nutritional benefits but can contribute significantly to obesity or overweight.

Smoking

Many people immediately think of lung cancer when they think of the harmful effects of smoking, but coronary heart disease affects many more people. Young adults smoking 20 cigarettes daily are three times more likely to develop coronary heart disease than non-smokers, and the risk increases significantly with more cigarettes smoked. Other arteries supplying body parts are also affected, particularly the leg arteries (peripheral arterial disease) and the brain (strokes).

Genetic disposition

People with a family history of heart disease and strokes, particularly before the age of 50, are recommended to have their cholesterol levels checked regularly. Some families are known to have metabolic disorders that give rise to high levels of blood lipids or fats, particularly cholesterol, causing life-threatening disorders.

Lifestyle

Stress is another important influence in heart disease, although most doctors think that this is secondary to the factors already listed. People with 'type A' personalities – always rushing from one job to the next, looking at their watches, needing to get on with things and do things well – are thought to have an increased risk of heart disease and hypertension, but these people are also busy and active, which may in itself help to keep them healthy.

Overweight and obese 'couch potatoes' are more likely to develop heart disease than people who exercise regularly and use up the energy from fats in their diet.

There is some evidence that depression, grief, redundancy or other personal crises can affect the progress of cardio-vascular disorders.

General principles and value of diagnostic techniques

Various methods of obtaining information about the structure of the heart and the way in which it functions have helped doctors to diagnose cardiac disorders for many years. Although listening to the heart sounds and counting the heart rate provided valuable information, modern techniques such as electrocardiography (ECG), chest X-rays, echocardiography, angiography, CT scanning, MRI, cardiac catheterisation and specialised blood tests have meant that the study of the heart has developed into a whole new branch of medicine, known as cardiology.

Diagnostic imaging techniques

Chest X-rays
A simple, painless chest X-ray, often carried out as an out-patient or even by a mobile unit in the workplace, can reveal the outline of the heart and major blood vessels. These structures appear white, as they are more dense to the rays passing through and this distinguishes them from the darker lungs and ribs.

The position, size and shape of the outline can reveal, to the trained eye, whether there is any enlargement or wasting (atrophy) of parts of the heart and blood vessels. Any calcification (a hardening due to calcium deposits) in major vessels or valves will show as very dense patches.

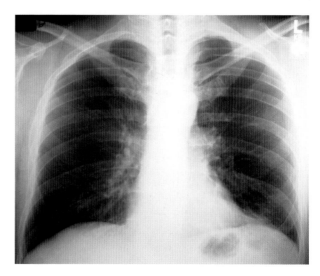

A chest X-ray

Echocardiography
This technique uses ultrasound (high-frequency sound waves) to display images from the echoes bounced back from different parts of the heart. As it does not use radiation, it is extremely valuable in assisting diagnosis, particularly in obtaining information on congenital abnormalities and heart valve operation. Blood flow across heart valves can be measured using this technique.

Coronary angiography
This is useful to show the chambers of the heart and the state of the coronary arteries. The patient is injected with a contrast medium (which is opaque to X-rays) into the blood stream. X-rays are taken to display the heart and its blood supply. It is particularly valuable in congenital heart disease and coronary artery disease.

CT (computerised tomography) Scanning
Modern CT scanners are able to take still images of a heart beat and get valuable information to diagnose a wide variety of cardiac disorders. However, at present there is a long wait for scans, and other techniques are more readily available.

MRI (magnetic resonance imaging) scans
MRI scans provide very high quality images of the heart, as these become more common it is likely

that techniques such as angiography may be used less. In some cardio-thoracic specialist centres, MRI equipment is provided in a 'containerised' vehicle for transport between centres. It is often used to assess the progress of coronary by-pass operations.

Blood pressure monitoring

You have already learned about the value of monitoring blood pressure to detect early signs of hypertension and subsequent heart disease and strokes. Many GPs check blood pressure on a patient attending for something unrelated. People are advised to have an annual blood pressure check, more often for patients with a family history of heart disease or a borderline hypertensive state.

ECG (electrocardiogram) traces

Like monitoring of blood pressure, ECGs can be carried out almost anywhere because machines can be light and portable. A form of tape recorder can be attached to the patient to obtain continuous 24-hour recordings.

The electrical activity of the heart can be detected by electrodes attached to the chest, wrist and ankles. You will recall that the S–A node (under the guidance of the sympathetic and parasympathetic nerves) sends out nervous impulses that excite the atrial muscle and then follow the conducting tissue around the heart. It is this activity that the electrodes are recording, immediately before the heart muscle masses contract. Many heart disorders produce abnormal electrical activity and the ECG is, therefore, a useful tool for diagnosis. Heart disorders detected by ECG include:

* coronary thrombosis

* coronary artery disease

* heart muscle disorders (cardiomyopathy)

* arrhythmia (variation of rhythm, such as fibrillation and heart block)

* ectopic beats (extra beats).

As the ECG trace is timed and recorded, unusual heart rates known as **tachycardia** (faster than normal) and **bradycardia** (slower than normal) can be identified.

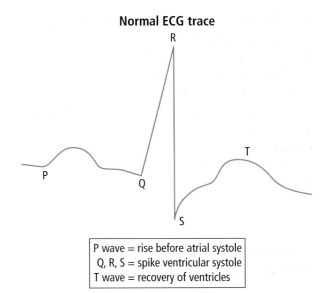

Normal ECG trace

| P wave = rise before atrial systole |
| Q, R, S = spike ventricular systole |
| T wave = recovery of ventricles |

FIGURE 12.15 *Normal ECG*

Try it out

Many people have had ECGs – ask someone you know what happened and how it felt. Your teacher may be able to ask a hospital technician to show you some abnormal ECGs and demonstrate how it is done.

Cardiac catheterisation

A catheter is a slim tube used to drain fluid (usually urine), inject fluid or apply pressure to a vessel. Cardiac catheters are used to investigate heart disorders.

What if?

What would you do if you needed to investigate the right side of the heart? Would you insert the tube into an artery or a vein? What about an insertion into the left side of the heart? Justify your answers.

Under a local anaesthetic, a small cut is made into the appropriate blood vessel and the catheter inserted and gently passed along until it is in position in the heart. Once there, it can be used to measure pressure in the chambers, take biopsies of the heart lining, collect samples of blood for oxygen levels or introduce radio-opaque material to show up on X-ray.

Cardiac catheters are used to investigate congenital heart disorders and coronary heart disease. Sometimes a balloon catheter can be used as treatment to open up a narrow valve or blood vessel.

General principles and value of treatments

Treatment of heart conditions includes any measure that will prevent or cure a disorder, or relieve symptoms to obtain a better quality of life. Many heart treatments will also involve accompanying changes in lifesyle. Heart surgery has only evolved over the last 50 years; before that it was dangerous and rarely done.

Heart by-pass surgery

This is more commonly known as a coronary artery by-pass operation and is just that – a by-pass using a length of leg vein joined to the aorta at one end and the coronary artery beyond the blockage at the other.

The surgeon has viewed a cardiac angiogram previously to ensure that the patient's heart is suitable for surgery. Some individuals have more than one blockage by-passed (double or triple by-passes). When the patient's leg veins are not suitable, synthetic tubing can be used.

There are often two surgical teams, one working on the leg and the other on the heart. The patient is placed on a heart-lung machine which replaces the functions of both the heart and the lungs while the repair is being carried out. The operation takes several hours and the patient has to be deemed well enough to undergo the surgery. Care in an ICU (intensive care unit) for about 10–12 days follows the operation. This type of operation is now carried out world-wide with over 10,000 operations annually.

Heart pacemakers

You have learned about the S–A node and its rhythmical excitation producing the heartbeat; the pacemaker is an artificial device implanted into a patient's chest to maintain a regular rhythm. It is used when the S–A node is malfunctioning or when there is an interference with the conduction of natural impulses. Advanced pacemakers can adapt the rhythm to exercise. An insulated wire is guided through a major vein so that the electrode end lies within the heart muscle. The battery end is located in a pocket of skin under the collar bone or abdomen. The service user can lead a normal life and batteries last many years. Replacing batteries means just a minor operation.

Heart transplant surgery and prevention of rejection

Transplantation means replacing a diseased part of the body, usually an organ, with a part from another individual, alive or recently deceased. This sounds like a simple technique to regain full or near full function. However, unless the donor individual is a very close blood relative, the body's immune system treats the donated part as foreign material and begins to destroy it. This destruction process is called rejection.

The first heart transplant was carried out in 1967 and the welfare of the patient was monitored by worldwide media every day. The patient survived

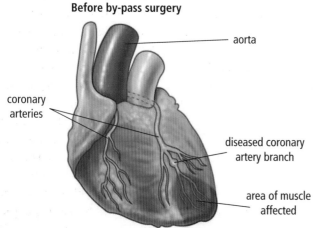
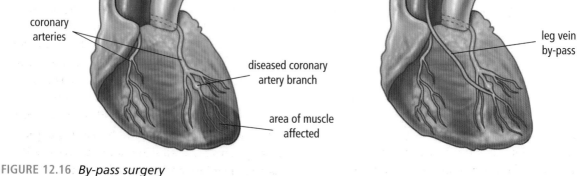

Before by-pass surgery

aorta

coronary arteries

diseased coronary artery branch

area of muscle affected

After by-pass surgery

leg vein by-pass

FIGURE 12.16 *By-pass surgery*

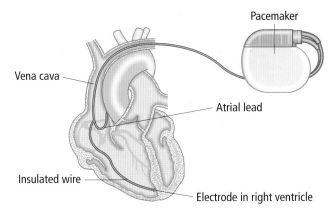

Pacemaker

Vena cava

Atrial lead

Insulated wire

Electrode in right ventricle

FIGURE 12.17 *A fitted pacemaker*

several weeks, but sadly died later. During the 1970s and 80s, more and more heart transplants were carried out and the success rate improved significantly. Although surgical techniques and heart-lung machines have improved dramatically over the years, a major factor is the development of effective suppressors of immunity to prevent rejection.

In the UK, heart transplants can only come from donors who have been pronounced clinically dead, whereas living close blood relatives may donate a kidney quite successfully. Kidney transplants are far more common than heart transplants. Individuals requiring a heart transplant may be in poor health having suffered for several years, whereas kidney patients have dialysis (an artificial back-up filtering system) to assist in maintaining health.

The donor heart is kept carefully in chilled saline and is transported to the recipient deemed most suitable to receive it. They will have been '**tissue-typed**' on joining the waiting list for transplant surgery. By matching tissue types of donor and recipient as closely as possible, the risk of rejection is reduced. No two people other than identical twins have identical tissue types, but close relatives often have similarities. Antigens on the surface of body cells, most particularly on leucocytes, are identified and recorded as a tissue type.

The patient is attached to a heart-lung machine to maintain the blood supply to vital organs. Nearly all the diseased heart is removed and the new donor heart is connected to all major blood vessels. The patient must then be placed on an immunosuppressive drug regime (to prevent an immune reaction), chiefly the drug cyclosporine, and remain so for the remainder of their life.

Infection must be guarded against because of the reduced immunity, so the individual must have clear instructions on how to proceed when infection is suspected.

Lifestyle changes

When coronary arteries are affected by atherosclerosis, it is highly likely that other arteries are affected, such as those supplying the legs and the brain. It makes sense to change to a healthier diet and:

* avoid heavy consumption of most fat (particularly animal fat)

* avoid convenience foods loaded with salt, sugar and fat

* move towards a healthy balanced diet featuring complex carbohydrates such as wholegrain foods, fruit and vegetables, fish, white meat, fibre and water.

Another reason for changing to a healthier diet is that a high fat and sugar diet also causes obesity, promoting hypertension and heart disease.

The situation with regard to smoking and its dangers must be clearly explained. The patient can be assisted and supported to stop smoking by helplines, chewing gum, patches and/or lozenges. They must be supported psychologically as well as physically during the period – preferably, this should have started before treatment commenced. Smoking is dangerous for patients with atherosclerosis because it raises blood pressure and increases atheromatous deposits in blood vessels as well as damaging lung tissue.

Alcohol consumption should also be kept within recommended limits or preferably to only occasional use, for it also raises blood pressure and causes palpitations leading to coronary heart disease.

A sensible exercise regime should be undertaken with professional guidance, to reduce fatty deposits, keep body weight in balance and stimulate the circulation and respiratory function.

It is almost impossible to have a stress-free life, and indeed a small amount of stress is beneficial from time to time, but stress should not be continuous. An organised life without rush and bother should be the aim, and for some people, this might involve reducing hours at work, with less responsibility and more delegation.

Thomas is 12 years old and small for his age. He has never been interested in playing sport. Now he is at secondary school, sports sessions are more intensive and he finds it impossible to participate much because he gets breathless and feels ill. The school nurse has spoken to his parents and advised them to consult health professionals. The doctors feel that he might have a congenital malformation in his heart as they have heard a murmur in his heart sounds, and further investigation is required.

1. What is a murmur? What does it usually indicate?

2. Thomas is to have a cardiac catheterisation and blood samples will be taken for analysis. Explain the purpose and value of a cardiac catheterisation.

3. Blood samples on the left side of Thomas's heart have a lower oxygen level than normal.

There are no problems with his respiratory function. Explain how blood on the left side of the heart could have a lower oxygen level than normal.

4. When the heart chambers are displayed using radio-opaque material, a small open defect in the atrial septum can be seen. Using your knowledge of the heart structure, describe the normal flow of blood through the heart and how Thomas will have been affected by this 'hole' in the septum.

5. Thomas has had surgery to repair the heart structure. In the cardiac rehabilitation centre, he has been given advice for the care of his heart and his adult lifestyle. Explain and evaluate the advice on blood pressure monitoring, diet, exercise, smoking, drinking and stress that Thomas would have heard.

Summary

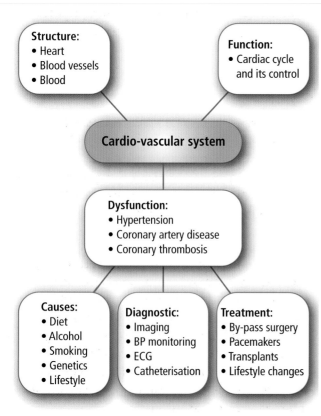

Structure:
- Heart
- Blood vessels
- Blood

Function:
- Cardiac cycle and its control

Cardio-vascular system

Dysfunction:
- Hypertension
- Coronary artery disease
- Coronary thrombosis

Causes:
- Diet
- Alcohol
- Smoking
- Genetics
- Lifestyle

Diagnostic:
- Imaging
- BP monitoring
- ECG
- Catheterisation

Treatment:
- By-pass surgery
- Pacemakers
- Transplants
- Lifestyle changes

Section 3: Digestive system

The purpose of the digestive system is to break down the large complex molecules that make up our food into small molecules capable of being absorbed through the wall of the gut or alimentary canal into the bloodstream. Once in the blood, these small molecules act as raw materials to build body structures, or for energy release in internal respiration. Energy is needed for work such as breathing, pumping blood around the circulation, transmitting nerve impulses, etc.

To break down large complex molecules in the laboratory we would use heat (as in cooking) or the addition of chemicals such as acids or alkalis. These processes are not possible in the human body, or cell and tissue structures would be destroyed or severely damaged.

Body cells are able to produce 'magical' substances called **enzymes** that can alter the rate of chemical reactions to build up or break down other molecules without using heat or harmful chemicals.

Enzymes are specific to the material on which they act (called a substrate). For example, a protease only acts on protein and a lipase only acts on lipids or fats. You may have noted that adding -ase at the end of the substrate name signifies that it is an enzyme. Not all enzymes follow this way of naming, but most do.

Enzyme reactions have some special features.

* Enzymes are sensitive to temperature. At low temperatures they work very slowly, if at all; at high temperatures, they become distorted (called denatured) and permanently stop working. Enzymes work optimally at body temperature.

* Enzymes are sensitive to the acidity or alkalinity of their surroundings, known as pH. Some digestive enzymes like pepsin (also known as gastric protease) work best in an acid environment. The stomach lining secretes pepsin and hydrochloric acid for maximum efficiency in breaking down proteins. Lipase prefers alkaline conditions and the pancreas secretes alkaline salts such as sodium hydrogen carbonate, to provide optimal conditions. Salivary amylase prefers neutral, or pH7, conditions. *Amylum* is the Latin name for starch, so amylase works on starch.

* Relatively few enzyme molecules are required to break down lots of large food molecules because they are catalysts.

Gross structure of the organs and glands of the alimentary canal

The alimentary canal is a tube that extends from the mouth to the anus. It is dilated, folded and puckered in various places along its length. You will need to know the names of the various regions, their main purpose and the outcome of their activities. Many glands are associated with the alimentary canal, and have important roles to play in digestion.

Ingestion is the act of taking food and drink into the mouth. Food is mixed with saliva, chewed, or masticated, by the action of the tongue and teeth, rolled into a small ball known as a **bolus**, and swallowed. This process is called mechanical digestion and is an important part of physically breaking the food down at an early stage. Saliva contains an enzyme known as salivary amylase, which begins the digestion of carbohydrates.

People do not chew food as much today as they did in the past, because many foods are well-cooked or ultra-refined, meal-times are rushed, many meals are convenience foods and 'mushy' in texture, and generally people are not brought up to chew food well as they did in Victorian England. This means that not only is there less physical breakdown, but salivary amylase is not adequately mixed into the food.

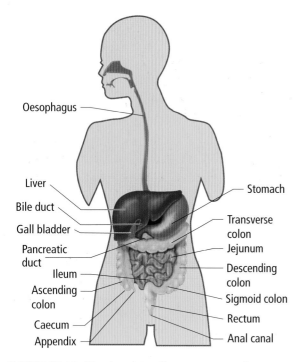

Oesophagus

Liver

Bile duct

Gall bladder

Pancreatic duct

Ileum

Ascending colon

Caecum

Appendix

Stomach

Transverse colon

Jejunum

Descending colon

Sigmoid colon

Rectum

Anal canal

FIGURE 12.18 *The human alimentary canal*

The stomach is the widest part of the alimentary canal, tucked mainly behind the rib cage under the diaphragm on the left side and receiving food from the mouth by way of the oesophagus, or gullet. The swallowed bolus is in the oesophagus for a few seconds only and no enzymes are secreted here, although salivary amylase will continue to act during this brief journey. The oesophagus is mainly a muscular transit for food boluses. Food can stay in the stomach for up to three hours, with a protein meal remaining the longest and food not containing protein passing through relatively quickly. During this time, the strong stomach walls roll and churn the food around and pour on secretions from the gastric glands. The resulting paste-like material is called chyme. Gastric glands produce juice that contains gastric protease and hydrochloric acid. This gastric juice works on proteins. In babies, another enzyme, rennin, solidifies and digests milk protein. The pH of the stomach is 1–2; this is strongly acidic. The stomach empties the chyme in spurts through the pyloric sphincter, a thick ring of muscle which alternately contracts and relaxes.

The next part of the alimentary canal is the small intestine, so-called because of its small diameter (certainly not its length, it is about six metres long). The first c-shaped part, the duodenum, is mainly concerned with digestion, and it is helped by two large glands that pour their secretions or juices into this area.

The liver

This is a large dark-red organ occupying the top right half of the abdomen and partly overlapping the stomach. It has many vital functions in the body, one of which is to produce bile. Bile contains no enzymes, but it provides important bile salts that cause fats (or lipids) to emulsify. Protein and carbohydrate have already experienced enzymic action. Lipids, like all fats, do not mix readily with water, so the enzymes have only a small water/lipid surface on which to work. The emulsification causes the fats to form millions of tiny globules, each with a water/lipid surface, so that enzymes can work efficiently over a massively enlarged surface area. Bile also contains bile pigments: bilirubin and biliverdin. These are the waste products of degraded haemoglobin from old, broken red blood cells. They give the brown colour to faeces. Bile is secreted continuously by the liver and temporarily stored in a sac called the gall bladder. When a lipid-rich meal arrives, the gall bladder releases bile into the small intestine.

The pancreas

This is a slim, leaf-shaped gland, located between the intestines and the stomach, close to the duodenum. It secretes enzyme-rich pancreatic juice as well as the alkaline salts referred to previously. Pancreatic enzymes work on all three macronutrients (protein, fat and carbohydrate).

The intestinal wall also contains glands which secrete enzyme-rich juices that continue the digestive process. These work either on the surface or inside the epithelial lining cells.

The remainder of the small intestine, also known as the ileum, is mainly concerned with the absorption of the now fully-digested food. It is specially adapted for this because of its:

* long length

* folded interior

* lining covered in many thousands of tiny projections called villi

* epithelial cells of villi covered in microvilli, projections so small that they can only be detected using an electron microscope.

These adaptations increase the surface area for absorption of nutrients from digested food to enormous proportions. Each villus is lined by columnar cells and **goblet cells** only one cell thick with an internal extensive capillary network and a blind-ended branch of the lymphatic system called a lacteal.

The chief products of protein and carbohydrate digestion pass into the capillary network which drains to the liver by the hepatic portal vein. Those of fats pass into the lacteal and eventually, via the lymphatic system, into the general circulation.

In the right-hand lower corner of the abdomen, the small intestine meets the large intestine, and

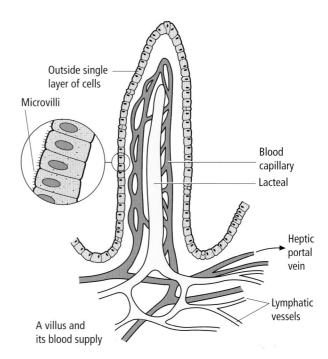

FIGURE 12.20 *Structure of a villus*

Did you know?

Food and chyme move down the alimentary canal by a process known as peristalsis. Note that in Figure 12.21 there are two sheets of muscle surrounding the tube – one sheet runs in a circular fashion around the tube while the other runs down the tube. Behind the bolus or chyme the inner circular muscle contracts (and the longitudinal muscle relaxes) pushing material in front of it. This is rather like your fingers pushing toothpaste up the tube. In front of the material, the circular muscle relaxes and the longitudinal contracts to hold the tube open to receive the food. Two sets of muscles acting in this way are said to be antagonistic.

Even if you stand on your head, peristalsis will still push your food down your alimentary canal! Strong peristaltic waves will cause abdominal pain, called colic, and the food is hurried down the intestines.

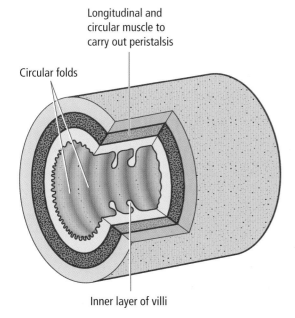

Small intestine showing the internal folds and the villi

FIGURE 12.19 *Section through the small intestine*

there are two biological remnants at this point, the caecum and the appendix. In grass-eating animals the caecum is a large structure with the worm-like appendix at the end. In man, neither the caecum nor the appendix has any function, although the appendix can become inflamed or pustulous and threaten life – a condition known as appendicitis.

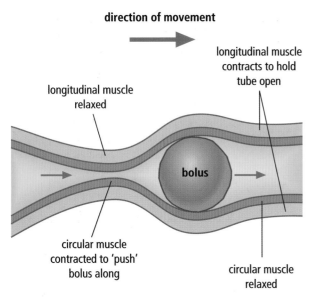

direction of movement

longitudinal muscle relaxed

longitudinal muscle contracts to hold tube open

bolus

circular muscle contracted to 'push' bolus along

circular muscle relaxed

FIGURE 12.21 *Peristalsis*

Did you know?

Sometimes when explorers or military personnel are going to remote areas for a lengthy stay, they will have their appendix removed beforehand – just in case!

The large intestine runs up the right side of the abdomen and turns to travel across to the left side before ending in a short tube called the rectum which opens to the exterior in the centre of the lower buttocks, guarded by a muscular sphincter, the anus. There are no enzymic juices in the large intestine.

Most of the large intestine, also known as the colon, has a puckered appearance because the longitudinal muscle splits into three bands and the circular muscle bulges out between the bands. During the journey down the alimentary canal, many glands have poured watery juices onto the chyme. The body cannot afford to lose too much water and the purpose of the large intestine is to slow down the passage of food waste (food waste is all that remains at this stage because all the nutrients were absorbed in the small intestine). Therefore water can be reabsorbed and the motion, or faeces, becomes semi-solid and can be eliminated by muscular action of the rectum and relaxation of the anus at a convenient time.

Did you know?

When toxins from pathogens affect the digestive system, the body often responds by rushing waste along the large intestine. There is insufficient time to reabsorb the water, and the effect is colic and diarrhoea. The beneficial side of this is that the pathogens are speedily removed from the body.

Faeces contain:

* cellulose (fibre or roughage) from plant cell walls from fruit and vegetables

* dead bacteria, including the usually harmless bacteria living in the large intestine which have died naturally, and other bacteria, which are often killed by the hydrochloric acid in the stomach

* scraped-off gut lining cells.

Mucus is secreted, by enormous numbers of goblet cells in the gut lining, to reduce friction as chyme and waste is moved along by peristalsis.

Basic functions of the digestive system

You have learned about many of the functions of the digestive system along with its structure, but Table 12.3 will help to consolidate your knowledge of the actual digestive processes.

Try it out

You have just eaten a meal of fish and chips – write an account of the processes involved in the digestion of this meal.

When the nutrients from food have been absorbed in the small intestine, amino acids and glucose pass via the capillaries of the villi to the hepatic portal vein, sometimes called the portal vein (see Figure 12.20).

Key concept

A *portal vein* is one which begins in capillaries (in the villi) and ends in capillaries (in the liver). Most blood vessels have capillaries at one end only.

LOCATION	GLAND AND JUICE	CONTENTS	SUBSTRATE	END PRODUCT	OTHER COMMENTS
Mouth	Salivary glands/ saliva	Salivary amylase	Carbohydrate: starch	Disaccharides: 'double' molecule sugars	Salivary amylase mixed with food during mechanical digestion. Requires a neutral pH to function efficiently
Oesophagus	None	None	None	None	Salivary amylase still acting on short journey to stomach
Stomach	Gastric glands/ gastric juice	Pepsin*, hydrochloric acid Rennin in babies	Protein	Amino acids and peptides (like double amino acids)	pH of gastric juice is acid for pepsin to work. Food churned into chyme. Bacteria in raw food killed by acid
Small intestine a) Duodenum	Intestinal glands/ intestinal juice (succus entericus)	Peptidase Various carbohydrases	Peptides 'Double' molecule sugars	Amino acids Glucose and other simple, soluble sugars	Alkaline medium (pH 8)
b) Liver, an associated gland, not part of alimentary canal	Liver/ bile	No enzymes Bile salts Bile pigments	None	None	Bile salts important in emulsifying lipids or fats. Converts small intestine contents from acid to alkaline.
c) Pancreas, an associated gland, not part of alimentary canal	Pancreas/ pancreatic juice	Lipase Pancreatic amylase Pancreatic protease* (formerly called trypsin) Alkaline salts	Lipids or fats Carbohydrates Proteins and peptides	Glycerol and fatty acids Glucose Amino acids	An important digestive gland. Salts convert acid stomach secretions to alkaline pH so that enzymes work optimally
d) Ileum	None	None	None	None	Main area for absorption of the end-products of digestion through millions of villi
Large intestine a) Colon	None	None	None	None	Main area for reabsorption of water
b) Rectum	None	None	None	None	Muscular walls expel semi-solid faeces through anus at periodic intervals

*Gastric protease and pancreatic protease are secreted as inactive precursors; they become activated by other substances once they are mixed with chyme in the lumen (hole) of the tube.

TABLE 12.3 *The main digestive processes, locations and outcomes*

Amino acids may travel via the bloodstream to areas of need in body cells. They are important in making enzymes, some hormones, plasma proteins, new cells (growth), and in repair processes. Surplus amino acids are broken down in the liver as they cannot be stored. Some parts of the molecules are used for energy, but the nitrogen-containing part is converted into urea and excreted by the kidneys (see Section 5).

Glucose is either transported to cells to be broken down in internal respiration to release energy, stored in liver and muscles as glycogen, or converted into fat to be stored around organs or under the skin.

Glycerol is used for energy or reconverting fatty acids into a form of fat that can be stored. Fatty acids travel from the lacteals, through the lymphatic system, into the main veins of the neck; this circuitous route enables smaller quantities of potentially harmful lipids to enter the circulation gradually.

Dysfunctions of the digestive system

There are many conditions associated with dysfunction of the digestive tract, and you will learn about three of them. Understanding the processes of digestion and absorption and the functions of the large intestine will enable you to analyse the signs and symptoms associated with such disorders.

Irritable bowel syndrome

This disorder is aptly named for it is characterised by bouts of abdominal pain, and disturbance of bowel habit such as constipation and diarrhoea. The abdomen can feel distended or bloated and little relief is gained from passing wind or faeces. The condition seems to appear in early and middle adulthood, affecting more females than males. It is one of the most common conditions affecting the digestive tract.

> **Key concept**
>
> *Syndrome:* a collection of signs and symptoms which together make up a clinical picture of a diagnosis.

Gastric ulcers

Also known as peptic ulcers, these can occur in the stomach, lower end of the oesophagus, and duodenum (sometimes called duodenal ulcer). A patch of lining, usually around a centimetre across, is eroded away to leave a raw area; this is often thought to be due to excess hydrochloric acid. Most individuals develop gastric ulcers in middle adulthood. A gnawing pain in the abdomen, burping and feeling bloated are the usual symptoms, although some people will have no symptoms.

Gall stones

One-fifth of women have gallstones at post-mortem, demonstrating that this is a common disorder. Men are less affected. Many gall stones cause no symptoms until they get stuck in the bile duct, when they cause intense pain in the upper right area of the abdomen and sometimes nausea and vomiting.

Causes of dysfunction

The causes of these disorders are generally due to diet and psychological causes. Some types of gastric ulcer have been found to be the result of a bacterial infection easily treated with an antibiotic.

Irritable bowel syndrome

People with this condition show no abnormalities of the intestine and are usually not underweight or malnourished. There may be some disturbance of the muscle walls of the intestine, but the actual cause is unknown. Some doctors believe that anxiety and stress are major factors in the development of this disorder.

Gastric ulcer

Gastric protease or pepsin is an enzyme that digests protein when activated by hydrochloric acid. Body structures, including the stomach wall, are mainly made of protein too, but are normally protected by a thick ropy type of mucus. This protection may break down allowing ulceration if:

* too much acid is produced

* mucus secretion decreases

* the patient has an inherited family disposition to ulcers

* there is reliance on the aspirin group of drugs
* the patient smokes
* the stomach wall is irritated by alcohol, caffeine or bile
* there is bacterial infection
* there is psychological stress.

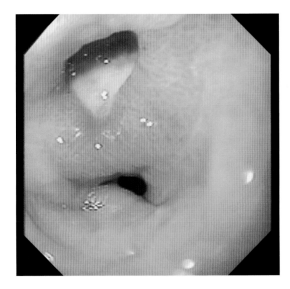

Gastric ulcer

Gall stones

The most common forms of gall stones are made up of cholesterol, although bile pigments and calcium salts may also be found. When too much cholesterol is passed into bile by the liver, precipitation may take place, forming stones. This is more likely to occur with a cholesterol-rich diet, which in turn is more common in obesity. Some doctors believe that not eating for long periods may cause bile to stagnate and form stones.

Effects of dysfunction

Most disorders of the digestive tract have certain common features such as pain, loss of weight, and poor absorption of nutrients and/or water.

Irritable bowel syndrome

Intermittent pain, as well as excessive wind, are common features of this disorder. Malnourishment tends not to happen, but there is clearly poor absorption of water during bouts of diarrhoea. Sufferers often have a poor appetite

during such bouts and this, together with the diarrhoea, may lead to weight loss.

Gastric ulcer

A gnawing pain, which can be so severe as to wake people who are sleeping, and weight loss are regular features of a gastric ulcer.

Gall stones

Severe pain when a stone impacts in the bile duct is an important feature, although many people have symptom-less stones in the gall bladder itself.

When there is a reduction in the quantity of bile entering the duodenum, fats will not be fully emulsified, enzymatic digestion will be reduced and fats will pass out of the body in faeces. There is not likely to be much weight loss unless there is a long wait for treatment.

General principles and value of diagnostic techniques

With the development of **endoscopy,** where the gut can be visually examined and samples of lining tissues taken for biopsy without surgical intervention, diagnostic techniques have undergone a major revolution. Previously, reliance was placed on X-rays with radio-opaque meals and enemas, and exploratory surgery known as laparotomies. These techniques are still used, but endoscopy has caused a great reduction.

Key concept

Endoscopy: a collective term for viewing a cavity or tube with a flexible, fibre-optic endoscope which can have many attachments for cutting, grasping, snaring and removing cells or tissue for pathological examination. Many endoscopes have cameras attached to the lens and images can be viewed on a screen. When an endoscope is used for viewing the stomach, it is known as a gastroscope whereas in the colon, it is called a colonoscope.

Gastroscopy

The patient is asked to fast for at least six hours prior to the examination so that the stomach is

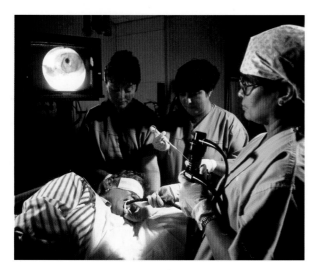

An endoscope

empty. A sedative drug and local anaesthetic throat spray are given to ease discomfort and ensure relaxation as the gastroscope is passed down the throat into the stomach. A gastric ulcer will be visible to the doctor.

Colonoscopy

To empty the colon, laxative drugs are provided and the patient is requested to drink several litres of a special cleansing agent. The patient is offered a sedative drug to help ease the discomfort and facilitate relaxation. The colonoscope is passed through the anus and the flexible tube can be threaded through the various parts of the large intestine. Small benign (non-cancerous) growths called polyps can be removed and evidence of inflammation noted. An individual with irritable bowel syndrome will have a colonoscopy to eliminate more serious colon conditions.

Tissue biopsies

As explained above, tissue biopsies can be taken with a special attachment on the gastroscope or colonoscope. The tissue is embedded in wax and then sliced extremely thinly for microscopic examination. The pathologist will look for any changes in structure and actively dividing cells, which may signify malignant (cancerous) changes.

General principles and value of treatment

Treatment for ulcers

Lifestyle changes

Many people can change their lifestyle to heal ulcers themselves. This involves:

* avoiding irritants of the stomach lining (see causes on pages 128–9)

* not smoking

* eating small meals more often

* avoiding drugs that irritate the stomach lining.

Medication

When the problem is thought to be acid over-secretion, there are antacid medicines to neutralise the acid, blockers to stop acid being produced and different drugs to form a protective coat over the ulcer. If bacterial infection is present, antibiotics will bring about a cure in most cases.

Surgery

When all other treatment fails and the ulcer is affecting the quality of life of the individual, a partial gastrectomy may be performed to remove the part of the stomach containing the ulcer.

Irritable bowel syndrome

Lifestyle changes

Irritable bowel syndrome has no cure, but dietary changes (adopting a high fibre diet) and measures to relieve anxiety and stress can help. Reassurance, psychotherapy or **counselling** may be undertaken and in appropriate cases drugs may combat anxiety. The individual may need help from professionals to identify and deal with the source of anxiety.

General surgery

As a last resort, some people's quality of life is so affected by irritable bowel syndrome that they elect to have part of the large or small intestine removed. Part of the diseased colon is removed and the open end brought to the surface of the skin where an artificial opening or stoma is made. A light-weight bag is attached by adhesive strips to the skin to receive the faeces. This is known as a colostomy. The bag is easily changed after a motion. This is a serious operation and a stoma nurse supports the individual before and after the operation in the management of the stoma and bag, diet and lifestyle. Faeces discharge once or twice a day and after recovery and training, the individual should be able to lead a normal life.

An ileostomy is the same procedure, but this time the ileum is brought to the surface.

Gall stones

Lifestyle changes

With gall stones, an individual needs to ensure that their diet is not unduly high in sugar and fat and to maintain their ideal weight for their height. Clearly, if overweight or obese they would be advised to alter their diet and take more exercise.

General surgery

Removal of the gall bladder may be necessary if there are repeated attacks. This will cure the majority of cases of gall stones.

Try it out

Using your knowledge of the digestive system, identify the differences between the management of a colostomy and an ileostomy.

Summary

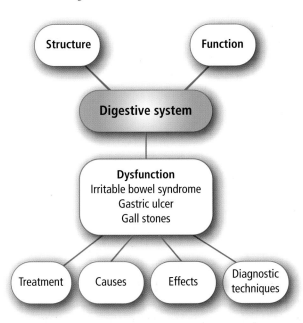

Consider this

Sarah is 45 years old and verging on obese. She has several children and the weight appears to have piled on after each pregnancy. She works as a teaching assistant at the local primary school and has very little time to prepare meals except at weekends. The children are always hungry and most meals are made of convenience foods. Last week, Sarah had to call the doctor because she had a bad pain in her right side, felt sick and nauseated. She has noticed that her faeces are paler than usual and look greasy. She had a similar bout last year, but didn't call the doctor.

1. Can you identify a possible diagnosis?

2. Can you identify the clinical or laboratory investigations that might have been carried out if she had visited the doctor last year?

3. Explain why the character of her faeces has changed with this pain.

4. Explain why the doctor has referred Sarah to a general surgeon.

Explain the principles and value behind the operation that Sarah will shortly have.

Section 4: Reproductive system

The reproductive system consists of all the male and female organs and tissues that are essential to producing offspring to ensure continuity of the species. Each contains an organ, which is also a gland, for the production of gametes and various tubes and tissues for ensuring that the two gametes can fuse to form an embryo. The female also has organs for nurturing the embryo (foetus) until birth occurs.

Structure of the female reproductive system

The female reproductive system comprises the ovaries, Fallopian tubes (or oviducts), uterus and vagina, and is located in the pelvis.

Ovaries are oval-shaped bodies that produce ova or egg cells (the female gametes), and female sex hormones. A baby girl is born with ovaries that contain thousands of immature follicles, each with a primitive ovum. She will not develop any more during her lifetime.

Ovaries are closely associated with oviducts (Fallopian tubes). The end of each oviduct nearest the ovary has finger-like processes, called fimbriae, closely applied to the surface of the ovary. The oviduct merges with the uterus at the other end.

The uterus is an inverted pear-shaped muscular organ with a special lining called the endometrium. The thickness of the endometrium varies at different parts of the female sexual, or menstrual cycle. The muscle, or myometrium, is able to contract and relax, but also to retract or shorten the length of the muscle fibres. This is important during childbirth so that during relaxation, the foetus doesn't return to its former position, but is gradually forced out.

The lower end of the uterus protrudes into the vagina, and this is called the cervix. The cervix is a tight muscular ring with a small opening into the uterus, normally closed by a plug of mucus. The uterus nourishes and anchors the embryo and foetus during pregnancy and the muscular walls expel the foetus in childbirth. The vagina is an extensible muscular tube capable of accommodating the male penis during sexual intercourse.

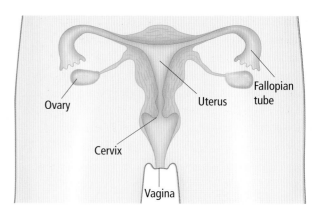

FIGURE 12.22 *The female reproductive system*

Structure of the male reproductive system

The male reproductive system comprises testes in skin sacs called scrotums, epididymes, sperm ducts (or vas deferentia), urethra and penis. There are associated glands known as the prostate gland and the seminal vesicles.

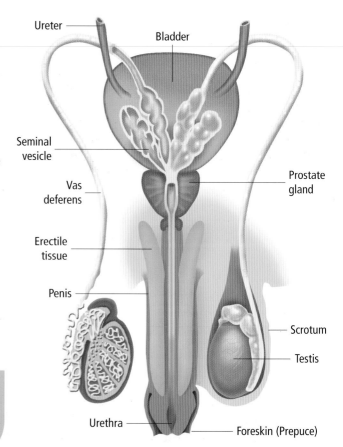

FIGURE 12.23 *The male reproductive system*

Like the ovary, the testis produces both gametes and sex hormones. The male gametes are called spermatozoa (often shortened to sperm; the singular is spermatozoon). The testis is divided internally into a number of sections, each containing masses of coiled seminiferous tubules in which the sperm are formed. Cells between the coiled tubes, the interstitial cells, produce testosterone, the sex hormone in males. Unlike the ova, sperm are formed continuously, often into old age.

Sperm cannot form properly at body temperatures, so the testes hang outside the body cavity in skin sacs called scrotums.

Once formed, the sperm are released into the lumens (central holes) of the seminiferous tubules into the epididymis to mature before emerging into the vas deferens of each side.

During sexual intercourse sperm are moved by rhythmical contractions down the vas to the urethra, deep inside the penis. During this journey, the prostate gland and the seminal vesicles add their secretions, and the resulting fluid is known as semen.

The penis consists of the urethra, down which urine and semen pass (but not at the same time), and columns of special erectile tissue. Erectile tissue has large spaces which fill with blood when sexually aroused so that the penis becomes stiff and erect and able to pass into the vagina to deposit semen. In the unexcited, so-called flaccid or limp state, this is impossible.

The prostate gland secretions provide sugars and protein for the sperm and the seminal vesicles provide sugars such as fructose, which activate the sperm.

Basic function of the reproductive system

Menstrual cycle

Preparing for ovulation

After puberty, ova come under the influence of the follicle-stimulating hormone (FSH) produced by the pituitary gland at the base of the brain. Each month, about 20 immature follicles begin to grow and produce oestrogen, another hormone. One follicle outstrips the rest, and releases the ovum (ovulation) about 14 days later. The remaining follicles atrophy (waste or fade away). The follicle cells surrounding the 'champion' ovum can measure about one centimetre just before ovulation and are now producing a lot of oestrogen. The oestrogen inhibits FSH by a negative feedback mechanism, allowing another pituitary hormone called luteinising hormone (LH) to flourish.

Ovulation

LH causes ovulation and converts the remaining follicle cells in the wall of the ruptured follicle into a glandular structure called the corpus luteum. Secretions from the corpus luteum are rich in another sex hormone called progesterone.

The cycle starts again

Progesterone, as it increases in concentration, inhibits LH, allowing FSH to increase once again, stimulating about 20 more immature follicles into growth. During this time the endometrium is breaking down in menstruation due to a lack of oestrogen and progesterone and the unfertilised ovum passes out with the menstrual tissue and blood.

Key concept

Negative feedback mechanism: a mechanism in which an increased output of a substance stimulates a change, which in turn inhibits the increasing output and the norm is re-established.

Female sex hormones and their role in the menstrual cycle

FSH and LH, from the pituitary, act on the ovary causing follicle growth and ovulation/corpus luteum formation respectively. They are called gonadotrophins, which means acting on gonads – ovaries and testes.

Oestrogen and progesterone are ovarian, or female, sex hormones that prepare the female body for pregnancy if the ovum is fertilised. They do this by acting on the breasts and endometrium of the uterus. Oestrogen promotes growth of cells and progesterone promotes gland formation.

In the first half of the menstrual cycle, when oestrogen is produced from follicle cells, the endometrium builds up in thickness. After ovulation, when progesterone increases and oestrogen declines, the newly thickened endometrium becomes glandular ready to nourish any developing zygote.

After about three-and-a-half weeks, when no fertilisation has taken place, the corpus luteum in the ovary begins to decline and oestrogen and progesterone levels in the blood drop significantly. The thick, glandular endometrium cannot survive without these hormones and begins to peel away with small loss of blood. This is known as menstruation; the whole cycle is called the menstrual cycle, although the female sexual cycle is a more correct term. For study purposes, although not so precise in real life, the cycle is deemed to start at day 1 and finish at day 28; menstruation lasts 5–7 days and ovulation occurs on day 14.

Fertilisation

For fertilisation to take place, sexual intercourse should occur in the period around ovulation. Sperm survive only about 48 hours in the female reproductive tract. The ovum is normally fertilised about one-third of the way down the Fallopian tube.

During foreplay, caressing and kissing, both partners feel sexually aroused. Feelings are very strong and powerfully-driven by nature. The male's penis becomes hard and erect as the erectile spaces fill with blood and the female's vagina becomes slippery with mucus. The male inserts his penis into the vagina and generally thrusts up and down until a climax or orgasm is reached and ejaculation of semen takes place high in the vagina just below the cervix. The ejaculate is only about 3 cm³ in volume, but this contains around 300 million spermatozoa as they are so small.

However, many spermatozoa fall out of the vagina, and the journey through the cervix and Fallopian tubes is so hazardous that out of this huge number only about 100 ever reach the vicinity of the ovum. Sperm try to penetrate the few layers of follicle cells still surrounding the ovum. When one sperm manages to get through

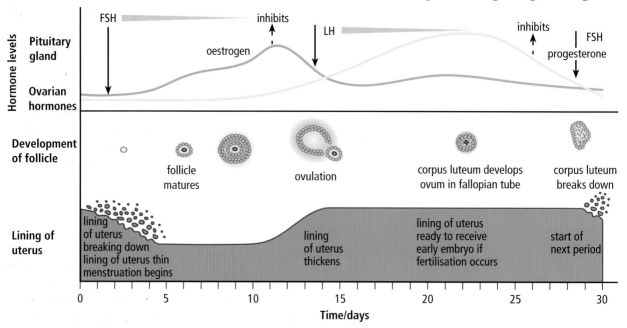

FIGURE 12.24 *The menstrual cycle*

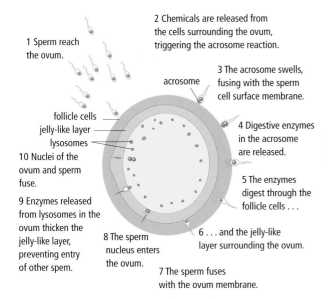

1 Sperm reach the ovum.

2 Chemicals are released from the cells surrounding the ovum, triggering the acrosome reaction.

acrosome

3 The acrosome swells, fusing with the sperm cell surface membrane.

follicle cells
jelly-like layer
lysosomes

4 Digestive enzymes in the acrosome are released.

10 Nuclei of the ovum and sperm fuse.

5 The enzymes digest through the follicle cells . . .

9 Enzymes released from lysosomes in the ovum thicken the jelly-like layer, preventing entry of other spem.

8 The sperm nucleus enters the ovum.

6 . . . and the jelly-like layer surrounding the ovum.

7 The sperm fuses with the ovum membrane.

FIGURE 12.25 *Fertilisation of ovum by a spermatozoon*

the follicle cells and ovum membrane, a chemical reaction occurs in the cell membrane and further sperm cannot get through. The successful sperm nucleus, leaving its tail behind, moves towards the nucleus of the ovum and there the two nuclei fuse. This is the moment of fertilisation, or conception.

After a short rest, the fertilised ovum, now called a zygote, starts to divide – first two cells, then four, eight and so on, until a ball of cells is formed. Meanwhile it is still travelling down the Fallopian tube and takes a whole week to reach the endometrium of the uterus.

On arrival in the cavity of the uterus, it will come to rest on a patch of thick, glandular endometrium and begin to burrow down using new finger-like processes. By the eleventh day after ovulation, the burrowing or implantation is complete and the ball of cells is buried deep in the endometrium. The woman is pregnant, but this is a dangerous time for the new life as the time of menstruation is near, and if menstruation took place it would be swept away. To prevent this, a hormone produced by the embryo, human chorionic gonadotrophin (HCG) is released into the mother's uterine blood which stimulates the corpus luteum into further growth, increasing oestrogen and progesterone production to prevent menstruation.

Pregnancy

The enlarged corpus luteum of pregnancy maintains the endometrium for the first 12 weeks, by which time the embryo and its coverings (amnion and chorion) have grown and a placenta has been formed. The placenta has many functions, one of which is to secrete large amounts of oestrogen and progesterone so that the corpus luteum is no longer needed by the twelfth week.

What if?

If the placenta is not mature enough to produce the high levels of oestrogen and progesterone needed at 12 weeks, there will be a fall in the levels of these hormones and the endometrium will begin to break down. This is called a miscarriage and the pregnancy will stop. This is why the third month is a critical time in pregnancy.

What temporary treatment could you suggest for a woman who has repeated miscarriages at the third month of pregnancy?

This is not the only cause of miscarriage.

The placenta and umbilical cord form an indirect link with the blood vessels of the mother's uterus so that:

* the foetus is able to move but is anchored to the uterus

* oxygen, glucose, aminoacids, hormones, vitamins, mineral salts, etc. can pass from the mother's blood to the foetus

* carbon dioxide, urea and other waste products can pass from the foetus to the mother's blood to be eliminated.

All the beginnings of the major organs have been formed by the eighth week of pregnancy, including a beating heart, and they grow and develop further during the remaining 32 weeks.

During pregnancy, breasts develop under the influence of oestrogen and progesterone and are prepared to produce milk within a few days after delivery of the baby.

Birth

Somewhere near the end of 40 weeks gestation or pregnancy, birth occurs. The foetus is usually head down in the pelvis and is said to be 'engaged'. Oestrogen and progesterone levels fall and a new pituitary hormone, oxytocin, causes muscular contractions of the uterine wall. The contractions start slowly (about every 20 minutes) and then become more frequent (every 2–3 minutes).

The first stage of labour is to widen the cervix (called dilatation) and it takes between 4 and 12 hours. At some stage, there is a 'show' – this is a reddish-brown discharge caused by the release of the mucus plug from the cervix. This is followed by 'the waters breaking' – the release of the amniotic fluid in which the foetus has been lying. The uterus, cervix and vagina now form a continuous birth canal and the baby's head is pushed out of the cervix into the vagina.

The second stage of labour begins as the strong contractions aided by the mother pushing with her abdominal muscles help the baby's head to be born. The head is the widest part of the baby, as the shoulders can flex.

The rest of the baby follows quite quickly, the whole process taking from 10–60 minutes. The baby takes a few breaths or cries to re-oxygenate the blood after the journey through the birth canal. The umbilical cord connecting the baby to the placenta is clamped and cut.

The third stage of labour is the delivery of the placenta. This occurs after a short rest interval, when contractions re-commence. The placenta has peeled away from the slack uterus and passed down the birth canal. It is carefully examined to ensure that it is whole and no bits have been left inside to become a focus for infection.

Dysfunctions of the reproductive system and their causes

Between one in four and one in six couples in the UK are infertile. You might think that this would keep the population in check, but statistics show that there are around 14 births per thousand people (1992). This is a moderate birth rate, but the death rate is also falling and people are living longer. The UK population is, therefore, an ageing population.

Many couples and individuals choose to have their families later in life, when they have the homes they desire and their careers are well developed. It is more difficult to conceive as you get older and if this trend continues, the birth rate may fall further.

Infertility

> **Key concept**
>
> *Infertility:* the inability to produce children or offspring or achieve conception.

Causes of infertility

To become pregnant, there are certain fundamental requirements:

1. the female must be able to produce heathy ova
2. the male must be able to produce mature, mobile spermatozoa in sufficient quantities
3. sexual intercourse must take place
4. there should be no obstruction for the sperm to reach the ovum in the Fallopian tube
5. a spermatozoon must be capable of fertilising the ovum
6. the zygote must be able to implant in the uterus
7. the embryo must be healthy
8. the hormonal requirements must be adequate for further development of the embryo
9. the pregnancy must be maintained by the appropriate hormonal environment.

Approximately 40 per cent of infertile couples have problems in both partners; the remainder is equally split between male and female causes.

The most common cause of infertility in males is a lack of healthy sperm. Sperm may be weakened, short-lived, abnormal, sparse or completely lacking due to inflammation of the testes at some stage, mumps, cystic fibrosis or sexually-transmitted diseases. Smoking, drugs and toxins can lower the sperm count. Failure to deposit the semen containing the sperm high in the vagina as a result of impotence is also common (see below).

The most common cause of infertility in females is failure to ovulate. The cause may be unknown, or it may be due to hormonal imbalance, stress, ovarian cyst or cancer. Fallopian tubes may be blocked because of previous inflammation, sexually-transmitted disease, or congenital abnormalities. One or both tubes might have been removed due to ectopic pregnancies (see below). The following uterine conditions can also contribute to infertility:

* endometriosis (patches of shed endometrium which have lodged outside the uterus, in the pelvic cavity)

* fibroids (benign muscular tumours in the wall of the uterus)

* 'hostile' mucus in the cervix that produces antibodies to the partner's sperm.

Ectopic pregnancy

Ectopy means an abnormal placement, and in ectopic pregnancy the implantation of the zygote takes place somewhere outside the uterus. This maybe the abdomen or pelvis or most commonly, in the Fallopian tube. An ectopic pregnancy can be life-threatening, as shock, internal or vaginal bleeding can occur as well as rupture of the tube. It is most likely to occur where there is an abnormality in the uterus or tube, or where infection has caused blockage.

Try it out

From your knowledge of the menstrual cycle and pregnancy, suggest why ectopic pregnancies are so dangerous. Explain why ectopic pregnancies might occur.

Impotence

This is the failure to reach or maintain an erection to carry out sexual intercourse. Impotence is the most common sexual dysfunction in males. Psychological causes may stem from depression, anxiety, guilt, stress and fatigue. Physical disorders such as diabetes, endocrine or neurological malfunction and alcohol dependence can also result in impotence. Side effects of certain drugs can cause impotence.

General principles and the value of diagnostic techniques

Blood tests

A blood sample can give valuable clues about hormone imbalance as hormones travel via the bloodstream. This might yield information about certain causes of infertility and impotence

and may provide evidence for the diagnosis of ectopic pregnancy. However, in many cases blood tests are negative. Pregnancy tests using blood rather than urine are expensive to perform and rarely used. Blood can also reveal antibodies and be used to check on the general health of the individual and exclude other conditions that might have an influence on fertility.

Ultrasound

This procedure is easy to perform, causes no pain and is safer than X-rays. It uses high-frequency sound waves from a transducer (a device that transfers energy from one source to another) that is gently moved to and fro over the skin surface. The sound waves bounce off soft tissue and fluid-filled organs and the echoes are converted into images seen in two dimensions on a viewing screen.

The fluid-filled pregnant uterus is an ideal subject for ultrasound scanning and most people will have seen a photograph of the image of a foetus in the uterus of a mother-to-be.

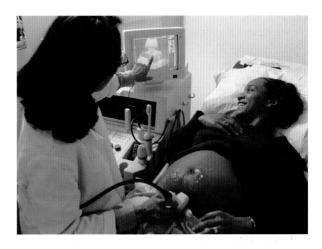

Ultrasound scan in pregnancy

Try it out

Ask someone you know if you can have a photocopy of their baby's ultrasound scan. An enlarged copy would be much better. Try to identify parts of the foetus, the placenta and umbilical cord. It is quite difficult sometimes! Perhaps between you, your class could get hold of several examples to give you more experience in the interpretation of parts.

Hystero-salpingogram

Hysteros is the Greek word for the uterus – hysterectomy means removal of the uterus. *Salpinx* means a tube – in this case, the Fallopian tube. Hystero-salpingography is the examination of the uterus and Fallopian tubes using X-rays after a radio-opaque fluid is introduced through the cervix. The cavities of the uterus and tubes appear white and any uterine abnormalities and tube blockages are shown as the fluid either outlines the structures or cannot pass and will appear black.

General principles and value of treatment

Infertility treatment

Infertility treatment varies with the causes, and about 50 per cent of couples treated become parents. The principle is to introduce sperm to the ova by avoiding mechanical or psychological barriers. In some cases, this means extracting ova from the ovaries and mixing with semen outside the body.

Male infertility

Males who cannot produce spermatozoa cannot become fathers other than by adoption or artificial insemination by a donor (AID). The anonymous donor's semen is screened for micro-organisms and a careful medical history is taken to ensure that the donors are in good health and as free from physical and mental disorders as possible.

For males with low sperm counts, artificial insemination using the husband's sperm (AIH) can be tried. AIH is also used where psychological factors or antibodies hostile to sperm exist.

Female infertility treatment

Specific drugs can stimulate ovulation, alternatively, Fallopian tubes, uterine abnormalities or fibroids can sometimes be repaired or removed.

IVF (in vitro fertilisation) involves fertility drugs to stimulate ova to maturity. The development of the ova can be monitored by ultrasound scanning. The mature ova are then removed by a laporoscope (a type of endoscope inserted through a skin incision into the abdomen) and fertilisation is attempted by mixing with the partner's semen **outside** the body. In vitro means 'in glass' referring to the glass dishes which fertilisation takes place in. After a short delay and incubation, the dish is examined to see whether embryos are developing. Several embryos are placed in the female's uterus through the vagina. Any unused ova can be deep stored for other attempts.

Success rates for IVF are improving, but few women become pregnant straight away. IVF can be tried several times, but the procedure is expensive.

A similar procedure called gamete intra-Fallopian tube transfer, or GIFT, involves obtaining ova as for IVF and after examination replacing them with a sample of semen in the Fallopian tubes. This is both less expensive and less complicated than IVF.

Blood tests

Gonadotrophin hormones, often synthetically produced, can be given where there is a failure to ovulate and monitored by analysis of blood samples.

Summary

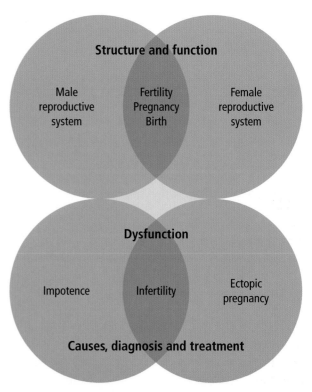

Section 5: Renal system

The renal system is essential for life as it is a major route for eliminating waste products of metabolism from the body, maintaining the correct water balance and maintaining the acid-base balance in the body. The system is very important in homeostasis, maintaining the internal environment of the body, i.e. around the cells.

Gross structure of the renal system

The renal system comprises two kidneys, their tubes (known as ureters), the bladder and the urethra.

The kidneys lie on the posterior (back) wall of the abdomen, above the waist and partly protected by the lowest ribs. There is one on each side of the vertebral column.

The bladder is a central pelvic organ connected to the kidneys by two ureters 20–30 cm in length. Both bladder and ureters have a lining of transitional epithelium, surrounded by muscle and fibrous tissue.

The bladder is connected to the exterior by the urethra, which is much longer in males than females. In males, the urethra just below the bladder is completely surrounded by the prostate gland (see Figure 12.23), it forms part of the penis.

Each kidney is surrounded by a capsule of fibrous tissue and body fat for protection. Two small glands cap each one and these are known as the adrenal glands. Each kidney is 10–12 cm long and supplied by a branch of the aorta (the renal artery). The renal vein returns blood to the vena cava. Within each kidney, the arterial blood vessels break up into small branches, which supply approximately one million units called nephrons. These are the filtering units of the kidney. A section through a kidney shows a dark outer area known as the cortex and an inner, paler, area, the medulla. The cortex contains most of the Bowman's capsules, glomeruli and renal convoluted tubules. The medulla contains mainly loops of Henle and collecting ducts.

The function of the renal system

Although there are some minor functions of the renal system, the two major tasks are to produce urine (to eliminate excess water, salts and waste products of metabolism), and to effect homeostasis.

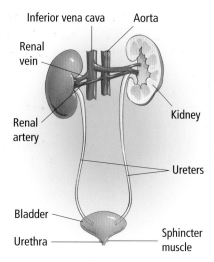

FIGURE 12.26 *The renal system*

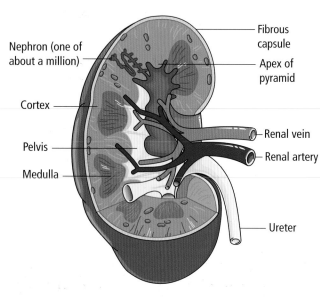

FIGURE 12.27 *Section through a kidney*

Urine production

The first part of a nephron is a cup-shaped Bowman's capsule (made of single-layered squamous epithelial cells) into which a tangle of capillaries fits very closely. The capillaries emanate from the branches of the renal artery.

This knot or tangle of capillaries is called a glomerulus and its exit vessel (efferent capillary) is narrower than the entry vessel (afferent capillary). This means that a 'traffic jam' of blood occurs in the glomerulus under high pressure and a protein-free plasma filtrate (approximately 10 per cent of plasma) is forced out of the glomerulus into the Bowman's capsule, called glomerular

filtrate. This process is called ultra-filtration. Behind the Bowman's capsule is the first part of the renal tubule, sometimes called the first convoluted tubule because it is so intricately wound. This tubule is closely associated with a capillary network formed from the exit vessel or efferent arteriole coming from the glomerulus.

Did you know?

Amino acids (nitrogen-containing compounds) cannot be stored in the body as raw material so, when there is a surplus, it is broken down chemically to urea (which still contains the nitrogenous material) and other materials. Urea is always present dissolved in plasma but, if levels increase significantly, it acts as a poison. Urea is produced in the liver and eliminated from the blood by the kidneys to be excreted in urine.

Important changes happen to the glomerular filtrate as it flows down the first renal tubule:

* $\frac{7}{8}$ths of the water is reabsorbed into the capillary plexus

* all the filtered glucose and amino acids are also reabsorbed

* $\frac{7}{8}$ths of the salts are reabsorbed, mainly sodium and chloride ions.

It is important to recognise that:

a) Plasma proteins and blood cells are too large to be filtered out through the epithelial cells of the capillary and Bowman's capsule.

b) Both ultrafiltration and reabsorption in the first renal tubule are non-selective – in other words, this will happen even if the body contains too much water or salt.

c) Glucose and amino acids are too important to the body cells to be passed out in urine, so they are reabsorbed here.

The filtrate then passes into a long loop of Henle and is already reduced in water and salts, but still contains urea.

The loops of Henle are sandwiched in the medulla between the last parts of the nephron, the collecting ducts. The deeper parts of the cortex have a special sodium concentrating process located in the loops. The function of this will be apparent later. The loop of Henle leads into the second convoluted renal tubule, and it is here that the filtrate begins to be 'tailored to fit the requirements of the body' for the first time.

An important hormone from the pituitary gland called anti-diuretic hormone, or ADH, allows water to be reabsorbed through the tubular cells. When the body needs water to be conserved, such as after sweating on a hot day or after intense physical activity, ADH secretion is high and water is reabsorbed into surrounding capillaries. When there is a surplus of water, say from drinking a lot or when the weather is cold and there is little sweat produced, ADH secretion is minimal. In this case the tubular cells act rather like waterproofed tubes and the excess water is passed on into the urine.

In a similar but more complex way, another hormone from the adrenal glands, called aldosterone, regulates the sodium **ions** in the body. Filtrate moves on to the collecting ducts, which run into the pelvis of the kidney and into

the ureter. Remember that the collecting ducts are sandwiched in the cortex in a high sodium area formed in the loops of Henle. In the presence of ADH, water passes out of the filtrate (by osmosis) and further concentrates the urine.

The ability to concentrate urine is extremely important for people living in desert regions where water is sparse. It is also essential to get rid of surplus water so the blood does not become too dilute.

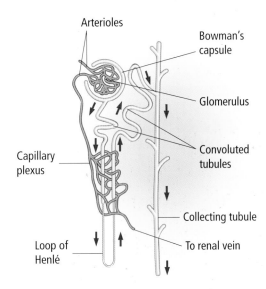

FIGURE 12.28 *Structure of a nephron*

Urine leaves the kidneys via the ureters, moving partly by peristalsis and partly by gravity to the bladder where it is stored temporarily. The bladder holds about half a litre of urine before sending nerve impulses to the spinal cord to activate the emptying reflex. Urine then leaves via the urethra at periodic intervals. The base of the bladder is guarded by a muscular sphincter.

Homeostasis

Tissues and organs can function efficiently only within a narrow range of variables such as temperature, pH (acidity/alkalinity), blood pressure, blood glucose, heart rate, respiratory rate and osmoregulation (basically water balance in the body).

To keep these variables balanced, receptors (receiving cells) must detect external change and transmit information to a control centre (most often, the brain), which corrects the deviation by means of effectors (action cells or 'doing' cells – the actions of the effectors are usually gland secretions or muscular responses). This is known as negative feedback, as the external change is damped down or reduced to return the system to normal behaviour.

You have already learned how water is regulated by the kidneys and the action of ADH. Receptors (osmoreceptors) present in the brain monitor the osmotic pressure of the nearby blood flow. When the blood becomes more dilute (low osmolality) the osmoreceptors are not stimulated and little ADH is produced, leaving surplus water to pass out in the urine. When osmolality rises, osmoreceptors are stimulated and cause ADH secretion from the pituitary, water is reabsorbed and osmolality returns to normal.

Regulation of the pH of body fluids is partly carried out by the lungs and the kidneys. The process comprises several complex chemical reactions. Relatively small but significant quantities of acids enter the body each day, some from food and drink, such as vinegar, citrus fruit, etc., and others as a by-product of metabolism. The kidney conserves ions like sodium and disposes of excess acid **ions** (H^+ ions) by secretion from the second renal tubule. Under these conditions urine becomes acidic.

Dysfunction

Renal failure

This condition arises when the kidneys cannot effectively remove waste products from the blood and remove them from the body in urine. It also arises when water, salts and blood pressure are

not regulated by the kidneys. The condition can be acute, resulting from shock or haemorrhage or chronic, resulting from progressive, long-term damage.

Signs and symptoms might include:

* decreased urine production
* fatigue
* weakness
* nausea, vomiting and loss of appetite.

Renal infection

Any obstruction to the flow of urine will cause urine to stagnate and become a focus for infection, known as pyelonephritis. Thus, kidney or ureteric stones (see below), enlarged prostate gland in males, tumours or congenital defects, may result in kidney infection. In females, in particular, bacterial infection of the kidneys may result from cystitis (an inflammation of the bladder) because the infection has spread from the bladder up the ureters to the kidneys. Cystitis is more common during pregnancy. Back pain and high temperatures result from pyelonephritis.

Kidney stones or calculi

Various chemicals like calcium can precipitate out of filtrate/urine and form hard bodies known as calculi or kidney stones. Some doctors think that stones may result from dehydration, particularly in hot weather, or from a previous infection. Males appear to be more affected than females. Kidney stones can exist without symptoms, but stones in the ureters and bladder can be excruciatingly painful to pass.

Prostate enlargement

Although not strictly part of the renal system because of its role in the male reproductive system, enlargement of the prostate produces urinary problems due to its position encircling the urethra at the base of the bladder. Prostatic enlargement occurs mainly in men in middle to later adulthood. Although prostatic cancer is a possible cause, prostatic enlargement is more often a benign enlargement without a known cause.

Symptoms include difficulty in passing urine (dysuria), reduced flow of urine, dribbling from an overfull bladder progressing to incontinence. Sudden abdominal pain, with only a few drops of urine produced, is life-threatening and needs emergency treatment. This is known as acute retention of urine. As previously mentioned, obstructed flow of urine and stagnation can lead to kidney infection.

Causes of dysfunction

The causes of renal problems may be many and varied, such as long-term use of pain killers and allergic reactions, including some that are as yet unknown. A few examples are included in this section.

Diabetes

Diabetes is a condition that can affect blood vessels in many parts of the body, including the small arterioles that supply the kidney glomeruli. These vessels may be partly obstructed resulting in renal failure and hypertension. High levels of blood glucose also predispose to bacterial infection, which may result in pyelonephritis.

Raised blood pressure

Hypertension causes kidney damage and kidney damage causes hypertension. This can be a vicious circle – raised blood pressure from an unknown cause can cause kidney damage that leads to an even higher BP.

Lifestyle

You have already learned about the effects of lifestyle on raised BP, including diet, alcohol and smoking, and most of these are appropriate to renal disease. For example, not smoking, keeping alcohol intake low, minimising stress levels, taking regular exercise and eating a healthy, balanced diet are all important for patients with renal disease. Not having BP or blood glucose checked regularly may lead to diabetic or renal damage.

Drinking plenty of water is important for kidney function. Many people feel that any form of kidney disease means that they should not drink as much fluid as normal. In fact the reverse is true as vulnerable kidneys find it hard to concentrate urine so drinking plenty of fluid helps to eliminate waste products more easily. However, patients undergoing regular dialysis must adhere to the recommended dietary and fluid regime set.

Diagnostic techniques

There are more ways to diagnose disorders of the renal system than most body systems, including the usual X-ray techniques, those with radio-opaque materials, and ultrasound scanning. Both blood and urine reveal abnormal chemical constituents, and endoscopy through the urethra can be undertaken to assess the interior of the urethra and bladder.

Diagnostic imaging techniques

X-rays
X-rays will reveal calculi and the outlines of the kidneys demonstrating size and gross abnormalities.

Angiography
X-rays using radio-opaque material injected into renal arteries or veins will show up the kidneys' blood supply.

Intravenous urography, formerly known as IVP (intravenous pyelography)
This is similar to angiography; injection into veins will reveal the internal structure of the kidneys and calculi. The rate of excretion of material from the kidneys can also be investigated.

Ultrasound scanning

Excellent kidney images can be gained by this technique; size, cysts, tumours and obstructions can be clearly revealed. This technique is also used to check progress after kidney transplantation.

CT scanning

Sections through the kidney by CT scan are used to identify abscesses and tumours.

Blood tests

As well as routine blood tests, special tests showing how the rates of certain substances, such as creatinine and urea (both nitrogenous materials), are 'cleared' from the blood and eliminated in urine provide useful information as they can be compared with normal figures.

Urine dipsticks

There is a wide range of dipsticks for testing the presence of protein, blood, glucose, bile and pH. The sticks are chemically treated to change colour when the appropriate substance is present. Some sticks can show a range of colours to indicate the concentration of substances.

Try it out

Obtain some dipsticks testing for as many properties as possible and test your own urine for the presence of substances. One box of dipsticks will provide enough for all the group.

Urethroscopy

A urethroscope is a type of slim endoscope used for viewing the interior of the urethra. A cystoscope visualises the bladder, and both can be used for removing obstructions such as prostatic enlargement, polyps and benign tumours.

Treatment

When kidney function is poor and/or failing, there is dialysis, associated dietary restriction and medication to 'take over' kidney function. This is usually a temporary measure, short or long-term, until transplantation can occur. Although transplants are expensive, the operation is a one-off cost whereas dialysis, also expensive, is a continuous cost.

Dialysis

There are two main types of dialysis, haemodialysis and CAPD (continuous ambulatory peritoneal dialysis). Haemodialysis involves attaching a patient to a kidney machine for at least four hours a day, three or four times a week. A patient requires a 'fistula' operation several months beforehand; this is usually in the arm. A fistula is an artificial connection between an artery and a vein, into which the needle attachment to the kidney machine is made. Multiple layers of special membrane material separate the patient's blood from dialysing fluid in the kidney machine.

Any substance (waste products, toxic materials and excess water) needing to be removed from the blood is in low or zero concentration in dialysate so that the substance passes across by diffusion and osmosis. Any substance not requiring elimination can be kept at a high concentration in the dialysate. The dialysate is drained off as waste and the 'cleaned' blood is returned to the patient.

CAPD uses the inner lining or peritoneum of the abdomen as the dialysing membrane and the dialysate is introduced through a special tap and catheter. The process of emptying the old dialysate and introducing the fresh dialysate takes about one hour, twice a day. The patient may walk about with the dialysate inside

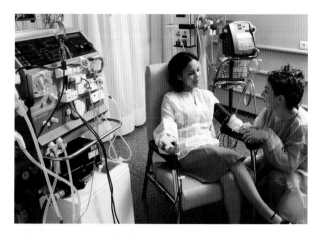

Patient using a kidney machine

(hence use of the word 'ambulatory') and carry on with work. Although peritoneal dialysis can take place in hospital, most patients carry out CAPD at home and work. Conversely, a few patients have home kidney machines, but most haemodialyse in hospital.

Kidney transplant

In the UK, most transplant organs are only available from recently deceased persons or close relatives. The composition of the recipient individual's antigenic make-up is determined from blood tests and matched to a donor's make-up so that they are as closely matched as possible. This process is called **'tissue-typing'.**

Failing kidneys are usually left in place and the new kidney placed in the pelvis and connected with the bladder by the donor's ureter. The donor blood vessels are connected to branches of the lower aorta and vena cava. The patient begins immuno-suppressant therapy to prevent rejection and monitoring is carried out by urinalysis, blood tests and ultrasound scanning. The chief danger of rejection is in the first few months after the transplant. More than 80 per cent of transplants are successful enabling the patient to live a normal life while continuing on immuno-suppression.

Summary

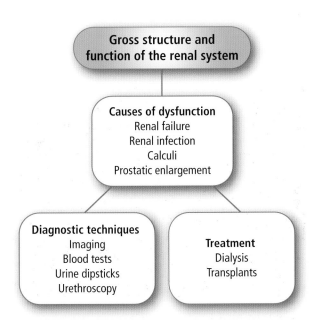

Gross structure and function of the renal system

Causes of dysfunction
Renal failure
Renal infection
Calculi
Prostatic enlargement

Diagnostic techniques
Imaging
Blood tests
Urine dipsticks
Urethroscopy

Treatment
Dialysis
Transplants

Consider this

After many years on medication for high BP, Graham was surprised to learn that his lethargy, poor appetite and fatigue was considered by his doctors to be due to failing kidneys. Doctors advised that he should have a fistula put in his arm ready for dialysis in the future. Eighteen months later, Graham started haemodialysing three times each week. He had dietary restrictions of protein, salt and potassium-rich foods as well as water.

1. What is the relationship between high BP and kidney failure?

2. What is the nature and purpose of a fistula?

3. Explain how urine is produced by a normal kidney.

4. Explain how haemodialysis can replace some kidney functions.

5. Explain why fluid and dietary restrictions are necessary in an individual undergoing dialysis.

6. Evaluate the benefits of dialysis and kidney transplant as methods of treatment.

Section 6: Musculo-skeletal system

The axial skeleton comprises the bones which lie in the midline of the body, namely, the skull, spinal column, ribs and sternum. The appendicular skeleton consists of the limb bones and their respective pectoral (shoulder) and pelvic girdles. Skeletal muscle is attached to the bones of the skeleton and at least two muscles are involved in moving a bone. Muscles can only pull, never push – so one muscle contracts to displace the bone and another is needed to return the bone to its original position. These muscles are said to act antagonistically. To cause movement, muscles must act across a joint, as the bones themselves cannot bend.

Support

The musculo-skeletal system supports body weight against the downward pull of gravity. You may know that you are taller at the beginning of the day than at the end; that is why it is important to take height measurements in a research study at the same time of day. This loss of height during the day is due to gravitational pull. The skeleton is important in preventing body organs from becoming progressively compressed due to gravitational pull. In ideal posture, the body weight is evenly distributed about the skeleton, but this is difficult to maintain, particularly with movement. The skeletal muscles exert muscle tone or firmness and are continually contracting minutely to maintain this even distribution.

The musculo-skeletal system also gives support to other structures in the body, such as the rib cage which supports the lungs so that breathing can take place efficiently. The brain is supported by the base of the skull.

Movement

Clearly, movement is a fundamental basic of all animal life enabling us to find food and water, take shelter, reproduce, etc.

You have already learned how peristalsis moves food, chyme and waste through the alimentary canal. This type of muscle is not attached to the skeleton and is generally known as smooth muscle (also called involuntary, unstriped or unstriated muscle). You have also learned how cardiac muscle contracts and relaxes

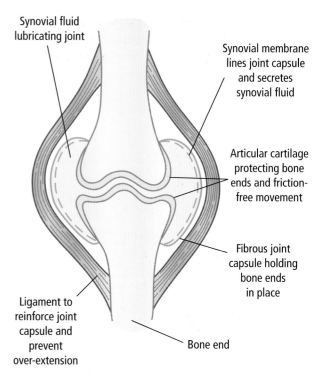

Synovial fluid lubricating joint

Synovial membrane lines joint capsule and secretes synovial fluid

Articular cartilage protecting bone ends and friction-free movement

Fibrous joint capsule holding bone ends in place

Ligament to reinforce joint capsule and prevent over-extension

Bone end

FIGURE 12.29 *A synovial joint*

to drive blood around the circulation. The third type of muscle is that attached to the skeleton, often called skeletal muscle (other names are voluntary, striped or striated muscle). Cardiac and involuntary muscle works without conscious thought, whereas skeletal muscle works in response to the will; i.e. it is said to be voluntary.

Voluntary movement

A voluntary muscle consists of contractile muscle fibres packed closely together. At one end is the origin and the other is the insertion, both of which are tendinous or fibrous and attached to bone. When a muscle contracts it shortens, enabling movement by pulling on the bone over the joint.

When a muscle contracts to move a joint, another muscle working in an opposite way contracts to return the bone to its original position. An example of muscles moving (flexing) and returning (extending) the forearm is shown in Figure 12.30.

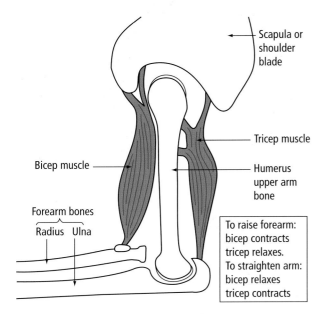

Bicep muscle

Forearm bones
Radius   Ulna

Scapula or shoulder blade

Tricep muscle

Humerus upper arm bone

To raise forearm:
bicep contracts
tricep relaxes.
To straighten arm:
bicep relaxes
tricep contracts

FIGURE 12.30 *Movement at the forearm*

Protection

The skeleton protects many vital organs. Some of the major organs of body systems and their protective skeletal parts are shown in Table 12.4.

Dysfunction of the musculo-skeletal system

Movement is essential to a good quality of life, as it enables us to carry out daily activities. Therefore, any dysfunction of movement severely affects physical, emotional and mental health.

Arthritis

Pain, stiffness and swelling of one or more joints is known as arthritis. There are several different types of arthritis, but you will learn about two of the most common.

Osteoarthritis

Osteoarthritis, the most common arthritic disease, generally affects people in middle and later adulthood. It arises from wear and tear on the joint, overgrowth of bone at the joint edges and thinning or absent areas of the articular cartilage. All these can

BODY SYSTEM	ORGAN PROTECTED	PART OF THE SKELETON
Nervous system	Brain	Cranium of the skull
	Spinal cord	Spinal column
	Sense organs, e.g. eye, ear, tongue	Skull
Respiratory system	Lungs and bronchi	Rib cage, spinal column and sternum
Cardiovascular system	Heart and major blood vessels	Rib cage, spinal column and sternum
	Spleen	Rib cage
Renal system	Kidneys	Rib cage and spinal column
	Bladder	Pelvis
Digestive system	Liver	Rib cage
Reproductive system	Ovaries, uterus	Pelvis

TABLE 12.4 *Major organs and their skeletal protection*

mean that friction, stiffness and pain is experienced with movement, and the bone ends become worn away. Large weight-bearing joints are often the first to show degeneration although previously injured joints can display arthritic changes earlier.

Rheumatoid arthritis

Rheumatoid arthritis can occur at any age, even in childhood. Joints become red, inflamed and swollen during attacks and there may be a slightly raised temperature and other aches and pains. Small joints like those in the fingers, wrists and toes are most frequently affected. The frequency and severity of attacks can vary and the condition is more common in females.

Osteoporosis

Bone consists of a protein background of collagen on which calcium salts become impregnated. Collagen provides a degree of flexibility while the calcium salts give bone its hardness. In osteoporosis, the collagen background becomes reduced, making the bone brittle and more liable to fractures. The dysfunction is more common in older women, although in both sexes it can form a natural part of the ageing process.

Parkinson's disease

Strictly speaking, this is a disease of the nervous system, but many of the signs and symptoms affect the musculo-skeletal system. The first signs are tremors of hands, arms or legs, more noticeable at rest. Later, there is stiffness and weakness of the muscles followed by a fixed, so-called 'wooden' expression on the face, a rigid, stooped posture and a shuffling walk. Movements are slowed, muscles have more tension and there is often accompanying depression.

Multiple sclerosis (MS)

Previously known as disseminated sclerosis, this is also a disease of the nervous system with signs and symptoms affecting the musculo-skeletal system (see below).

This condition is marked by periods of remissions and relapses; the frequency of both is very variable and it is not unknown for someone to be diagnosed as having MS and not suffer another attack. Generally, the signs and symptoms vary with the part of the brain affected by patchy demyelination. Females are affected slightly more than males, and it commonly affects young adults.

Patients may present with dragging of one leg (affecting walking), double vision, loss of sensation or muscle power, etc.

Did you know?

Myelin is the lipid/protein material that sheathes many nerve fibres and forms the white matter of the brain. The main function of myelin is to speed up the rate of the passage of nerve impulses although it also has a protective effect.

Causes of musculo-skeletal dysfunctions

Arthritis

Osteoarthritis

Anything that causes extra wear and tear on joints is a contributory factor for osteoarthritis, including:

* being overweight or obese
* occupational hazards – osteoarthritis is more common among people who have worked as e.g. a footballer or other sport professional, dancer, window cleaner, etc.
* skeletal deformities or misalignment of bones
* injuries to joints or joint inflammations
* normal ageing process (over 60 years).

Many of these are lifestyle factors.

Rheumatoid arthritis

This is considered to be an auto-immune disease; it might have been triggered by a streptococcal infection in chidhood. An auto-immune disease, of which there are several, is one in which the individual develops **antibodies** against their own tissues. In this case, the synovial membrane becomes inflamed and thickened and this may spread to the underlying cartilage and bone.

Osteoporosis

This condition is most common in women after the menopause because oestrogen (which declines after the menopause) is not present in sufficient quantities to maintain the consitency of bone. Other causes include heavy smoking and drinking (lifestyle causes), poor calcium intake and hormonal disorders. There is a genetic influence as daughters of mothers with osteoporosis are more at risk.

Parkinson's disease

A definitive cause is not known, but certain psychological medications and illegal drugs can lead to this condition. Cardiovascular disease and a rare brain infection are also known to be predisposing factors.

Multiple sclerosis

Although the definitive cause is unknown, there is a strong genetic influence as relatives of people with MS are eight times more likely to develop symptoms. Environment is also important as the disease seems to be one associated with temperate climates, and some theorists believe that a virus contracted in early life may play a part. Others classify this condition as an auto-immune disease.

Diagnostic techniques

X-rays can confirm both types of arthritis together with the signs and symptoms of the condition. In osteoarthritis, bone overgrowths and increased density of bone ends are significant.

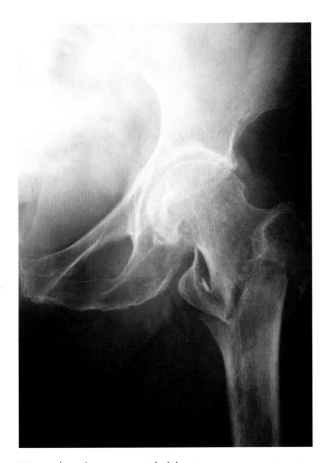

X-ray showing osteoarthritis

X-rays and sometimes blood tests are used to diagnose osteoporosis. Neurological conditions such as Parkinson's disease and multiple sclerosis are usually diagnosed on signs and symptoms.

However, newer techniques such as CT scanning and MRI are helpful in the diagnosis of conditions like MS.

Treatment

Common medications

Pain-killer (analgesic) drugs such as aspirin, and non-steroidal anti-inflammatory drugs (NSAID) such as ibuprofen are used to treat arthritic pain and stiffness. Corticosteroids may be injected into joints to provide relief.

Hormone replacement therapy with or without calcium tablets can be used to treat osteoporosis. Steroid drugs may be used to reduce symptoms of an attack of MS, and Levadopa, converted to dopamine in the body, is used to treat Parkinson's disease.

Joint replacement

The medical term for this is arthroplasty, and it is undertaken when a joint is very painful, deformed or diseased and unstable. Hips and knees are the most common joints to be replaced by plastic or metal artificial joints that are cemented in place after the diseased joint and its socket have been removed. Shoulder, elbow and finger joints are also replaced on a regular basis. Antibiotic cover ensures that there is no infection.

Physiotherapy

In most musculo-skeletal disorders, exercise and physiotherapy is important to prevent joint stiffness, ease pain and keep muscles active. Arthritis sufferers are encouraged to take non-weight bearing exercise such as swimming.

People with MS should lead as active a life as possible and exercise to strengthen muscles. Exercise is particularly beneficial for building bone, and long, brisk walks are recommended for patients with osteoporosis or those with a risk of developing osteoporosis through a family history.

Physiotherapy exercises can be active, to strengthen particular muscle groups, or passive, where the therapist moves the part. This keeps joints mobile. Other treatments may involve massage, infra-red heat treatment and hydrotherapy (exercising in water).

Summary

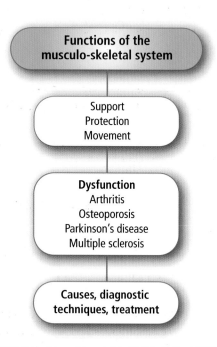

Functions of the musculo-skeletal system

Support
Protection
Movement

Dysfunction
Arthritis
Osteoporosis
Parkinson's disease
Multiple sclerosis

Causes, diagnostic techniques, treatment

Consider this

Vijay had complained of aches and pains in his bones for several years, but in the past two years the pain in his left hip has become so bad that he has become quite inactive. He uses a walking stick when he does move around. Vijay played first class cricket in his younger days and is now 62 years old. At last, his wife has persuaded him to see his GP. The GP arranged for him to have X-rays at the local hospital and see him again in three weeks. Meanwhile she prescribed analgesic drugs to relieve the pain.

1. Can you identifty the likely cause of Vijay's pain?
2. Give two factors that have contributed to the condition.
3. Why has Vijay's GP sent him for X-rays?
4. What changes will the GP or radiologist expect to see in the X-rays to support the diagnosis?
5. Why is it important for Vijay to become more active?
6. Evaluate the options available to Vijay and his GP or consultant to improve his quality of life.

UNIT 12 ASSESSMENT

How you will be assessed

✳ The assessment of this unit consists an examination lasting for 90 minutes. The total number of marks allocated to the paper is 100. Each question or part question displays the number of marks allocated in brackets at the end of the question.

✳ The total mark gained from the responses you give to the questions will be the mark for this unit.

✳ Questions may involve the use of illustrations, photographs and case studies as scenarios.

✳ All questions need to be answered.

Preparation

When you attend for examination, try to be fresh after a good night's sleep and breakfast/lunch and make sure that you have the writing materials for the examination.

Make a revision plan several weeks in advance of the examination, allowing time to cover all the material several times. Do not try to do too much in one session and test yourself repeatedly. It is a good idea to have a revision 'buddy' and test each other, if you can. It is useful to write a little quiz after revising and put it to one side for two or three days before trying to answer it.

The space after a question is also a guide to the information required although it must take into account both large and small handwriting.

Make sure that you write legibly for examiners can only mark what they can read.

It is very important that you take note of the number of marks allocated to the queston, or part of the question, as this will provide a guide for both the quality and quantity of your answers. The following is an example:

George has been referred to a cardiologist (heart specialist) because he has been having chest pains when he exerts himself. The cardiologist sends him for an ECG. Identify three ways in which an ECG is helpful to the cardiologist in forming a diagnosis. (6)

In this part question, you will need to state the three pieces of information obtainable from the ECG and then explain how it might be useful in diagnosing coronary heart disease.

For example:

a) heart rate can be measured; this might show an abnormally slow or fast rate indicative of dysfunction

b) heart rhythm will be shown, this might show irregularities like fibrillation due to heart disease

c) the P Q R S T waves might be abnormal indicating that there is disease in an appropriate part of the heart.

Such a response would earn 3 x 2 marks. If you fail to provide the relevant explanation for each 'way', you will gain only 3 or half marks.

You will need to read a question through more than once and ask yourself what the examiner is looking for as a response. You are rarely asked for information more than once so, if you are tempted to repeat an answer, go back and check that you answered the first question correctly and try to find different information for one of the questions.

When you are asked to describe something, you are being requested to 'paint' a picture using words and phrases.

An explanation requires reasons to be given for your statements and if you are requested to discuss – positive and negative aspects are required. A written evaluation means teasing out the values or strengths and weaknesses and forming a conclusion. Words like state, describe, explain etc. are called command words and you cannot afford to ignore these as the mark allocation is built upon these and your knowledge. Many candidates offer bullet points when asked to explain, discuss or evaluate and these will gain only a few of the marks.

Try not to leave any questions unanswered – you never know whether you might gain a few marks and make a difference to your grade.

When a question is taking you a long time to find the answer, pass on but do not forget to return to it at the end. Keep an eye on the time!

Always read your responses through when you think you have finished.

Test questions

Please note that these assessment questions are designed to contribute towards practice for your candidates' assessment but are not written to mirror OCR's A2 Level questions.

1. List the parts of the digestive system, in order from mouth to anus, in a table and describe the function of each part in a second column. (10)

2. Explain the differences between a colostomy and an ileostomy. (4)

3. a) Describe the characteristic features of enzymes in the digestive tract. (4)

   b) How and where is protein digested in the alimentary canal? (4)

4. Karen has renal failure as a consequence of long-term hypertension.

   a) Explain the meaning of renal failure. (2)

   b) Explain the meaning of hypertension. (2)

   c) Karen has been told that she must be prepared for dialysis in the near future.

       i) Describe the difference between the two forms of dialysis that are available. (6)

       ii) Under what circumstances might Karen be able to stop dialysis in the future? (2)

5. Describe three different diagnostic imaging techniques and provide an example of the use of each. (6)

6. Endoscopy is used for the investigation of many conditions. Name two types of endoscopy and provide an example of a dysfunction that might be investigated using each of the named endoscopes. (4)

7. Explain the dysfunction known as ectopic pregnancy and its possible causes. (8)

8. Describe the possible treatment for a couple presenting with infertility if the man's investigation has revealed a low sperm count. (4)

9. Explain how lifestyle choices can be reponsible for coronary heart disease. (10)

10. Misha is 54 years of age and she is worried about developing osteoporosis after the menopause because her mother suffered from the condition. How could Misha protect herself as far as possible from osteoporosis in the future? (4)

References and further reading

After you have read this unit, you will need to dip into various sources to find extra information as there will not be a single source covering most of the topics. Many long-term illnesses have supporting organisations that supply extra material and can be found by typing the name of the condition into a search site on the Internet.

Other useful sources are:

Nursing Times magazines

Health Matters magazines

Smith, T. (2000) British Medical Association *Complete Family Health Encyclopaedia* London: Dorling Kindersley

Stoppard, M. (2005) *Dr Miriam Stoppard's Family Health Guide* London: Dorling Kindersley

GCE level Human Biology/Biology textbooks

GCE Health and Social Care textbooks

Useful websites

BBC
    www.bbc.co.uk/health
Department of Health
    www.dh.gov.uk
Enquiry sites
    www.howstuffworks.com
    www.ask.co.uk
    www.netdoctor.co.uk
Government Statistics
    www.statistics.gov.uk
Health Education Authority
    www.hea.org.uk
Health Protection Agency
    www.hpa.org.uk
Private health care
    www.bupa.org.uk

Child development

Unit 13

This unit covers the following sections:

13.1 Patterns of development

13.2 Factors that influence development and norms of development

13.3 Theories of play and how play can affect development

13.4 How to plan and make a learning aid for a child (0–8 years)

In this unit you will learn about the patterns of development of children from birth to eight years including the physical, intellectual, emotional and social development for each key stage. The range of factors that can affect development of children including the family, environmental factors, psychological factors and behavioural problems is also discussed.

Theories of play, how it can affect development and influence children's cognitive development including the theories of Piaget, Vygotsky and Bruner are covered. The benefits of play, its use as a therapeutic process, types, categories and stages of play are discussed. You will learn about the different environments in which children play and the effects these may have on their development.

An understanding of how to plan and make a learning aid suitable for a child from birth to eight years and the aims, objectives and outcomes which can be achieved by the child using the aid you have designed is also required. The safety aspects of the learning aid, sources of feedback to evaluate the aid and evaluation of the learning aid are covered.

This unit has links with Unit 2: 'Communication in Care Settings'; Unit 6: 'Working in Early years Care and Education'; Unit 10: 'Care Practice and Provision'; Unit 11: 'Understanding Human Behaviour'; and Unit 12: 'Anatomy and Physiology'.

How you will be assessed

You will need to produce evidence as set out in the assessment objectives. Objective one (AO1) requires you to describe three patterns (milestones) in each area (physical, intellectual, emotional, social) of development of children from birth to eight years. The second and third objectives (AO2 and AO3) must be based on the study of a child you have chosen who should be at least eight years old. The fourth objective (AO4) links directly to the designing and making of a learning aid suitable for the child studied.

Section 1: Patterns of development

Children are expected to follow the patterns of development recognised by health professionals. However, every child is unique and develops at their own pace, some reach milestones more quickly than others. This can be for a variety of different reasons, including:

* the genes the child has inherited from its parents

* the amount of time and encouragement and interest given by the parents

* possible health problems

* the quality of the child's environment.

When a child is slow or 'delayed' in one area of development, they are often quicker or 'advanced' in another. There is usually no need for parents to get concerned because their child has not reached a milestone by the 'normal age'. However, serious delays in achieving the milestones of development can be an indication that the child may have underlying problems and should be investigated.

Growth and development are distinctly different although they are closely linked. Growth refers to the changes in size of a child when they gain height and weight. Development is directly linked to the acquisition of skills and gaining control of their bodies. Growth and development usually follow the same pattern, although some children grow without developing skills, which may be due to a problem or disability. It is important for health care workers, early years workers and parents to be able to recognise when children are not developing properly.

> ### Key concepts
>
> *Growth:* involves changing in size through gaining height and weight.
>
> *Development:* involves acquiring skills and gaining control of the body.

Physical growth

Physical growth begins when the baby is conceived and continues until the body matures at around 18 years of age. Growth does not usually occur at the same rate throughout this time for all parts of the body. Children experience 'growth spurts' when they seem to grow much faster than at other times. Parts of the body also grow more quickly at different times, resulting in the proportions of the body differing. At birth a baby's head is very large in proportion to the rest of their body. As the child develops the head becomes smaller in relation to other parts of the body.

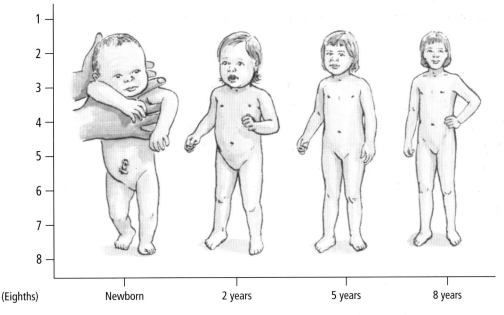

FIGURE 13.1 *The proportions of a child's body change during the growth period*

Centile charts

Centile charts are used by health professionals to monitor growth. Babies and children are measured and weighed by midwives and health visitors. The measurements are then plotted on the centile chart (also known as percentile chart) to monitor the rate of growth. The centile chart is used to compare the child's growth according to the 'norms' or average rate of growth. The charts differ for boys and girls because boys are known to be taller and weigh more than girls. Separate charts are usually used to record a child's height and weight.

Centile charts have three lines marked on them. The middle line, labelled 50 (**the 50th centile**), shows average growth. The top line, labelled 98 (**the 98th centile**), records children who are taller or heavier than average. Only 3 per cent of children would be expected to be above the 98th centile. The bottom line, labelled 2 (**the 2nd centile**), records shorter or lighter than average children. Only 3 per cent of children would be expected to be below the 3rd centile.

Figure 13.2 shows the weight and height of a 3-year-old girl. As both are recorded on the 50th centile this child would be considered to be of normal height and weight for her age.

Did you know?

Children inherit physical characteristics from their parents' genes. As this includes their height and weight there are noticeable differences between babies of different ethnic origins.

Key concept

Physical development: the process of gaining control of movements, and learning skills which will be perfected with age.

What if?

Age	Height (cm)	Weight (kg)
Birth	55	2.5
3 months	60	3
6 months	63	4.5
12 months	68	6.2
18 months	72	7
2 years	80	9.5
3 years	92	11
4 years	100	14.5
5 years	108	18.5

The chart shows George's height and weight from birth to 5 years. Plot George's height and weight on a centile chart. Compare George's growth with the expected pattern of development.

Physical development

Physical development can be divided into three main categories (see Tables 13.1–4):

* *fine motor skills:* smaller movements and manipulation

* *gross motor skills:* use of muscles to control the body and larger movements

* *sensory skills:* use of the senses: sight, hearing, taste, touch and smell.

Patterns of physical development

Infant: 0–1 year:

Fine motor skills

A newborn baby has a grasping reflex. When an object is placed in a baby's hand their fingers

2 to 8 years: Girls
Height-for-age and Weight-for-age percentiles

Name _____

Record Number _____

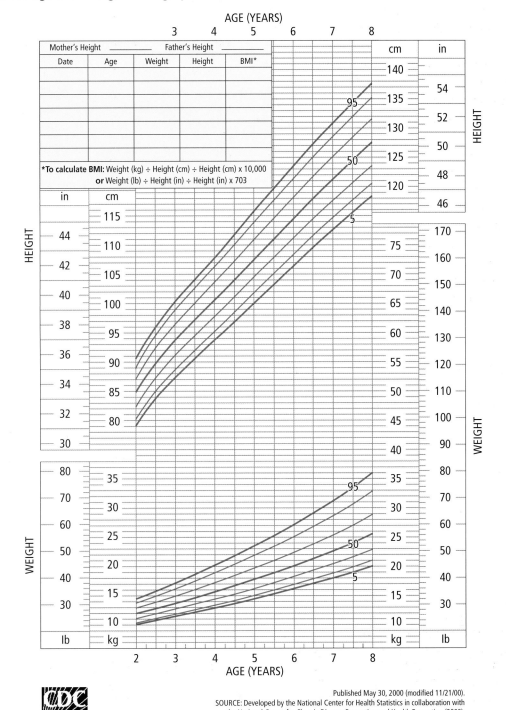

Published May 30, 2000 (modified 11/21/00).
SOURCE: Developed by the National Center for Health Statistics in collaboration with
the National Center for Chronic Disease Prevention and Health Promotion (2000).
http://www.cdc.gov/growthcharts

FIGURE 13.2 *Centile charts representing growth from 0–8 years with normal height and weight recorded for a 3-year-old*

curl around it, seemingly trying to hold onto the object. This reflex disappears after 3 months. At 3 months babies show a great deal of interest in their hand movements and spend much of their waking time watching the movement of their hands. When an object is placed into a baby's hand they may grasp it for a short time and then drop it, but this is different from the grasping reflex of a newborn baby. The baby may swing their hands in an unco-ordinated manner.

A 'pincer' grip, where the baby holds an object between finger and thumb, develops by 1 year of age. A 1-year-old will drop objects to the floor in a voluntary manner. At this age babies often point to objects, especially toys, they want.

Pincer grasp develops during the first year

Gross motor skills

Reflexes

When babies are first born they can carry out several unintentional movements (reflexes). These are automatic and they have no control over them. Reflexes help babies to survive until they gain control of their body and can make movements for themselves. Table 13.1 describes the basic reflexes.

REFLEX	DESCRIPTION
Swallowing and sucking	A baby will automatically suck a finger placed in their mouth. This helps the baby to feed as they suck on the breast or teat. This reflex disappears when the baby is 6 months old.
Rooting	When a baby's face is stroked gently with a finger it will turn its head towards the finger. This looks like the baby is trying to find a nipple or teat and is expecting a feed. This reflex disappears after 6 weeks.
Walking	When a baby is held in a standing position with the soles of the feet resting on a hard surface, the baby will make stepping movements as if trying to stand up straight. If the shins are placed against the edge of a table the baby will seem to 'step up' as if trying to climb on the table. This reflex disappears after 6 months.
Startle	If a baby is exposed to loud noises or bright lights it will close its hands into a fist and bend the elbows, bringing the hands close to the shoulders. Sometimes they may cry as well.
Falling	When moved suddenly a baby feels like it is being dropped. This makes them open their hands and throw their arms backwards. They then bring their arms inwards as if trying to catch a ball.
Blinking	A newborn baby blinks when a light is shone directly into their eyes.

TABLE 13.1 *Basic reflexes of a baby*

A baby's reflexes are checked when they are born, as if the reflexes are not normal this can be a sign of a problem.

Think it over

Why is it necessary for a baby to have reflexes when it is born? How do the reflexes help the baby to adapt to its new world?

Head control

The muscles in the neck must develop before a baby gains control of their head movements. A newborn baby has no control of the head because the muscles are very weak. If the baby is lifted into a sitting position the head will fall backwards. It is very important to always support a baby's head to protect it from injury. At 3 months, a baby begins to gain control of their head. The head will wobble slightly if a baby is held in an upright position. If a baby is pulled upwards into a sitting position the head will still drop back, but not as far as a newborn baby.

A 6-month-old baby will have complete control of their head. The head does not fall back when the baby is pulled into a sitting position, so the baby can hold their head up and look around.

Sitting up

To sit the baby must have control of the neck and back muscles. The ability to sit unaided is developed during the first year (see Table 13.2).

Lying on the stomach (prone position)

When lying on their stomach babies develop strength in their arms and legs, and from this position they learn to crawl.

When a newborn baby is laid on their stomach the head will turn to one side and the legs curl under the stomach, similar to the baby's position in the womb. Around one month the baby will start to hold their head up and the legs start to straighten. At three months the baby lies with legs straight and pushes up on the arms to lift their head and shoulders. The arms gain strength and are straight at 5 months so that the baby can lift both head and chest off the floor. A baby can also roll from front to back. By 6 months old a baby

AGE	DEVELOPMENT OF SITTING
Newborn	A newborn baby held in the sitting position rolls forwards. The back bends and the head falls forward.
3 months	The baby needs to be supported in the sitting position. The back is held much straighter and although the head is wobbly, the baby will keep the position for a short time.
6 months	A baby can sit up straight with the support of a chair or pram. It is possible for a baby to sit unaided for a short time with their hands on the floor between their legs to give support. The muscles are still weak and this position cannot be held for long.
9 months	The baby can sit without support and pull up into a sitting position unaided.
1 year	The baby can now sit unsupported for a long time, turn to the side and stretch out to pick objects up without falling over.

TABLE 13.2 *Development of sitting*

can roll back onto the front again. A 9-month-old baby starts to move about the floor, often shuffling on its bottom in a sitting position, by pulling with arms in the prone position or by rolling. A 1-year-old is usually crawling quickly on hands and knees or even hands and feet. Sometimes children miss out the crawling stage and walk straight away.

Walking

The legs of a newborn baby are not strong enough to carry the weight of their body and the muscles in the legs, hips and thighs are too weak to be supportive. The baby also must be able to co-ordinate the muscles and the movement of the legs to balance.

A newborn baby appears to walk during the first few weeks but this is simply a reflex action.

At 3 months a baby has developed some strength and will support a little of their weight with help, but the knees and hips quickly give way and the baby tends to crumple. By 6 months, babies often enjoy being bounced up and down and can support their body weight. From 9 months a baby starts to walk. This is often sideways at first, holding onto furniture, or with both hands held. From 9 months babies can pull themselves upright using furniture or trousers for support. By 1 year old they can walk holding a hand for support. They usually keep their feet wide apart to give a wider area of support, and they fall over a lot.

Sensory skills

From birth babies use their senses to develop an awareness and understanding of their surroundings. They respond to stimuli in the form of light, sound, touch, taste and smell and they learn as they look, listen, feel, taste and smell. This means they turn their head towards a bright light, startle when there is a loud noise, nuzzle when the side of their face is stroked or reject the teat of a bottle if they are used to the taste of a nipple. Vision is closely linked to the development of fine-motor skills and hand-eye co-ordination, hearing to language development, taste and touch to intellectual development and smell to social and emotional development.

Newborn babies can see things near to them, their focus is limited to around 20–25 cm. Objects further away appear blurred. They are fascinated by the human face and tend to stare at their mother's face when being fed. They are very sensitive to light and will close their eyes tightly when a bright light is shone in their face. They will look at patterns for longer than solid colours.

FIGURE 13.3 *The different stages of walking*

They can also notice movement and will follow an adult or larger object moving in front of them. By 1 month babies are attracted by brightness and will turn their face towards the light from a window or a bright shiny object. They follow the movement of a bright, dangling toy moved in their field of vision.

A newborn baby can hear, and following birth is often held by the mother on her left side, where the baby can hear her heartbeat (the same sound they hear in the womb) which has a calming effect. A baby can recognise their mother's voice before they are a week old. Babies cannot hear very soft sounds when they are born. By 1 month old babies tend to blink in response to sounds and are startled by loud noises. They may turn their heads towards the source of sound, but cannot locate it. Young babies are soothed by the sound of certain music and singing, for example, lullabies.

Breastfed babies can distinguish the smell of their mother's breasts from those of other women. They show a preference for sweet tastes over salty or sour ones. A baby's skin is sensitive to different textures and changes in position.

By 3 months babies have a greater range of focus and can see slightly further. Control over the movement of their eyes increases. Their hands become fascinating and babies tend to put them in their mouth. At 6 months the eyes work together, they begin to notice their surroundings and look around them watching nearby people. If a toy falls out of sight they will not look for it. They will turn towards the source when they hear sounds across the room, especially their mother's voice. At this age babies love to explore objects with both their hands and mouth. At 9 months babies will look in the correct place for an object which has fallen out of sight. They are becoming more alert and will follow people who are moving around the room. A baby looks around for quiet sounds which are made out of sight.

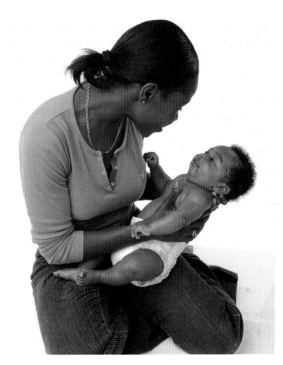

Babies recognise their mother's voice

Toddler 1–3 years

Fine motor skills

Hand control develops quickly during this stage. A child practises different fine movements. During play, fine motor skills are developed through manipulating different toys; for example, using shape sorters and jigsaws, building towers of blocks, drawing and turning the pages of a book. Through the child's desire to gain independence toddlers develop skills of holding a bottle or cup, turning door handles, pulling off shoes, using a spoon for feeding and dressing or undressing. At 15 months a child can build a tower with two bricks and turns several pages of a book together. The tower increases to three bricks at 18 months, six bricks at 2 years and nine bricks at 3 years. At 2 years the child can hold a pencil and draws circles, lines and dots with no resemblance to anything in particular. Two hands are usually used to perform more complicated tasks.

Gross motor skills

Between the ages of 1 and 3 years children begin to develop control over their movements. They learn to move when they want to and become more independent.

Think it over

Which senses are most important to a newborn baby? Why do you think this is?

Walking

Usually by the time a baby is 15 months old walking is steadier and falling over is quickly becoming a thing of the past. Some children walk much earlier than this and others later. They often hold their hands in the air to help balance, and find stopping and turning corners difficult. Looking down can result in a fall. Crawling upstairs is fun but standing up and leaning backwards has painful results. At 18 months a child will walk upstairs holding onto the rail tightly to balance. The child will climb the stairs putting two feet on each stair.

At 2 years a child walks up and down stairs holding on and keeping two feet on each stair. The child can kick a ball without falling over and has developed the balance required to stand on tiptoe and jump, often landing one foot at a time. The child rides a tricycle by pushing it along with their feet, not using the pedals. By the time a child reaches 3 years old they can walk upstairs in an adult manner with one foot on each stair, but coming down is still a problem and both feet are needed to balance on each stair. Jumping off the bottom stair is great fun! The child may be able to balance on one leg and start to hop around.

Sensory skills

At 1 year a baby can see almost as well as an adult. Babies can focus on objects quite a long distance away. They watch people, animals and moving objects for long periods. Looking for lost or hidden toys is enjoyed. Babies of this age know and respond to their own name, and to familiar sounds and voices. Familiar objects can be recognised by touch alone. They turn, stroke and pat objects in their hands. Taste has developed to enable them to discern different foods and show a preference for sweet, salty and fatty flavours.

At 18 months children will see and pick up small objects, such as beads, with a pincer grasp. They enjoy looking at picture books and recognise bold, brightly coloured objects on a page and can see fine detail. They can recognise familiar people at a distance and in

Hide and seek is fun

photographs, and will realise they are looking at themselves in a mirror. Children at this age no longer take everything to their mouths to explore. By 2 years the child's sight has developed fully and they can see everything adults can. General conversation is listened to with interest.

Think it over

How can parents help their baby to develop fine and gross motor skills? What can parents do to ensure their baby is safe when they start moving around? How could having a physical disability affect a baby's development?

Pre-school child 3–5 years

Fine motor skills

Hand and eye co-ordination have developed well by this stage. Preference for using a particular hand may be evident from 3 years. The child can thread large beads onto a lace. Jigsaws with larger pieces are completed with ease. Using a spoon is perfected, with spillages occurring rarely. The pages of a book can be turned individually at this age. A drawing of a face is definitely recognisable. At 4 years the pre-school child can button and unbutton clothing. They use scissors to cut out basic shapes. Drawings develop to include a head, trunk and legs.

AGE	FINE MOTOR SKILLS DEVELOPED
Newborn	* has a grasp reflex which disappears after a few weeks * hands are kept closed in a fist most of the time
3 months	* hands are held open * looks at hands * plays with fingers * holds objects that are placed in the hand for a short time then drops them
6 months	* able to grasp an object without it being placed in the hand * grasps toys with whole hand (palmar grasp) * passes objects from hand to hand * turns objects over * puts objects into the mouth * splashes water in the bath * plays with toes when lying on back
9 months	* uses fingers and thumb to grasp an object (inferior/primitive pincer) * deliberately drops things on the floor * looks for fallen objects * picks objects up with index finger and thumb (pincer grasp) with difficulty
1 year	* uses pincer grasp easily to pick up small objects * points to objects wanted using index finger * starts to show a preference for using one hand * able to place small objects into a container * throws things on purpose * able to bang bricks together
15 months	* claps hands * can place one block on top of another * drinks from a cup using two hands to hold it * grasps crayons with whole hand and makes marks on paper * holds a spoon but often misses mouth * turns spoon upside down before reaches mouth
18 months	* can turn the pages of a book several at a time * able to build a tower of three blocks * can put large beads on a string * uses pincer grasp with confidence * begins to hold pencils and crayons properly * can take shoes off but not put them on
2 years	* can turn pages of a book one at a time * can put shoes on * able to draw simple pictures * can turn door handles/knobs * able to build a tower of six bricks * can undo a zip * holds a pencil properly and can draw circles, lines and dots *continued on next page*

TABLE 13.3 *Norms of physical development: fine motor skills*

AGE	FINE MOTOR SKILLS DEVELOPED
3 years	* holds small crayons properly * can draw a face * eats with a spoon without dropping food * able to build a tower of nine or ten bricks * able to use toy scissors * able to dress but needs help with buttons * tries to undress but finds it difficult
4 years	* can build a tower of ten or more bricks * able to thread small beads on a lace * can hold and use a pencil in an adult manner * can draw a figure that resembles a person showing head, legs and body * can copy letters * eats with a spoon and fork * can fasten and unfasten buttons and zips * can put together large piece jigsaw puzzles
5 years	* can use a knife and fork with confidence * may be able to thread a large eyed needle and sew large stitches * has good control over pencils and paintbrushes * can draw a person with a head, a body, legs, a nose, mouth and eyes * can construct complex models * can copy a square * can do jig saws with smaller pieces * can dress and undress with little help * can cut out shapes using scissors more accurately
6 years	* can build a tower of cubes that is straight * holds a pencil correctly * able to write numbers and letters that are equal sizes * can write their last name as well as their first name * may begin to write simple stories * can tie shoe laces
7–8 years	* holds small crayons properly * is competent with their writing skills * uses colour in drawings to represent what they see e.g. blue for the sky * at the top of a page and green for the grass at the bottom * draw people with heads, bodies, hands, hair, fingers and clothes * can use a large needle to sew with thread

TABLE 13.3 *Norms of physical development: fine motor skills*

AGE	GROSS MOTOR SKILLS DEVELOPED
Newborn	* has stepping reflex but loses this after six weeks * head has to be supported when lifted * rolls in a ball when sat up * lies on tummy with head on one side and knees drawn up underneath
3 months	* can lift head when lying on front * can turn head from side to side when lying on front * pushes up on arms and lift shoulders off the floor * kicks legs strongly * can hold larger objects, e.g. rattle
6 months	* lifts head and chest above the floor * supports upper body on straight arms * can sit for long periods supported by a chair, pram or cushions * can sit unsupported for short periods of time but falls over easily * able to roll from front to back * can sometimes roll from back to front * starts trying to crawl
9 months	* crawls backwards first and then forwards * pulls into standing position using furniture to hold on to * walks sideways around furniture * can sit unsupported for longer periods of time * some start to crawl upstairs
1 year	* crawls very quickly * walking holding one hand or push along toys * some may be walking unsupported * can sit unsupported for long periods of time * crawls upstairs forwards * crawls downstairs backwards * can sit down from standing without falling over
15 months	* able to walk without support but swings arms to keep balance * can crawl downstairs on bottom, feet first * throws a ball * able to kneel without support * can stand without holding onto anything
18 months	* can walk with confidence * can pick things up from the floor without falling over * can sit on 'haunches' (squat) without falling over * can walk up and down stairs with support * runs but is unsteady * can use push-along toys confidently * pulls toys along
2 years	* can walk up and down stairs without support two feet to a step * climbing on furniture is fun * able to kick a ball * runs without falling over *continued on next page*

TABLE 13.4 *Norms of physical development: gross motor skills*

AGE	GROSS MOTOR SKILLS DEVELOPED
3 years	* can run and walk without problems * can balance on tip toes * can throw a ball * can catch a large ball with arms straight * can walk upstairs properly one foot to each stair * comes down stairs with two feet on each stair * can hop * can pedal a tricycle * able to jump with two feet together
4 years	* has a good sense of balance * can stand, walk and run on tiptoe * can catch, kick, throw and bounce a ball * can use a bat * hops on one foot * bend at the waist to pick up objects from the floor * enjoys climbing * run up and down stairs one foot per stair * can ride a tricycle with skill and make sharp turns
5 years	* can run and dodge by changing direction quickly * can skip with a rope * can stand on one foot for about 10 seconds * may ride a two-wheeled bicycle with stabilisers * shows good co-ordination * dance with rhythm * can hop forwards and backwards
6 years	* can jump off apparatus with confidence * can run and jump * can kick a ball from a distance * can catch and throw a ball accurately * may ride a two-wheeled bicycle without stabilisers * can skip in time to music
7–8 years	* can hop on either leg * can balance and walk on a thin line * may be expert at riding a two-wheeled bicycle * able to use roller skates * may climb on apparatus with skill * able to swim without arm bands * can catch and throw a ball with one hand only * can control their speed when running

TABLE 13.4 *Norms of physical development: gross motor skills*

FIGURE 13.4 *Fine motor skills make learning fun*

Gross motor skills

Riding a tricycle using the pedals is a skill that is mastered around 3 years. By 4, the child can stand, walk and run on tiptoe with confidence. Climbing is enjoyed either on furniture or play equipment. Hopping is perfected at 5 years and the child enjoys ball games. The child develops balance sufficiently to walk along a balance beam.

Sensory skills

A child begins to recognise different colours. By 3 a child can match two or three primary colours. Red and yellow are usually the first known colours, blue and green the next. At 3 a child will listen intently to stories they like and will want to hear favourites repeatedly. At 4 years a child will match and name four primary colours. They will listen to stories intently and may follow stories with their eyes, identifying words and pictures.

School age 5–8 years

Fine motor skills

Children will have developed a preference for using one hand or the other by this stage. Most children are right-handed, with around 10 per cent of boys and fewer girls being left-handed. A very small number

What if?

Imagine you are a nursery nurse. What activities would you use to help a pre-school child to develop gross motor skills? How could you help their development of fine motor skills? What could you do to improve their sensory skills?

of children can use either hand with the same level of accuracy and are referred to as ambidextrous. At 5 years old the child can draw a clear picture of a person with the head, trunk, eyes, nose and mouth apparent. Control of pencils and paintbrushes will be good. The child can dress and undress easily. Cutting out is fairly accurate. By 6 the child can catch a ball with one hand and hold a pencil in an adult manner. At 7 years old children can form letters well and their writing is clear. Drawings become more detailed towards the end of this stage. Colouring-in is more accurate with the child able to keep within the lines. At 8 years writing will be regular, with joined-up letters. The child will be able to tie and untie laces. Precise skills are perfected, for example, sewing.

Gross motor skills

The school-aged child gains confidence and is very reassured in using gross motor skills previously developed. At 6 years the child has good balance and can ride a two-wheeled bicycle. The enjoyment of ball games and the ability to kick a football is enhanced. Running and jumping

Balance gives a child freedom

are combined, with the child able to make running jumps. By 7 to 8 years the child can climb and balance well on play equipment and apparatus.

Sensory skills

At 5 years a child will be able to name and match 10 to 12 different colours. Their vision, hearing, taste and smell will be fully developed to adult level.

Think it over

What activities could help a school-aged child to develop fine and gross motor skills? Make a list under each heading. Compare your activities with others in your group. Are there any differences between activities available for children who live in rural areas compared with those living in towns or cities?

Intellectual development

A child's mind is very active from birth. As children learn to think, reason and explain, their intellectual development progresses (see Tables 13.5–8).

Key concept

Intellectual development: the development of the mind.

FIGURE 13.5 *How children learn*

Think it over

What activities could help children's intellectual development?

How are children encouraged with their intellectual development in a nursery? How does this change when they go to primary school?

Intellectual development can be divided into two main strands:

* cognitive development (understanding)

* language development, including verbal and non-verbal communication.

The development of these is very closely linked to the physical, social and emotional aspects of development. The pattern of intellectual development usually follows the same sequence. A child must pass through one stage before progressing to the next. Intellectual development relies, to some extent, on the development of physical skills. Before a baby is mobile, only the immediate surroundings can be explored. As soon as the baby can crawl and walk, a whole new world which allows the baby's experiences and understanding to expand opens.

Intellectual development can be affected by inherited patterns; a family history of 'late-development' may be repeated. Inherited learning difficulties could also affect the sequence of intellectual development.

Language development

Children use language to express their needs, to socialise and to share information with others. The way a child develops language depends on their opportunities to practice speaking. Children develop language or verbal communication by watching and copying those around them. A baby quickly learns that smiles are nicer to experience than frowns and often imitates them without understanding exactly what they are doing. Frustration is common in babies before they begin to talk as they find it hard to communicate with their carers. Verbal communication makes life much easier.

AGE	INTELLECTUAL SKILLS DEVELOPED
Newborn	* aware of feeling of hunger and responds by crying * recognise their mother's or main carer's voice * explore using senses and movement * copy adults who open their mouth or stick their tongue out * respond to high-pitched tones by moving their limbs * respond to brightly coloured or shiny objects
3 months	* uses mouth and touch to explore * look around to explore their surroundings * smiles in response to speech * shows an interest in play things, e.g. mobiles, rattles, chime balls * likes to explore different textures, e.g. on an activity mat or play gym * laughs and vocalises with meaning
6 months	* makes noises to voice displeasure or satisfaction * understands objects and knows what they can do * learns by using senses like smell, taste, touch, sight, and hearing * repeats actions and copies sounds, e.g. animal noises * puts things in his/her mouth to explore
9 months	* recognises and looks for familiar voices and sounds * understands the meaning of 'no' * focuses eyes on small objects and reaches for them * recognises familiar pictures * looks for fallen toys * explores objects by touching, shaking, banging * babbles expressively as if talking
1 year	* finds objects which have been seen and then hidden away * plays 'peek-a-boo' * enjoy looking at picture books * uses trial and error to learn about objects * watches and copies actions of others, e.g. 'clap hands' * scribbles to and fro
18 months	* can identify pictures of named objects, e.g. cup, ball, dog * looks for objects that are out of sight * can point to parts of the body * starts to show a preference for using one hand * can take things out of a container one by one * able to scribble on paper * refer to themselves by name
2 years	* learns by trial and error * able to put together a 3-piece puzzle * able to match different textures * starts to use everyday objects for pretend play, e.g. a cardboard box * able to stack beakers in order * scribbles in circles, may make vertical lines and V shapes * know their full name * interested in the names of people and objects

continued on next page

TABLE 13.5 *Norms of intellectual development*

AGE	INTELLECTUAL SKILLS DEVELOPED
3 years	* listens attentively to short stories and books * enjoys repeating simple rhymes/stories * understands concepts of time; 'now', 'soon', and 'later' * asks who, what, where and why questions * able to put together a 6-piece puzzle * can sort objects into simple categories * understands the concepts of 'one' and 'lots' * can count up to 10 * can identify primary colours; red, blue and yellow * able to distinguish, match and name colours * knows his/her age * knows and can name correctly three different shapes, e.g. circle, square, triangle * can copy a circle * drawings of people may have a head and one or two features
4 years	* can sort objects using more different categories * can place objects in a line from largest to smallest * can name 6–8 colours and 3 shapes * able to solve problems using trial and error * understands the concepts of 'tallest', 'biggest', 'same', 'more', 'in', 'under', and 'above' * beginning to understand why things happen * asks questions constantly * knowledge increased * able to remember significant events, birthdays holidays etc. * drawings become more detailed * confuse fantasy and reality – may have an imaginary friend * use writing to communicate
5 years	* understand past, present and future * understands 'more', 'less' and 'same' * can recognise own name and write it * respond to books and enjoy stories * understands that stories have a beginning, middle, and end * interested in reading * can count to 10 * able to draw things they see with increasing detail * can understand time concepts like yesterday, today and tomorrow
6 years	* start to understand mathematical concepts – time, weight, length, capacity and volume * understands the days of the week * increasing interest in why things happen * beginning to read independently * concentration improving * has good problem solving ability
7–8 years	* can perform simple calculations involving addition and subtraction * may be able to tell the time from a watch or clock * developing an ability to reason – knows that something may happen because of a certain action * understands that the number of objects remains the same however they are presented

TABLE 13.5 *Norms of intellectual development*

Language includes common features:

* it is a way of communicating between people
* there are certain rules which must be followed
* it is constructed of sounds, gestures and symbols understood by those using them
* it allows those using it to be creative and express themselves fully.

Language is made up of composite parts which link neatly together:

* verbal communication
* listening
* gestures
* facial expression
* writing
* reading
* other forms of communication, e.g. sign language, pictures.

Verbal communication

When children learn verbal communication they learn the rules of grammar as well as the meanings of the words. This is not something which can be learned quickly. Verbal communication takes a lot of practice to get the sounds right and express them in a meaningful way. Certain activities can help with the development of language:

* people talking to the child
* listening to voices
* practising sounds
* copying sounds
* learning what different sounds mean.

Children develop verbal communication at different speeds, which are much more noticeable than in any other area of development. Some children will be well ahead of the average ages for developing speech, others may be a long way behind. Girls usually talk earlier than boys do. The development of language can be divided into two distinct stages:

* pre-linguistic
* linguistic.

The 'pre-linguistic stage' occurs between birth and 12 months. At this time babies cry, smile and use facial expressions to gain attention. Babies seem to use the pre-linguistic stage to learn about the rules of how to communicate. They understand what is being said to them and start to communicate through pointing and crying.

Children use various methods of communication to attract attention

FIGURE 13.6 *The language chain*

The 'linguistic stage' is when speech develops and words are used to label objects, e.g. dog, cup, ball. From here children progress to simple and then to more complex sentences. Children use holophrases initially, when a single word has several different meanings, for example 'dog' is used to name any animal. They then progress to put words together to form mini-sentences as a form of telegraphic speech, for example 'dada gone'. These sentences enable children to express themselves more clearly. Eventually verbs and nouns are incorporated and sentences become more complex and meaningful.

AGE	LANGUAGE DEVELOPMENT
Newborn	Cries to communicate. At 1 month small sounds are made in the throat, called guttural sounds. By 5 or 6 weeks the baby starts to coo and gurgle when someone is speaking to them. At around 8 weeks eyes and head move towards a sound.
3 months	Raises head in response to sounds. Learns to control the muscles in lips, tongue and voice box (larynx) and makes a wider range of sounds. Gurgling and babbling occur more often and there seems to be a two-way 'conversation' with other people.
6 months	Cooing may stop. The variety of sounds increases. The noises made can seem to represent words, 'goo', 'adah' (often thought to be baby's first word of 'dada'), 'der', and 'ka'. Laughing, chuckling and squealing when playing are common. Screams when annoyed.
9 months	Babies begin to copy the sounds made to them by adults. Can repeat the same word several times, 'dad-dad', 'mum-mum' and 'bab-bab' are favourites. These are not usually spoken with meaning, more often because the baby is getting used to making sounds. Imitates sounds, e.g. blowing raspberries.
1 year	Words are spoken with understanding and sometimes in response to instructions, like 'give it to daddy' – the baby responds with 'dad-dad'. Babbling sounds more like speech. Imitates simple words. Begins to point which shows understanding of words, e.g. when asked, 'where is the ball?' the baby points to the ball.
2 years	New words are learned very quickly. The toddler can use 50 or more words and can put together two or three words to make simple sentences, e.g. 'me want ball'. Starts to use pronouns, e.g. me, I, you. At this time questions are asked constantly.
3 years	Vocabulary is large. A simple conversation can be held with longer sentences used. The child often talks non-stop. Uses language to describe experiences and express their feelings. Sometimes gets the ending of words wrong, e.g. drawed, sleeps. Asks inquisitive questions; Why?, Where?, What?, How?
4 years	Child is able to sound like adults because they can copy the speech patterns they hear. People who don't know the child can understand what is being said. Sentence structure is usually accurate, although errors involving tenses can occur. Nursery rhymes are remembered and enjoyed. Questions are asked constantly.
5–8 years	Child has learned the basics of language and now develops their vocabulary and perfects their use of language. Mistakes occur rarely and complex sentences are used with added confidence. Writing and reading develop well. Child enjoys reading, writing and talking socially by 8 years of age.

TABLE 13.6 *The pattern of language development*

Facial expressions and gestures

Children increase their use of facial expressions and gestures as verbal communication develops. Expressions and gestures form an important part of the use of language throughout life; both can be used to enhance the words said. Gestures are

Listening is an essential skill

Listening

Listening is a skill which children must learn to communicate effectively. Listening to the other person's contribution is essential to ensure the conversation flows and the child understands the information they have been given. Learning also takes place by listening to others; it is therefore essential for a child to have mastered this skill by the time they start school.

Non-verbal communication

Babies love to communicate with other people from a very early age, using various non-verbal communication methods:

* using their eyes to make contact with their carers

* using varying tones – crying, screaming and gurgling are all used to portray different messages

* using facial expressions to show they are happy, unhappy, content

* using gestures with their hands – pointing, throwing, pushing, pulling and clinging to inform others of their wishes.

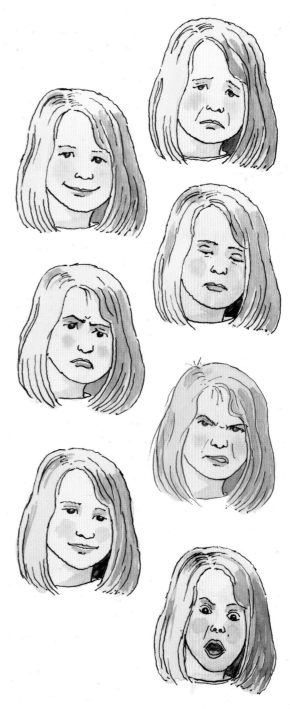

FIGURE 13.7 *Facial expressions can give various messages*

often used to replace words, as they can have a greater impact. It is important to learn quickly the meaning of facial expressions and gestures to be able to communicate effectively with others.

Sign language

Children who have hearing problems or difficulty talking may use sign language as an alternative means of communication. There are two types of sign language which are commonly used. Makaton is very basic and is often used with children. It is often used to encourage language ability in hearing people. British Sign Language (BSL) is more complicated and can be used to convey complex messages. BSL is a complete language system not associated with the English language and developed by deaf people – it is central to the deaf community. Sign language has relatively limited vocabulary so gestures and facial expressions are used to improve the communication process.

Communication gives freedom

Pictures and writing

Pictures are often used by children to express their feelings. The ability to draw also progresses in stages similar to language. As children get older their pictures become more recognisable. By the time children can read and write fluently they are less likely to favour drawing as a communication method. Pictures are also a method

What if?

What different types of language problems could a child suffer from? How could a child with language problems be supported to overcome them?

AGE	DRAWING AND WRITING DEVELOPMENT
15 months	* Grasps thick crayon half way up * Uses palmar grasp with either hand * Scribbles to and fro
18 months	* May use either hand to draw. Could begin to show a preference for one hand or the other * May demonstrate a primitive tripod grasp (thumb and first two fingers) * Scribbles and dots
2 years	* Tries to hold the pencil nearer the point with a primitive tripod grasp * Vertical lines and circular scribble forming * May write a 'V' shape
2 years 6 months	* Improved tripod grasp * Can draw a recognisable circle * Horizontal lines and circles are favoured * May write a 'V' and 'T' *continued on next page*

TABLE 13.7 *The pattern of drawing and writing development*

AGE	DRAWING AND WRITING DEVELOPMENT
3 years	* Has good control of the pencil between two fingers and thumb * Shows a preference for right or left hand * Can copy a circle but does not always join it up * May write 'V', 'H' and 'T' * Draws a person (head with one or two features, eyes, nose, mouth)
4 years	* Holds a pencil like an adult and has quite good control * Can colour in pictures but not always within the lines * 'V', 'H', 'T' and 'O' may be copied * Begins to trace shapes, letters and numbers by joining dots * Draws a potato person with a head, legs and trunk, may have arms and legs with digits (fingers and toes) * Names drawings
5 years	* Good control of pencil * Can copy circles, squares and triangles * May write 'V', 'T', 'H', 'O', 'X', 'C', 'A', 'L', 'U' and 'Y' * May write own name and simple words * Can draw a house with windows, door, chimney and roof * Can colour in a picture and stay within the lines * Pictures may have background, i.e. sky
6 years	* Able to write letters of a similar size * Can write their last name as well as their first * May begin to write simple stories * The body becomes more important than the head and the legs have feet
7–8 years	* Individual letters are easier to differentiate * Capital and lower case letters are in proportion * Draws people including fine details; a head, body, hands, hair, fingers and clothes * Pictures are more detailed to include houses, animals, cars and other objects of interest * Can express themselves clearly in writing * Punctuation and grammar are improving * May use joined up writing

TABLE 13.7 *The pattern of drawing and writing development*

of communication for children with physical disabilities who cannot speak or use sign language.

Try it out

What activities do children do when they start school to help them develop their writing and drawing skills? Design an activity which would help a child who has difficulty writing. Explain to others in your group how your activity would help. Compare your activity with others in the group. How do activities encourage the development of different skills?

Cognitive development

Cognitive development enables children to understand the environment around them. The development of concepts, problem-solving skills, creativity, imagination, memory, object permanence and concentration are keys to successful cognitive development.

Key concept

Cognitive development: the development of the mind through thinking and learning skills.

FIGURE 13.8 *Good facilities help children's development*

Concepts

Children have to learn many different concepts. They learn through seeing them, experiencing them and through adults providing activities, equipment and support.

Through exploring their surroundings in a variety of different ways children develop a range of concepts.

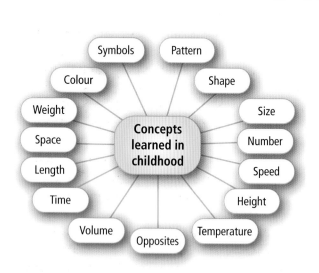

FIGURE 13.9 *Concepts learned in childhood*

Problem-solving skills

Problem-solving skills give a child the ability to solve both easy and complicated problems. As a baby they may learn to put shapes into a shape sorter and as a child learn to ride a bicycle. The ability to solve problems follows a pattern (see Figure 13.10).

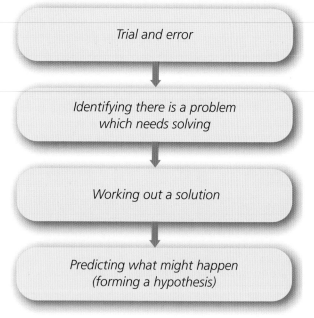

FIGURE 13.10 *Problem solving*

Problem solving is linked to a child's ability to reason. They understand that certain actions will produce specific results, for example, if a button is pressed on a toy it will make a noise.

Creativity

Creativity provides a child with the ability to use their imagination to express their ideas. Children

Pretend play helps to develop a child's imagination

demonstrate their creativity when they paint pictures, make collages, make models, dance, sing, and make music.

Imagination

A child's imagination gives them the ability to see things when they are not in front of them or even when they do not exist. A child uses imagination to play pretend games, make up stories or talk to an imaginary friend. They also use it when dancing, dressing up, drawing, painting, reading, designing, model making, etc.

Memory

Memory enables a child to store and retrieve information, ideas and things that have happened to them. Short-term memory is used to remember trivial things like shopping lists. Long-term memory stores information, like names and places, until it is needed. Psychologists have many theories about the development of memory; however most agree that children and adults develop different strategies to store and retrieve information that has been stored previously.

Psychologists believe people can store information in their short-term memory for between 15 and 30 seconds, although this can be extended through a process known as 'rehearsal' by repeating something, for example, a telephone number. Children develop this strategy around 7 years of age, this is why simple instructions are often forgotten before this.

Long-term memory is thought to have unlimited capacity. Retrieving information from long-term memory often involves the use of 'encoding' or triggers which release the information. Triggers could be a picture, letter, word or even a smell.

Children's memory span improves dramatically throughout childhood. They practice rehearsal and become more efficient at using this process to support their memory. They also become more adept at carrying out processes such as 'encoding' automatically.

Object permanence

This is the ability to understand that an object still exists even when out of sight. Children love to play games where a toy is hidden and they have to find it. At first they think it has disappeared completely but as they develop object permanence they take great delight in searching for the toy.

Jean Piaget's (1896–1980) theory of development (see Unit 11 Section 2) links the progression of a child through four stages of cognitive development.

The **sensorimotor** stage begins soon after birth with a baby relying on inbuilt behaviours of sucking, crawling and watching. The sucking reflex is necessary for a baby to get milk from its mother to survive. This behaviour develops to explore their surroundings through sucking fingers, toys and clothes. During this stage the baby slowly adapts to the world around, building knowledge and understanding with every experience. Piaget believed that babies could not use mental images of objects to remember them. Towards the end of this stage at around 18 months to 2 years a child can remember images and understand the objects they see. The sensorimotor stage ends when a child understands that objects have permanent existence and are still there even when they cannot see them.

Between 2 and 7 years Piaget believed that children could not operate in a logical or rational way – this stage he called **pre-operational.** Children between two and four have the ability to use words but do not necessarily understand what they are saying. They may use the word 'cat' to describe any animal they see, not specifically a cat as adults know it. By 5 a child will name objects correctly as their understanding has developed. They do not, however, understand the logic behind what they say and often get the meaning of words wrong. Pre-operational children do not understand mass, number and volume. If they see a tall thin glass full of milk compared to a short wide glass, they will say the tall glass has more in it because they cannot conceive volume. Children at this stage are also very self-centred, or egocentric, as they are only capable of thinking of themselves.

The **concrete operations** stage occurs between 7 and 11 years. This is when a child thinks about everything in a logical manner. Logical thought processes are used to solve problems. Children at this stage cannot cope with abstract thought, or with forming hypotheses or theories to explain the world around them. A child may be able to imagine an object from another viewpoint but may find it difficult to explain their ideas using language. Children of this age enjoy collecting factual information about topics they are interested in.

The final stage, **formal operations,** is when children and adolescents develop formal logical thinking which enables them to use their imagination and understand beyond the limitations of reality. They can use this to solve problems by developing hypotheses and testing them out. They can go further than 'here and now' and progress to predict the future, which opens a world of possibilities.

Concentration

Concentration is the ability a child has to spend time and pay attention to a task. The concentration span of a newborn baby is a few seconds. As the baby develops concentration increases. A child who is interested in an activity will concentrate for longer than a child who lacks interest. Children need to be able to concentrate so that they learn more and store the information in their memories.

Internal factors can affect a child's concentration. A child who is:

* *tired* will not pay attention as readily as when they are wide awake

* *ill* will not concentrate on something which they normally find interesting when they are well

* *uninterested* in a particular event will lose concentration

* *deprived* will only concentrate if the activity or stimulus will satisfy their immediate need.

Patterns of intellectual development

Infant: 0–1 year

During their first year babies develop an understanding of their surroundings and their carers, and communicate their needs through crying. They are totally dependent on their carers. They use their senses to raise awareness and develop an understanding of the world. They watch adults closely and explore objects using their mouth and touch. Copying and repetition are used to develop understanding. They are gaining information all the time and new objects interest them more than those they know well. As soon as a baby can move around they will want to explore even more.

Toddler: 1–3 years

Children's intellectual development progresses quickly between 1 and 3 years. They gain an understanding of their surroundings and the foundations of future learning are made. During this stage children learn by trial and error. They repeat actions they have enjoyed and take notice of everything that is happening around them. Imitation of other children and adults increases. They begin to understand the consequences of their actions, for example, if they tip a drink over it will make a wet patch. Reasoning skills may begin to develop. With the development of language skills they begin to ask questions like 'What?' and 'Who?'.

Pre-school child: 3–5 years

At this stage children show more reasoning skills and ask 'How?', 'Where?', 'When?' and 'Why?' constantly. These questions help them to develop their understanding of the world. They begin to understand about people and places they have never seen. Their concentration is improving and they will spend more time doing activities that interest them. They begin to recognise shapes and letters, and use some in their writing. Problems tend to be solved through a combination of reasoning and trial and error and they begin to understand why their actions are successful. Imagination is featured highly when playing, for example, in the home corner and dressing up. Memory skills are developing and they can remember special activities like birthday parties and familiar songs and stories.

School age: 5–8 years

Children now show more understanding and use reasoning based on personal experience. They continue to use some trial and error for learning. Reading and writing continue to improve. Understanding of past, present and future and the concept of measuring time, weight, length, capacity and volume develop. They are interested in why things happen and like to test their own ideas (hypotheses).

Concentration increases and they can work at a task without being distracted for longer periods. Ability to perform calculations using addition and subtraction improves. Their memory is developing rapidly along with their understanding. The foundations of learning have been well established and children continue to make progress in line with their potential.

Try it out

Suggest three different activities which could support a child's intellectual development. Explain how each would help. What other skills could each activity help the child to develop?

Social and emotional development

Babies are born with the need for company and are very sociable. A baby who is lonely will cry for attention and can usually be consoled by a cuddle from their carer. A baby's social development follows a particular pattern.

* Interaction with their main carer – making eye contact, smiling and babbling.

* Knowing that they are part of a family – recognising the difference between people they are familiar with and strangers.

* Mixing with other people in a group and co-operating – following instructions, copying actions, playing with other children and sharing.

The social skills are developed at first with the child's parent or main carer, and the child then goes on to develop social skills required to interact with others. Emotional development is all about the way we feel about ourselves, other people and the things we do. Children have feelings of fear, excitement, affection, pride, jealousy, sadness and contentment. They show these and many more depending on their experiences. It is important that children develop the ability to recognise and control their feelings through their emotional development.

Everyone likes to feel they belong and get on well with the people around them. The ability to mix with others is referred to as 'socialising'. If a child lacks the skills and attitudes necessary to socialise with others in their community they are likely to become very lonely. Children are happier and healthier if they get on with the people around them.

Patterns of social and emotional development

Infant: 0–1 year

During their first year babies quickly develop an emotional bond with their parents and carers. This is instinctive as they recognise their mother's smell and the sound of her voice is soothing. Their personality begins to emerge and they start to socialise with those close to them. Using eye contact, smiling, crying and laughing they interact with their parents and carers and learn important skills of socialisation.

A newborn baby's behaviour is controlled by reflexes. At 1 month old babies learn to smile at a voice or face and respond to a voice and smile. By 2 months babies are able to communicate through noises. They may stop crying when they are picked up and sleep less during the day and more at night. At 3 months old babies take interest in their surroundings and take notice of sounds and familiar faces, but they may cry if their mother moves out of sight. They can clearly express their feelings of pleasure, fear, excitement, contentment and unhappiness. At 6 months babies are more aware of themselves in relation to other people. Babies prefer to be with their mother or primary carer, reaching out to them when they want to be picked up. A fear of strangers develops which is demonstrated through body movements and crying. At 9 months the attachment with their primary carer is very strong. They enjoy playing and are very responsive. They still cry if they are hungry or need changing, but use their voices more to attract the attention of an adult. By one year they are affectionate towards parents and familiar adults, like to play simple games and will wave goodbye.

Toddler: 1–3 years

During the next year children learn that they are a separate individual from their primary carers. They recognise their own name and begin to use it. They begin to explore their environment independently when they can crawl and walk. Babies at this age can understand and obey simple commands. Around 2 years they only see things from their own point of view and will show anger and frustration if their needs are not met straight away. Tantrums are a big feature and the 'terrible twos' is common. They have no understanding that other people have needs which have to be met as well. Mood swings are common, changing from angry and upset to happy and supportive. Children have to come to terms with their yearning for independence and their inability to fully express their desires. When children develop more physical skills, independence and language skills their tantrums gradually disappear and they become more contented. They like to play near other children but not with them. Concern for others is sometimes shown, for example sympathy if a person is hurt or telling their mother if the baby is crying. This may be because they understand how the other person is feeling.

Pre-school child: 3–5 years

When children reach 3 years old they have become more sociable individuals with a strong self-identity. They are able to express their feelings and become more confident. Friendships develop and they are happier to be left with adults other than their primary carers. Social skills are developed; for example, taking turns and sharing toys. They may be willing to wait for their needs to be met. Children continue to need reassurance at this age and may still argue and have tantrums if they do not get their own way. They show concern for other children who have hurt themselves or are upset. Between 4 and 5 years children are friendlier, have greater self-confidence and are more trusting. They are quite sociable individuals and enjoy spending time with their friends.

School age: 5–8 years

At 5 years children start to understand gender roles and tend to play with children of the same

AGE	SOCIAL AND EMOTIONAL SKILLS DEVELOPED
Newborn	* enjoys feeding, being talked to and having cuddles * likes to feel close to mother * imitates facial expressions, e.g. smiles at parents * gazes into parent's or primary carer's eyes * moves whole body to express enjoyment * shows signs of inborn temperament (excitable or placid)
3 months	* smiles and coos to express enjoyment * likes to be cuddled * recognises familiar people, smiles at strangers * shows enjoyment at different activities, e.g. bath time
6 months	* enjoys playtime and laughs when enjoying activities * wary of strangers, gets upset when mother leaves * recognises other people's emotions, cries and laughs when others do * will pass toys to others * able to feed self with fingers
9 months	* prefers to be near a familiar adult * can distinguish between family and strangers * expresses fear of strangers by crying * content with own company * enjoys songs and action rhymes * comfort objects, like a blanket or teddy, become important * enjoys being noisy * expresses likes and dislikes at mealtimes * dislikes going to bed * can drink from a cup with help
1 year	* shows affection for family * likes to be with people he or she knows * plays alone * able to wave bye bye * shy towards strangers * plays games with others like pat-a-cake * often depends on comfort objects * may have mood swings – happy one minute, upset the next * enjoys social side of meal times * learning to feed self * may help with dressing
18 months	* happy to play alone, but likes to be near a familiar adult * shy of strangers * wants to be independent * can take clothes off and try to dress themselves * can use a cup and spoon reasonably well * show emotions clearly, fear, anger, joy, happiness * temper tantrums start * may start to be toilet trained * senses others' concerns for them, e.g. when climbing * may get frustrated easily * enjoys repetitive stories and rhymes * begins to use words to express themselves

continued on next page

TABLE 13.8 *Norms of social and emotional development*

AGE	SOCIAL AND EMOTIONAL SKILLS DEVELOPED
2 years	✳ able to express their feelings ✳ keen to try out new activities and likes to help with chores ✳ can be very clingy and dependent on carers ✳ can be confident and independent ✳ gets frustrated easily if cannot express themselves ✳ temper tantrums are common ✳ able to dress and to feed themselves without spilling much ✳ can go to the toilet on their own, may need help to pull pants up ✳ likes to have their own way and has strong sense of self-identity
3 years	✳ begins to show interest in making friends with other children ✳ understands gender and age ✳ can show concern for others ✳ gaining confidence ✳ likes to be independent and do things for themselves ✳ shows feelings for younger brothers/sisters ✳ able to use the toilet on their own ✳ happy to share toys and take turns ✳ able to pretend and imagine but fears develop, e.g. of the dark ✳ enjoys pleasing adults and helping out ✳ can use a fork and spoon to feed themselves
4 years	✳ very affectionate towards family, friends and familiar people ✳ beginning to play with others and likes to be with other children ✳ will share toys ✳ will play on their own for longer periods without adult attention ✳ can wash and dry their hands and brush their teeth ✳ beginning to dress and undress themselves ✳ shows a sense of humour ✳ likes to be independent and are strong-willed
5 years	✳ dresses and undresses themselves ✳ has definite likes and dislikes ✳ enjoys responsibility, e.g. caring for pets ✳ chooses own friends ✳ understands the rules of play and takes turns in play ✳ plays happily with other children and shows sympathy and comforts friends ✳ is more confident
6 years	✳ chooses friends for their personality and interests ✳ can hold a long conversation with another child or adult ✳ begins to compare themselves to other people ✳ carries out simple tasks around the house ✳ takes responsibility for own possessions
7–8 years	✳ learns how to control emotions and may criticise own achievements ✳ able to keep own thoughts private ✳ begins to think of what they would like to be in the future ✳ independent in washing, dressing and toileting ✳ may be able to speak for themselves at the dentist or doctor ✳ forms close friendships, mainly with own sex

TABLE 13.8 *Norms of social and emotional development*

sex. They like to choose their friends and lasting friendships may develop. They understand rules and the need for fair play and will take turns in activities. Imitation is great fun, using both words and actions. Emotionally, children are usually confident and proud of their achievements. Between 6 and 8 years children are more willing to share equipment and materials. They tend to be more critical of their achievements and may 'give up' if they do not feel their work is of the right standard. They are increasingly influenced by adults and children who are not family members, and understand others' points of view. Friends are very important and they may get upset if they are left out of a game or group activity. They have become very good communicators and their social skills are well-developed by the end of this stage. Children compare their achievements with others and may get upset if they are not doing as well as their friends. By 8 years they will have developed their own identity and personality. Their attitude towards life will be established and they will have learned many of the skills required for independence.

Summary

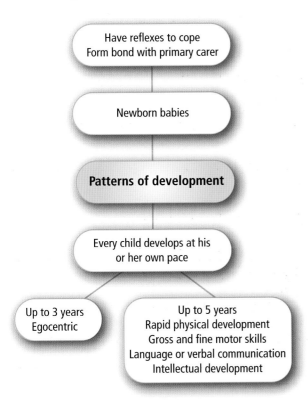

Section 2: Factors that influence development and norms of development

Factors that influence development

Family structure

Children live in a range of family structures for many reasons. The 'normal' family of children living with two married parents is an image of the past. With increased divorces and many partners living together outside marriage, the range of family structures has expanded. Whatever structure of family a child lives in, it is important for them to have love, care and attention.

There were 17.0 million families in the UK in 2004 and around 70 per cent were headed by a married couple. Although married couples were the main family type, the number of married couple families fell by 4 per cent (0.5 million)

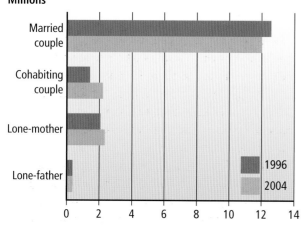

All families: by family type, 1996 and 2004, UK

Millions

Legend: 1996, 2004

Categories (top to bottom): Married couple, Cohabiting couple, Lone-mother, Lone-father

Axis: 0, 2, 4, 6, 8, 10, 12, 14

Source: National Census, 2001, Office for National Statistics

FIGURE 13.11 *Types of families*

between 1996 and 2004. This decline occurred despite an overall increase of 3 per cent (0.5 million) in the total number of families. Over the same period the number of cohabiting couple families increased by over 50 per cent to 2.2 million, while the number of lone-mother families increased by 12 per cent to 2.3 million. Children in lone-parent families were more likely to live with their mother than with their father. In 2004, nearly 90 per cent of lone-parents were mothers.

Nuclear family

A nuclear family is where children and their parents live together. The parents are usually the primary carers for the children. The children may have contact with grandparents and other relatives who may live in different parts of the country or even the world.

Extended family

Parents, children and other relatives live together in the same house or very close together. Grandparents or other relatives may help care for the children. The upbringing of the children is seen as the responsibility of the whole family, not just the parents. Children are able to develop a strong relationship with several members of the family and often develop a strong sense of security.

Lone-parent family

Children live with only one of their natural parents. This could be for a variety of reasons:

* one parent has died
* parents have separated or divorced
* a woman may have chosen to become a single-parent
* a teenager may have become pregnant and her partner did not want the responsibility of a child.

Reconstituted families

Reconstituted families are increasing as parents who separate, divorce or lose a partner often remarry. One natural parent, a step-parent and the children formulate a reconstituted family. If the step-parent has children, the child will have step-brothers or sisters, and if the couple has more children they will have half-brothers or sisters. This type of family can often be confusing for young children or outsiders to comprehend.

It is not uncommon for children to live in different family types through their childhood. This is a result of changes in relationship and childbearing patterns, such as the rise in births outside marriage and the growth in divorce and cohabitation. Children can be affected by the breakdown of marriage and cohabiting partnerships, and the creation of new partnerships. In 2003, 153,500 children under 16 were affected by their parents divorcing in England and Wales. Just over one in five were under 5 years old.

Did you know?

In 2001, 10 per cent of all families with dependent children in the UK were reconstituted families. There is a tendency for children to stay with their mother following the break-up of a partnership. Over 80 per cent of step-families consisted of a natural mother and a step-father.

Married-couple step-families were more likely than cohabiting-couple step-families to have natural children in the family as well as stepchildren (57 per cent compared with 35 per cent in 2001).

Roles and responsibilities of parents/carers

Parents and carers have the responsibility to look after their children both physically and emotionally, teaching them what they must know to become accepted as members of their society. Parenting includes ensuring the child's physical, intellectual, emotional and social needs are met, teaching them the norms and values of their culture and providing children with the basis to become economically independent as adults.

A child's development is dependent on being provided with food, warmth and shelter. Parents and carers also have a duty to look after children when they are sick and comfort them when they are unhappy. Parents need to encourage social skills so that children understand the difference between right and wrong and appropriate behaviour and attitudes in their culture. Parents should provide opportunities for learning so children develop the skills, knowledge and understanding required to survive alone as independent adults.

The ways parents behave towards their children may impact on their development. The warmth and love a child experiences allows them to feel security and attachment, and to form trusting relationships with others as they grow.

Parents should listen to their children's opinions and ideas and take them seriously to build confidence. Parents who accept a child for who they are and support them without making unreasonable demands upon them will allow the child to build their self-worth and confidence. For example, a hard task will be made easier if a child is given encouragement and support while completing it.

Environmental factors

Location

Where a child lives can have a huge impact on their development. Families who live in rural areas have limited access to facilities like libraries, swimming pools and parent-and-toddler groups. Public transport is often scarce, which could make travelling to local amenities difficult. These limitations can be balanced by the impact of a more natural environment without pollution or the pressures of living in a town or city. Although children living in towns or cities may have access to a range of facilities, the cost of these could be a barrier for some. Those living on housing estates may have other difficulties to cope with, including peer pressure or conflicts between groups of people.

Location and social exclusion

According to the government social exclusion department, children and young people are especially vulnerable to the effects of **social exclusion.** They may be exposed to crime as victims, or drawn into early offending. They may be faced with multiple problems, skip important stages of their education and face illiteracy and unemployment. Their long-term prospects may include homelessness, mental health problems and chronic debt. Children growing up in the most deprived areas of the UK are most at risk of social exclusion.

Housing

Housing can also have a direct impact on a child's development. The following aspects of housing can all have an effect on children's development.

Size and number of rooms in a house

Where space is short and children must share a bedroom they may feel a lack of privacy. If children are unable to have their own personal space there may be increased tension in the house, leading to disagreements and arguments.

Damp or dirty housing

This can affect a child's health, because there is increased risk of germs and bacteria which could lead to illness. Damp housing can lead to respiratory problems such as asthma.

Access to outdoor play

Children who do not have access to a garden or public outdoor play area may lack opportunities to develop their physical skills. They may also lack opportunities to meet friends and develop their social skills and confidence.

Stability and security

Children who move house constantly may not develop long-term friendships and may feel insecure.

Nature versus nurture

The nature versus nurture debate refers to the influences which affect a child's development. Some people believe that it is inherited (genetic) factors (nature) which have the greatest impact, others believe it is the quality of environment in which a child is brought up and the care they receive (nurture). In reality, psychologists have shown that both factors influence a child's development.

The environment where a child lives is one key factor which interacts with many others to influence life chances. Factors connected with nurture, including housing, parenting, family, education and socio-economic factors, also link with the child's inherited genetics, their nature. This includes physical features, temperament, susceptibility to certain inherited diseases and intelligence. Nature cannot exist without nurture – both have an impact on development and can provide both positive and negative effects.

Social and economic factors

Social class

Social class is used to differentiate between groups of people. The 2001 National Census carried out by the Office for National Statistics classified the population into eight different groups.

The class a child's family belongs to can have a direct impact on their development. Although social class is often linked to income, the occupations which people have provide an indication of their position within the community. The unemployed are often the most disadvantaged due to the effects this can have on their health and expectations. A child who lives in a family where unemployment is seen as the 'norm' may feel there is little point in working hard at school as they won't get a job anyway. Alternatively, this may make them work harder because they do not want to suffer the same deprivation throughout their lives or make their own children have the same experiences.

Financial status

The financial status of a family is directly linked to the amount of money they have. Sources of income could include:

* earnings from employment

* government benefits

* investments

* profits from the business if self-employed

* profits from sale of goods or property.

SOCIO-ECONOMIC CLASSIFICATION		
Analytic Classes		**Examples**
1	Higher managerial and professional occupations	
1.1	Large employers and higher managerial occupations	Chief Executives of major organisations
1.2	Higher professional occupations	Doctors, lawyers
2	Lower managerial and professional occupations	Middle management in bigger organisations, departmental managers or customer services, teachers, physiotherapists
3	Intermediate occupations	Clerks and bank workers
4	Small employers and own account workers	Painters and decorators, or small manufacturing company owners
5	Lower supervisory and technical occupations	Builders, joiners
6	Semi-routine occupations	Unskilled labouring jobs
7	Routine occupations	Assembly line workers
8	Never worked and long-term unemployed	

FIGURE 13.12 *Socio-economic classification of the Office for National Statistics, 2001*

The amount of 'disposable income' is the money which a family has after paying any taxes, national insurance and pension contributions. This money pays for essentials including housing, food and clothing, before money can be spent on desirable items like toys, holidays and social activities like swimming or gym clubs.

A child's development could be affected by the amount of income the family has. Income can influence a child's development positively and negatively in a variety of different ways. According to the Office for National Statistics there are fewer children living in poverty in recent years. In 2002–03, 17 per cent of the population in Great Britain lived in low-income households (before deduction of housing costs). Children are disproportionately present in low-income households. The number of children living in low-income households rose to a peak of 27 per cent in the early 1990s, the proportion doing so fluctuated. It fell from 1997–98 to 2000–01, and then levelled at 21 per cent for each of the three years to 2002–03 when 2.6 million children were affected.

Access to consumer goods and services is one indicator of children's living standards. For those goods that only became available in the last decade or so, there is a strong link with household income. In 2001–02, 86 per cent of households in Great Britain in the highest income group (weekly disposable income of £1,000 or more) had access to a home computer. This was almost six times the 15 per cent of households in the lowest income group (£100 to £200 per week). The gap was even wider for Internet connections. Access to a computer and Internet access can have a direct impact on a child's education and achievements.

More established goods such as washing machines and central heating, once regarded as luxuries, are now common across all income groups and household types. However, they are still less likely to be found in lower- than in higher-income households. On average, 91 per cent of households had central heating in their homes in 2001–02. The lack of efficient heating can impact on health and well-being.

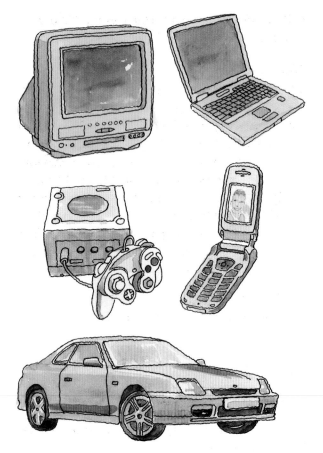

FIGURE 13.13 *Consumer goods impact on a child's development*

Car ownership is closely related to income, as well as to sex, age, stage of lifecycle and location. High proportions of households without access to a car were found among lone parents (43 per cent). For many people, lack of access to a car can cause difficulties in getting to the shops or health services. In 2000–01, 11 per cent of households without access to a car said they had difficulty in accessing their GP. This compares with 4 per cent who had access to a car.

Gender

Children's gender can affect the expectations others have of them. Girls may be made to feel weaker and less important, boys made to feel stronger, more powerful and tougher. The pressures placed on children to conform to the expectations of their gender can affect their development. Boys often suppress their emotions because they have been told that it is not right for boys to cry. Boys may try to seem 'hard' to fit in with a group of friends because they believe that is what is necessary for them to be liked. Emphasis on equal opportunities has removed many barriers which were once experienced; both girls and boys should have the same opportunities if the legislation is being met.

Culture

Cultural beliefs are linked to family values. The cultural life of the family will affect a child's

> **Key concept**
>
> *Culture:* the human behaviour passed from one generation to another.

FIGURE 13.14 *Ways income can influence a child's development*

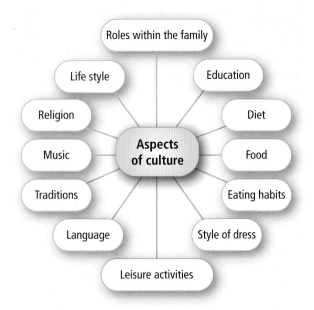

FIGURE 13.15 *Aspects of culture*

upbringing and therefore impact on their development. The national culture of the country where a child is brought up will also have an impact.

Children from ethnic minority groups may be made to feel different by their peers, particularly if their first language is not English. This could have a negative impact on their confidence and self-esteem and their overall development could suffer. The family and cultural environments interact with and can affect a child's development of skills, awareness and understanding. Children may hide differences in their culture rather than be proud of them, for example, not telling people when they are fasting. Children need to be proud of their cultural identity to achieve their full potential, they can get positive benefits from identifying with a strong culture.

The religious background of a family can influence their culture. Religion can provide a set of rules which are expected to be followed, sometimes linked to a behaviour and/or dress code. The religion may also set specific times for worship and festivals. Diet can also be influenced by religion.

Cultural beliefs impact on development

Among all families, those headed by a person of non-white ethnic background are more likely than white families to have children living in them. In 2001, nearly four out of five Bangladeshi families in the UK had dependent children compared with just over two out of five white families (the smallest proportion for any ethnic group). Over 70 per cent of black African, other black and Pakistani families also had dependent children. Indian and Chinese families had the fewest dependent children of any non-white ethnic group (58 per cent and 57 per cent had dependent children).

Discipline

The ways in which parents rear their children affect them. Some parents may be strict and exert strong authority over their children; others may be more tolerant. The ways they choose to bring up the child provide the basis of long-term behaviour in society. Children who have had the right sort of discipline will grow up to know right from wrong and will be able to exert self-discipline when they need to. Consistent discipline carried out in a firm and reasonable manner is most effective. Children will benefit from this because they will:

* feel secure
* know what is expected of them
* be safe
* develop self-control.

Children who have had no discipline are likely to:

* feel insecure because they do not know where the boundaries are
* be greedy because they expect everything they want
* be disobedient because they do not do what is asked
* always expect to get their own way
* have accidents because they do not understand danger.

Children can have too much discipline. This can have a negative impact on their development because their parents place demands on them which cannot be achieved. The child may then feel that they cannot do anything right, and become unhappy. This can lead to a breakdown in the parent-child relationship.

Psychological factors

Security

A child will feel secure if they are loved and have someone who cares for them because they feel safe, happy and wanted. Feeling this way helps a child to progress in their development. If a child feels unloved and unwanted and is left alone for long periods they will feel insecure because they do not have the comfort of knowing that they are cared for and they do not feel safe. A child who is insecure may become withdrawn or behave badly to get attention. Their behaviour problems and lack of attention will impact on their development.

Bonding

When a child develops strong feelings for the people who care for them they form bonds of attachment. This is often referred to as 'bonding'. Holding a baby close gives the baby feelings of comfort and security. A baby's first emotional bond is usually with their mother or primary carer. The more a baby is cuddled and loved, the stronger the bond becomes. Bonding forms the foundation on which emotional development is based.

Bowlby (1953) states: 'What occurs in the earliest months and years of life can have deep and long lasting effects.' Bowlby studied mothers and their babies in the mid-1940s and believed that there was a biological need for mothers and babies to be together during a critical period when an attachment, known as bonding, was formed. Bowlby felt that if the bond was broken through separation, the child would suffer lasting psychological damage. Bowlby believed that children who suffered in this way may grow up unable to love or show affection towards others and might also fall behind in their learning at school. Without bonding extreme consequences

could be that they could be more likely to turn to crime when they matured.

Nowadays there is less stress on the importance of the baby remaining constantly with the mother: care from and bonding with other carers is also possible. It is very important for babies to make a loving bond with primary carers. This early stage of their life sets the scene for future development. A lack of love as a baby could be a detrimental start for a child's emotional development.

Sibling rivalry

When a new baby arrives in the family, an older brother or sister is likely to feel jealous. The older child may feel that they have to compete for their parent's attention and be afraid that the new baby is a rival. They will have been used to having their parent's undivided attention up to the baby's arrival and may now feel left out because the new baby is getting a lot of attention, not only from the parents but also from other relatives.

Sibling rivalry can also occur in older children if a brother or sister achieves well or is more able. There can also be problems with sibling rivalry over toys, possessions or even friends. This type of jealousy can have a negative impact on development if it is not dealt with at the time. Comparison and competition are natural between siblings and can have a positive impact on their development. According to Dr Mandy Bryon, at Great Ormond Street Hospital, sibling rivalry is inevitable. It is a normal, healthy part of development and is, in

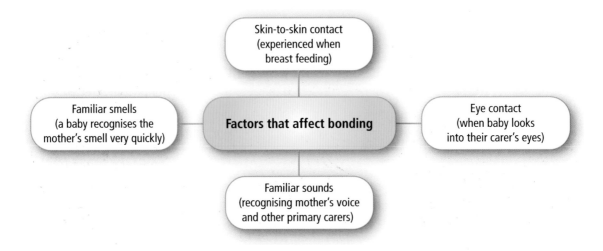

FIGURE 13.16 *Factors that affect bonding*

FIGURE 13.17 *Bonding is important*

FIGURE 13.18 *A new arrival can seem threatening*

fact, positively beneficial. 'Siblings have a unique relationship,' says Bryon. 'They share the same environment, the same genetic make-up (assuming they have the same parents), and have to learn to share their most treasured possession, usually their mother. With brothers and sisters they feel a sense of freedom and security that allows them to test out all sorts of emotions that they would not dare exhibit with anyone else.' The sort of relationship that children forge with brothers and sisters in the early years will determine their relationship in later life.

Fears

All children experience fears at some time. A baby will cry if there is a loud noise. At 9 months a baby develops a fear of strangers. From the age of 2 years other fears may develop, e.g. a fear of dogs, the dark, heights and almost anything they do not understand. Fears are linked to the fact that a child's imagination is developing and may get carried away. Adults can make children afraid of things by making threats to them or talking about scary things, like ghosts and fires. Children who are particularly fearful could develop problems with their emotional development or even develop obsessive compulsive disorders. Fears can also be beneficial to children, by enhancing their awareness of dangerous situations.

Nightmares

Some children have regular nightmares, others rarely have them. Nightmares can develop from a child's fears, e.g. a child who is afraid of dogs could have nightmares about being chased by a

FIGURE 13.19 *A child's fears are real to them*

dog. To a young child the nightmare is real. They may cry out in fear or even wake up. When a child has a nightmare an adult should comfort and reassure them.

Regression

When a child's behaviour returns to that of a younger child, this is called **regression.** It is most likely to happen when a child feels insecure, because they are afraid, feel unloved or unwanted. For example, if a child's parents separate the child may not understand the reasons why and blame him or herself (see Unit 11 Section 2). Regression includes:

* bed wetting
* wetting pants
* clinging to parents
* refusing to communicate
* using 'baby talk'.

Behavioural problems

Aggression

Children demonstrate aggression in various ways:

* kicking
* hitting
* biting
* head banging
* shouting.

Aggression can be a sign of frustration, jealousy, unhappiness, a method of attracting attention or a way of copying parents who hit children as a form of punishment. Children need to learn that aggressive behaviour is unacceptable as it could lead to social exclusion. Children who become out of control can become frightened and do not learn the boundaries to their behaviour.

Attention seeking

Attention seeking is often a sign that a child is insecure. This could be because they find it difficult to socialise with other children or it may be a habit which has been allowed to develop. Children demonstrate attention seeking by clinging to their parent or carer, constantly interrupting and wanting to be heard, answering back when told not to do something, or challenging authority when given instructions. Occasionally, attention seeking can be an indication that a child needs specialist help. A child who is harming themselves to attract attention could indicate a psychological problem which could be dealt with by a child or educational psychologist. A health visitor could also give advice to parents who are concerned about attention-seeking behaviour and may refer the child for counselling.

Temper tantrums

Around the age of two a child's intellectual and cognitive abilities are developing fast. They start to realise that they are separate beings and become increasingly independent. They begin to assert themselves through temper tantrums. Some children seem especially prone. Around 14 per cent of 1-year-olds and one in five 2-year-olds have two or more tantrums a day.

FIGURE 13.20 *Tantrums attract attention*

Children usually have temper tantrums as a result of frustration. This may be because they have been told they cannot have or do something, or it could be because they have not yet developed the skills required to express themselves properly. Tantrums are likely to occur in children who have a very determined character and a lot of energy; they are less likely in children who are easy going and placid.

In a tantrum a child will scream and shout, kick and even throw things. Occasionally a child can hold their breath, which is alarming for parents. They will not listen to anyone who tries to reason with them and will not follow any instructions given. The best way to deal with a temper tantrum is to protect the child from hurting themselves without reacting. As soon as a child learns that they will not get the attention they crave the tantrums will decrease and eventually disappear. Some toddlers can be distracted out of a tantrum, so it is worth showing them a favourite book or puzzle or turning on a music tape while talking about it in your normal tone of voice.

What if?

You observe a child throwing a temper tantrum when shopping in a supermarket. The mother becomes very frustrated and shouts at the child. The child's behaviour gets worse. The mother smacks the child. How could the mother have dealt with the situation in a more positive manner? Why would this have been effective?

Lying

Children often use their imagination to make up stories and play pretend games. Under fives do not know the difference between the real world and 'make believe'. Young children may tell 'lies' which are meant honestly and are not intended to deceive people. Children learn truthfulness over time, usually by their parents setting an example. At around 5 children know that unless they tell the truth people will not believe them. Children over 5 years who lie usually do so because they fear punishment if they tell the truth. Rassmussen (2004) stresses that lying is an innocent fantasy common to children who have yet to develop an understanding of truth and falsehood. Children lie for a number of reasons, and in many cases it is a normal part of development. They might lie because they are afraid of their parent's temperament. It is not surprising that constantly angry, shouting, rigid or restrictive parents often encounter compulsively lying children. Children might lie to impress others, to boost their self-esteem, to get something that they want, or even to protect someone they love. Parents should let their children know that telling the truth lets other people know they can be trusted. They should also let their children know that lying is dishonest, and there are often negative consequences for lying.

According to Dr John Busak, Professor of Psychiatry and Director of the Neuropsychiatry Center at the University of New Delhi, the environmental factor in childhood also plays an important role in determining whether or not a person grows up to be a chronic liar (2002). Those who come from chaotic and dysfunctional families have a greater tendency to lie than those who grew up in a caring household. Busak hypothesises that children from such families lie to change or modify reality so as to make life more tolerable – lying becomes a strategy for coping with the hostile environment.

Think it over

Remember an occasion when you told a lie. What made you lie? Did you feel better after lying? Were you caught out or did you get away with it? How should you have dealt with the situation? With hindsight, why do you think this would have been a better way?

Norms of development

What if?

Norms of development are the average ages when children develop certain skills. List as many reasons as you can think of why some children develop skills early and others later. Share your ideas with the rest of your group. Discuss your findings.

Summary

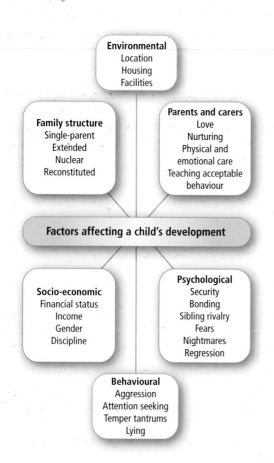

Section 3: Theories of play and how play can affect development

Play is central to the healthy growth and development of the child and is recognised as a basic human right for children, as stated by the United Nations Convention on the Rights of the Child, Article 31. The National Childcare Strategy (1998) recognises the importance of play:

'Childcare helps children grow up happy and confident and introduces them to the joys of play and books.'

All children should be encouraged to play frequently and spontaneously. Children play because they enjoy it; having fun is instinctive. They change activities often and their motivation, enthusiasm, concentration and determination can differ accordingly. Play has a direct impact on a child's physical, intellectual, emotional and social development. It is important that toys and play activities are appropriate to a child's stage of development; otherwise they may lose their motivation to play. If the toy is too simple the child will become bored and lose interest, if it is too complicated the child may not have the skills to play with it and may become frustrated.

How play influences physical development

Children learn and develop physical skills through play. Fine motor skills are developed through playing with small equipment. Gross motor skills are developed through more vigorous play. Children develop balance and co-ordination through play. They also exercise their body and limbs. The senses; sight, hearing, taste and touch all benefit from play. The exercise of play increases the heart rate and improves circulation, bones are strengthened, lung capacity is developed, a child's appetite is improved which encourages them to eat a balanced diet and also improves their digestion.

Through infancy (0–1 year), children use their hands and mouths to explore their environment and their mobility increases. Toys at this stage need to be small enough to be manipulated, yet safe to go in the mouth. Toys which stimulate the senses, like mobiles for sight and activity mats for touch, hearing and sight are excellent.

During the toddler stage of development (1–3 years) children develop physical skills very quickly. Toys help them to develop balance, co-ordination and muscular strength. As children's physical skills develop, toys help them to move around and use their hands with confidence.

Pre-school children (3–5 years) have advanced physical skills. Their balance and co-ordination are well developed. Larger toys help to encourage gross motor skills like climbing, jumping and skipping. Hand-eye co-ordination is enhanced by using constructions toys, painting, and model making. Playing with dolls and teddies can help children's fine motor skills and co-ordination, especially when they include clothes which have zips, buttons and laces, as they can transfer the skills developed to dress themselves.

At school age (5–8 years) children are interested in creating things, which helps to perfect their fine motor skills and hand-eye co-ordination. Physical activities and games help children to gain confidence in their physical skills and balance. Playing football, climbing frames, bicycles, roller skates, swings and slides are all enjoyed. Creativity develops finer detail as the child's fine motor skills develop and activities like cutting, sewing and construction toys with smaller pieces are beneficial.

Think it over

Children who go to a private nursery are thought to have an advantage over children who do not. Discuss this statement with others in your group. Explain to your tutor why you feel the statement is true or false.

Children explore the world around them

Play enhances a child's development in various ways

How play influences children's cognitive development

Play has a direct impact on the development of a child's mind, their ability to understand concepts and the development of language skills. Children learn about some concepts by seeing and experiencing them, but for others they need adult support. Adults can provide a range of opportunities to explore, investigate and discover, to play with different toys, games and activities. Children need adults to support them by playing with them, answering their questions and giving praise and encouragement. Cognitive development depends on a child developing the ability to classify, store and remember information. Playing with toys and games and experiencing other activities will help children to concentrate and memorise information.

Various psychologists have developed their own theories about children's cognitive development and the role of play within

FIGURE 13.21 *Adults support children when they play*

this. These include Piaget, Vygotsky and Bruner.

Piaget and learning through play

The most famous psychologist to work with cognitive learning theory is Jean Piaget (1896–1980). Piaget believed that children

AGE	TITLE	STAGE OF LEARNING
0–2 years	Sensory motor	Babies start to explore the world around them using their senses. They see the world from their own point of view only and are 'egocentric'. By around 8 months they start to understand that a person or object still exists even though they cannot see it. They learn mainly by trial and error.
2–7 years	Pre-operational	Children begin to have thought processes and use language to express them and ask questions. They start to use symbols in their play. They continue to be egocentric. They think that non-living things and animals have the same feelings as they do – 'animism'. At this stage children need to see and feel things to be able to understand them.
7–11 years	Concrete operational	Children begin to see things from another person's point of view – 'decentering'. Logical thinking develops, they can reason and are not taken in by appearances – able to 'conserve'. Rules of games can be followed. Children can use and understand symbols, for example, letters and numbers, and can use reasoning skills. They still need to use objects to help solve some problems. They understand that non-living things do not have feelings.

TABLE 13.9 *Piaget's stages of development*

develop logic based on everyday experiences, playing, socialising and trying to understand their experiences by drawing conclusions. Sometimes their conclusions may be wrong, and it is through further experiences, playing and socialising that they learn the correct information. Piaget set out three clear stages of development linked to children's chronological ages. He believed children could not progress from one stage to the next until they were ready to do so.

Vygotsky and the role of language

Lev Vygotsky (1896–1934) had similar ideas about children's development to Piaget, and believed that children were active in their learning. Vygotsky believed that language played an important role in cognitive development. He also emphasised the role of adults and a child's social development on their learning. He believed that children had potential which adults needed to discover and release. This is referred to as the **zone of proximal development** (ZPD) – the difference between a child's current level of achievement and what they have the potential to achieve. With support and nurturing from an adult, this potential could be released and become reality. Therefore, support and encouragement of an adult when a child is playing should have a positive impact on their cognitive development. Further information on Piaget and Vygotsky can be found in Unit 11 (see pages 80–84).

Bruner and modes of representation

Jerome Bruner (born 1915) agreed with much of the work of Piaget but concentrated on extending the work of Vygotsky. He also felt that children were active in their own learning, but he did not agree with Piaget's stages. Bruner felt that children developed different ways of thinking which he called *modes of representation*. There are three different modes (see Table 13.10). Children are born with one mode and gradually develop the other two; an adult uses all three modes of thinking. Bruner felt there was a definite link between language and thought. As a child begins to talk they can think in a symbolic mode because language helps to place things into categories. Bruner felt the role of adults is important in this process, since they can help children to understand the symbols that speed up the process of learning. Bruner talked about scaffolding, where adults help a child to reach the solution to a problem by giving them support, maintaining the child's interest and pointing them in the direction of information which enables them to increase their knowledge and reasoning skills. For example, an adult supporting a child playing with a shape sorter may talk to the child about different shapes and point to the relevant holes. Bruner also felt that older children who had progressed from one mode to another could support younger children in their development.

MODE	APPROXIMATE AGES	DESCRIPTION AND USE
Enactive	0–1 year	Information is stored according to physical movements. When something has to be remembered, the movement is recreated.
Iconic	1–7 years	Information is stored using images which may be based on smell, hearing or touch. A certain smell may trigger a memory.
Symbolic	7 years upwards	Not everything can be pictured so symbols of language, music and numbers are used to store information.

TABLE 13.10 *Bruner's three modes of representation*

Spiral curriculum: Bruner believed in this idea which refers to the ability of a child to look at subjects at different ages at different levels of complexity. A baby enjoys playing with water by splashing in the bath, as a toddler he enjoys playing in a paddling pool and pouring water during water play, later during pre-school or school age he may develop understanding of the concept of volume by pouring water into different sized containers.

Compare the theories of Piaget, Vygotsky and Bruner. Which theorist do you agree with? Explain your reasons.

Benefits of play

There are many benefits associated with play as shown in Figure 13.22.

Preventing boredom

Preventing a child from being bored is very important. A bored child will lose their motivation and enthusiasm, which could lead to the child becoming frustrated and angry. A child who is bored will find ways to occupy him or herself, which may involve being destructive. This could ultimately lead to a child having behavioural problems which are difficult to control later in life. Children who are not bored are usually happy and enthusiastic.

Reducing stress

A child who enjoys playing is less likely to suffer from stress than a child who does not have the benefits of relaxing through play. A child who is suffering from stress could be encouraged to relax through supervised play which diverts their attention from the cause of their suffering. Playing at 'schools' can help a child get used to the requirements of going to school and reduce their nervousness when the time comes. Dressing up and playing out the role of 'doctors and nurses' can prepare a child for a stay in hospital.

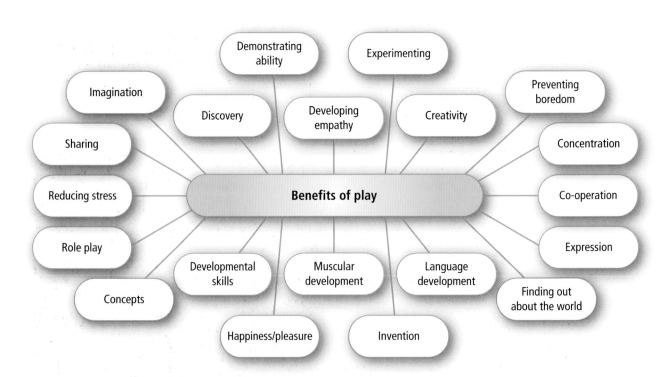

FIGURE 13.22 *The benefits of play*

Although the play may not precisely mimic real situations, a basic understanding is better than not knowing anything about what is going to happen. Through play based on a real-life situation the child will understand better what to expect.

FIGURE 13.23 *Play helps children to prepare for real situations*

Diverting aggression

A child with an aggressive nature can be helped to control this if they are given the opportunity to alter the direction of their aggression. A child who has a problem with kicking could be encouraged to kick a football instead of another child. A child who has aggression built up within them could be encouraged to use a hammer to construct a model rather than hurting someone or damaging property. Painting and drawing can be used to help children express their anger in a non-violent way, reducing tension, enabling them to relax. If a child has not developed the language skills to express themselves clearly they can often do so through pictures. Play dough can be squeezed, squashed, banged and battered enabling a child to relieve their aggression. Simply running around and chasing others can help a child to relax and remove any anger or frustration.

Creating happiness

A child who enjoys playing and is having fun will inevitably be a happy child. The satisfaction of achievement through play raises a child's self-esteem and gives them pleasure. Playing with other children and developing friendships also contributes to a child's emotional state as they can share their experiences and have fun. When a child receives praise and encouragement while they are playing, they will feel a sense of pride and satisfaction which makes them happy.

Helping children to find out about the world

Play also provides opportunities for children to learn about the world around them. It encourages investigation and experimentation, enabling the child to learn how things work and identify the results of their actions – 'what happens if …'. This in turn develops the inquisitive nature of children. Books are an excellent source of information and children can learn about different cultures by reading stories. Culture can be valued and experienced through play activities like dressing up and role play. Children can use their imaginations to pretend they are different people in a variety of situations, which helps them to understand the world they live in.

Think it over

What outings could a playgroup take the children on to enhance their understanding of the world around them? Which do you think would have the biggest impact on the children? Explain the reasons for your decision.

FIGURE 13.24 *Children love reading*

SKILLS CATEGORY	DEVELOPMENTAL SKILLS	SUITABLE TOYS/ACTIVITIES
Fine motor skills	Fingers/hand play	Baby gym/activity centre Rattles and squeaky toys Pram toys Activity mats with different textures Bath toys Mobiles
	Whole hand palmar grasp Passing toys from hand to hand	Bricks to hold and bang together Simple picture books Textured (feely) toys Rattles and squeaky toys Stacking bricks or beakers Cuddly toys Shape sorters Boxes, tins, containers Fabric books
	Inferior pincer grasp Primitive tripod grasp	Bricks Household objects (must be checked for safety first) Chunky crayons Board books Post boxes with different shaped holes Activity and musical toys
	Palmar grasp	Any toys which can be held with the whole hand Musical toys Chunky crayons Jack-in-the-box Sand pit Water play sets Bat and ball
	Pincer grasp Hand-eye co-ordination	Small toys Bricks Cars, trucks Shape sorters Threading toys Picture books Board puzzles Construction toys Play dough Kitchen and cooking sets Jigsaw puzzles Junk toys Bat and ball, swing ball Scissors, collage and cutting out sets
	Tripod grasp	Crayons, pencils, painting sets Stencils Black board and chalk Painting sets

continued on next page

TABLE 13.11 *How developmental skills can be encouraged through play*

SKILLS CATEGORY	DEVELOPMENTAL SKILLS	SUITABLE TOYS/ACTIVITIES
Fine motor skills	Dressing and undressing	Activity dolls with zips, buttons etc. Dolls and soft toys with clothes Shoe lacing set Dressing up clothes Fancy dress costumes
Gross motor skills	Rolling over Sitting up	Baby gym Play mats Mobiles Baby walker
	Crawling Standing	Small push along toys Ride and sit on toys Baby swings Large balls
	Walking	Push and pull toys Wheeled toys Trolleys Prams Balls Follow the leader
	Running	Balls Skate board Hide-and-seek Tag/chasing games
	Hopping Jumping	Pogo stick Trampoline Hop scotch Dancing Gymnastics
	Climbing	Large outdoor toys Climbing frame Slide
	Skipping	Skipping rope Hoops Dance classes Gymnastics
	Balance	Climbing frames Balance beam and benches Trampoline Tricycle Bicycle Roller skates/blades Dancing Gymnastics Swimming

continued on next page

TABLE 13.11 *How developmental skills can be encouraged through play*

SKILLS CATEGORY	DEVELOPMENTAL SKILLS	SUITABLE TOYS/ACTIVITIES
Gross motor skills	Throwing and catching Kicking	Balls of different sizes Hoopla Magnetic dart boards Soft balls Bean bags Hoops
Sensory skills	Sight	Mobiles Baby gym/activity centres Brightly coloured toys Toys that light up Glitter sticks Bold picture books Mirror toys Moving toys Shape sorters Hammer and peg toys Bricks Stacking beakers Construction toys Decorations in the child's room – posters, pictures, murals Story books Toys used to develop hand-eye co-ordination Painting/colouring Drawing Dot-to-dot
	Hearing	Musical toys Rattles Talking toys Story telling Singing Dancing Listening to music Conversation/talking Nursery rhymes
	Touch	Feely bags Textured toys Rattles Play mats Shape sorters Small toys Fabric books Balls Sponge/squeezy toys Construction toys
	Smell	Scented toys Guess the smell games Visits to places of interest e.g. the zoo, beach, countryside, aquarium, supermarket, markets

TABLE 13.11 *How developmental skills can be encouraged through play*

Encouraging developmental skills

Right from birth, play helps babies to develop skills. Toys and activities can be used to help developmental skills to be learned, practised and perfected. Children should be provided with toys and activities which stimulate their development. Many toys are labelled with suitable ages; however, the stage the child has reached should be considered and toys chosen accordingly. Toys should not be too easy or difficult as this will merely frustrate them. Children will work at learning a new skill, practice it and then go back to enjoy using it. It is not always necessary to use bought toys to engage a child and extend their ability; many household objects are safe and provide challenges which children enjoy. For example, an empty saucepan and wooden spoon make a great musical instrument for a baby or toddler, and an empty cardboard box could be used by a small child for climbing in and out of, or by an older child for junk modelling (see Table 13.11).

Try it out

Visit your local toy shop and observe the variety of different toys available for children to play with. The toys often have suggested ages on them to guide shoppers about which ones to buy for their child. What would be the disadvantages of buying toys which are for older children? What are the advantages of having guidelines of which toys are suitable for particular stages of development?

Choose three different toys. Explain to your group why you chose each toy and how it would help a child's development.

How play can be used as a therapeutic process

Children who are unwell, who have a disability or special needs, or who have experienced a trauma in their lives, can benefit greatly from play as a therapeutic process. Play distracts them from their personal situation, gives them a positive focus and enables them to feel equal to their peers. Play also helps children to express their feelings when talking about a situation could be too difficult or disturbing.

Children who are unwell

Children who have an illness may not be interested in any activities at first. Reading short stories to them is excellent when they do not have the energy themselves. As they recover they will become bored and frustrated if they have nothing to occupy their time. Activities which are straightforward and don't require much concentration should be first, for example, play dough on a tray or a simple puzzle. Board games, card games, colouring books and word puzzles can also be used.

Children with special needs

Toys and activities need to be carefully chosen for children with special needs. Their situation could be exacerbated if activities are too easy or too challenging. Toys can help children with certain conditions to improve their development.

A child with **autism** or Asperger's syndrome (see page 54) would become withdrawn if toys were too confusing. They need simple toys based on real-life situations, like train sets, cars, or farms. Linking visits, books and videos to the toys help these children to relate them to their everyday lives.

Children with **cerebral palsy** have difficulty controlling their movements. They require sensory stimulation through textured toys, books or musical toys. **Down's syndrome** children need toys which will stimulate them, as they tend to learn skills by accident and repeat things they enjoy.

Children with cystic fibrosis (see page 108) are often very intelligent although their physical ability may be impaired by their breathing difficulties. Toys and activities can be used to develop their talents through music, art and reading.

Children with sensory impairments need toys and activities which will offset their difficulties. Children with visual impairments, depending on their level of vision, need toys which are bold and bright, make sounds and have flashing lights. Toys which encourage them to use their hands are beneficial, particularly if they have very little sight, as new textures and objects can be frightening at first.

Children with a hearing impairment need a wide variety of toys to maintain their interest. Bright, colourful toys and those which move, light up or make a sound when the child makes a noise help them to learn that they are making sounds. Musical toys and instruments are a great way of helping them to develop motor skills and rhythm as they can 'feel' the music even though they may not be able to hear it. Sensory rooms provide children with the opportunity to enjoy and interact with lights, sounds, smells and textures.

A sensory room is therapeutic and aids development

A child who is a wheelchair user, due to medical conditions, or as a result of an accident, who can use their upper limbs needs to play in exactly the same way as other children. Their need for stimulation may be greater as they cannot take part in some physical activities which involve gross motor skills. They will need to be encouraged to develop intellectually, socially and emotionally through play.

Helping children cope with trauma

Play improves the emotional well-being of a child and is used to help them cope with difficult situations, life events and emotional problems. Play is particularly beneficial when children are unable to express themselves clearly, either because they have not developed the necessary language skills, or because they are too traumatised to speak. Therapeutic play is often used to prevent a minor problem worsening, for example, a bereaved child may be encouraged to draw pictures to remember the happy times they spent together, or they may be encouraged to play music which helps to relieve the stress they are experiencing. Play therapy enables children to explore their feelings and make sense of their life experiences. Therapeutic play helps children to express themselves safely and securely without feeling threatened. Speech therapists, physiotherapists, counsellors, music therapists, art therapists, child psychologists and many other health professionals use play in supporting a child to restore their health and well-being.

Think it over

What toys and activities would be suitable for the play therapists to use in the children's ward of your local hospital? Explain your choices.

Types of play

There are many different types of play. Some of the main categories are:

* spontaneous play – children play with whatever they want in a manner which suits them as an individual
* structured play – where children are given guidance and support
* solitary play – children playing alone
* interactive play – children playing together, sharing ideas and supporting each other
* heuristic play – using objects to support the play activities
* indoor/outdoor – according to the environment where the play takes place.

Piaget and Hughes have provided theories linked to different types of play.

Piaget's typology of play

Piaget believed that play helps to transform a child's thinking from the concrete to the abstract, and progresses from individual or solitary play, to social or group play. The types of play can be directly linked to his stages of development.

Practice play

During the **sensorimotor** stage (0–2 years) children focus on gaining control of their own bodies and external objects and participate in practice play. This enables children to develop skills by repeating movement or sound such as sucking, shaking, banging, babbling, and eventually peek-a-boo games. They keep repeating and trying until they have mastered the skill and then may repeat the activity for the pleasure it gives them. As children learn about the properties of objects and how to manipulate them, they begin to monitor the effects of play on their environment. Their relationship with that environment becomes increasingly systematic because they know that if they carry out a certain action there will be a resultant response, for example, when playing in a baby gym they know that certain buttons create a response like a sound.

Symbolic play

The **pre-operational** stage (2–7 years) is a time when children master symbolic functions, including the matching of objects with words, and the transition from a self-centred egocentric focus to awareness that events have causes outside of themselves. At this stage, children begin to take part in make-believe games using objects for purposes other than their normal function, e.g. a cardboard box becomes a car or rocket.

Games with rules

Between 4 and 7, when they still think intuitively rather than logically, children become interested in games which include rules, structure and social interaction. As they move through the **concrete stage** (7–11 years), during which activities are categorised and early logical operations occur, the types of rules involved in their play and the reasons for them change. At first, the rules focus on the sensorimotor aspects of play and provide structure and repetition. Gradually they become focused on the social aspects of play linked with acceptance by the participants, e.g. team games, board games, etc.

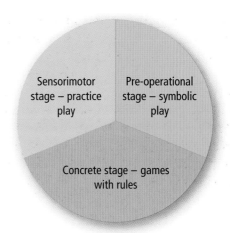

FIGURE 13.25 *Piaget's typology of play*

SCENARIO

Richard

Richard is 8 years old. He was born with a visual impairment and found balancing difficult. He was 18 months old before he walked independently. As a baby he enjoyed playing with his parents. Peek-a-boo was a favourite game. He liked toys which made noises and got a lot of pleasure from toys which made a noise or action when a button was pressed successfully. Once he succeeded he would repeat the action to gain the sense of pleasure, again and again. As he got older Richard enjoyed playing with cardboard boxes and would imagine they were a train one day, a racing car another and even a tractor on a farm. Richard went to a nursery school when he was 2 years old. He made friends easily and liked to play alongside them at first. He quickly learned that he could interact with the other children and his play became more interesting when he could work together with other children. Richard was very competitive and liked to win games like dominos and pairs.

Explain Richard's play using Piaget's typology.

Why was it important for Richard to be encouraged during play by his parents and carers?

How could Richard's sight problems have affected his ability to play?

Hughes' typology of play

According to Hughes (1996) there are 15 different types of play which children actively participate in.

Symbolic play

This is play which allows control, gradual exploration and increased understanding without being too advanced for the child, for example, using a piece of wood to symbolise a person or a piece of wool to symbolise a wedding ring.

Rough and tumble play

Close encounter play which is less to do with fighting and more to do with touching, tickling, gauging relative strength, discovering physical flexibility and the excitement of showing what children can do. For example, playful fighting, wrestling and chasing where the children involved are not hurting each other and are laughing, giggling and obviously enjoying themselves.

Socio-dramatic play

Acting out of real and potential experiences of a strong personal, social, domestic or interpersonal nature, for example, playing at house, going to the shops, mums and dads, organising a meal, or even having a row.

Social play

Play where the rules and criteria for social engagement and interaction can be revealed, explored and amended. For example, any social or interactive situation where all those involved will abide by the rules or protocols, i.e. games, conversation, making something together.

Creative play

This play allows a new response, the altering of information, understanding how materials can be joined together, with an element of surprise, for example, enjoying creation with a range of materials and tools purely for pleasure.

Communication play

Play using words, nuances or gestures, for example, mime, jokes, play acting, singing, debate, poetry.

Dramatic play

Play dramatising events in which the child is not a direct participant. For example, presenting a TV show, an event on the street, a religious or festival event, even a funeral.

Deep play

This play allows the child to encounter risky or even potentially life-threatening experiences, to develop survival skills and overcome fear. Examples are a zip wire, riding a bike on a parapet, balancing on a high beam.

Exploratory play

Play to access factual information using manipulative skills, such as handling, throwing, banging or mouthing objects. For example, playing with an object or area and, either by manipulation or movement, assessing its properties, possibilities and content, such as stacking bricks.

Fantasy play

Here a child rearranges the world in a way unlikely to happen to them personally. For example, playing at being a pilot flying around the world, or the owner of an expensive car.

Imaginative play

Play where the normal rules, which manage the physical world, do not apply. For example, imagining you are, or pretending to be, a ship or tree, or patting a dog which is not there.

Locomotor play

Play involving movement in any direction for enjoyment. For example, chase, tag, hide and seek, tree climbing.

Mastery play

Mastery play involves control of natural resources in the environment. Examples are digging holes, changing the course of streams, constructing shelters, building fires.

Object play

This play uses infinite and interesting sequences of hand-eye manipulations and movements. For example, examination and unusual use of an interesting object, e.g. cloth, paintbrush, cup.

Role play

Play exploring life experiences, although not normally of a deep personal, social, domestic or interpersonal nature. For example, brushing with a broom, dialling with a telephone, driving a car.

Happy days nursery

Happy Days Nursery provides various activities and toys to encourage the children to play. They have a dressing-up corner with doctors' and nurses' outfits, cowboy and fairy costumes. The children are encouraged to make various artefacts including scarecrows from old clothing, Humpty Dumpty using paper plates and tissue paper, and boats using pasta shapes. Sand and water play are fun; the children have water wheels they can pour the water through and funnels for the sand. There is a miniature telephone box and the children love to pretend they are calling the emergency services. Others pretend to be the emergency services and arrive making the relevant sound effects.

Every week the interest table is changed to include various objects which link to the theme of the week.

Outdoors there is a play area which includes a climbing frame, slide, hoops, rope ladders and a tunnel.

The routine at Happy Days is planned to enable the children to participate in a variety of activities throughout the day. Some activities are directed by the staff, others allow the children to decide for themselves and play freely.

How do the activities in the nursery fit Hughes' typology?

How do the activities encourage the children's development?

Why is it important for there to be a mixture of directed and 'free' activities?

Categories of play

Children enjoy participating in different activities during the day. They would become bored and their development may be delayed if they continuously experienced the same type of play. Children should be encouraged to play with different toys and activities to stimulate their development and encourage them to learn and practice various skills which contribute to their individuality. Types of play can be divided into different categories which all contribute to a child's development (see Table 13.12).

List five of your favourite play activities. Why did you like them? How did each activity help your physical, intellectual and social development?

CATEGORIES OF PLAY	ACTIVITIES	IMPACT ON DEVELOPMENT
Physical – play usually involves some form of physical activity. Physical play refers to the play activities which involve children using most or all of their bodies. They use their large muscles and exercise their bodies. Physical play is usually very active and involves strength and stamina.	✳ Team games, e.g. football, netball, hockey ✳ Slides, swings, climbing frames ✳ Riding tricycles and bicycles ✳ Roller skates/rollerblading ✳ Trampolining, swimming, dancing, gymnastics ✳ Hopscotch, skipping ✳ Crawling, jumping ✳ Throwing a ball	Physical – helps children to develop fine and gross motor skills, balance and co-ordination. Intellectual – children can develop concepts of size, speed, distance and awareness of the world around them. Emotional – boosts confidence and self-esteem, promotes pride in their achievements and allows children to release tension. Social – taking turns, sharing and interacting with other children. *continued on next page*

TABLE 13.12 *Categories of play*

CATEGORIES OF PLAY	ACTIVITIES	IMPACT ON DEVELOPMENT
Creative – children use different materials to make something using their own ideas. Children can experiment with different ideas and find out what is or is not successful. Children's achievements through creative play are their own work and may not be easily recognised by an adult – to the child it means a lot.	* Painting, drawing, colouring * Cutting out and sticking * Collage, junk modelling * Sand and water play * Play dough * Writing stories or poems * Construction toys * Sewing * Clay modelling	Physical – helps children to develop fine motor skills, sensory skills and hand-eye co-ordination. Intellectual – helps language skills, colour recognition, children learn about different materials and their properties, develops their imagination and helps understanding of various concepts including size and shape. Emotional – children can express their feelings without using words, builds their self-esteem and confidence. Social – when playing with other children, aids the development of social skills like manners and patience.
Imaginative – also referred to as pretend play or role play. Children pretend they are somebody or something else and take on that role in their games. They may use toys or clothes, or pretend boxes are objects like cars or rockets as props. The children are completely engrossed in their 'fantasy world'.	* Dressing up * Home corner * Dens * Puppet shows * Cardboard box toys * Shops * Kitchens	Physical – encourages fine and gross motor skills. Intellectual – develops children's imagination and encourages their use of language. Emotional – develops confidence and enables children to act out real fears and emotions in an 'unreal' situation. Social – helps children to learn how to share and think of others in different situations to themselves, for example, different cultures and adult roles.
Exploratory – when children endeavour to find out about things: they are exploring the world around them. Children discover ideas and concepts for themselves.	* Shape sorters * Feely bags * Activity centres * Baby gyms, play mats * Play dough * Sand and water play * Bricks * Stacking beakers * Puzzles * Musical instruments * Books * Painting * Junk modelling, collage * Visits to places of interest * Construction sets	Physical – development of fine motor skills, hand-eye co-ordination and sensory skills. Intellectual – understanding concepts of size, shape, space, distance, volume, weight, time, colour texture, what happens if things are dropped, increasing vocabulary, cause and effect. Emotional – satisfaction, pleasure, self-esteem, confidence, dealing with accidents. Social – sharing, taking care of possessions, social skills. *continued on next page*

TABLE 13.12 *Categories of play*

CATEGORIES OF PLAY	ACTIVITIES	IMPACT ON DEVELOPMENT
Manipulative – involves children using their hands to manipulate objects into different positions, through holes or joining them together in some way. The hands, eyes and brain have to co-ordinate to be able to achieve a successful result.	* Jigsaws * Shape sorters * Construction toys * Play dough * Rattles * Soft toys * Water sets * Sand pits * Model making * Threading beads onto laces * Tool kits * Cutting out * Cars and garages * Dressing and undressing dolls * Colouring books	Physical – development of fine motor skills, hand-eye co-ordination and sensory skills. Intellectual – encourages development of language skills, colour recognition, logical thinking, concepts of size, shape, volume, numbers and understanding of the world around them, valuing culture and diversity. Emotional – builds confidence and self-esteem, gives satisfaction for their achievements, enables children to cope with success and failure and teaches them to keep trying if they want to succeed. Social – develops social skills of sharing, taking turns, supporting each other and interacting, develops independence in being able to dress and feed themselves.
Social – when children are playing together in joint activities or games. Social play progresses through five stages: * solitary * parallel * looking on * joining in * co-operative (These stages are described in the *Stages of Play* below.)	* Board games * Card games * Climbing frames * Team games * Dressing up * Party games * Competitive games * Imaginative play * Table-top activities * Reading * Writing	Physical – fine motor skills, gross motor skills, sensory skills, balance and hand-eye co-ordination. Intellectual – the meaning of rules, winning and losing, the consequences of anti-social behaviour, concepts of time, space, size and distance. Emotional – how to deal with conflict, what happens to someone who cheats, satisfaction of team work, confidence, self-esteem. Social – children develop social skills including conversation, taking turns, the importance of following rules, manners, sharing, honesty, co-operation, responsibility and friendships.

TABLE 13.12 *Categories of play*

Stages of play

Social play develops through five stages.

Solitary play

Children play on their own up to 2 years. They are not interested in interacting with others because they are only able to think of themselves. Children at this stage of play enjoy exploring their environment and trying things out. They are happy to do this on their own as the social and language skills required to interact have not yet been developed. In this stage of play children may seek reassurance from adults and be happy to play adult-led games like peek-a-boo.

Parallel play

Children are more aware of each other and like to play alongside other children from the age of 2. They often play parallel to others and there is little, if any, interaction between them. Children know that others are playing close to them but are not able to co-operate as they are 'egocentric' and only think of themselves. They may be involved in the same activity but are concentrating fully on their own individual actions, for example, in a sand pit.

Looking-on play

Looking-on play usually happens when children are around 3 years old. They watch carefully what other children do and may try to copy them. Children at this stage may stand on the edge of older children's games. Observing other children can give a child the confidence to try the same activity for themselves.

Joining-in play

From around 3 years, children will join in games organised by adults, but do not take responsibility for themselves. Through joining-in play children learn how play can be more interesting when others are involved. They begin to develop social interaction skills and like to join in with their 'friends' and play the same games. They are not yet able to co-operate fully.

Co-operative play

Children will play actively together happily, taking turns and sharing from three-and-a-half years onwards. They will co-operate with each other, sharing ideas about games to play and taking on different roles. Sharing may only last for short periods of time and there are often arguments, as children of this age like to take control. Co-operative play helps children to learn the importance of being honest; they quickly learn that cheating and anti-social behaviour like kicking will not be tolerated and will lead to them being excluded. By the age of 7 co-operative play will include games with rules. When asked what they are doing, children of this age will be able to clearly explain what the game is about.

Solitary play

Looking-on play

Parallel play

Joining-in play

Co-operative play

FIGURE 13.26 *The five stages of play*

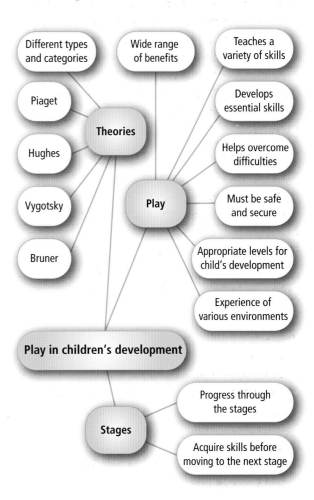

Environments in which children play

Children play in a variety of environments. The types of play experienced may vary according to the amount of space, facilities and equipment available.

FIGURE 13.27 *Environments in which children play*

Playing in different environments can help a child to develop a wider range of skills which enhance their physical and intellectual capability. They will meet and interact with other adults and children which will have an impact on their social and emotional development. Playing in different environments generally has a positive impact on a child's whole development.

Section 4: How to plan and make a learning aid for a child (0–8 years)

When planning a learning aid certain things need to be considered.

The needs of the child to be met

The learning aid should be planned to meet specific developmental requirements which could include physical skills, intellectual concepts, social skills and emotional needs.

The age of the child

The learning aid will need to be suitably challenging for their stage of development. If it is too simple the child will become bored and lose interest; if it is too difficult the child will become frustrated and give up.

The strength of the learning aid

Learning aids made of flimsy material or paper may not withstand a child's exuberance and may be destroyed before they benefit the child.

The learning aid should be stimulating and interesting

It may help a child to use their imagination, develop new skills, or learn new concepts, or it may be specifically relevant to the child. Whatever the aim, it should be exciting and fun to use.

The safety of the learning aid

The learning aid must be safe to use, with no sharp edges, small parts, or places for fingers to get trapped. It should have rounded corners and use non-toxic paint for colouring.

The resources to be used

Cost can influence which resources are used, and a learning aid does not have to be expensive to make – recycled materials which are safe and clean can be just as effective as new ones.

Aims, objectives and outcomes

The learning needs of the child should be identified using the information already gathered for objective two (AO2) and objective three (AO3). When comparing the child's development with the norms from birth to 8 years, you may identify an area or areas where the child would benefit from using the learning aid; for example, if the child was late developing certain skills, or had difficulty understanding particular concepts. The knowledge and understanding you wish the child to develop should be reflected in your aims, objectives and outcomes for the learning aid.

Aims

The aims will be broad goals which include what you intend the child to achieve through using the learning aid. They should sum up the purpose of the learning aid.

Objectives

The objectives break down the aims into smaller manageable pieces. Clearly identified, specific objectives are needed to ensure the aims are achieved. The objectives can be used to decide whether the overall aims have been met or not. They will enable the making of the learning aid to be achieved within a specified timescale. The objectives could link to certain features of the learning aid which will help achieve the aims, for example, use of colour.

Outcomes

Your outcomes should explain exactly how the learning aid will help your chosen child's development. This could include specific milestones and may cover more than one area of development (physical, intellectual, emotional and social).

Examples of learning aids available to buy

Table 13.13 shows examples of learning aids which are commercially available. The learning achieved represents the aims and suggests how each could be used to help a child's development. They could be used as a source of ideas for the designing and making of a learning aid.

LEARNING AID	LEARNING OUTCOMES	HOW THE LEARNING AID CAN BE USED
Dressing toys	A child will be able to develop fine motor skills whilst learning how to fasten buttons, zips and other fastenings used on children's clothes. Colour recognition and language could also be developed whilst playing with the aid. It could also help to develop imagination if the aid became an imaginary friend to the child.	Teaching the child how to dress themselves. This could be used by the child playing on their own or with a carer or friend. It could also help to stimulate conversation and develop imagination if the aid became an imaginary friend to the child.
Play mat/ baby gym	A child can learn hand-eye co-ordination, colours and sounds through the development of sensory skills.	This could be used with adult supervision or the child could be allowed to explore it on their own for short periods of time. When a child enjoys an activity they will repeat it, therefore developing co-ordination much quicker.
Books	A child can learn how to turn pages, learn nursery rhymes, learn concepts and language/reading skills. Learning to press buttons and turn pages develops fine motor skills. Books can vary in their complexity according to the age and level of understanding of the child. Emotional and social skills would be developed if books used in groups.	Books can be used independently, with a carer or in groups where emotional and social development would also be a bonus.
Building blocks	A child will learn how to build things up on top of each other, hand-eye co-ordination and develop fine motor skills. If the blocks are different colours the child would learn to recognise these. Blocks with the alphabet on encourage recognition of letters and language skills.	Building towers and knocking them down is great fun and the child does not realise they are actually learning. Putting the letters in order according to the alphabet would help with word and letter recognition. Sorting into groups of the same colour would aid colour recognition and categorising objects.
Textured toys	A child can learn different materials, sounds and colours. The fabrics are also different textures so the child will learn differences between them. Exploration and sensory skills would be developed alongside fine motor skills. Talking about the toy would help build language skills, also social and emotional development.	The child can explore the toy independently as it would hold their interest and is fascinating for them to use. This is ideal for solitary play but could also be used with a carer or friends.
Dominos	A child will learn the alphabet, number recognition and colours. Fine motor skills will develop through using and moving the dominos. Sharing and taking turns could be introduced to develop social and emotional skills. Mathematical skills could also be developed by counting the dominos.	This could be used independently, with a carer or in a group. Children could be encouraged to learn the rules of the game. Social and emotional skills would also benefit.

TABLE 13.13 *Examples of learning aids*

Method of making the aid, and resources used

The method for making the learning aid you have chosen should be listed as a set of step-by-step instructions. They should start with the raw materials used and end with the completion of the learning aid. Different methods could be appropriate including:

* using a computer, for example, to make a book, dominos, or a 'pairs' game

* woodwork, for example, a puzzle or building blocks

* sewing, for example, a play mat, baby gym, dressing doll

* paper maché, for example, a puppet

* drawing, for example, an activity book.

The resources list for the learning aid must include all the items required to complete it.

Safety aspects to be considered when making the aid

Safety is paramount in the design and making of the learning aid. All manufactured toys have

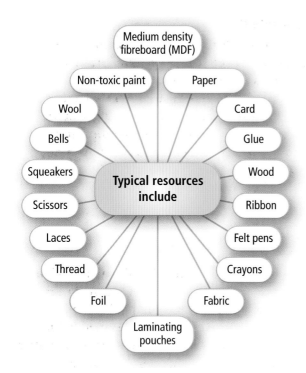

FIGURE 13.28 *Typical resources for making play aids*

Image labels:
Medium density fibreboard (MDF), Non-toxic paint, Paper, Wool, Card, Bells, Glue, Squeakers, **Typical resources include**, Wood, Scissors, Ribbon, Laces, Felt pens, Thread, Crayons, Foil, Fabric, Laminating pouches

to pass strict safety legislation and carry a safety mark; either the European Community (CE) symbol or the Lion Mark. Your learning aid must not expose children to health hazards or risk physical injury. The following points should be considered carefully:

* avoid small parts which could be swallowed and cause choking

* any paint which is used MUST be non-toxic

* avoid using fabric with lose hair or fur which children could choke on

* avoid sharp edges or points – round off corners

* avoid any parts where a child could trap their fingers

* loose ribbons should not be used for under threes

* batteries should be used with care.

Consider the safety of the area where the learning aid is to be used, for example, if the learning aid involves the use of water or paint the floor surfaces should be washable and not close to electricity.

Sources of feedback

You must gather feedback to enable you to evaluate the learning aid. The methods used to collect your information should be selected carefully to ensure your evaluation is thorough. You could use a combination of the following methods.

Observation

You should observe the child using the learning aid, this will enable you to assess whether the learning aid meets the aims, objectives and intended outcomes you set when planning it. You will be able to assess the child's reaction to the learning aid by observing them using it.

* Did they find it interesting?

* Were they able to use it effectively?

* Did they develop skills and achieve what you planned?

* Were there any unplanned outcomes, for example, benefits you had not planned or realised would be possible?

Parent/teacher reflections

The parent of the child would be a valuable source of feedback. They know their child well and will be able to ascertain whether the learning aid meets the child's needs. Asking the parent questions relating to your aims and objectives would help you to analyse the level of success. If the parent is not available when the child is using the learning aid, you could ask the child's teacher for their opinion.

Assessor records

Your assessor may use feedback from other students to assess the suitability and success of the learning aid. They may ask a range of questions about your learning aid to assist with their assessment which could include:

* Were your aims appropriate?

* Did you achieve your aims?

* Were your objectives appropriate?

* How far did you meet your objectives?
* Were the planned outcomes achieved?
* Was the learning aid suitable for the age, gender and development level of the child?

Questionnaire

You could design a questionnaire to help you gather the information required to assess the effectiveness of the learning aid. This could be used for peer assessment or with the child's parent/teacher. The questionnaire would enable others to reflect on your learning aid and judge it according to the parameters set within your questions.

Closed questions could be used to collect opinions about the learning aid and would be useful when gathering information on scaled responses. For example:

> **Does the learning aid help the child to develop number skills?**
>
> Circle the number according to judgement where 0 is low and 5 is high
>
> 0   1   2   3   4   5

Questions like this would be straightforward to analyse within your evaluation.

Open questions would allow people to freely comment on the effectiveness of your learning aid. For example:

> **How do you feel the learning aid would help the child with their development of number skills?**
>
> _____
>
> _____

Depending on the age of the child, if the questionnaire was constructed carefully you could ask the child to complete it.

Interview

You could interview the child, their parent, a teacher or your assessor to find out their opinions of your learning aid. A semi-structured interview, where you have planned your questions before the interview, would focus on the information you require. You should focus the interview around the aims, objectives and outcomes to be achieved by the child.

Evaluation of the aid

You must use the feedback gathered to evaluate the learning aid you have planned, made and used with the child. You must reflect on the aims, objectives and learning outcomes which influenced your design. Through your evaluation you must reflect on your performance and analyse the benefits of the learning aid to the child.

The child's response

Your evaluation must include information about the child's response to the learning aid. You should consider the following:

* What was their reaction when you first introduced the learning aid?
* Did they enjoy using it?
* Did they understand what they had to do?
* What did the child like about the learning aid?
* What did the child not like about it?

Achievement of outcomes

You must provide information about how well the learning aid met the outcomes you proposed. Consider the following:

* Did the learning aid enable the child to develop the skills you planned?
* Were there any weaknesses in the design?

* Was there anything which did not work out as planned?

* Were there any outcomes which you had not anticipated? If so, how did these benefit the child?

Effectiveness of purpose

When judging the effectiveness of purpose of the learning aid you will need to consider the following points:

* Was the learning aid suitable for the child's age?

* Was the learning aid appropriate for the child's level of development?

* Was the learning aid sufficiently challenging for the child?

* Was the design attractive?

* Was the design safe to use?

* Did the design hold the child's attention?

* Was there anything about the design which was too difficult for the child?

* How could the design be improved if you were to make it again?

* What sort of learning aid could be used to develop the child's skills further?

Summary

Aims and objectives
Reflect learning outcomes
State how the child will benefit

Making a learning aid for a child (0–8 years)

Development
Plan
Construct
Evaluate

Evaluation
Use different methods to gather information
Fully evaluate the benefits
Suggest improvements

Consider this

Choose a learning aid which is available to buy. Critically evaluate the strengths and weaknesses of the learning aid.

What age child would it be suitable for?

How would the learning aid help a child's development?

Do you feel the learning aid is good value for money?

How could the design of the learning aid be improved?

Share your evaluation with others in your group. Compare the different learning aids chosen by members of your group. Use your findings to help with the design of your learning aid.

UNIT 13 ASSESSMENT

How you will be assessed

This unit is assessed through a portfolio of work, with the mark you gain for that assessment being your mark for the unit. As part of your portfolio you will produce evidence based on the study of a child up to the age of 8 years. It is recommended that the child you choose to base your evidence on is at least 8 years old to enable you to provide the information required. Your evidence will include:

* a description of three patterns (milestones) in each area of development of children, described from birth to 8 years

* an explanation of the factors that have influenced the child studied and how they have affected his or her development, comparing their development with the norms

* research relating to two theories of play and how they can be reflected in the development of the child studied

* records of the planning and making of a learning aid for the child studied to use and an evaluation of the effectiveness of the aid and the benefits to the child studied.

To help you to fully understand how your work will be assessed, guidance on what you need to include in order to achieve the highest marks for each assessment objective have been included (see below).

Key things to think about

Evidence for this unit could be gathered using primary or secondary sources. Primary sources could include work experience in a nursery, play group or primary school, part-time employment, or younger members of your own family or other relatives or friends. If you do not have access to a child you can study in this way, you could use secondary sources or a case study provided by your assessor. If you do this, you can observe a child of a similar age using the learning aid which you design.

You could consult with the parent(s) or primary carers of the child to help you to gather the information you require. Child record books, if kept by the parents, could provide an excellent source of information which could be used to compare the child's development to the norms. If photographic evidence is used to support your work you must obtain permission from the child or their primary carer.

It is essential for confidentiality to be maintained at all times. You should not provide details of the case study which would enable those involved to be identified by others who read your work. Do not use real names. Addresses or contact details are not required.

You will need to include information on the factors that have had an effect on the child you have studied. Mind-mapping could be used to identify the factors initially, then discuss how these factors have actually affected the child's development. Remember 'development' refers to physical, intellectual, emotional and social aspects. You will need to apply this knowledge and understanding to compare the child's development with the norms and may use factors to justify variations of development from the norms (advanced or delayed).

An understanding of the theories of play will be required before you can apply two of them to the child studied. Three sources of information need to be used, these should be recorded in your reference section/bibliography. Your analysis of the reflection of theories of play in your child's development needs to be detailed and include two examples of each theory. Observations of the child playing in different environments, for example, home and nursery/school could be used to enhance your understanding. Theories of play could include those of Piaget, Vygotsky, Bruner and Hughes (see Section 3) or they may be based on the influences of play, categories of play, stages of play, benefits of play or use of play as a therapeutic process. Your choice of theories will be influenced by the links with your chosen child.

The learning aid you design and make must be relevant for your chosen child at some point in their development between birth and 8 years old. (It doesn't have to be relevant for the age the child is now.) For example, the aid could be used to help the child develop a social skill such as dressing or feeding. It could be something to help the child overcome a particular difficulty, for example colour recognition or reading through using a book. You must evaluate the use of the learning aid and analyse the benefits to the child studied. Recommendations for improvements also need to be included.

Assessment objectives

You will need to produce evidence as set out in the assessment objectives (AOs). The number of marks allocated is shown in brackets.

AO1: a description of **three** patterns (milestones) in each area of development of children, described from birth to **8** years

You identify the key stages and describe **three** patterns (milestones) in each area of development of children, described from birth to **8** years. You must cover physical. Intellectual, emotional and social development. Language and cognitive development must also be included. Your understanding of the patterns of development will help you to gain higher marks. (10)

AO2: an explanation of the factors that have influenced the child studied and how they have affected his or her development, comparing their development with the norms

You need to give descriptions of the factors that have affected the child's development. You must apply your knowledge of the factors which have influenced the child's development, both positively and negatively. Comparison between the child's development and the norm for each area must also be covered. Any variations from the norm need to be explained.

The writing used to present your information should convey meaning and use specialist vocabulary. (10)

AO3: research relating to **two** theories of play and how they can be reflected in the development of the child studied

You must use **three** sources to gather your information, e.g. existing toys, books, catalogues, and keep a detailed record of the sources used.

You must analyse how **two** theories of play can be reflected in the development of the child studied **Two** examples for each theory must be included. Judgements have to be included to access the higher marks. (15)

AO4: records of the planning and making of a learning aid for the child to use and an evaluation of the effectiveness of the aid and the benefits to the child studied

You must plan and make a learning aid for the child studied. This will include aims, objectives and planned learning outcomes. You need to explain the methods you will use to make the learning aid, including the resources required and timescales to be followed. You will then need to use the learning aid with the child and gather feedback from others, for example the child, parents, teacher, assessor or peers. Evaluate the effectiveness of the learning aid and its benefits to the child, making recommendations for improvement. (15)

References and further reading

Beaver, M., Brewster, J., Jones, P., Neaum, S., Tallack, J. (2002) *Babies and Young Children* Cheltenham: Nelson Thornes

Bowlby, J. (1953) *Child Care and the Growth of Love* Harmondsworth: Penguin

Brennand, H, Fairclough, J., Hall, V., Nicholson, E., Rees, E. (2001) *Child Development* London: Hodder & Stoughton

Bruce, T., Meggitt, C. (2002) *Childcare and Education* London: Hodder Arnold

Bryon, M. see www.ich.ucl.ac.uk/gosh_families/ask_do_jane_collins/relationships/sibling_rivalry.htm

Busak, J.J. (2002) *Why People Lie*

Fisher, A., Seamons, S., Blackmore, C., Snaith, M. (2005) *OCR Nationals Level 2* Oxford: Heinemann

Gilbert, P. (1997) *A Textbook of Nursery Nursing The Essentials* Cheltenham: Stanley Thornes

Hobart, C., Frankel, J. (1995) *A Practical Guide to Activities for Young Children* Cheltenham: Stanley Thornes

Hughes, B. (1996) *A Playworker's Taxonomy of Play Types*, 2nd edition London: Playlish

Meggitt, C., Sunderland, G. (2000) *Child Development An Illustrated Guide* Oxford: Heinemann

Minett, P. (2004) *Child Care and Development* London: John Murray

Rasmussen, V Ph.D, (2004) *Starting a Day Care Centre* (www.startingadaycarecenter.com)

Tassoni, P. (2000) *Certificate Child Care and Education* Oxford: Heinemann

Tassoni, P., Bulman, K., Beith, K., Robinson, M. (2005) *Children's Care and Development NVQ Level 3* Oxford: Heinemann

Tassoni, P., Beith, K., Eldridge, H., Gough, A. (2000) *Diploma Child Care and Education* Oxford: Heinemann

The Truth About Lying (www.bbc.co.uk)

Useful websites

Family statistics
    www.statistics.gov.uk
    www.surestart.gov.uk
    www.underfives.co.uk
Play Therapy
    www.playtherapy.org.uk
Toy Safety
    www.familyrapp.com
    www.rospa.com

Social trends

This unit covers the following sections:

15.1 Social trends and patterns in family life

15.2 Reasons for change in the strucutre of the family and the roles of individuals

15.3 Changes to service provision available to the family and individuals

15.4 Using data to explore and draw conclusions about the trends and patterns of family life

The family is widely believed to be the most important unit of social organisation, and an individual's family situation has a profound effect on their health and welfare. Within British society there is now a great variety of different types of family, and evidence suggests that the nature of the family is changing.

This unit develops your skills in analysing demographic data so that you can understand any social trends affecting the family and individuals. In particular, the unit focuses on analysing secondary sources of data to explore how family structure is changing, including increases in the rates of divorce, remarriage and cohabitation. The unit also looks at the health and social care services available to support families and individuals.

Many of the statistics used come from the 2005 edition of the government publication *Social Trends.* To prepare for the unit test and to improve your ability to analyse data, it would be useful to look at this publication on the Internet and perhaps download the first two chapters that cover population and households and families.

This unit builds on the knowledge and skills developed in Unit 1, Promoting Quality Care; Unit 7, Health as a Life Style Choice; and Unit 9, Caring for Older People. This unit also has links with Unit 11, Understanding Human Behaviour; and Unit 13, Child Development.

Assessment

This unit is assessed externally. A sample assessment is included at the end of the unit.

Section 1: Social trends and patterns in family life

In this section you will analyse data to examine the changes in the structure of families and households over the last 50 years. The data does not stand alone, as it represents significant changes in population and age structure in the UK in the last 50 years. Social trends are linked to social changes which have affected every aspect of daily life in the last 50 years.

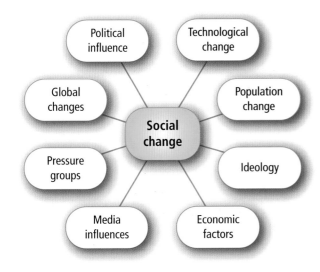

FIGURE 15.1 *The factors affecting social change*

Think it over

Look at the following changes in family life that have occurred in the last 50 years and decide whether they have been influenced by technological, economic, ideological or political factors, or a mixture of several factors.

1. lower birth rate
2. increased life expectancy
3. one-parent families
4. more people staying on for higher education.

We can see from these examples that social change occurs for a variety of reasons. In this section we examine in more detail the changes in the structure of families and households which reflect wider changes in society.

Study skills: understanding statistics

We will be looking at a range of data from various sources, including government statistics. It is important to be aware of how statistics are presented, and the meaning of the terms used in the tables. When you look at a table for the first time you should ask yourself certain questions:

1. Where was the data derived from?

2. When was the data collected?

3. If the data comes from a government department or a political party, what do we need to be aware of? Is there a political bias?

4. What are figures in the table – are they in percentages (%) or thousands ('000s)?

5. Are there any terms used that you aren't clear about? If so, you may need to refer to a dictionary or glossary, but you will find that there are often definitions given at the foot of the table.

Mean, median and mode

In many statistics that relate to averages, the terms **mean**, **median** or **mode** may appear. The **mean** average is worked out by adding all the values and dividing by the total number of values in the set (e.g. the mean of the values 5, 7, 6, 7, 5, 5 is 5.8; in other words, 35 divided by 6). However the mean average is not always a good representation of the data. For example, if you were calculating the average salaries of people in the UK and included very high incomes and very low incomes, the resulting mean could be very misleading. For this reason, in many of the tables we will be looking at, you will find that the **median** average is used. The median average is the middle value of a set of numbers arranged in ascending order. If the set has an even number of values then the median is the mean of the two middle numbers. So in the case of the set 5, 7, 6, 7, 5, 5, we would rearrange the numbers from lowest to highest (5, 5, 5, 6, 7, 7) and find that the median is the mean of 5 and 6; in other words, 5.5. In some statistics it may not matter too much whether the median or the mean is used – for example in looking at the height of policemen in London at the time when there was a minimum height requirement there would be a limited range. The modal average refers to the value that appears most frequently. In this example the modal average would be 5. This type of average is not usually used in official statistics. In this unit you will find that most averages are the median average.

Is a monastery a sort of family?

We will look in more detail at a range of family groupings in this section.

As we saw with defining 'family', there are always problems with definitions and it is important that terms are clearly defined. This is especially the case with the data that we use in this unit.

The nuclear family

The nuclear family is a family unit consisting of an adult male and female and their dependent offspring. Some sociologists who have studied the family see the nuclear family as the basic universal form of family structure. Before industrialisation in the UK, most people worked on the land and depended on the family for material support; the family form was extended, with several generations working together to support each other. According to some research studies the nuclear family developed from the need for a mobile workforce that could move around the country to find work in the towns and factories. There is still a great deal of dispute about family forms during the nineteenth century in the UK, but in the last 50 years there have been changes in family structure, particularly related to the nuclear family. The nuclear family was a very common unit of social organisation in the UK 50 years ago, now a range of other types of family has increased in importance, and the relative importance of the nuclear family has declined.

A traditional nuclear family

The number of children

The relationship between marriage and children has changed in the last 50 years. With the development of effective contraception, and changes in the role of women, the numbers of children being born (the fertility rate) has declined.

The decline in the average number of children per woman (family size) among women born in the mid-1930s onwards is the result of fewer woman having large families and more women remaining childless. Of women born in 1920 in England and Wales, 31 per cent had given birth to three or more children by the end of their childbearing years. Women born since the 1950s have waited longer before starting a family: 38 per cent of women born in 1948 were still childless at the age of 25 and this increased to 65 per cent of women born in 1978.

Think it over

Why do you think women are waiting longer to have their first child? Factors such as:

✱ being in education for a longer period

✱ developing a career

✱ being able to support yourself economically

✱ reliable contraception

could all be seen to be important factors.

Can you think of anything else?

Extended families

An extended family is a nuclear family that has been added to – either vertically, with the inclusion of grandparents and grandchildren, or horizontally with the inclusion of brothers and sisters of the original couple (i.e. the children's uncles and aunts). Family structures in the UK are becoming more diverse with the development of a multi-cultural society, and also because of a range of family forms.

Reconstituted families

A reconstituted family is a family in which one or both adults have been previously married and therefore children are living with a step-parent and perhaps step-brothers and step-sisters. The increasing rate of divorce is making this type of family more common.

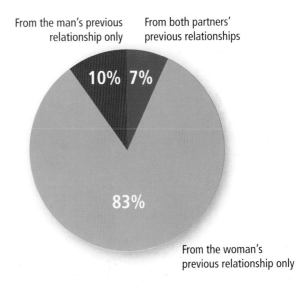

Step-families[1] with dependent children,[2] 2003/04
Great Britain

[1] Family head aged 16 to 59.
   Dependent children are persons under 16, or aged
[2] 16 to 18 and in full-time education, in the family unit,
   and living in the household.

Source: General Household Survey, Office for National Statistics

FIGURE 15.2 *Step-families with dependent children*

One-parent families

The numbers of children living in one-parent families tripled between 1972 and 2004. In 2004, 76 per cent of children lived in families headed by a couple.

Factors such as the increased level of divorce, the social acceptability of single mothers, and the levels of benefits available to single parents, may all partly explain this increase. However, there are many problems faced by single parents and their children. A high proportion of one-parent families live on low incomes, and therefore one-parent families are likely to experience various sorts of deprivation which can affect their health and well-being.

Dual-worker families

This term relates to a partnership in which both parties work. Many women combine working and looking after the home and family, and studies show that women who are working still take on most of the household and childcare tasks. Although dual-worker families may have a relatively high income, they may suffer from other stresses (particularly if trying to balance a full-time job with housework and childcare). The numbers of dual-worker families have increased over the last 50 years; social factors including

GREAT BRITAIN	PERCENTAGES				
	1972	1981	1992	2001	2004
Couple families					
1 child	16	18	17	17	17
2 children	35	41	38	37	37
3 or more children	41	29	27	24	23
Lone-mother families					
1 child	2	3	5	6	7
2 children	2	4	6	8	9
3 or more children	2	3	5	6	6
Lone-father families					
1 child	-	1	1	1	1
2 children	1	1	1	1	1
All children	100	100	100	100	100

Source: General Household Survey, Census, Labour Force Survey, Office for National Statistics

TABLE 15.1 *Increase in lone-mother families 1972 and 2004, and dependent children living in different family types*

occupation, class and ethnicity affect which couples are most likely to be dual workers. Many dual-worker families do so because of financial commitments rather than choice.

Childless couples

Fertility rates have fallen since the late 1960s and 1970s. Women have started childbearing at a later age and more women are remaining childless. About one in five women in England and Wales currently reaching the end of their fertile life are childless.

What if?

If fewer children are being born what effect will this have on:

* family structures?
* children's services?

Same-sex couples

Many same-sex couples live in stable relationships in the UK. Historically, some same-sex couples have taken part in 'marriage' ceremonies, although marriage between same-sex couples has had no legal standing. Prejudice against same-sex relationships has declined with a gradual changing of previously negative attitudes towards gay and lesbian people, and this has developed further with the 'coming out' of well-known figures in entertainment and politics. In some states in the USA and Australia, same-sex partnerships are recognised by law.

On 5 December 2005 the Civil Partnership Act came into force in the UK. This allows civil marriages between same-sex couples to take place in register offices. The Civil Partnership Act allows same-sex couples to make a formal, legal commitment to each other by forming a civil partnership. Before the Act, same-sex couples had no way of gaining formal legal recognition of their relationship and this caused a range of problems that heterosexual couples did not experience, especially those linked to inheritance when one partner dies.

The Act covers:

* employment and pension benefits
* the provision of support and maintenance for each partner and for any children of the family
* fair treatment for life assurance.

If the civil partnership breaks down a formal court-based process for its dissolution can occur.

At the moment it is difficult for a same-sex couple to adopt a child jointly; this will also be changed in England and Wales when the Adoption and Children Act (2002) is fully brought into force.

Single-person households

Since 1971 the number of single-person households has increased from 18 per cent to 29 per cent of all households. In the mid-1980s and 1990s these households consisted mainly of older women. This reflected the higher life expectancy of women compared with men, and the tendency for women to outlive their husbands.

In Table 15.2 we can see that 60 per cent of women over 75 were living alone. However in recent years the number of younger people living on their own has increased, particularly in the age group 25–44.

Think it over

Can you think of reasons for this change? Some possible factors are:

* increased divorce, when couples who split up tend to form two new households
* women earning more money and being able to support themselves
* people tending to marry later and staying single for longer.

Can you think of any more?

GREAT BRITAIN	PERCENTAGES				
	1986/87	1991/92	1996/97	2001/02[1]	2003/04[1]
Males					
16–24	4	4	5	7	6
25–44	7	9	11	17	15
45–64	8	9	10	15	14
65–74	17	18	21	19	19
75 and over	24	32	31	32	29
All aged 16 and over	9	11	12	16	15
Females					
16–24	3	3	3	3	3
25–44	4	5	6	6	8
45–64	13	13	12	14	15
65–74	38	37	39	35	34
75 and over	61	60	58	59	60
All aged 16 and over	16	16	16	17	17

[1]Data from 2001/02 onwards are weighted to compensate for non-response and to match known population distributions

Source: General Household Survey, Office for National Statistics

TABLE 15.2 *People living alone by sex and age*

Homelessness

Homelessness can result from changes in a person's circumstances. These can include disagreements within the family who may no longer want to support someone, the breakdown of family relationships, or financial problems leading to rent or mortgage arrears. Local councils have a statutory duty to ensure that suitable accommodation is available for applicants who are homeless through no fault of their own. Families with children, and households who include someone who is vulnerable because of old age, pregnancy, or physical or mental disability, have priority and councils have a 'homelessness duty' to provide accommodation for these groups.

According to the statistics, there is a disproportionate number of homeless people from ethnic minority groups. This means that the percentage of homeless people from ethnic minorities is far greater than the percentage of ethnic minorities in the population as a whole. For example, if 10 per cent of households in the UK population are headed by people from ethnic minorities, you would expect a similar figure in homeless figures. In 2003–04, 22 per cent of applicants accepted as homeless in England were from an ethnic minority group.

Think it over

Why do you think this is the case? Possible reasons could include:

* ethnic minorities, especially from Pakistani or Bangladeshi groups are more likely to be on low incomes or to be unemployed

* racial discrimination could affect their access to housing and employment.

ENGLAND	PERCENTAGES
One person	
Males	18
Females	19
Lone parent with dependent children	
Males	3
Females	35
Couple with dependent children	15
Other households	10
All households	100

[1]Households accepted as homeless and in priority need by local authorities

Source: Office of the Deputy Prime Minister

TABLE 15.3 *Homelessness*[1] *by household composition 2002/2003*

Think it over

Look at Table 15.3 and describe the pattern you see. We can see that the greatest number of people who are accepted as homeless are lone mothers.

Most households that are accepted as homeless by local councils are provided with temporary accommodation. Since the mid-1990s there has been a steady increase in homeless households, from 41,000 in March 1997 to 97,000 in March 2004. Reasons for this increase could include the following:

* less rented accommodation provided by the local councils

* breakdown of families

* more single-parent families.

In March 2004, 11 per cent of homeless people were accommodated in hostels or women's refuges and 7 per cent were living in bed and breakfast hotels. In April 2004, the Homelessness (Suitability of Accommodation) (England) Order (2003) came into effect. This order means that local councils in England can no longer place families with children in bed and breakfast hotels for more than six weeks. As a result, the number of homeless households living in bed and breakfast hotels fell.

Think it over

What are the problems for families with children who have to live in bed and breakfast hotels?

What could be the effects on:

* their health?

* their education?

* their diet?

Families who move around a great deal may not register with a GP, and they may have difficulty finding places in a local school. The lack of facilities in a bed and breakfast hotel can affect their physical and mental health because of limited living space, lack of cooking facilities and lack of privacy.

Economic activity and employment

In the 1950s unemployment was low as the UK was recovering from the war and traditional industries were in full production. In some industries there was a labour shortage and workers from the Commonwealth were encouraged to immigrate to the UK. These industries included the textile industry in the Midlands, the car manufacturing industry, the transport industry in London and also the NHS, which recruited workers from the Republic of Ireland and from the Caribbean. In the last 50 years, there have been changes with the decline of traditional industries due to competition from other countries, and the closure of many factories in the manufacturing sector. The work force itself has also changed with more part-time workers and fewer full-time permanent posts. Many part-time posts, in particular, are filled by women. The unions have less influence and fewer workers belong to a union. All these factors have had an impact on the levels of employment and unemployment in the last 50 years.

In the last ten years employment rates have continued to be high in the UK. However, the percentage of men in the UK who are economically active has declined, from 89 per cent in 1984 to 84 per cent in 2004 (Labour Force Survey). The percentage of women who are economically active has increased from 67 per cent in 1984 to 73 per cent in 2004. These changes are due to a range of factors including the decline of the manufacturing industry, changes in technology, changes in the skills required of the work force and the changing role of women.

The economic activity rate (i.e. percentage of people in the work force) is linked to the economic cycle. As the UK experiences economic growth, the number of jobs increases and unemployment falls. As the economy slows and goes into recession, unemployment tends to increase. The recession in the 1990s had a greater impact on unemployment among men than among women, as traditional manufacturing industries were most affected. The number of people deemed to be unemployed in 2004 was 1.4 million, but these figures are problematic, as the 'economically active' figures include those who are actively looking for work but are unemployed.

> **Key concept**
>
> People are considered to be *economically active* or 'in the work force' if they are aged 16 and over and are either in work or actively seeking work.

Unemployment

Reasons for unemployment (or economic inactivity) vary with age. Long-term sickness and disability are the main reasons for economic inactivity, particularly among 35–49-year-olds. In 2004 there were 7.8 million economically inactive people of working age in the UK; 60 per cent of these were women.

> **Did you know?**
>
> Long-term sickness and disability was the most common reason given for economic inactivity by men of working age in 2004. For women, the most common reason was looking after family or home. Of lone-parent households, 42 per cent were workless in 2004.

> **Think it over**
>
> Look at Table 15.4 and describe the pattern you see.
>
> Can you think of any additional information that would be helpful in analysing the figures?

We have already seen that ethnic minority groups are more likely to be in low-income households. If we had ethnicity included in the table it might give us additional understanding of factors affecting unemployment.

Unemployment rates vary across the UK. Unemployment is low in Southern and Central England, but some inner city areas such as Newham in London and parts of Manchester, the North East, East Anglia and Cornwall have high unemployment rates. Northern Ireland and Scotland also have high unemployment. Unemployment can be linked to the decline of traditional manufacturing industries in some areas. The collapse of the Rover car company in 2005 will have a great impact on unemployment in the Birmingham area and also on companies supplying Rover.

Unemployment and educational achievement

One of the key factors affecting unemployment is educational achievement. In 2004, men with no qualifications had a 45 per cent rate of unemployment; women with no educational qualifications had a 44 per cent rate.

Migration and emigration

> **Key concepts**
>
> *Migration:* the movement of people from one area to another.
>
> *Internal migration:* the movement of people to another region within the same country.
>
> *External migration:* the movement of people from one country to another.

| PERCENTAGES | | | | | |
UNITED KINGDOM	16–24	25–34	35–49	50–59/64	All aged 16–59/64
Males					
Long-term sick or disabled	5	38	60	53	37
Looking after family or home	1	12	17	4	6
Student	84	25	4	–	30
Retired	0	0	–	31	13
Other	10	26	18	12	14
All males	100	100	100	100	100
Females					
Long-term sick or disabled	4	10	24	42	21
Looking after family or home	22	72	59	27	45
Student	64	8	4	1	19
Retired	0	0	–	15	4
Other	10	10	11	16	12
All females	100	100	100	100	100

Data are not seasonally adjusted and have been adjusted in line with population estimates published in spring 2003.

Source: Labour Force Survey, Office for National Statistics

TABLE 15.4 *Reasons given for economic inactivity by sex and age, 2004*

The UK figures on migration are split into two categories:

* *Emigration:* the movement of people from the UK to another country

* *Immigration:* the movement of people from countries abroad to the UK.

The pattern of people entering and leaving the UK has changed during the twentieth century. As we have already discussed, immigration into this country increased in the 1950s. In the 1960s and 1970s various immigration controls were put in place that restricted immigration. Since 1983 there has been a net migration into the UK. If you look at the Table 15.5, you can see that more people are entering the country than leaving it. In 2003 an estimated 151,000 more people arrived to live in the UK for at least one year than left to live elsewhere. Net international immigration is projected to remain at a high level over the next 25 years. Nationals of the European Economic Area (EU plus Iceland, Liechtenstein and Norway) have the right to live in the UK provided they are working or able to support themselves financially. Nearly all other overseas nationals wishing to live permanently in the UK have to be accepted by the Home Office for settlement (grants of settlement). Between 2002 and 2003 the number of people accepted by the Home Office for settlement rose by 26,000 to 144,000. Figure 15.5 shows the number of people accepted through grants of settlement.

Look at Figure 15.5 and describe what you see. In 2003, 28 per cent of grants of settlement

UNITED KINGDOM	THOUSANDS					
	1993–1997			1998–2002		
	INFLOW	OUTFLOW	BALANCE	INFLOW	OUTFLOW	BALANCE
Work related	59.2	85.3	-26.1	103.4	92.8	10.6
Accompany/join partner	72.3	64.0	8.2	77.2	51.1	26.0
Formal study	61.8	13.0	48.8	91.2	13.7	77.5
Other[1]	93.2	70.6	22.6	164.6	99.3	65.3
No reason stated	20.6	23.8	-3.2	27.7	49.2	-21.5
All reasons	307.1	256.7	50.4	464.0	306.0	158.0

[1]Includes those looking for work, working holidaymakers, asylum seekers, those visiting friends and family, taking a long holiday or travelling for religious reasons

Source: Office for National Statistics

TABLE 15.5 *Average annual international migration by main reason for migration, 1993–1997 and 1998–2002*

Grants of settlement: by region of origin
United Kingdom

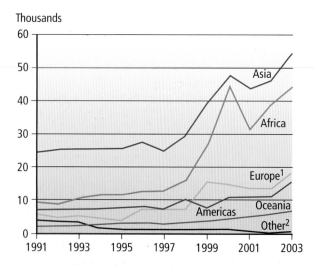

[1] European Economic Area (EEA) nationals may apply for settlement, but are not obliged to do so. The figures do not represent the total number of Europeans eligible to stay indefinitely in the UK. Data on EEA nationals granted settlement have not been recorded since 1998.

[2] Includes British Overseas citizens, those whose nationality was unknown and, up to 1993, acceptances where the nationality was not separately identified; from 1994 these nationalities have been included in the relevant geographical area.

Source: Home Office

FIGURE 15.3 *Number of people accepted through grants of settlement*

were to Asian nationals, with a further 31 per cent to African nationals. Between 1998 and 2002 the main reason given for immigration was 'other'; this includes asylum seekers.

In this section we have looked at a range of social trends in the family which are linked to demographic changes in the population and age structure of the UK. As life expectancy increases, and fewer children are being born in families, the age structure of families will alter and this will impact on family relationships. These trends are also linked to other factors that influence social change including political and economic influences. The family can be said to reflect the society in which it exists.

Think it over

Think about current story lines and characters in *EastEnders* or another soap opera you know. How far do they reflect the social trends affecting the family we have looked at in this section?

Changes in relationships within the family

The changes in the family have not only been ones of structure, but there have also been changes in the relationships of family members. For your assessment you need to be able to interpret data on patterns of family life in the UK in the last 50 years. Changes in the patterns of family life can have an impact on its members.

Look at this scenario and identify the changes that have occurred in family life that have impacted on the relationships in this family.

SCENARIO
Stella

Stella is 60. She has just retired and she was looking forward to spending her time with her husband doing various activities. She has two daughters and four grandchildren who live nearby. One daughter, Louise, is divorced and the other, Tracy, is a single parent. Both daughters are working.

Now Stella has retired, her daughters assume that Stella will help to look after her grandchildren (who are all under 8 years of age) so they can increase their hours at work.

Stella's mother, who is a widow, recently had a fall at home. She has been discharged from hospital but she still needs help with cooking, cleaning and shopping. Stella feels she must help her out.

Stella's husband, Dennis, is annoyed that the time he looked forward to being with his wife is taken up with family responsibilities.

You may decide that the following factors are relevant:

* increased life expectancy means older people are living longer and are often on their own

* the increase in single-parent families puts pressure on other members of the family to help out

* the increase in divorce has a financial impact on family life

* as married women continue to enter the workforce, childcare is an issue.

Try it out

Look at a selection of problem pages in magazines and identify examples where changes in the family and in the relationships of family members have caused problems.

What if?

If you were appointed Minister for the Family, what support would you try to give families? How much should the state support families and how much should we encourage families to help each other?

Trends that have changed family relationships

Births outside marriage

Marriage and childbearing have become less strongly associated over the last 35 years in the UK, with 41 per cent of births in 2003 occurring outside marriage. Much of this increase is due to cohabiting couples rather than to single mothers. In the 1960s there was a great deal of stigma attached to having an 'illegitimate' child. Nowadays this term is never used. In the media you see plenty of examples of celebrities having children before being married or not getting married at all.

Cohabitation

Cohabitation is a fairly recent trend. Since 1986 the number of unmarried men and women under the age of 60 living together has increased. Before that time cohabitation was not socially acceptable. With the increase in divorce, and changes in society's attitudes towards marriage, cohabitation has increased but it is still difficult to establish the true picture of cohabitation, as if a woman lives with a man this may affect her benefits.

There are several factors you could discuss:

* the average age of marriage is rising and many people may decide to live together before they get married

* with the increase in divorce, many divorced people may not wish to remarry

* with children from a previous marriage to consider, some people feel that their children would not like them to marry.

Conjugal roles within the family

Conjugal roles are the roles played by husband and wife within a marriage. The increase in cohabitation has led to the term 'conjugal roles' being increasingly replaced by 'domestic division of labour'. The roles taken by men and women are increasingly shared; i.e. either men or women may do domestic jobs, take the children to school, and do the weekly shopping. However, according to the *UK 2000 Time Use Study*, women still undertake most of the household chores and childcare. Adults who were 16 and over were asked to keep a diary of how they spent their time on a particular day during the week and a particular day during the weekend. The survey found a significant difference between men and women on certain activities.

Think it over

Look at Table 15.7 and describe the patterns you see. What may be the problems with conducting a survey in this way? How could you check that the findings are reliable?

Studying the family can present problems for the researcher, as family life is private. You can ask people to fill in a questionnaire about their family and their relationships but you may not get truthful answers. In all research, you need to ensure that any information you get is kept confidential, and the identity of the person is not revealed. When studying family lives that are different from our own, we must be careful not to judge others. Issues about research are more fully covered in Section 4.

SCENARIO
Mary's story

'My husband died when he was 55 and I was left with four children, aged between 14 and 22. I managed well financially because he had a good job and I had his company pension. I also worked myself. I had a lot of supportive friends. I was not really looking for another partner but I met Bill. He was divorced and had four boys aged between 9 and 15. All the children got on well. His boys lived with their mother after the divorce. Bill did not have much money after the divorce as his wife had the family home and he was paying her maintenance. Bill moved in to live with me as the two oldest children had left home. It seemed OK but it was a strain at times, and one of his sons came to live with us for a while. Once all the children had left home, I sold the house and bought a property with Bill. The children were worried about their inheritance and what would happen if I died. It all caused a lot of trouble so in the end Bill bought his own place that we use at weekends. None of our children would like us to marry, and I don't see the point of it at our age.'

GREAT BRITAIN	PERCENTAGES	
	MALES	FEMALES
1986	11	13
1991/92	19	19
1996/97	22	22
2001/02[2]	25	28
2003/04[2]	25	27

[1]Aged 16 to 59. Includes those who described themselves as separated but were, in a legal sense, still married.

[2]Data from 2001/02 are weighted to compensate for non-response and to match known population distributions.

Source: General Household Survey, Office for National Statistics

TABLE 15.6 *Non-married people[1] cohabiting by sex*

Summary

There have been many changes in family structures in the last 50 years. Demographic changes have led to changes in the structure of the population as a whole, as well as changes to the age structure. These changes

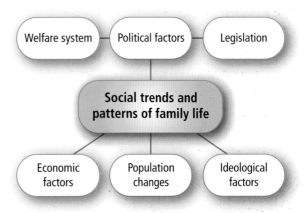

UNITED KINGDOM	HOURS AND MINUTES PER DAY	
	MALES	FEMALES
Sleep	8:23	8:33
Leisure		
Watching TV and Video/DVD	2:41	2:17
Social life and entertainment	1:16	1:33
Reading and listening to radio and music	0:36	0:35
Hobbies and games	0:26	0:16
Sport	0:18	0:11
All leisure	5:17	4:52
Employment and study[2]	4:17	2:42
Housework and childcare	2:17	4:03
Personal care[3]	2:07	2:19
Travel	1:28	1:21
Other	0:09	0:10

[1]Adults aged 16 and over
[2]Includes voluntary work and meetings
[3]Includes eating, drinking, washing and dressing

Source: Time Use Survey, Office for National Statistics

TABLE 15.7 *Time spent on main activities[1] by sex 2000–2001*

have influenced social and economic aspects. Relationships between family members have also changed. Traditional models of family life have been affected by changes in attitudes towards childbirth, marriage and homosexuality.

Section 2: Reasons for change in the structure of the family and the roles of individuals

In this section we will discuss some of the reasons for the changes in the structure of the family and how the roles of family members have changed. In your assessment you will be tested on changes in family structures in the last 50 years.

Divorce

Marriages and divorces[1]
United Kingdom

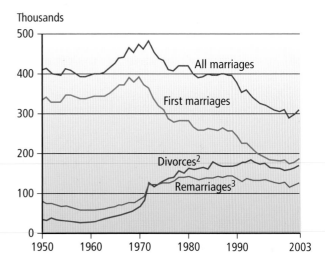

Thousands

1 For both partners.
2 Includes annulments. Data for 1950 to 1970 for Great Britain only.
3 For one or both partners.

Source: Office for National Statistics; General Register Office for Scotland; Northern Ireland Statistics and Research Agency

FIGURE 15.4 *The rates of marriages and divorces in the UK between 1950 and 2003*

Look carefully at Figure 15.4 and describe the pattern you see between 1970 and 2003. In 1969 the Divorce Reform Act introduced a single ground for divorce, the irretrievable breakdown of the marriage. This could be based on adultery, desertion, separation, or unreasonable behaviour. The Act came into effect in 1971 in England and Wales. From Figure 15.4 it is clear that marriages as a whole have declined in number during this period and divorces have increased.

Think it over

Can you think of reasons for these changes?

Factors could include the decline of the influence of religion and the increase in the acceptability of other forms of partnerships, including cohabitation.

Remarriage

Following divorce, people often form new relationships and may remarry. Looking at remarriages in Figure 15.4, we can see that the number of remarriages since 1990 has tended to remain fairly constant at around 120,000.

Think it over

Discuss within your groups the possible impacts on individual family members of this pattern – on children, grandparents, in-laws and former partners.

Contraception

One of the reasons for the falling birth rate has been the development of effective contraception. In the 1960s the contraceptive pill was developed, and this is still the contraceptive of choice for women aged between 16 and 49. The type of contraception a woman uses varies with her age. Women under 35 are more likely to use the pill. As a woman gets older she is more likely to be sterilised, or she will have a partner who has had a vasectomy. Many younger women aged 16 to 17 use the pill. The development of effective contraception has affected women's roles. Women are more able to choose when they have their children and they can develop their careers in their 20s. However, it has also meant that many women are putting off having a family until they are in their 30s or 40s. If you look at *Social Trends* you will see how the age at which women have children has increased.

The teenage pregnancy rate in the UK is the highest in Europe and the government has developed a teenage pregnancy strategy to try to reduce this. Many health trusts offer an informal contraceptive advice service to young people. The problem with this approach is that young women are targeted when young men should also be made more aware. Ideas such as a 'Love Bus' touring local youth clubs and estates and giving advice have been tried. Secondary schools also offer an advice service, but this may be a problem for certain religious groups who do not approve of contraceptive advice being offered in an educational setting.

Think it over

If women are having their children when they are older, what positive and negative effects will this have?

Think it over

How could you promote contraception to young people? Sexual health is an issue in the UK nowadays with the increase of STDs (sexually transmitted diseases) among young people. The pill may offer protection from pregnancy, but does not protect against STDs and HIV. Condom use could be seen as an ethical problem among some groups who do not approve of artificial birth control methods.

Emergency contraception

The 'morning after' pill has been obtainable from chemists, walk-in centres and minor injuries units since 2001. Most women use their own GP to obtain this pill, and women under 30 are more likely to use this. Condom failure is usually given as the reason for obtaining this pill. Details about contraception and sexual health are available on the National Statistics website (www.statistics.gov.uk).

Abortion

The Abortion Act (1967) came into effect in 1968 and allows the termination of a pregnancy by a registered doctor under certain conditions. Before the Act came into effect, many women had 'back street' abortions which often resulted in infections and the death of the mother. A legally-induced abortion must be certified by two registered doctors as justified because the continuation of the pregnancy would involve risk to the life of the pregnant woman, to her physical or mental health, or to her family.

The number of legal abortions in England and Wales has increased from 23,641 in 1968 to 186,274 in 2001, (Abortion Statistics 2001, Department of Health).

Abortion rates:[1] by age
England & Wales

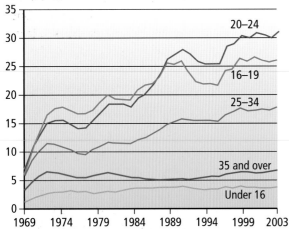

Rates per 1,000 women

[1] The rates for girls aged under 16 are based on the population of girls aged 13–15. The rates for women aged 35 and over are based on the population of women aged 35–44.

Source: Office for National Statistics; Department of Health

FIGURE 15.5 *Abortion rates by age*

Look at Figure 15.5 carefully and identify the pattern you see. Do these figures relate to the changes we have already seen in family life?

Cultural and racial diversity

The UK is now seen as a multi-cultural society. In the 2001 census, about 10 per cent of the population were from an ethnic minority background. Ethnicity is a difficult concept to define as it includes religion, culture and way of life, including dress and language used. Because of this problem groups of people are often defined by culture rather than ethnicity, so the Welsh and the Irish can also be said to belong to a separate culture.

Ethnic or racial monitoring takes place in education and employment. This is one way of ensuring that people are treated fairly, whatever their racial background. One method of ethnic monitoring is to ask people what ethnic group they belong to. This can cause problems, as people may see themselves as belonging to one group but an outsider may see them as belonging to another. In this census people were asked to say what their ethnic group was and therefore, the figures from the census may not reflect the true numbers of black and ethnic minority people in the UK.

In family life, cultural diversity means that different groups will have different family forms; for example, West Indian families are often headed by a female and include other older women. In some Asian families the eldest son takes responsibility for his older parents. Italian men tend to live with their parents until they get married, and grandparents may also live with them. Health and social care workers need to be aware of different family forms and also customs including diet, washing practices and religious observance that reflect the culture of different groups.

An increasing older population

As we have already seen, the number of births is declining and life expectancy is rising. With these two factors together the population is changing so that an increasing percentage of people in the population are over 65.

Think it over

In your groups think about the consequences of this pattern for:

* housing
* health and social care services
* employment
* government policy.

Smaller workforce

One result of an ageing population is that there will be fewer people in work, and a larger number of people who are retired. People who are in work pay income tax and other taxes. People who are retired claim pensions, and may have less money to spend (and pay correspondingly lower taxes). They may also be entitled to benefits which are funded through taxation.

Look at Figure 15.6 carefully and describe the patterns you see. What are the implications of these patterns?

Pensioners'[1] gross income: by source[2]
Great Britain

£ per week at 2002/03 prices[3]

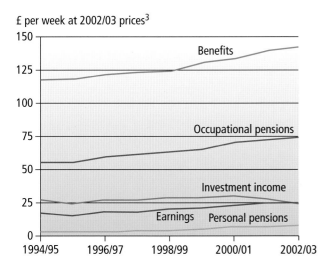

[1] Pensioner units are either pensioner couples where the man is over 65, or single pensioners over state pension age (65 for men, 60 for women).
[2] Excludes 'other income'.
[3] Adjusted to 2002/03 prices using the retail prices index less local taxes.

Source: Pensioners' Income Series, Department for Work and Pensions

FIGURE 15.6 *Composition of income for older people*

Economic factors

In the last 50 years many economic factors have affected changes in the structure of the family. These interlink with factors such as changes in women's role, the trend towards home ownership, the cost of childcare and the cost of maintaining a child from birth to adulthood. As more students enter university, parents support their children financially for longer. With the current student loan system students leave university in debt, this means that older children are tending to leave home later as they cannot afford to buy a property or to rent while they are still repaying debts. This can also affect when they get married or cohabit, and when they have children. As we have already seen, people are marrying later, if they marry at all, and they also have children later.

Another example of economic factors affecting households is the increase in divorce. When partners split, the mother and children are usually awarded the family home by the courts. Instead of one household, the family now has two households with the same amount of income but more expenditure, which will affect the standard of living for all members of the family. Single parents are more likely to live in poverty.

The changing role of women

The traditional role of women after the Second World War was as mother and home-maker. The 1944 Education Act provided free secondary education for all children, and this meant that children who won places in grammar schools could go there. Grammar schools were single sex, and girls' grammar schools offered the educational opportunities they needed to enter higher education and take on a wider range of roles in the workforce.

The roles of both men and women are changing, with men taking on roles that were associated with women in the past – childcare, working in primary schools, shopping and cooking. Compared with 50 years ago, it is now much more common for women to have higher-paid jobs and return to the workforce after having their children.

The changing concept of childhood

Childhood is defined by sociologists as the time during which the person has not reached adult status. Every society has a different concept of what childhood means, and this changes from society to society and from one chronological period to another. In the Middle Ages children were seen as young adults. Childhood, as we know it, evolved with the development of the educational system. The official school leaving age is now 16, but during the twentieth century it rose from 11 to 13 to 15, as a result of legislation.

In some countries children work from the age of 5. Legislation in the UK reflects the view that children are vulnerable and need to be protected, but the age when children can do certain activities varies. For example, the ages at which you can buy cigarettes, drink in a pub, or have sexual intercourse are laid down by law, but actual practice may not reflect the legal situation.

Try it out

Interview a friend or family member who was a child or teenager during the 1950s, to find out how they perceive the differences between life for young people then and now.

Changes in educational provision

In the last 50 years there have been many changes to the way people access education and study. Education has expanded at both ends of the age spectrum, with increasing provision for nursery education as well as rising numbers of older people returning to study.

Children under the age of 5 are starting school younger, and with the extended hours' policy, schools are staying open longer so that parents can go to work and then collect their children on the way home. Childcare places are expanding for the under threes to enable single parents to return to work.

Think it over

Can you think of some effects of these changes on the family and the child?

Special needs children have been encouraged to enter mainstream schools, instead of attending special schools. They are **statemented** and their needs assessed, and schools must provide support for them. Many parents of special needs children feel that special schools provided well-qualified staff to support their children, but others thought that by attending mainstream schools special needs children would be more easily integrated in society.

Think it over

What do you think about the policy of educating special needs children in mainstream schools? Draw up a list of the good things and bad things about this policy from the point of view of the children, parents and staff.

Higher education

Government policy since the 1960s has been focused on the expansion of higher education. Nowadays more people take A levels and go on to university than ever before. University places have increased and former further education colleges and polytechnics have become recognised as universities.

There has also been an increase in older people becoming students and studying for a degree or other qualification. The government's policy on life-long learning encourages everyone to continue studying and developing their skills.

In the last 50 years, changes to education and training may have resulted in more people achieving academic qualifications, but the decline in vocational training and apprenticeship schemes has led to a skills shortage in the UK.

Educational attainment

There are still notable differences in the educational qualifications achieved by different groups on the basis of:

* social class
* ethnicity
* gender
* regional differences.

The National Curriculum operates in England and Wales. Scotland and Northern Ireland have their own curricula. In 2004, the proportion of boys in England reaching the required standard for reading and writing in Key Stage 1 and English at Key Stages 2 and 3 was lower than that of girls.

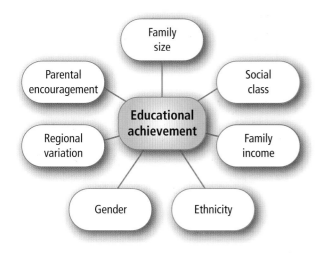

FIGURE 15.7 *Some factors that affect educational achievement*

At GCSE level, girls continue to out-perform boys in all subjects; in A levels the same pattern occurs.

Research into differences in educational achievement

Research has looked at reasons for differences in educational achievement. The Green Paper *Work and Parents* suggests that children who have limited contact with their father will perform less well. Children under 5 whose mothers go to work achieve exam results that are below those whose mothers stay at home (research quoted in *The Sunday Telegraph,* 4 February 2001).

The child's position in the family has also been linked to educational achievement – the eldest child in a family tends to do better than younger siblings because it is assumed that they have more attention given to them by parents and they also act as teachers to their younger brothers and sisters (University College London, 2005).

We can see from these examples that research tends to focus on either the school itself or on the family. Government policy has tended to focus on schools but recent initiatives, such as Sure Start, focus on supporting the whole family and how this support can help learning.

The Department for Education and Skills White Paper *Schools Achieving Success* (2001) sets out the government's strategy for improving

What if?

If you were going to do a piece of research to find out why these differences exist, how would you go about it? Previous research into differences in educational achievement has focused on:

* the attitudes of young people towards education

* the interactions that take place in the classroom

* the educational qualifications of parents and their attitudes towards education

* differences between mixed- and single-sex classes

* ethnicity and social class differences.

We can see from the quantitative data in government statistics that these differences do exist but statistics do not tell us the reasons behind the differences.

Would you use qualitative and quantitative data in your study?

Qualitative data could include:

* interviews with students and parents

* group discussions with students in single-sex or mixed-sex groups

* asking students to record their feelings about studying in some way – like a diary.

Quantitative data could include the following:

* attendance patterns using the register

* results of tests and marks for homework

* questionnaires.

As with all research, you would need to make sure that the method you choose answers the research question asked. You would need to gain permission for your study and to ensure confidentiality. You would also need to think about how to analyse and present your findings.

schools. As part of the Neighbourhood Renewal programme the department aims to:

* raise achievement in schools and encourage young people to continue in education and training
* reduce achievement gaps between ethnic groups, social classes, gender and regions
* encourage people who have left school to return to education
* promote equal opportunities for everyone in schools.

Aims of the White Paper

Primary education

Standards in maths and English will be raised so that by 2006 the number of schools where pupils achieve Level 4 or above rises.

Secondary education

Standards in English, maths, ICT and science will increase so that 85 per cent of 14-year-olds will achieve level 5 or above by 2007 (80 per cent in science). By 2006 at least 25 per cent of students should achieve the equivalent of five GCSEs grades A to C.

Educational attainment in higher education

Increasing numbers of students have gone into higher education in recent years. In 2002–03 there were 2.4 million students in higher education, 56 per cent of whom were female. Young people in manual social classes are under-represented in higher education in Great Britain and the gap in attainment between students from manual and non-manual backgrounds has increased. People from Black African-Caribbean and Bangladeshi backgrounds are less likely to have a degree than people from other groups.

As more people achieve A levels and degrees we should have a more skilled workforce, but often the skills used in the workplace are more practical than the skills taught in secondary and higher education. With the closure of many apprenticeship schemes, there is a shortage of skilled manual workers in plumbing, carpentry and engineering. Many of these workers now come from the EU where training schemes still operate. However, there are government initiatives such as the Modern Apprenticeships Schemes and Return to Work retraining schemes which may help solve this problem. *The Foster Report on Further Education* (November 2005) recommended that further education colleges should be relaunched as skills training centres.

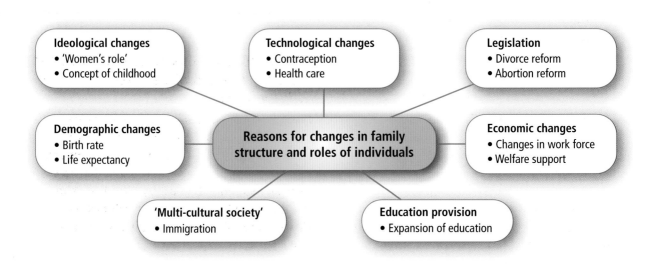

1. In 2005 increasing numbers of students went to university. What effects may this have on:

    * the individual

    * the family structure

    * society?

2. Many women are choosing to concentrate on their careers and put off having children until later. What effects may this have on:

    * the individual

    * the family structure

    * society?

3. Demographic trends show that there is a rising older population in the UK. What effects could this have on:

    * the individual

    * the family

    * society?

4. The Divorce Reform Act of 1969 led to an increase in the numbers of divorces taking place in England and Wales. What effects may this have on:

    * the individual

    * the family

    * society?

Summary

In this section we have looked at the many changes in family structure and in the roles of family members over the last 50 years.

Section 3: Changes to service provision available to the family and individuals

As the structure of the family changes, the provision of services will vary to meet the needs of the family and its members. In this section we will cover the different types of services available to support the family, and consider how service provision is changing. We will also look at the main roles and responsibilities of health and social care professionals who work with families.

The statutory, private and voluntary sectors

Services that are available to families and individuals are provided by three sectors – statutory, private and voluntary.

Main roles and responsibilities of health and social care professionals who work with the family

The main focus of responsibility for professionals who work with families and children is to protect children and support family members. This can be seen clearly in Figure 15.8, which gives an example of a visit by a health visitor soon after the birth of a child, with factors affecting the child, mother and whole family being considered.

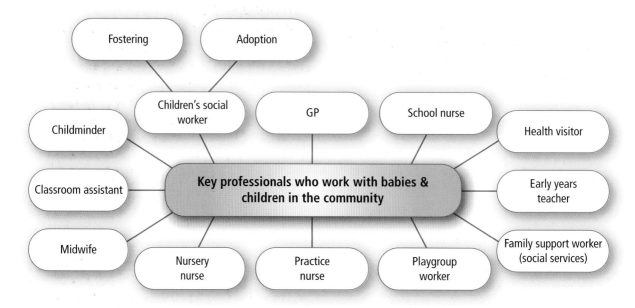

FIGURE 15.8 *Some key professionals who work with children*

Specific responsibilities of health and social care professionals who work with the family include:

* liaising with other professionals
* referring to other agencies if required
* reporting issues of concern
* maintaining confidentiality
* promoting healthy living
* providing information regarding benefits and other support
* maintaining a child-centred approach at all times.

This is covered in more detail in the section on child protection.

With the development of interagency working, key professionals work together supporting children and families as a team, with frequent meetings planning care for the families in their area. Individual case conferences vary greatly, but if there is a child-protection issue, a case conference will be held where professionals working with the family and child will discuss written evidence documenting the situation. Professionals might include the health visitor, the family support worker (social worker), the school nurse and family

doctor. The parents or carers of the child have a right to be informed that the conference is taking place and the chair of the meeting (who would be a senior member of the children's services team) would decide whether it is appropriate for parents to attend. If parents do attend they have the right to bring along an advocate, or someone else who can support them. Children's services are now organised as a separate department from adult social services and there is close working between health and social care.

The aim of the government is to develop Children's Trusts which will include everyone involved in supporting families. In 2005 there were 35 Pathfinder (or Pilot) Children's Trusts in England. By 2008 there will be Children's Trusts in all areas. A Children's Trust in one London borough has been set up to support children with disabilities and long-term health needs but in the future it will be extended to provide support to all children and families in the area.

Services to reduce family breakdown

Many factors can contribute to family breakdown. As part of the multi-agency approach to supporting families and children, a variety of agencies provide support to families in the case of breakdown.

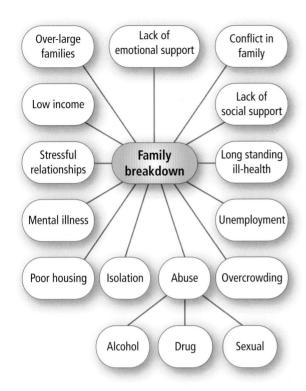

Parenting skills

Many parents who find it hard to cope have had disruptive childhoods themselves – perhaps they were in care, or their parents had died or divorced. People in this situation often find it difficult to cope when they have their own children. This can put pressure on the family. Apart from the help provided by voluntary organisations such as Home-start, there are also other sources of help available locally, such as parenting courses run by health visitors.

Try it out

The website for Home-start (www.home-start. org.uk) lists all the local groups. Find the one in your area and find out what they do. Look at their annual report and you will find that they are closely involved in helping families and they work closely with colleagues in health care and social work.

FIGURE 15.9 *Factors that can contribute to family breakdown*

Look at Figure 15.10 and describe what you see. You can see that there is a mixture of health and social care support, including the voluntary sector.

Children with behavioural problems

Behavioural problems can put a strain on the family. To help with this, there are child-centred support programmes provided by NHS psychologists

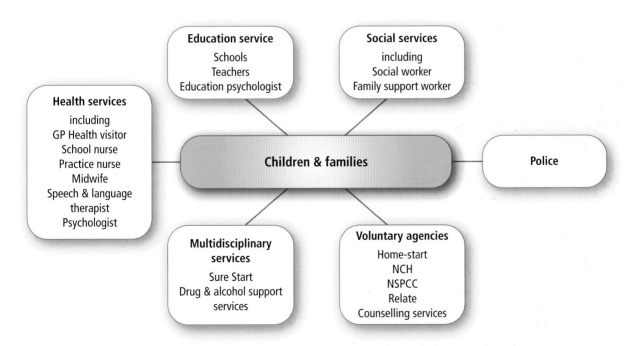

FIGURE 15.10 *The agencies that may support children and families*

Home-start

Home-start is a national voluntary organisation that offers informal and friendly support for families with young children. The support is free, confidential and non-judgemental. Many families are referred to Home-start by health visitors or social workers, but families also refer themselves.

Home-start relies on volunteers to visit families. Volunteers are trained and supported by a mentor when they first start. Volunteers are people who have had children themselves and know that childcare problems are quite usual. They help with children, doing simple activities such as taking them out to the park. This support can be particularly welcome if there are several children under five. The volunteers encourage and support parents and offer practical help and reassurance.

Parents contact Home-start for a variety of reasons. They may feel isolated if they have no close family near them; they may be finding it hard to cope because of their own or their child's physical or mental illness; or they may need a friendly face to discuss their concerns with. Many people feel more comfortable talking to a volunteer rather than to a health professional who they may feel will judge them or refer the child to social services. As well as providing practical support and help with children, Home-start also sets up parents' groups.

Home-start volunteers give active support to parents who are struggling, including taking children on outings

and voluntary organisations to support children and families. In one family centre, children who are aged between 3 and 8 years old are supported and encouraged to express their feelings through art, play and role-play without the need for verbal communication. Children who use this centre:

* have suffered domestic violence
* have a parent or carer who suffers from depression
* have experienced loss or separation
* have parents or carers who misuse drugs or alcohol
* experience abuse
* have a parent with mental health problems
* experience harassment.

The family centre mentioned above takes referrals from GPs, health visitors, schools and social workers. An initial meeting would take place with the child, the family and the key worker. As part of the assessment process the psychologist would meet the family in their

SCENARIO

A parent's story

When my health visitor suggested that I attend this Home-start group due to the fact that I had severe post-natal depression, my first reaction was 'not another group!' I couldn't have been more wrong. From day one I was made to feel welcome and at last there were people with similar problems and for the first time I didn't feel abnormal just because I couldn't cope with my own children.

home, followed by a further meeting with the child and the key worker. In this centre children are supported in groups, but if it was felt necessary the child could receive individual sessions. The group work sessions last for one hour for 16 sessions.

What if?

Children who are experiencing these problems often cope by displaying certain behaviours. If you were working in a nursery class, what behaviour would you think may indicate there was a problem? You need to be careful about this, as very often children with stressful situations may not show any unusual behaviour.

Warning signs could include:

* aggressive outbursts – physical or verbal

* temper tantrums

* soiling themselves

* uncommunicative behaviour.

Sure Start Centres

Key concept

Sure Start: a government programme covering children up to the age of 14 (16 for those with special needs). Sure Start services are organised jointly by the statutory and voluntary sectors. Services include children's centres and extended schools. These services are covered in greater detail on page 252. More information is available on the Internet (www.surestart.gov.uk).

Family services will be offered within Sure Start programmes at Sure Start Centres, so all services for families and children are in the same location. Referral will be easier and support should available at an early stage once a problem is identified.

Assistance during family breakdown

A range of services assist families that are in danger of breaking down. A website gives information on advice to parents and this page gives links to services that are available (www.direct.gov.uk).

Counselling

Counselling can be arranged either for one partner or a couple. Counselling is available on the NHS and a GP refers people, but this is usually for six weeks at most and there may be a waiting list. The voluntary sector, including churches, may offer counselling. Relate is a voluntary organisation that offers counselling to couples who are experiencing difficulties. Although Relate is a voluntary organisation, it employs psychologists and counsellors, and clients are asked to make a contribution towards the cost of the service. Currently the cost of a counselling session is £50, but clients with a low income would be asked to give what they can afford.

Mediation

Family mediation helps those involved in family breakdown to communicate better with one another and to reach their own decisions about all or some of the issues arising from separation or divorce. Issues would include arrangements about children, property and finance. The National Family Mediation (NFM) service is available to help divorcing couples reach agreement without bias. The NFM can also help people who are trying to save their relationship. More details about the organisation are available on their website (www.nfm.u-net.com).

Divorce

If parents separate or divorce and can't agree on arrangements for their children, they may refer their dispute to a family court for a decision. Most court cases involving children are about disputes between parents over where the children should live and what contact they should have with the absent parent. After the Children Act (1989), the term 'custody' is no longer used and terms 'parental responsibility' and 'residence' are used instead. 'Parental responsibility' means the rights and responsibilities a parent has in respect of the child. A 'residence order' sets out who the child should live with. Residence orders can sometimes be shared. The term 'contact' replaces the previous term 'access'. Contact is when the child spends time visiting or staying with the parent or other people such as grandparents. The Children and Family Court Advisory and Support Services (or

CAFCASS) safeguards and protects the welfare of children involved in family court proceedings. It advises the court so that decisions are made in the best interests of the children concerned. CAFCASS gets involved when parents cannot agree about the arrangements for their children and they ask the court to decide the arrangements. CAFCASS would ask a Children and Family Reporter to help. These are trained social workers with a special interest in families and children. They are independent of social services and other agencies and their main concern is the welfare of the child. The CAFCASS website gives details of how the system operates and it may be useful for you to look at this (www.cafcass.gov.uk).

Apart from divorcing or separating couples, CAFCASS may also be involved when someone applies to adopt a child or when social services are trying to take a child into care. In every instance the main concern of CAFCASS is the interests of the child.

Supporting children during a divorce

Divorce or separation is a difficult time for all the family and children can often feel it is their fault the family has broken down. Parents can help their children by:

* explaining what is happening

* maintaining routines – going to the same school, clubs and activities as usual

* reassuring the child that it is not their fault.

In a research project 'the KIDS Project' (Robinson and Scanlay, Cardiff University) researchers listened to 104 children between the ages of 5 and 16 whose parents' marriage had broken down. The children enjoyed taking part, because they could talk about things they could not discuss with their parents and they felt they could talk through their problems. They also felt that by taking part in the project they could help other children who may be affected by family breakdown. The study included the following findings:

* Divorce disrupted the sense of continuity children had in their lives. They responded by trying to control the impact of events and by seeking to follow a 'normal' way of life as soon as possible.

* Communication between children and parents was not always effective. Children acknowledged they did not always understand what parents were trying to say and they were aware of their own difficulties in asking for information.

* Children's understanding of the legal process was poor and they tended to rely on knowledge gained from misleading television or cinema portrayals.

* Children often felt excluded from the decisions which directly affected them and expressed a wish to be considered and consulted at all stages.

* Children often sought to talk to others, especially friends, to secure reassurance and advice or to be listened to. They felt they would have benefited from direct access to information they wanted and to people who would listen, accept and understand.

Child protection services

In recent years there have been major developments in policy and practice in children's services, influenced by the *Safeguarding Children Report* (2002) and the *Laming Report* (2003) which was a report on the way in which child protection services should be organised following the death from abuse of Victoria Climbie. The Children Act (2004) was the basis for the national framework for local change programmes that had to be implemented by all organisations offering services to children. This programme was called *Every Child Matters: Change for Children*. More details are on the website (www.everychildmatters.gov.uk). Current policy and practice related to children has to ensure that five key areas are addressed:

* *being healthy:* enjoying good physical and mental health and living a healthy life style

* *staying safe:* being protected from harm and neglect

* *enjoying and achieving:* getting the most out of life and developing the skills for adulthood

* *making a positive contribution:* being involved in the community and society and not engaging in anti-social or offending behaviour

* *achieving economic well-being:* not being prevented by economic disadvantage from achieving their full potential in life.

In the past, many cases of child abuse were undetected because the different organisations involved, such as the police, schools, health and education services, did not communicate with each other. As a result of current government guidelines, organisations that used to work separately now work in partnership so that communities can develop strategies to prevent social exclusion, anti-social behaviour, ill-health and abuse.

Current guidelines define 'vulnerable children' as those disadvantaged children who would benefit from extra help from health and social workers, as well as other agencies such as schools, in order to maximise their life chances. 'Children in need' are defined as a highly vulnerable group of children who are already receiving help from social services and elsewhere. The Government estimates about 36 per cent of the child population are vulnerable and 2.7–3.6 per cent of the child population is in need. In one London borough, the 0–19 population is 45,750. If we used government estimates, this would mean 16,500 vulnerable children and up to 1,600 children in need in the borough.

Roles and responsibilities of child protection workers

To develop an effective system of child protection, councils and health workers need to:

* support parents and carers

* have an early intervention system so that vulnerable children are identified early so that they can be protected

* work together but have a key worker who is the lead professional

* have a common assessment approach to assess children at risk

* develop children's centres based on the Sure Start model

* have joint inspections of local children's services (up to nine inspectors from different professional groups can be involved in Joint Annual Reviews).

Figure 15.11 shows the Child Concern Model that is being adopted by several areas in order to protect children.

Role of professionals within the model

Health visitors are the first contact with a family, but many other professionals are also involved. School nurses and nursery nurses also work developing children's services in the community, particularly with the extended schools programme. In the core service health visitors, nursery nurses, school nurses and registered nurses work together to support the family and protect the child. Each visit has a specific aim from antenatal contact to contact in secondary school. At each home visit the health professional will assess the following areas (see Table 15.8):

* mental and physical health of child and parent or carer

* the family situation and home environment, including housing, employment, income, benefits, family support and social integration.

As a result of problems in the past with sharing information about children at risk of abuse, Area Child Protection Committees (ACPCs) have been set up to encourage effective working relationships between different services and professional groups. One way of achieving this is through the development of records on children seen to be 'at risk' that will be shared by all members of the team.

Joined-up record keeping

In one PCT, working in partnership with the social services, the professional workers developed a system of colour coding records that applied to all agencies dealing with children. Colour coding helps the workers to identify the children with the greatest needs in their case load.

Children and families who are assessed as not in need will have clear folders but those children assessed to be vulnerable and in need of support and extra services will have coloured folders according to the need.

	NEW BIRTH VISIT
Purpose	* To offer information, advice and support to the family * To provide opportunities for parents to raise issues and concerns * To observe and support baby's health, feeding and progress * To identify vulnerability and unmet need
Content	**Child** Parental concerns General Health – medical conditions/illness – hospital follow-up Assessment of physical health by observation and/or questions to include: * Skin * Fontanelle * Eyes/ears * Mouth * Umbilicus * Muscle tone/Responsiveness * Hearing * Bowels and micturation Weight, length and head circumference – document on PCHR centile chart Confirm Guthrie, haemoglobinopathies, hypothyroidism tests Immunisations – advice and information Feeding method/pattern Sleep/routines Accident prevention/cot death risk factors/'Handle with care' Use of Personal Child Health Record (PCHR) **Parent/Carer** Parents physical/emotional health Basic care Breastfeeding support (as appropriate) Diet/rest Family planning/contraception Ensuring safety – advice and information Emotional warmth – interaction with the baby Stimulation Stable pattern of care **Family/environment** Update family health needs assessment Smoking status Family support networks Housing Employment/income Social integration **Community resources – post natal groups etc**
Who	Health visitor
Timing	10–14 days after birth

TABLE 15.8 *Example of an assessment made by a health visitor*

CHILD CONCERN

A FRAMEWORK FOR INFORMATION SHARING, ASSESSMENT AND SUPPORT

STAGE 1

Low level
of vulnerability.
Need for advice,
guidance and support.

Assessment of need
and service
by single agency.

STAGE 2

Problems persist despite
support. Needs are severe
or complex enough to require
more than one agency.

Single-agency assessment
informed by consultation.
Referral for service from
another agency.

Some co-ordination
of referrals.

STAGE 3

Problems worsen – current
support inadequate.

Co-ordinated multi-agency
assessment, service plan
and review process.

Use existing multi-agency
meetings or child
support meeting.

Some co-ordination
of referrals.

STAGE 4

Needs remain
unmet – not
benefiting from
help.

Threshold for
specialist assessment
that may be statutory.

Some shared records.

BASELINE

Children and young people
make good overall progress.

Family meets children and young
people's needs with universal health,
education and community services.

STAGE 5

Highest level of vulnerability.
Specialist assessment has
confirmed the need for specific,
sustained and intensive support.

Some shared records.

Common assessment framework
Multi-agency
Agreed lead
Specialist assessment

FIGURE 15.11 *The Child Concern Model*

Assistance with care for family members

Many different types of assistance are available to support older family members with specific needs, as well as children. However, the example below focuses on services available to support parents of young children. Parents who are finding it hard to cope may use the voluntary services such as Home-start and Sure Start programmes that are set up by a partnership between health and social care.

The extended school

The head teacher of this school is in charge of 52 children. At the moment there are four babies aged between 3 months and 2 years and the rest of the children are 3 to 5 years of age. Over 50 per cent of the children are from ethnic minorities. The school is open from 8 am until 6 pm. Children have their breakfast, lunch and tea at the school. The babies are sometimes playing with the older children, so there is a family feel to the school. There is a range of activities for the children to do, and there is also a rest room where they can sleep. There is a sensory room, with a range of soft play objects, and patterns and shapes are projected on the walls. This area is used by all the children, but children who have behaviour problems are encouraged to use it as it has a calming effect.

The school is seen as part of the community. Parents have a drop-in session to discuss any problems and the school has a number of professionals who support children and parents with difficulties. There is also a child minder drop-in session. The head teacher is the nominated Child Protection Officer for the school. The following professionals are part of the team that works with the head teacher:

* a health visitor
* a paediatrician
* an educational psychologist
* a special educational needs teacher
* a social worker
* a speech and language therapist.

The voluntary sector is also involved. Home-start volunteers offer support to parents of children at the extended school. The school refers children to different professionals such as the GP, the mental health team or the child day care team, with the agreement of parents. Parents are also advised about any benefits or other financial payments that may be due to them.

The head teacher has many concerns about the children in her care. Many children start at the school when they are 3 years old and they are still wearing nappies, they have poor dental health, they never sit down to eat at a table at home and they are unable to use a knife and fork. Some children have been used to looking at television for most of the day and they don't know how to play. Playing with these children is seen as a crucial aspect in their emotional and physical development. There is a range of play materials in the rooms and the garden is full of different play areas which will help children develop their motor skills. The importance of children interacting and playing together is stressed, as their social skills may be rather limited.

The school has a healthy-eating programme and all meals are prepared on the premises. Chocolate has been banned. Every child has a key worker who supports them, and works with the parents to help their child attain their full potential. Children with special needs are assessed via **statementing** and their needs provided for. In this school there is a special session with the special needs worker for children who have autistic tendencies.

As part of the Sure Start programme, Sure Start Circle children's centres are also developing to support children and families. The centre that is described here is one of the first to open in the UK.

The Sure Start Circle Children's Centre

In the same estate a children's centre is also operating. The services are offered at a range of venues in the area, co-ordinated by the central office. The services are only available for certain post code areas which have been identified as those most in need. There is close working between the centre and the extended school, with workers from the centre running activities at the school. Children's centres are committed to:

* giving the best start in life for every child
* offering better opportunities for parents
* providing affordable, good quality childcare
* encouraging stronger and safer communities.

These centres offer a range of services including:

* full day care and early education
* family support

Sure Start

This is a government initiative to support families, carers, parents-to-be and children under 5 who are living in poverty. The support to families is provided by health and social care professionals as well as voluntary organisations. As part of the Sure Start programme, extended schools and Sure Start Centres are developing.

In one area there are two children's centres – one based in a nursery school and one based in a purpose-built annex to an existing infants' school. These two centres are based in areas where there is a great deal of deprivation, on a large pre-war council estate which has numerous problems including alcohol and drug abuse, as well as high rates of teenage pregnancy and truancy. Many people in this area suffer poor health including lung and heart disease. Children's centres are models of integrated service provision, where primary care trusts (PCTs), local authorities, Jobcentre plus, education, childcare providers, social services and voluntary groups all work together to provide services for children under 5 and their families.

As part of the Sure Start programme, extended schools have developed in some deprived areas in the UK, and it is expected that this provision will extend to all areas in the future. The government's definition of an extended school is one that provides a range of services and activities to meet the needs of its pupils, their families, and the wider community. Extended schools offer a range of activities, breakfast clubs and after school learning. Some extended schools for older groups work with health and social care and the police.

* child and family health services
* support for children with special educational needs
* support for training and employment for family members
* links with local childminders.

There are case conferences on the children and families the team is supporting. There is an emphasis on healthy pregnancies with antenatal care and 'stop smoking' workshops for pregnant mums.

In cases involving children, the children's needs must come first and if these are not being met, social services have a duty to plan and provide services to support the child. A key

The extended school offers a range of facilities for young children and their families

SCENARIO
Jamie's story

Jamie was referred to the school when he was 3 by a charity that works with families in the area. He has special educational needs. Two months before he was born, his father died in a car accident, and his mother, Anne, has had severe depression since then. Anne has had bereavement counselling, but still finds it difficult to cope with general day-to-day life – getting Jamie to school on time and looking after him. He is a demanding child because of his special needs as he has been diagnosed as having ASD (Autism Spectrum Disorder). Anne relied on her own parents a great deal, but they have now moved out of the area and the teacher is concerned she is becoming more isolated, which is a problem for both herself and Jamie. Through building a trusting relationship with Jamie and Anne, the teacher has been able to offer support and to develop a holistic approach to the support for this family through the professional team based at the school. The isolation of single mothers is seen as an issue on the estate but with the various parents' drop-in groups and other support groups it is hoped this will improve in the future.

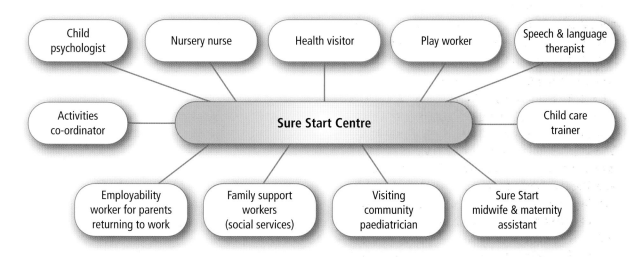

FIGURE 15.12 *The members of the Sure Start children's centre multi-disciplinary team who work together*

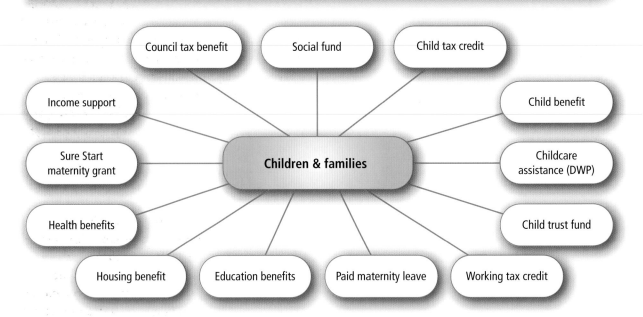

FIGURE 15.13 *Sources of financial support for children and families*

worker will be appointed for every child on the Child Protection Register and their progress will be reviewed regularly.

Financial support for children and families

There have been many government programmes to help support mothers with child care to enable them to return to work. These are continually changing. If you go to the DWP website you will find details of a range of financial benefits for children and families.

Summary

In this section we have examined how service provision to the community changes in response to the changing needs of society. Through the delivery of services using the mixed economy of care, the roles of health and care professionals are continuously changing.

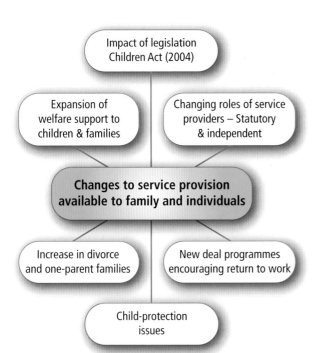

Impact of legislation
Children Act (2004)

Expansion of
welfare support to
children & families

Changing roles of service
providers – Statutory
& independent

**Changes to service provision
available to family and individuals**

Increase in divorce
and one-parent families

New deal programmes
encouraging return to work

Child-protection
issues

Section 4: Using data to explore and draw conclusions about the trends and patterns of family life

In this section we will cover the skills you need
to interpret and understand secondary sources of
information to examine demographic and social
trends affecting the family and individuals. You
will also need to evaluate the data and explain
problems associated with studying the family
and individuals.

Quantitative data

This is data which is expressed in numerical form.
This includes numbers, tables and percentages. We
have already looked at a lot of this type of data in
this unit. Most government policy is developed as
a result of analysing quantitative data. However,
numbers alone may not tell the whole story
although they are useful for looking at trends over
a period of time, such as the changes in marriage
rates, birth rates and death rates.

Qualitative data

This is data that expresses the thoughts and
feelings of an individual or a group. Although
the quantitative unemployment data may
tell us about the numbers of people who are
unemployed, qualitative research would focus on
the experience of being unemployed and will use
the words of unemployed people themselves. Ann
Oakley (1974) did a famous qualitative study on
housewives, when she asked ten housewives to
tell her about their daily routines and how they
felt about being a housewife.

Reliability, validity and bias of primary and secondary data

In this unit we have been looking at a range of
secondary data.

Key concepts

Primary data: data that is collected by a researcher and can include interviews, questionnaires, tape recorded information and observational records. An example of primary data would be the interviews collected by Ann Oakley in her study.

Secondary data: data used by researchers which has been collected by other agencies. It includes census figures (collected every ten years), and official statistics compiled by government departments, including the Office for National Statistics. It also includes historical documents, books and films, as well as research reports.

Reliability and validity

In both primary and secondary data, reliability is seen as a key issue. Research is said to be reliable if, when repeated using the same method, it produces the same results. Reliability is a concept used when evaluating quantitative data. Some sociologists who follow the positivist approach, argue that large-scale surveys such as the census are more reliable than small-scale research using a few subjects discussing feelings. However critics of **positivism** argue that **validity** is more important than **reliability.**

Key concept

Validity: is concerned with establishing whether the data collected gives a true picture of what is being studied. The personal experiences of people could be collected in a variety of ways, including unstructured interviews and life histories.

Statistics may show trends over a period of time but may not reflect reality. For example, definitions of unemployment have changed numerous times over the last 30 years so these statistics can be said to be both unreliable and invalid, as they have been manipulated and cannot be taken to represent the true picture. In 2005 people who were unemployed but were looking for work or were on training programmes were not included in the unemployment figures.

Key concept

Positivism: this approach argues that research into society and social issues should be undertaken in a scientific manner so that evidence gathered can to be used to explain events. Positivists would prefer quantitative data.

SCENARIO

The eleven plus

In a London borough, children in the final year of junior school take the eleven plus test to decide whether they will enter a local grammar school. Statistics show that there is the same pattern of results each year, with most students falling into the middle grades and a few either achieving low or very high grades. This pattern is called the normal curve of distribution (see Figure 15.14).

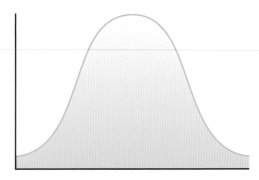

FIGURE 15.14 *The normal curve of distribution*

We could say that the eleven plus test is very reliable because the same pattern emerges every year. However, we could also argue that the test is invalid. Validity is the ability of a test or research method to measure what it sets out to measure. The eleven plus is used as a measure of intelligence and to predict future performance. The scores may be affected by a variety of factors. Some parents may pay for their children to be coached, or children may do lots of practice tests to improve their performance, but this may not be a true indicator of intelligence and potential. In the same way, IQ tests (measuring intelligence) may be reliable but lack validity.

Data sampling methods

If a researcher is going to conduct a survey into a particular topic, they will need to decide what group of people they will choose to take part in the research. This group is called the **sample.** The sample will be drawn from a **sampling frame,** which could be the electoral roll, doctors' lists, a school register or any other collection of names or addresses. Sampling is a very important part of the research process, as the sample used should reflect the population that is being studied. If the population being studied consists of a certain age range, gender and ethnic mix, the sample should contain the same. So that if the population being studied had a 10 per cent ethnic minority population, a male/female split of 50/50, and more people aged over 65, the sample should reflect this. If the sample reflects the population as a whole we can say that the sample is representative of the population being studied, and therefore we can generalise from the findings. However there are problems with this. If the sample is chosen but some people refuse to take part, then this may make the sample unrepresentative and can affect the reliability of the research. Many critics of quantitative research would say that much of this research is unreliable and also lacks validity because it does not reflect the reality of what it is trying to measure. Apart from the problem of an unrepresentative sample which affects reliability, the researcher will have devised questions that are of interest to him and may not reflect the interests of the subjects and this will affect the validity of the research. There are several ways of developing a sample for research purposes.

Random sampling

In **random sampling** each member of the survey population has an equal chance of being chosen to participate. Random sampling is seen to remove bias as people are chosen at random and everyone has an equal chance of being selected. For example, if you decided to conduct some research in your doctor's surgery about the care patients received, you may decide to interview every fifth person on the doctor's surgery list.

Stratified random sampling

The **stratified random sampling** approach is supposed to remove the problems that you may experience using the straightforward random sampling approach. If you were using the doctor's list as a sampling frame, you would look at the pattern of the survey population, and divide the list into males/females, different age groups and ethnic groups. Then you would draw a sample from each of the groups, the size of the sample in each being in proportion to the numbers of members of that group in the survey population. By using a stratified random sample you would hope that the sample you finally end up with is more representative than a basic random sample.

The pros and cons of random sampling methods

Pros

* aims to ensure that results can be generalised to the whole population

* sampling errors can be assessed and quantified mathematically

* stratification can include the inclusion of small but important groups

* stratification can minimise the chance of selecting biased samples.

Cons

* researcher must be able to obtain a sampling frame

* simple random sampling may still give a biased sample

* implementing random sampling methods can be time-consuming

* stratification requires prior knowledge about the proportions of different types of people in the population.

Quota sampling

In **quota sampling** the researcher has a list of characteristics required of respondents and a given quota of each to select and interview. This approach is widely used in market research when manufacturers want to test the response to an advertising campaign, and they may want to see if there is a different response to the campaign from men and women, or between different social classes. The researcher's quota would probably be 50 men and 50 women. Within each of these groups the researcher would have to interview 20 manual workers, 20 white-collar workers and 10 professional workers. Within each working group there would also be a given number of people in particular age bands. However, because the choice of the respondents is left to the interviewer, they may choose to interview more approachable looking people, so there could be bias. Another problem could be making sure that the respondents fit the quota. You could spend a whole Saturday

afternoon trying to find a male professional of a certain age in order to finish the quota.

The pros and cons of quota sampling

Pros

* no need to obtain a sampling frame

* refusals do not prevent the required sample size being achieved

* can be a quick method to implement

* may be the only way to sample views on an exhibition or event.

Cons

* not a truly random sampling method

* interviewer's choice will influence sample selection

* quota setting requires prior knowledge of the proportions of the groups in the population

* misses people who are difficult to access; people who are housebound or are in hospital.

Methods of collecting primary data

There is a variety of ways of carrying out primary research and each has strengths and weaknesses. In this section we will be looking at the main approaches.

Experiments

Experiments are often used by psychologists as a way of discovering how individuals behave. Scientists also use experiments to test theories and hypothesis. Experiments in health and social care are very different from those taking place in the controlled environment of a laboratory. Experiments in psychology involving individuals can be difficult as individuals tend to react differently to the same stimulus. For example, memory tests on people may be affected by factors such as their education and training, as well as the skills they need for their job. For example, members of the police force tend to have a better visual memory than members of the general public, because of their training. Ethical issues are a key issue in experiments in health and social care, as the scenario on page 259 shows.

FIGURE 15.15 *The joys of quota sampling*

Patients for research

The local research and ethics committee has been asked to approve research into a new surgical procedure. This procedure involves placing a new device in the heart to reduce the possibility of a heart attack due to the irregular beating of the heart. Patients who attend the local cardiac clinic who have atrial fibrillation (irregular heart beats) will be approached and asked to participate in the research programme. Using a random approach, 20 patients will be given the new device (the experimental group) and 20 patients will be given the standard defibrillator (the control group). The patients will not be told which type of device they have been fitted with. Patients will be given a patient information sheet which clearly explains the research. They are told they can withdraw from the study at any time and their treatment will not be affected if they decide not to take part.

Ben

Ben has **autistic** spectrum disorder. His behaviour in the playground is very aggressive. A psychologist has decided to try various approaches to see if he will respond and become less aggressive. With the consent of Ben's mother and other parents of the children in the group, Sue (the psychologist) videos Ben in the playground over a period of two weeks. Immediately before play time, she does specific activities with Ben, and then sees if there is a change in his behaviour. If a particular activity seems to have a positive result the classroom assistant will continue with this activity programme.

What are the ethical problems here?

Informed consent is a key issue. Do the patients fully understand the research? How will the selection of patients in the two groups take place? In some studies, patients are allocated a number and these numbers are used to allocate the patients at random. If the new device works more effectively, will patients be allowed to switch to the more effective model?

There are many problems related to experimental research in health and social care, and these will increase with the development of new treatments and drugs. In some research, when new drugs are tested on an experimental group and are shown to be effective, there may be problems when the research ends and the funding for the new drug also ends, as the hospital or primary care trust may be unwilling to pay for an expensive drug. The main issue is to ensure that the patient is not harmed in any way, either physically or emotionally, and new European Directives are now in force to ensure patient safety and informed patient consent in research in health and social care.

Experiments can also be carried out looking at behaviour, especially of children as illustrated in this scenario.

What are the problems here?

* Ben's behaviour may change but it may not be in response to the programme.

* Ben's behaviour may change because he is getting more attention as he is being videoed.

* The other children may also be affected by the filming.

Individuals respond differently to stimuli and also it would be difficult to control all the factors that affect Ben's behaviour and know that the programme is responsible for changes in Ben's behaviour.

Pros and cons of experiments

Pros

* can be designed to test very specific theories and hypotheses

* the experimenter can control the circumstances in which the experiment takes place

* data collected is nearly always quantitative allowing statistical interpretation of the results

it is possible for other researchers to duplicate the experiment and test the repeatability of the results.

Cons

* range of enquiry limited to the specific aims of the experiment

* difficult for the experimenter to control all factors affecting the behaviour or responses of subjects

* artificial circumstances of the experiment may distort the subjects' behaviour

* scientific conduct of the experiment and presentation of statistical results may give more weight to the work than it deserves.

Questionnaires

Questionnaires are one of the most commonly used methods in research in health and social care, and they have several advantages:

* they can give information using a large sample of the population you wish to study and they are cheap to reproduce and to distribute

* because the questionnaire is self-administered there is less 'interviewer effect' on the responses made

* postal questionnaires may be a useful way of contacting a large number of people

* questionnaires are quick and usually quite straightforward to fill in.

Questionnaires are designed to provide quantitative data. This means they are easy to analyse and compare results.

Look at Figure 15.16 carefully. Can you think of any problems with it?

Feature of the service	Level of importance					How well it is provided				
	Low				High	Poorly				Very well
	1	2	3	4	5	1	2	3	4	5
1. Length of time to get an appointment with GP	☐	☐	☐	☐	☐	☐	☐	☐	☐	☐
2. Approachable GP	☐	☐	☐	☐	☐	☐	☐	☐	☐	☐
3. Access to GP out of surgery hours	☐	☐	☐	☐	☐	☐	☐	☐	☐	☐
4. Time spent with GP in consultation	☐	☐	☐	☐	☐	☐	☐	☐	☐	☐
5. Local to my home	☐	☐	☐	☐	☐	☐	☐	☐	☐	☐
6. Able to easily make an appointment	☐	☐	☐	☐	☐	☐	☐	☐	☐	☐
7. Being seen promptly at time of appointment	☐	☐	☐	☐	☐	☐	☐	☐	☐	☐
8. Effective diagnosis skills	☐	☐	☐	☐	☐	☐	☐	☐	☐	☐
9. Friendly receptionist	☐	☐	☐	☐	☐	☐	☐	☐	☐	☐
10. Range of services available e.g. physio	☐	☐	☐	☐	☐	☐	☐	☐	☐	☐
11. Able to obtain repeat prescriptions	☐	☐	☐	☐	☐	☐	☐	☐	☐	☐
12. Conveniently surgery opening times	☐	☐	☐	☐	☐	☐	☐	☐	☐	☐
13. Up-to-date patient information available	☐	☐	☐	☐	☐	☐	☐	☐	☐	☐
14. Incorporating complimentary medicine	☐	☐	☐	☐	☐	☐	☐	☐	☐	☐
15. Willingness to refer to specialist services	☐	☐	☐	☐	☐	☐	☐	☐	☐	☐

FIGURE 15.16 *An example of a questionnaire used by a primary care trust*

Here are some hints to help you.

* Are the instructions clear?
* Do you understand how you have to complete it?
* Do the categories you have to tick fit in with your responses?
* Are there any questions you feel a patient may have a problem answering?
* Are there some people who would have difficulty completing this questionnaire?

The pros and cons of self-completion questionnaires

Pros

* data can be collected cheaply from a large number of respondents
* no problem with the behaviour or appearance of the interviewer affecting results
* respondents have time to consider answers and to consult others if necessary
* postal methods may be the only way to contact certain groups
* may be more acceptable to some groups than an interview.

Cons

* postal questionnaires have a poor response rate
* responses may be largely from people who have strong opinions on the subject
* no check on whether the subjects have understood the questions
* no control over who actually completes the questionnaire
* no opportunity to observe respondents' reactions to the questions

* no control over the order in which questions are answered
* the questions limit the responses that are possible, even if there are a number of options given and the true views of the subjects may not be revealed.

Structured interviews

Interviews involve the researcher meeting individual subjects and collecting data directly from them. Interviews can be formally structured, following a particular schedule. Structured interviews are well defined, and each subject will be interviewed in exactly the same way. The aim of structured interviews is to ensure lack of interviewer bias as each interview is carried out in the same way. Interviewers follow an interview schedule, which contains a lot of questions laid out rather like a questionnaire.

Closed and open questions

In both questionnaires and interviews, questions can be either closed or open. **Closed questions** usually have a limited response and can cover basic data about the person, such as age, marital status, number of children, type of work done, etc. This type of information is easily analysed and presented. However many questionnaires and structured interviews also make use of open questions. Examples of these would be:

* How do you feel about…?
* What is your relationship like with your parents/siblings/partner?
* How do you spend your leisure time?

Very often an interviewer may prompt the subject for further information such as

* Why do you say that?
* Is there anything else?
* Can you tell me more about that?

Open questions require skill on the part of the interviewer, especially if personal and sensitive issues are being covered. They give a great deal of useful information, but both open and closed questions must be relevant to the purpose of the study rather than an excuse for the interviewer to be intrusive.

In-depth interviews

Many aspects of feelings and attitudes are difficult to explore through a set of structured questions. Sensitive and personal issues about which people have deep feelings are difficult to research in a set format. Each person has an individual way of looking at their situation and each has experiences that are particular to them and cannot be explained using a set formula. In-depth interviews give qualitative data when the centre of the research focuses on the individual's personal experience and how they make sense of what happens to them. Ann Oakley in her study spent about ten hours with each subject, exploring how each woman felt about her experience as a housewife. The researcher may prompt the subject, but the data is drawn from the subject's own personal viewpoint, rather than from the perspective of what the researcher feels is significant. In the relationship between the researcher and the subject, there is more of an equal partnership.

In-depth interviews provide a great deal of rich data and can be said to be valid as they reflect the reality of the personal experience of the interviewee. However, because they tend to produce a great deal of data, they can be difficult to analyse. Researchers who favour a more scientific approach would say they are subjective and biased, and that they are unreliable because they cannot be replicated as each subject will respond differently. Therefore, generalisations cannot be made. Interviewer influence can also be a problem. By spending so much time with a subject the researcher may develop a rapport with the person and they could feel that when they write up the research they want to show the person in a favourable light. Bias can also occur in the way the data is analysed and presented. The researcher usually would use categories to put the responses in some kind of framework, and the researcher could be accused of manipulating the data so that it reflects the views of the researcher. Ann Oakley was a feminist and when she had her baby and became a housewife herself, she found the role boring and monotonous. In the schedule she used to ask housewives about their feelings she included the question 'Do you find housework monotonous?' This could be seen to be a biased question. Perhaps she should have asked a more open question such as 'How do you feel about housework?'

Pros and cons of in-depth interviews

Pros

* subjects have the freedom to give an answer in their own words

* a large amount of information can be collected from each respondent

* answers can be a valid representation of the respondents' own thoughts and feelings

* respondents have time to open up on sensitive issues

* interviewers are free to explore any interesting issues that arise.

Cons

* interviewers must have well-developed communications skills

* each interview is time-consuming and it is only possible to carry out a few

* personal characteristics of the interviewer can affect the answers given

* time and privacy are needed to carry out the interview

FIGURE 15.17 *Interviewers need to make sure that the questions they ask are relevant to the purpose of the study*

* qualitative nature of the data collected and small sample size limit the possibility of making any generalisations.

Direct observation

Direct observation could be said to be similar to bird-watching. Subjects are watched as they go about their daily lives, while the researcher remains detached. Observation means studying by looking, but observation in research needs to be structured. The data collected must be organised so that relevant and useful information is sought and recorded. Many studies have been done on the interactions that take place between children in a playground, noting if different behaviours occur between different groups, such as comparing the behaviour of boys and girls.

There are ethical problems with observing people if they are unaware of it and also if they have not given consent. There are also difficulties as the researcher may interpret behaviour in a different way depending on their own experience of childhood, for example, and this may not reflect what is happening as far as the children in the study are concerned. In order to remove observer bias, two researchers may observe and compare notes and they may also ask the children in the study about their interpretation of what is happening.

The pros and cons of direct observation

Pros

* observers see what subjects actually do, not what they say they do

* subjects are studied in their natural environment

* can detect behaviour that subjects are unaware of

* can look at group behaviour and interactions between group members

* may be the only suitable method with non-literate subjects, e.g. children.

Cons

* observers may miss important behaviour while note-taking

* secretive observation leads to significant ethical problems

* incorrect inferences can be drawn from observed behaviour

* lack of control over the sample observed limits broader applicability of results.

Participant observation

Participant observation means that the researcher becomes part of the group being studied. This can be difficult as the researcher would have to be similar to the group being researched in aspects such as age, social class and gender. A white middle-aged woman would have difficulty becoming accepted by a West Indian male group. Participant observation has been used when studying a variety of groups, and joining a group of 20-year-olds may be possible if you were investigating a topic such as leisure activities of this age group. However, it would be difficult to use participant observation to study aspects of family life.

This type of research is very time-consuming. To be successful you need to be accepted by the group. You will need to decide how you are going to record events without drawing attention to yourself. If the group does something illegal you would need to decide whether you would go along with this or not. You may become so closely involved with the group that you 'go native'. That is, you become so much part of the group that you stop being an observer and become a full participant.

When the research ends, you need to decide how you will leave the group. Writing up the research afterwards is also difficult. You need to ensure confidentiality by changing names and the area in which the research took place. You would have the same difficulties in selecting and presenting material as when using other sorts of qualitative data. Those who favour a scientific approach to research would criticise the lack of reliability in such research, as even if you research another group in the same way, the outcomes would be different so you could not replicate the study.

Pros and cons of participant observation

Pros

* can produce very valid and accurate data

* may be the only method with closed or hostile groups

* less likely to misinterpret data.

Cons

* researcher needs time, commitment and excellent interpersonal skills

* researcher needs skills of objectivity and detachment from the group being studied

* researcher's influence on group behaviour could be a problem

* observers may be unknowingly ignorant of important aspects of the group's behaviour

* secretive participant observation leads to serious ethical difficulties.

Suitability of methods for collecting data

In this section we have looked at a range of methods for collecting data. Each method has advantages and disadvantages.

Problems with methods used for collecting the data

When you decide to do a study you need to focus on several practical aspects.

* Is there a time constraint?

* Is the information you need easily available?

* Are there ethical issues of confidentiality because of the nature of the study?

All data collection methods have their drawbacks, but you need to choose the best methods for your particular study. For example, if you wanted to do some quick research to find out how local people in a particular age group use their leisure time, it might be best to use questionnaires and interviews. You probably wouldn't find much help in secondary data, because your study is a local one and the best way to find out about it is to ask people directly. You probably wouldn't want to conduct an experiment to help with your study, because it would be very difficult to construct an appropriate and ethical one. You might consider using direct or participant observation, but both of these methods might prove more time-consuming and less reliable than questionnaires and interviews. When designing any research project, you need to select the data collection methods that will give

you the most reliable and valid data in the most efficient way.

Think it over

Look at the following proposed research projects. Would primary or secondary data be used? What methods would you use? or could you use a combination of methods?

* finding out how first-time mothers experienced childbirth

* finding out how people spend their leisure time

* finding out the population profile of your local area

* finding the divorce and remarriage rates in the UK

* finding out how people cross a busy street in your area

* finding out whether people are living in rented or owner-occupied accommodation.

In all these examples you need to think about the research question that is the basis of the study. You would also need to think about the purpose of the study. Is it to reach greater understanding of a person's experience or is it to record changes in patterns of family life?

Ways of overcoming data-collection problems

One way of improving both reliability and validity of research is to use a range of methods. If you wanted to explore the issue of older children who still live with their parents, you could start using data from *Social Trends* publications and then interview people who are still living at home with their parents. Statistics are useful to show trends, but they do not give explanations for *why* older children are continuing to live at the family home.

Another way of dealing with problems of interviewer bias in interviews is to show the transcript to the subject and ask them if this is a true reflection of their account. In observation studies you should always use two researchers so that you can cross-check what you see, and then you could interview the observed participants to see if they agree with your interpretation of events.

Ethical issues involved in collecting data and researching families and individuals

There are two main ethical issues involved in doing any research – preserving the subject from harm and distress, and confidentiality.

Preserving the subject from harm and distress

This is a key issue in research. The subject should have a free choice whether or not to take part, and should be able to stop at any time if they wish to. The researcher must explain the research fully and truthfully so that the subject understands what will happen and can give their informed consent to the research. Researchers must not coerce people into taking part, by using their position to influence the decision, for instance. For example, if a doctor wanted to include one of his patients in a research project, they must make it clear to the patient that refusal to take part will not affect their future treatment in any way.

Confidentiality issues

This is another key ethical issue. The subject has a right to confidentiality. Research reports should never identify the subject personally and should be written in such a way that the person can not be identified. In most studies, subjects are given another name or number so that they cannot be identified. The Data Protection Act (1998) safeguards people's rights when data about them is collected and processed. If you are using a computer to process data you need to follow safeguards so that unauthorised people cannot gain access to the names and addresses of the subjects. Sensitive personal data is covered by the Act and includes data about the physical or mental health of a person, as well as the sexual life of the person.

Summary

In this section we have explored a range of methods used in research. These methods allow us to explore issues related to the family and to society and to draw possible conclusions about trends and patterns of family life.

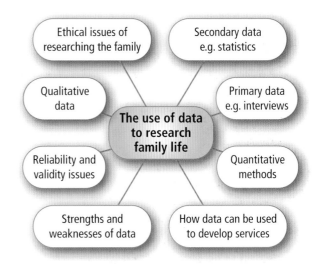

Consider this

1. GPs are concerned about the number of patients who fail to turn up for appointments at local surgeries.

   What data could you use to find out the extent of the problem?

   What primary data could you use to find out why patients don't turn up?

2. Decide which methods are most appropriate for conducting research into the following issues:

   * violence in the family

   * the number of older people in the area

   * the birth rate in the area

   * why people decide to contact social services.

   Give reasons for your choice.

3. Researchers discuss the reliability and validity of different types of data. Define these terms and discuss how you could ensure reliability and validity in a study researching patterns of family life – for example, the position of older people in the family.

4. Official statistics are often used to identify trends in family patterns.

   What are the problems of using official statistics?

UNIT 15 ASSESSMENT

Unit 15 is assessed by an externally assessed test paper of 90 minutes. You will be sent materials before you do the test. These will include statistical tables from *Social Trends* which you need to familiarise yourself with. Each question or part question displays the number of marks allocated in brackets at the end of the question. Please note that these assessment questions are designed to contribute towards practice for your candidates' assessment but are not written to mirror OCR's A2 Level questions.

Test questions

1.

Population[1] of the United Kingdom							
							Millions
	1971	1981	1991	2001	2003	2011	2021
United Kingdom	55.9	56.4	57.4	59.1	59.6	61.4	63.8
England	46.4	46.8	47.9	49.4	49.9	51.6	54.0
Wales	2.7	2.8	2.9	2.9	2.9	3.0	3.1
Scotland	5.2	5.2	5.1	5.1	5.1	5.0	5.0
Northern Ireland	1.5	1.5	1.6	1.7	1.7	1.8	1.8

[1] Mid-year estimates for 1971 to 2003; 2003-based projections for 2011 and 2021

Source: Office for National Statistics; General Register for Scotland; Northern Ireland Statistics and Research Agency

TABLE 1.1 *Population of the UK*

Using the information in Table 1.1 answer the following questions.

a. What was the population of the UK in 2001? (1)

b. In what area of the UK is the population expected to increase? (1)

c. By how much did the population of England increase between 1971 and 2001? (2)

d. Describe the trend for the population of Scotland between 1971 and 2001. (2)

e. The data for 2011 onwards are projections. What is a projection? (2)

f. Give two reasons why projections are likely to be accurate. (2)

g. Give two reasons why the projections could prove inaccurate. (2)

h. Give four factors that could affect population change. (4)

i. Looking at Table 1.1, there is a change in the population of England between 1991–2003 from 47.9 million to 49.4 million. Give two reasons why there may be problems with the accuracy of this data. (2)

2. The Primary Care Director of a local PCT has decided that she wants to evaluate the provision of health services to older people in the area from the patient's perspective. It is decided that a questionnaire will be distributed to all older people. There are 50,000 people in the area who are over 65. The questionnaire will provide quantitative data but this will be supplemented with structured interviews with 30 older people.

Answer the following questions.

a. Give two ways that this type of quantitative data could be used and explain how they could help. (4)

b. The questionnaires could be left in the surgeries and handed out by staff or they could be returned in the post. How could you ensure a good response rate? (2)

c. If the response rate is 25 per cent how will this affect the reliability of the research? (2)

d. There are several problems experienced with questionnaires. Look at these problems and suggest solutions:

 ✳ questionnaires in English being given to non-English speakers

 ✳ people concerned about being identified from the information they give

 ✳ very long questionnaires that people can't be bothered to complete

 ✳ ambiguous questions

 ✳ too many closed questions giving people limited opportunity to give information

 ✳ confusing number of possible responses (Strongly disagree, Agree somewhat, etc.)

 ✳ questionnaire difficult to read. (7)

e. What criteria should be used when deciding on the sample of 30 follow-up interviews? (5)

f. The PCT could use either structured or unstructured interviews. Discuss the advantages and disadvantages of each approach using concepts of validity and reliability. (10)

3.

Households by size					
Great Britain					Percentages
	1971	1981	1991	2001	2004
One person	18	22	27	29	29
Two people	32	32	34	35	35
Three people	19	17	16	16	16
Four people	17	18	16	14	14
Five people	8	7	5	5	5
Six or more people	6	4	2	2	2
All households (=100%) (millions)	18.6	20.2	22.4	23.8	24.1
Average household size (number of people)	2.9	2.7	2.5	2.4	2.4

Source: National Census, Labour Force Survey, Office for National Statistics

TABLE 3.1 *Households by size*

Using the information given in Table 3.1 answer the following questions

a. What was the average household size in 1971? (2)

b. How many households were there in Great Britain in 2004? (2)

c. What was the approximate population size in Great Britain in 2001? (2)

d. What percentage of people lived in households of 4 or more in 1971? (1)

e. What percentage of people lived in households of 4 of more in 2004? (1)

f. Give four reasons why households of 4 or more are less common in 2004 than in 1971. (4)

4.

Households: by type of household and family					
Great Britain					Percentages
	1971	1981	1991	2001	2004
One person					
Under state pension age	6	8	11	14	14
Over state pension age	12	14	16	15	15
One family households					
Couple[1]					
No children	27	26	28	29	29
1–2 dependent children[2]	26	25	20	19	18
3 or more dependent children[2]	9	6	5	4	4
Non-dependent children only	8	8	8	6	6
Lone parent[1]					
Dependent children[2]	3	5	6	7	7
Non-dependent children only	4	4	4	3	3
Two or more unrelated adults	4	5	3	3	3
Multi-family households	1	1	1	1	1
All households (=100%) (millions)	18.6	20.2	22.4	23.8	24.1

[1]Other individuals who were not family members may also be included

[2]May also include non-dependent children

Source: National Census, Labour Force Survey, Office for National Statistics

TABLE 4.1 *Households by type of household and family*

Look at Table 4.1, Analyse the data to identify trends in the number of one-person households who are over state pension age and those who are under state pension age since 1971. (4)

Discuss the factors that have influenced these changes. (10)

5. Describe how the role of women has changed in the last 50 years. Analyse the possible reasons for this. (14)

6.

Population of under 16s and people aged 65 and over
United Kingdom

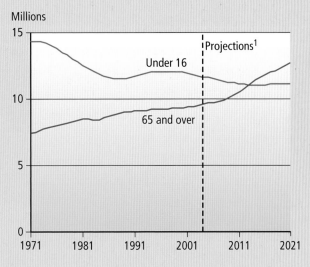

¹ 2003-based projections for 2004 to 2021.

Source: Office for National Statistics; General Register Office for Scotland; Northern Ireland Statistics

FIGURE 6.1 *Number of under 16s and people aged 65 and over*

Look at Figure 6.1.

a. Identify the patterns that you see in this figure. (2)

b. What are the implications for this pattern for the following:

　❋ the family　❋ the work force　❋ early years services　❋ services for older people
　❋ government policy? (10)

References and further reading

Guide to the Social Services in 2005/06 (2005) London: Waterlow Publishing

HM Government Green Paper *Every Child Matters* (2003) London: HMSO

HM Government Green Paper *Work and Parents* (2001) London: HMSO

HM Government *The Laming Report* (2003) London: HMSO

HM Government *Safeguarding Children* (2004) London: HMSO

HM Government *Social Trends 35* (2005) London: HMSO

HM Government *Schools Achieving Success* (2001) London: HMSO

Moonie, N. (2000) *Advanced Health and Social Care*, Oxford: Heinemann

Moonie, N. (2005) *Health and Social Care AS level*, Oxford: Heinemann

Oakley A. (1974) *Housewife*, London: Allen Lane

Robinson, M. and Scanlan, L. *KIDS Project* Cardiff University (www.law.cf.ac.uk)

Useful websites

Children and Family Court Advisory and Support Services

    www.cafcass.gov.uk

    www.dwp.gov.uk

    www.dh.gov.uk

Government Statistics

    www.statistics.gov.uk

Local Change Programmes

    www.everychildmatters.gov.uk

National Voluntary Organization

    www.home-start.org.uk

    www.direct.gov.uk

Office of the Deputy Prime Minister

    www.odp.gov.uk

Sure Start Programme

    www.surestart.gov.uk

Research methods in health and social care

Unit 16

This unit will give you an appreciation of the key purposes of research, and particularly its use in practice in the fields of health and social care. The ethical issues involved in conducting research, and ways in which faulty design or problems in implementation can result in error or bias in the results are discussed.

A range of research styles and methods is described. Practical advice on the design and administration of different types of data collection tools is included. The analysis and interpretation of data is explained in some depth. Finally, guidance on how to conduct a research project is set out, from the planning stage through to implementation and evaluation.

How you will be assessed

This unit is internally assessed. You must produce a research proposal, implement the research project and then produce a written report. You have the option to support your final report with an oral presentation.

You will need to follow the criteria as set out in the assessment objectives. Objective one (**AO1**) requires you to state the purpose of the research project, give a description of the research methods and the rationale for the research. Other objectives require additional discussion on ethical issues, sources of errors and bias (**AO2**); research to be carried out with analysis and presentation of findings (**A03**); and an evaluation of the research (**AO4**).

A full description of the assessment objectives is given at the end of the unit. There is also a reading list and a list of relevant websites.

Section 1: Purposes and methods of research

The purpose of research in health and social care

Research is vital in the development of health and social care practice. Worldwide, hundreds of journals are devoted to reporting the findings of research projects relating to new developments in medicine, health care or the impact of new initiatives in social care. Numerous websites are devoted to new research, and the many books published annually on related topics rely heavily on research findings to give authenticity and weight to their authors' arguments. News bulletins (whether on TV or radio) report the outcomes of significant pieces of research, and almost every day newspapers refer to newly-published results from research in health and social care.

questionnaires may be used to find out how people respond to the provision of a new service; or the observation of behaviours might be employed to give an insight into the impact of a certain environment on the ways that people interact.

Key concept

Research: a systematic enquiry that is designed to add to existing knowledge and/or to solve a particular problem (Bell, 1993).

Researchers will choose and adapt from a range of approaches and methods in order to seek answers to the questions or hypotheses they wish to test. The important thing about all research is that whatever method is used, the findings are reported systematically and scientifically, in as clear and honest a fashion as possible.

Try it out

Choose a quality newspaper such as *The Independent*, *The Guardian* or *The Times*. Scan it daily for a week, and note how many references there are to pieces of research in health and social care.

Sometimes, reference is made to a website giving further information about a particular study. Choose one of these items that interests you, and look at the website to see what the researchers have to say about their work.

Doing research involves making a systematic inquiry to add to existing knowledge or to solve a specific problem

What is research?

Over time, specific approaches and methods for carrying out research have developed, some of which are linked to particular disciplines. Laboratory experiments, for example, are often used when developing new drugs; or clinical procedures might be set up in a controlled environment to assess, say, the impact of damage to the human brain following a stroke. Outside the laboratory environment,

Who does research?

Anyone can do research: A brief trawl through the Yellow Pages to find names and addresses of all the local dentists is, in a sense, a piece of research. However, in this unit, we consider more elaborate research projects. Some of the main bodies undertaking research in health and social care are:

* universities
* hospitals
* national bodies, such as the Medical Research Council
* The Research Council for Complementary Medicine
* The Prince's Foundation for Integrated Health
* private organisations such as large pharmaceutical companies.

In social care, there are a number of bodies in the UK that sponsor or promote research. The Joseph Rowntree Foundation, for example, sponsors research that will impact on the development of social policy, as does the Institute for Public Policy Research (IPPR). These are only two of a number of bodies and organisations that promote social care related research.

Try it out

Search the Internet to see how many organisations you can identify that conduct research into health or social care related issues (the Joseph Rowntree Foundation publishes a list of useful sites).

Go into one of these sites to find out what research is going on at the moment.

* Who is paying for this research?
* What are the aims?
* What difference might it make when the findings are published?

In the UK, the government initiates a great deal of research, sometimes in-house (i.e. within specific government departments) and sometimes commissioned from outside organisations or independent researchers. Each government department, such as the Department of Health, has its own website, and details of ongoing and published research can be easily accessed. The Office for National Statistics (ONS) is the government department that deals with information from the National Census, the most recent of which was in 2001. Their website (www.statistics.gov.uk) has data on the population of England and Wales, with links to data for Scotland and Northern Ireland. The study of population characteristics is known as **demography.** Demographic data provides an essential background to research studies of many kinds.

As well as national government departments and agencies, local authorities may also have research units or departments. Demographic data is vital to the effectiveness of government, whether local or national.

Key concept

Demography: the study of the characteristics of given populations, e.g. of the whole of Scotland, or of the people who live in the city of Swansea.

The use of demographic data in local government

For example, consider a local council which has received Sure Start funding for a new day centre for single parents with young babies. The council's research unit processes data from the 2001 census to identify areas of greatest potential need within its boundaries. The data reveals a significant concentration of lone-parent households with dependent children in two Output Areas (these are the small local divisions within which census data is counted). These Output Areas lie adjacent to each other. The council therefore decides to look for suitable premises in either of these two small areas.

Did you know?

Sure Start is a government initiative that provides funding for projects designed to help very young children.

Year	Numbers			Rates per 1,000 population of all ages		
	Live births	Deaths	Natural change: live births minus deaths	Live births (crude birth rate)	Deaths (crude death rate)	Natural change
1993	673,467	578,799	94,668	13.2	11.4	1.9
1994	664,726	553,194	111,532	13.0	10.8	2.2
1995	648,138	569,683	78,455	12.6	11.1	1.5
1996	649,485	560,135	89,350	12.6	10.9	1.7
1997	643,095	555,281	87,814	12.5	10.8	1.7
1998	635,901	555,015	80,886	12.3	10.7	1.6
1999	621,872	556,118	65,754	12.0	10.7	1.3
2000	604,441	535,664	68,777	11.6	10.3	1.3
2001	594,634	530,373	64,261	11.4	10.1	1.2
2002	596,122	533,527	62,595	11.3	10.1	1.2
2003	621,469	538,254	83,215	11.8	10.2	1.6

FIGURE 16.1 *Population change in the United Kingdom, 1993–2003. National Census data is essential to local planning*

Purposes of research in health and social care

Reviewing and monitoring changes

When money and time have been invested in the provision of new services, it is vital to conduct evaluative studies to assess the impact and effectiveness of the changes.

Such studies might use a mixture of qualitative and quantitative research methods (see pages 281–3). Consider the example of the new Sure Start project described above. After receiving funding for this project, and spending time on its development, both the local council and the government department that supplied the funding would need evidence of its effectiveness.

Quantitative data would show, for example, how many people were using the new centre, how far they were travelling to get there and the most popular attendance times and activities.

Qualitative data would also be needed, and it would be a good idea to ask the centre users what they thought of the new service, whether there were things that could be done better, and what other things they would like to see in place there. Such evidence could be used to justify further

development of the project, either by application for more funding, or by the local council making financial provision within its own budget to continue the service.

Key concepts

Qualitative data: data which cannot be expressed simply in terms of numbers. It is often concerned with people's values, attitudes and/or opinions.

Quantitative data: data which is expressed in numerical form. It can be presented in tables, bar charts, pie charts, graphs, etc.

A real-life study of this kind can be investigated on the Joseph Rowntree Foundation website. The Joseph Rowntree Housing Trust has developed the UK's first Continuing Care Retirement Community, Hartrigg Oaks, a new concept in residential provision for older people. The scheme is experimental not only in its provision of a community environment in which residents are expected to be active in running the facility, but also in its promotion of imaginative financial arrangements to fund the development. Hartrigg Oaks opened in 1998, and the Joseph

Rowntree Foundation then commissioned the University of York to evaluate its effectiveness.

hartrigg oaks

Introduction to Hartrigg Oaks

Hartrigg Oaks, the first Continuing Care Retirement Community in the UK, is an ideal retirement option for people aged 60 plus who want to live life to the full. This unique environment enables individuals to live in a vibrant, stimulating environment, alongside like minded people who share a real sense of neighbourliness.

Well situated in the garden village of New Earswick, Hartrigg Oaks is only two miles from York City Centre and is within walking distance to shops and amenities.

Benefits

Hartrigg Oaks offers a range of benefits that can contribute to a full and active life for older people:

- extensive communal facilities
- a secure environment with beautiful landscaped gardens
- care when needed
- a range of financial options to suit a variety of needs and wishes
- a vibrant and stimulating community

Evaluative studies of new initiatives in care are essential. (Reproduced by permission of the Joseph Rowntree Foundation)

The University of York study used a range of data collection methods to provide both qualitative and quantitative data. The first report, published in 2003, provides qualitative data in the form of tables and bar charts, giving basic statistical information (numbers of residents, age profiles, short-term use of the facility, etc.), and also information about satisfaction levels. Some of this expressed quantitatively (e.g. a bar chart showing satisfaction levels) while qualitative data is given in the form of direct quotations from residents' observations and comments. Researchers used two postal surveys, face-to-face interviews and discussion groups with both staff and residents to gather the evaluative data. The full report can be accessed via the Joseph Rowntree Foundation website.

Exploring the specific needs of local populations

We have already seen how a local authority used census data to find the right location for a new

Sure Start Centre for single parents with young babies (page 274).

Demographic and epidemiological data is used constantly by politicians and service planners to explore the characteristics and needs of local populations, and to make informed decisions about new service developments or health interventions. An excellent example of the use of such data is provided by the Annual Report of the Chief Medical Officer (CMO), which can be accessed via the Department of Health website. This report presents the recommendations of the CMO on a number of issues, based on research which is explained and fully referenced. Some of these recommendations are general to the whole population, such as the impact of smoking on skin ageing, the economic case for creating smoke-free workplaces and public places, and the importance of early diagnosis of HIV (CMO's Report, 2003). However, some recommendations are specific to more local

Try this out

What does your community look like?

Access the National Census data for your country of residence (there are a number of possible access routes – see References section at the end of this unit).

Then search the data for details of your locality (this might be a town, a city or even one or more small Output Areas).

Can you identify:

✳ the total population

✳ the population in terms of males and females (gender)

✳ how many people are aged over 75 years

✳ how many lone-parent households there are

✳ how many people have a limiting long-term illness?

populations. In 2003, the report highlighted certain regional areas of concern for England, including that of the dental health of 5-year-olds in the North East. Using epidemiological data from dentists, the CMO's report notes a wide variation in the rates of decayed and filled teeth, from Hartlepool (average 0.86 per child) to South West Durham (average 2.82 per child). The report concludes that related factors are deprivation and the presence (or otherwise) of fluoridation, and notes that 'the provision of fluoridated water remains a priority in tackling inequality' (CMO Report, 2003).

Exploring hypotheses

Research is often designed to test out hypotheses in both health and social care. An example of a piece of research designed to test a hypothesis is described in the following scenario.

Key concept

Hypothesis: an assumption or theory made as the basis for further investigation.

SCENARIO

Stress and the common cold

Cohen and colleagues (1991) studied 420 volunteers (men and women) who agreed to be given the common cold virus via nasal drops. All the volunteers were housed in a residential unit in Salisbury, at the British Medical Research Council's Common Cold Unit.

Before doing this, the stress levels of each person were measured using standard psychological methods. In particular, researchers noted significant life events during the preceding year, the emotional state of the subject at the time of the experiment and each person's perception of how well they could cope with the ups and downs of life.

Cohen found that the people with the highest stress measures were more likely to:

(a) become infected with the virus

(b) develop colds.

Cohen is one of a number of scientists who are seeking to explore the hypothesis that psychological factors affect susceptibility to illness. This field of research is known as psychoneuroimmunology (PNI). In this case, volunteers are isolated (to reduce the risk of infection from other sources and with other viruses), and then exposed to the same virus. The same measures of stress are applied to each one. The study is systematic, and is experimental in design.

Key concept

Experimental method: involves comparison between groups of subjects, to assess the impact (or otherwise) of a particular factor. Experiments are designed so that they may be easily repeated.

Social science based hypotheses may also be tested by research. In a recent study, the possibility that Ecologically Based Family Therapy (EBFT) can have an impact on substance misuse in young people was tested over a period of time (Slesnik and Prestopnik, 2005). EBFT is a relatively new approach in which the impact of the environment, as well as other factors, is considered when working with people who have significant difficulties. In this study 124 young people with substance-related, mental health and family problems took part. All of them had run away from home. They were randomly assigned to one of two interventions: EBFT or a 'service as usual' (SAU) system available via a shelter. Researchers reviewed their subjects' situation at the start of the study, just after the end of the intervention, and then at 6 and 12 months afterwards. They found that those who had received the EBFT reported greater reductions in substance misuse than the young people in the control (SAU) group.

Key concept

Control group: in an experiment, the group which does not receive the new treatment or intervention is the control group.

A comparison can then be made between those subjects who experienced the new treatment, and those who didn't.

Did you know?

Ecologically Based Family Therapy (EBFT) is a method of working with someone to solve their problems. It takes into account everything about that person, including where she or he lives, who else lives there, relationships, lifestyle, etc. It is a holistic approach to working towards solutions in someone's life.

The investigation of care-related situations often involves the collection of qualitative data of some kind. The research into EBFT would have involved the collection of a great deal of qualitative data, which in this case would have been supported by basic quantitative information.

Extending and improving practice and collective knowledge

Research into medical treatments and knowledge is continuous and exhaustive. Worldwide, scientists in research laboratories seek to establish the mechanisms underlying certain diseases or medical conditions, or to test the reliability or effectiveness of specific drugs or treatment methods.

Such studies often involve the collection of quantitative data. This is data that can be expressed in terms of numbers, percentages, and so on, and is often used in medical and scientific research (although qualitative data often provides essential additional insights).

Key concept

Intervention: in medicine, an intervention can involve treatment with drugs or surgery, or involve physical work such as physiotherapy.

In social care, an *intervention* might be referral to a counselling service, to art or music therapy, or to therapies such as Family Therapy or EBFT.

Any planned work with a patient or service user, designed to help with a specific problem or condition, can be referred to as an intervention.

Currently, the 'gold standard' for the testing of medical knowledge and treatments is the **randomised clinical controlled trial** (RCCT). Research methods will be discussed later in more detail, but here it is enough to note that a randomised trial is based on a sample, randomly selected, who receive a particular drug or treatment. Another set of people, the control group, receive either the standard treatment, or no treatment at all, and outcomes for the two groups are compared. When a large number of such trials have taken place, researchers can then look at all the results by means of a **systematic review**.

Key concepts

Randomised clinical controlled trial (RCCT): a research method involving more than one sample group. The subjects of the trial are randomly selected. One sample group of subjects receives the treatment being investigated, the other doesn't and the results are compared.

Systematic review: a thorough and systematic comparison of the results of RCCTs to produce convincing evidence for the effectiveness (or otherwise) of a particular drug or treatment.

Sometimes, the results of research are inconclusive or even controversial. The debate on the safety of the combined MMR (measles, mumps and rubella) vaccine is an interesting example of this. In the late 1990s, Dr Andrew Wakefield published studies in *The Lancet* suggesting a possible link between the MMR vaccine and the condition known as autism, together with associated bowel and gut abnormalities (Wakefield, 1998). When this research received media coverage, many parents stopped having their children vaccinated with the combined drug. This alarmed health officials, who feared that uncontrolled outbreaks of diseases like measles might result. Since 1998 a great deal of attention has been paid by researchers (and the press) to the question of whether or not the MMR vaccine can have serious and undesirable consequences. The Department of Health has concluded that the vaccine is 'safe and extremely effective'. Despite this, there are still researchers who dispute these conclusions, and the debate continues. The government's position, together with lists of research articles, can be accessed via the Department of Health website. A conflicting view can be explored via the What Doctors Don't Tell You website (see the References and further reading section at the end of this unit).

Types of research study used in health research

Worldwide, there is considerable ongoing research into medical and other treatment interventions. Hospitals and university departments, charitable organisations (such as Cancer Research UK) and private companies invest considerable resources into testing existing procedures and pharmaceutical products, and searching for new and more effective interventions.

The Research Council for Complementary Medicines has published *An Introduction to Research* (1999) which sets out the range of types of study that can be conducted into health interventions (see Table 16.1).

Case reports describe a particular case in detail, particularly if the case is very rare, or perhaps if a practitioner has observed a new phenomenon.

Surveys are also descriptive, but their scope is broader than only one patient. Studies of dental health in children such as those referred to in the Chief Medical Officer's Annual Report include survey data.

Cohort studies are essentially a series of case studies. They might be used, for example, to study the impact of a treatment among a group of patients. A new drug such as beta interferon (now used in the treatment of some people with multiple sclerosis) would be administered to a defined group (a cohort), and its impact carefully monitored. The validity of the findings is limited by the absence of a control group, and there is always the possibility that changes in patient health may be due to factors that the study does not pick up.

In contrast a **clinical trial,** particularly when the subject group is **randomised,** is a more rigorous method of determining the effectiveness of a specific intervention. A clinical trial of the drug beta interferon would involve giving the drug to one group of patients, and comparing their progress with a second group who do not receive it. The second group may receive no treatment, another 'standard' treatment, or they may be given a **placebo.** A placebo is something that looks like a medical intervention (e.g. an injection or capsule), but in fact does not contain any active treatment. Clinical trials are also randomised, in that patients are selected according to a number of criteria (e.g. medical condition, age, gender) and then randomly allocated to either the treatment or the control group. Clinical trials are deemed to be even more effective if the researchers do not know which patients are receiving the real treatment, and which are receiving the placebo. In such cases, the researchers are said to be 'blinded'.

It is unlikely that one clinical trial will be conclusive. Researchers will attempt to replicate and refine the findings of other trials on the same subject. This, in turn, enables **systematic reviews** of the research into the same topic to be made. Such a review will attempt to assemble the evidence for a particular intervention, in a range of settings and patient groups. This kind of research activity is called **meta-analysis,**

Types of research study	
PURPOSE	**METHOD**
To describe something	Case reports Surveys Cohort studies
To explain something	Qualitative research (e.g. interviews, surveys)
To test a hypothesis	Quantitative research (e.g. clinical trials)
To make generalisations	Multi-centre trials Systematic reviews of trials

Source: Research Council for Complementary Medicine (1999)

TABLE 16.1 *Research into Health Interventions*

and it can sometimes reveal a common 'global' outcome from specific research. In the UK the Cochrane Collaboration (an online research facility established in 1993), systematically collects and makes available existing reviews of research about the effects of healthcare interventions. This organisation also promotes clinical trials and other studies of such interventions. The Cochrane Library is a collection of evidence-based medicine databases. Although full access is by subscription, some of the Cochrane's services are free, including details of the findings of systematic reviews.

In practice, researchers may make use of several methods of data collection. A clinical trial, for example, may be preceded by qualitative data collection about the subjects of such a study, to ensure that all the parameters have been considered. It might also be supplemented by qualitative data from people taking part in the study, to make sure that patients are not being adversely affected by, for example, environmental issues.

The scenario above demonstrates the advisability of supplementing quantitative research with qualitative information.

Systematic reviews are extremely important in the production of guidance for practitioners.

The National Institute for Health and Clinical Excellence (NICE) provides guidance in England and Wales on the promotion of health and the prevention and treatment of ill-health. NICE uses a range of methods, both qualitative and quantitative, to produce technology appraisals, clinical guidelines and advice on interventional procedures. NICE's guidelines are based on reviews of clinical and economic evidence. It also invites interested parties such as manufacturers, patients, carers and health professionals to give evidence on the use and effectiveness of specific interventions and treatments. The resulting guidelines are then publicly available to patients, professionals and carers.

Try it out

Choose a medical condition that interests you. Make an Internet search to find out what organisations currently sponsor or conduct research into that particular condition.

What kinds of research are being done (qualitative, quantitative, clinical trials, etc.)?

Research methods

Key concepts in research

The key distinction between qualitative and quantitative research has already been discussed. Another key distinction is made between primary data and secondary data.

Primary and secondary data

Primary data is the information collected by a researcher during the course of a study. Such information might include:

* information from questionnaires

* notes made during the observation of a person or group of people

* notes/transcripts/recordings made during an interview

* experimental data.

The collection and analysis of primary data will be discussed in more detail below.

> **Key concept**
>
> *Primary data:* the actual data collected by a researcher during the course of a study.

With respect to the project undertaken for this unit, primary data will be the information you collect directly in relation to the topic you are investigating.

Secondary data is that collected by people other than the researcher. Someone doing research will collect data from other sources to put their investigation into context, to make comparisons or to draw analogies. Sometimes, a researcher will make particular reference to other studies that appear to lend support to the findings of their own piece of work.

> **Key concept**
>
> *Secondary data:* data collected by people other than the researcher of a given project, and found in other published or Internet sources. Sometimes, unpublished work can provide a source of secondary data.

SCENARIO
What difference has it made?

Nas is studying the impact of a series of reminiscence sessions in a residential unit for older people.

His primary data includes: notes made when observing one of the sessions, the views of people attending the sessions (collected by questionnaire), and the views of both the unit manager and other staff (collected by an informal interview).

1. What other methods of data collection might Nas consider?

2. What else should Nas bear in mind when collecting this data?

A piece of primary research, such as the evaluative study of Hartrigg Oaks commissioned by the Joseph Rowntree Foundation (page 275) becomes secondary research when it is cited by someone else in another study.

Quantitative data

The key concepts of qualitative and quantitative data were introduced earlier in this unit (page 275). Broadly speaking, quantitative data is that which can be expressed numerically (i.e. it can be quantified), whilst qualitative data is that which is concerned with abstract concepts such as values, attitudes and opinions. Consequently it is harder (but not impossible) to express

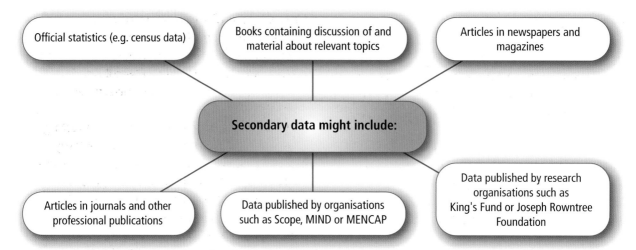

FIGURE 16.2 *Examples of secondary data*

purely qualitative data numerically. In this unit, a number of examples of quantitative data have already been cited.

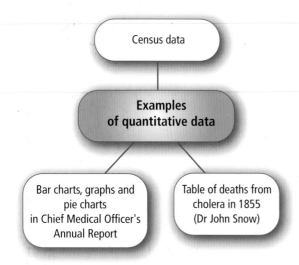

FIGURE 16.3 *Examples of quantitative data*

Such data is useful to a researcher because it allows conclusions or inferences to be drawn from the information collected. The interpretation of data will be discussed more fully below (Section 3). The production of quantitative data is an important element of scientific enquiry. For example, it would be unscientific to say that 'most of' the patients in a piece of research responded well to a certain treatment. This means little in scientific terms. It is more meaningful to quantify this and to state that, for example 80 per cent of patients in a clinical

trial of 3,000 people responded well to the same treatment. Note, too, that in a well-conducted research study, both the results of the treatment and the total number of people in the sample are quantified (see page 284 for sampling methods).

Qualitative data

Qualitative data cannot always be expressed numerically. It is data that is expressed by the subjects of a study in their own words, and is often concerned with how people feel, how they view particular issues or events, what they would like to do or what kinds of service they would like to receive.

In social research projects, researchers often leave space on the questionnaire for people to add their own comments. Qualitative information can be very useful in the design stage of a piece of research; it is good practice to obtain the views of people who are likely to be involved. Such opinions can alert researchers to key issues, and help avoid serious errors of judgement with respect to the design and implementation of the research. This is true for both evaluative and experimental research. In the scenario on page 280 the example was given of poor design with respect to a clinical study of a particular disease. Although the ultimate focus was to produce quantitative data about the incidence of a particular disease, failure to collect qualitative information about the feelings of the women taking part resulted in a high drop-out rate, so the results were not as comprehensive as they might have been.

A question of quality

A private research company has been asked to evaluate the impact of a new community centre on an estate where there are a number of high-rise blocks.

At a very early stage in planning the project the researcher, Jon, attends several local group meetings (e.g. the pre-school playgroup, the residents' association) and meets with a number of other people, such as the local community police officer, to explain the research and to ask people what they think. He tape-records what people tell him, and then uses the information to plan his research.

1. What basic principles should Jon observe before and during this initial fact-finding exercise?

2. How might he prepare for each of these meetings?

In this example, Jon has started his enquiries with an open mind. He doesn't ask people to fill in questionnaires at this point, but he does have some questions of his own. By asking open questions such as 'What do you think about the new community centre?', or simple specific questions such as 'Who do you think I need to talk to?' he starts to build a general picture of the situation. From this initial enquiry, he can focus in on key people and issues to investigate in a more structured way.

Qualitative data can also be useful to supplement quantitative material. The Hartrigg Oaks research (page 275) uses the actual comments of residents to augment and explain the more numerical information expressed in tables and bar-charts.

Think it over

When planning your own research project, it is a good idea to consider how you will use both qualitative and quantitative data.

Structured and unstructured data

The terms **structured** and **unstructured** are used with respect to methods of data collection. Broadly speaking, data which is collected in a structured way can be quantified, whereas unstructured data cannot.

Jon, in the example above, began collecting qualitative data about his research in a fairly unstructured way. He didn't use questionnaires to standardise the responses of the people he consulted, and made no attempt to quantify what he was told. He was content to record the responses, listen and accept information in whatever format people wished to express themselves. In the next phase of the project he began to devise ways of standardising responses. The issue of questionnaire design is discussed more fully below (page 286). Here it is enough to note that there are several ways to standardise responses to questions, including ticking boxes or circling numbers. This is what is meant by structured data, and used appropriately it can provide a way of quantifying qualitative responses, as Figure 16.4 shows.

COMMUNITY CENTRE:
user satisfaction survey

1. How many times a week do you visit the centre?
   (*Please enter number in box*)

2. Do you consider the service provided to be:

   Good

   Average

   Poor

3. Use this space to make any comments you wish about the community centre.

FIGURE 16.4 *User satisfaction survey*

The first two questions on the form collect structured data which can be analysed numerically. Once all the questionnaires have been completed (either by the researcher asking questions, or by giving out questionnaires for people to complete themselves), the researcher can add the number of answers to each question, and then express the results in numbers or percentages. For example, the results might show that 40 per cent of respondents considered the community centre offered a good service, 40 per cent felt the service was average, and 20 per cent thought it was poor.

In contrast, the last part of the questionnaire makes no attempt to structure what people want to say and, in theory, any responses are possible here. It is possible to classify these 'free-ranging' responses into broad areas. The researcher might be able to say, from such an analysis, that about 30 per cent of respondents would like to see different opening hours, or that 23 per cent found the centre difficult to access because they had mobility problems. However, because of the unstructured nature of the way this information is collected, any conclusions drawn will have to be cautious, and may need further investigation.

Try it out

Design a very short questionnaire for people to complete themselves. The task is either to find out what medication or what services respondents receive. The subjects are a group of people aged over 75 years.

Using primary research methods

One of the first tasks when conducting primary research is to define and select the subjects for your study. Identifying who to include in your research depends on the objectives of your study, and the topic chosen. The total numbers of people who are the subjects of your study are referred to as the 'population'. The population of a study can be composed of households rather than individuals.

Case studies and defined populations

In a small-scale study such as the one you will carry out for this unit, the choice of population

Key concepts

Subject: as well as meaning a 'topic' (such as maths or English), the term subject(s) is used in research methodology to indicate the person or people who are being studied in a particular piece of research.

Population: as well as meaning the people who live in a particular country or area, this term is used in research methodology to indicate the total number of people who are being studied.

may be straightforward. In the demographic study described on page 274 (research to support the choice of location of a new Sure Start day centre) the researchers needed to find out about all single parents in the borough. Census data enabled them to establish the geographical location of this particular population. In the study of Hartrigg Oaks (page 275), the population of the two postal surveys included all the residents of this community for older people. In the case study scenario described on page 281 the researcher, Nas, is studying the impact of reminiscence sessions on older people in a residential unit. His main population for study is all those residents who attended the sessions.

Sampling

Sometimes it is not possible to include all relevant subjects within the scope of a piece of research. It would be very difficult, for example, to measure the physiological changes resulting from smoking by studying every single smoker in the UK. This would involve testing possibly hundreds of thousands of individuals, and the logistical problems would be immense. For larger-scale studies such as this, a procedure known as **sampling** is necessary in order to reduce the population to a manageable size.

Key concept

Sampling: the selection of a representative cross-section of the population being studied.

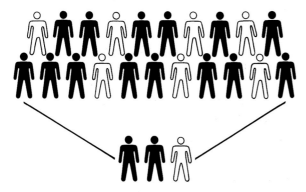

FIGURE 16.5 *The sample should be as representative of the population as possible*

Opportunity sampling

Sometimes, even when a population is well-defined, the researcher may have to be content with whoever is available to form the subject group. Not everyone may be prepared to take part in a survey, for example, and some people may be willing but unable to attend. Similarly, members of a group being observed may not all be present when the observation is made. This is very likely to be the case in a small-scale study where time and human resources are limited.

Random sampling

Researchers may use a number of different sampling methods to arrive at the population of a study. One such method is known as **random sampling.** Before it can be done, a **sampling frame** must be drawn up. This is basically a comprehensive list of potential subjects.

If, for example, researchers want to monitor the effectiveness of a new diagnostic technique designed to pick up early signs of cancer in older women, the total population may be defined as all women living in a certain area aged 50 plus. One way to make a random sample would be to ask all GP surgeries in that area to print lists of their female patients of that age. This list would be the sampling frame. The next stage would be to select names from that list, perhaps every tenth name, to give a smaller-scale list of subjects for study. A better way to ensure a truly random sample would

be to generate a random list of numbers by computer, and then to ask GPs to produce names corresponding to the numbered places on the sampling frame list.

Stratified random sampling

Sometimes, researchers will want to use a different sampling technique, especially if it is important to make sure that key sub-groups within a population are properly represented.

Suppose that the objective is to establish satisfaction levels amongst people using a new community outreach scheme. An initial survey might be done using a very simple questionnaire, but there might be too many users to interview everyone. The sampling frame would be the list of all people known to use the service. However, the list shows that 70 per cent of users are women. The sample chosen for in-depth interviews needs to represent this 70:30 gender split, so if 100 people are selected for interview, 70 must be women and only 30 should be men. This technique is known as **proportionate stratified sampling.**

Another kind of stratified random sampling is known as **disproportionate stratified sampling.** If a very small number of people using the outreach scheme are from a particular ethnic community, perhaps only five people, they represent less than 1 per cent of the population of the study. Using proportionate stratified sampling, only one of the hundred people selected would be from this group. However, if cultural issues were felt to be important, the researchers might want to ensure that all five people in this cultural group should be interviewed. There might be important reasons why people from this group were not using the facility, and interviewing all five users might provide important information for service planners.

In this case, the researchers deliberately structure the way in which subjects are selected to ensure that small but significant groups within the study population are properly represented. The data from such small groups can also be analysed and presented separately, to highlight any differences between them and the rest of the study population.

Quota sampling

Another sampling technique is **quota sampling.** This is often used by market researchers, who might be instructed to speak to a specified number of people in a particular category. If, for example, a council wanted to assess reactions to a new one-stop shop facility in a shopping centre, the quota sampling method might involve interviewers stopping 100 men and 100 women as they left the premises, to get their views on the service.

It will not be necessary for you to demonstrate use of these more sophisticated sampling techniques in your study for this unit. However, knowledge of how populations are sampled may help you to evaluate some of the secondary research collected.

Triangulation

Sometimes, particularly in larger studies, researchers will cross-check their findings by collecting data from a number of different sources and informants. A case study of group behaviours in a mental health day centre, for example, may be compared with data from a centre elsewhere. Such a comparison will allow a more balanced account to be made of observed behaviours. This process is known as **triangulation.**

Think it over

If you can get additional data from a different source on the same subject as your research project, you can use triangulation to modify or enhance your own findings.

Methods of data collection

Questionnaires

Some of the data for your research may be best collected using a questionnaire. You will have to decide whether it will be self-completed (by the population of your study), or whether you will complete them in an interview-type situation with each subject. Interviews will be considered more fully below (page 290).

Key concept

Respondent: a person who takes part in a survey, and who 'responds' to the questions (either by self-completion of a questionnaire, or during an interview).

The advice in this section applies mainly to the self-completion situation. When questionnaires are self-completed, clear instructions must be given, and the form must be user-friendly and easy to complete. Short, simple forms are more likely to be completed fully than long, complicated ones.

FIGURE 16.6 *'I'll never get this in an envelope, even if I do complete it'*

Types of question

The distinction between structured and unstructured data was discussed above, and a mini-questionnaire gave examples of questions designed to collect both types of data. Just to remind you, structured data is that which can be expressed numerically, whilst unstructured data is less easy to quantify.

Questions to collect unstructured data

Unstructured data is usually collected by means of verbal or open questions. Open questions cannot be answered simply by 'yes' or 'no', so a respondent has to answer in their own words. Open questions usually begin with the words 'what', 'why' and 'how'.

> **Key concept**
>
> *Open question:* a question which cannot be answered by 'yes' or 'no', and requires a response to be made in someone's own words.

Open questions are useful for collecting qualitative data, such as respondents' views or opinions, or where researchers are interested in exploring all angles of an issue, including some that they may not have thought of. Some examples are:

* What are your views about the meals on wheels service in your locality?
* What differences have you observed as a result of taking this drug?
* Why did you choose to use this service?
* How are you feeling as a result of having acupuncture?

Open questions are often used on questionnaires to get qualitative information in addition to the quantitative data collected in the structured part of the form. Sometimes, such data can be analysed and expressed numerically, especially if the researcher can detect a trend in the responses. However, you need to be very experienced in order to do this well, particularly if there are a lot of questionnaires to analyse.

Questions to collect structured data

There are several different options when collecting structured data by questionnaire, six are set out in Table 16.2 (following Bell, 1993).

The straightforward closed question can also be used on a self-completion questionnaire. A closed question can be answered 'yes' or 'no', and can be useful in determining which categories a respondent falls into. Some examples are:

* Do you use medication to control your condition?
* Does your child need physiotherapy?
* Do you need help in getting in and out of bed?

The closed question can also be used in conjunction with a technique known as routing. If a respondent answers in a certain way to a closed question, then they can be redirected on to a different part of the form, as the following example shows:

---

3. Do you use medication to control your condition?

If 'no', please go straight to question 7.

(Questions 4, 5 and 6 would then deal with aspects of taking medication. The person who answered 'no' at this point would not need to answer these particular questions.)

The *list* (Table 16.2) is useful to establish which of several options applies to each of your subjects. A respondent can tick as many items as are applicable. You may also want to pre-code items in the list for ease of analysis (Section 3). This can be done easily by allocating a number or a letter to each item on the questionnaire.

With the *category* type of question, a respondent will tick only one of a number of boxes and again, you may wish to pre-code each item for future analysis. As with lists, it is often useful to add the category 'other' to allow for options that you may not have anticipated.

The *ranking* question is normally used to establish the relative importance a respondent attaches to specific characteristics, qualities, or even services. You might use this method to discover which activities potential users of leisure services might value and use. The *scale* has a similar use, and can be used to ask respondents to attach values to specific characteristics or

Types of question

TYPE	EXAMPLE
List	Which of the following services do you use? (Please tick all that apply to you) Home care Meals service Residential care Other (please specify)
Category	Which of the following age groups do you belong to? (Please tick one category only) 19 years or under 20–25 years 26–30 years 31 years or over
Ranking	Place the following leisure activities in order of their importance to you by giving a number to each (1 = least important, 5 = most important): swimming movement and music art classes drama group craft activities
Quantity	How many times have you visited your GP in the last six months? (Please enter the number of times in the box)
Scale	The service given at my local GP surgery is: Excellent Good Average Fair Poor 1 2 3 4 5 (Please circle the number that most closely corresponds to your opinion)
Grid	See Table 16.3 for an example of a grid to collect data.

TABLE 16.2 *Structured data collection*

services. In the example above, people have been asked to rate the service provided at the local GP surgery. Here, respondents have been given a choice of five scores, allowing them to select a mid-point score if they feel ambivalent about an issue. Some researchers would offer only a four-point scale (e.g. excellent, good, fair, poor), as it is claimed that a five-point scale allows people to sit on the fence, and leads to meaningless scores of 'average'. However, others criticise the four-point scale on the grounds that it can polarise scores artificially; people may be genuinely ambivalent about certain issues, and should have the opportunity to express this. Making them choose between 'better' and 'worse' ends of a scale might not necessarily lead to meaningful scores.

The grid can be used to express more than one parameter at the same time, and does the job of collating the data into more than one category. Using the grid in Table 16.3, for example, would mean that the researcher could produce tables to show the total number of people using types of service, and the number using each type of supplier. Preferences towards particular suppliers would show up, for example, if the people in the sample preferred the Age Concern facilities to those provided by the council.

Using one or more of these types of structured questions will provide data that can be analysed numerically, even if it concerns people's views and opinions of something. In practice, researchers often use a number of different types

Grid form of question

Please indicate by ticking the appropriate boxes which services you receive and who provides them.

	COUNCIL	AGE CONCERN	NHS	PRIVATE COMPANY	DON'T USE THIS SERVICE
Day facilities					
Meals service					
Chiropody					
Community nurse					

TABLE 16.3 *Structured data collection using a grid*

of question on the same questionnaire, although they keep it simple by grouping question types together. Structured questions can be supplemented by unstructured data collection on the same form.

Questionnaire design and layout

It is important to give careful consideration to the design of a questionnaire, which should not be too complex, or too long. Points to consider include:

* type the questionnaire rather than handwriting

* consider the font size and design: will any of your respondents have visual problems?

* use plenty of white space: this aids clarity

* make instructions clear

* explain abbreviations, acronyms and specialised terms (jargon)

* if using tick-boxes, align to the right-hand side of the sheet

* leave complex questions to the end.

Piloting the questionnaire

Even in a small-scale study, it can be useful to have a 'dry run' to test out the questionnaire before collecting 'real' data. Asking other people to complete the form may highlight unforeseen ambiguities or problems.

This scenario shows a pilot exercise involving three centre users. It reveals that Andrea's questions are too vague to produce reliable data.

SCENARIO

A bit too vague

Andrea is studying transport use by people who attend a day facility for people with physical and sensory disabilities. She wants to find out about the frequency of use of the council's buses.

Her first attempt is:

How much do you use the council's bus service?

(Please tick) ☐
Very often ☐
Sometimes ☐
Not very often ☐

1. What problems might be anticipated if this wording is used?

2. How might the questions be improved?

Andrea's revised question is:

How many times a week do you use the council's bus service?

(Please enter a number in the box. If you do not use this service, please enter a zero.)

QUESTION TYPE	EXAMPLE	NOTES
Leading question	In your opinion, why is the council's decision a good thing?	Expects respondent to agree that this decision is indeed a good thing.
Presuming question	Why should CAMS be available on the NHS?	As above, makes assumption that respondent agrees with the proposition (i.e. that complementary therapies should be available on the NHS).
Double questions	Do you use physiotherapy and the day hospital service?	If a respondent uses only one of these, it is unclear how to respond.
Hypothetical questions	If you satisfied the eligibility criteria, which services would you choose?	Unlikely to give anything worth measuring.
Sensitive questions/ insensitive wording	Are you too disabled to access this building?	This question labels the respondent; it would be better to ask, 'Do you have problems accessing this building?'

TABLE 16.4 *Questions to avoid*

Each choice is open to personal interpretation. 'Very often' to one person might mean every week, whilst to another it might mean every day. On reflection, she opts for a quantity-type question, which limits respondents to specific choices which can be quantified.

There are several other potential problems with the wording of questions, some of which are set out in Table 16.4 (see Bell, 1993).

Try it out

Go back to the questionnaire you designed earlier (page 284).

In the light of what you have studied in this section, consider whether you might revise this questionnaire to include others types of question. Would you alter the layout, or change the number of questions. Redesign the questionnaire accordingly.

Interviews

Interviews can be structured, unstructured, or semi-structured in their design and execution. Whichever method you use, an important pre-consideration is to value and respect your interview subjects.

Facilitated sessions are often used to empower people with learning disabilities to express themselves

Conducting interviews

Thorough planning is essential to conducting successful interviews. There are a number of practical considerations to bear in mind, and these are set out in Checklist 1.

Types of interview

An interviewer may use a combination of structured, semi-structured or unstructured

CONSIDERATIONS	NOTES
Time	Choose times that are convenient for interviewees and yourself. Make sure your interview sessions don't clash with normal activities.
Pacing	Don't do too many interviews at once. Conducting even one interview can be very tiring, depending on its length and content.
Venue	Choose a venue convenient for everyone involved. It should be suitable for holding private, quiet conversations. The room needs to be comfortable, neither too hot nor too cold, and well ventilated.
Furniture	Furniture should be comfortable, but not so as to cause drowsiness. Consider whether you will need a table to take notes on, or whether you will have your papers on a clip-board.
Accessibility	If you or your respondents have mobility problems, for example, make sure that everyone can access to the building/room you have chosen easily.
Additional help	Will you need a signer (for any deaf people), or an interpreter? You may have your own sensory or language needs. In either case, check whether the venue is adequate to accommodate yourself, your subject and any helper who is present. People with learning disabilities may require the presence of an advocate or carer. When interviewing service users, you must be supervised by an appropriate professional worker.
Recording unstructured data	Consider whether you will: * use a tape recorder * take notes * bring a helper to take notes. NB The interviewee must be quite comfortable with whatever method of recording you choose.

CHECKLIST 16.1: *Preparing to conduct an interview session*

techniques, using two or even all of these approaches.

Structured and semi-structured interviews

In the *structured interview*, the researcher uses a schedule which might be very similar to the self-completion questionnaire. The interviewer will read out each question, completing or ticking the boxes, and circling the relevant responses as required. If the respondent doesn't understand something, the interviewer can explain as required. There are a number of advantages in using a structured interview, as far as the quality of data is concerned:

* all or most of the questions are likely to be answered (in a self-completed questionnaire, respondents may leave unanswered questions)

* the risk of misunderstanding of questions is minimised

* the risk of collusion between respondents is avoided

* the interviewer can dictate the pace of the interview

* additional responses/reactions may be observed by the interviewer

* problems of reading, writing and comprehension can be overcome

* quantitative data will be produced in a standardised way

* sensory and physical problems can be overcome.

In a structured interview, the researcher aims to ask the questions in the same way for each respondent. This is to make sure that data collected is standardised, and to minimise bias (for more on bias, see Section 2).

The interviewer may also have a list of prompts or probes to help respondents provide further detail in specific areas, for example:

TOPIC	OPEN QUESTIONS/PROMPTS
Social circumstances	Tell me about yourself. What's it like where you live?
Health	Tell me about your current state of health. What's your state of health like at the moment?
Service use	Why do you come to this drop-in centre? Tell me about the things you do here.

TABLE 16.5 *Collecting semi-structured data*

---

6. Do you consider that you receive enough practical support?

| Yes | Go to question 7. |

| No | Why is this?_____
Would you like to get your existing service more frequently? _____
What else would you like to receive? |

In this example, the technique of routing is also used (see page 287). If the respondent answers 'Yes' to question 6, then the interviewer moves straight on to question 7. If the answer is 'no', then the interviewer moves to a series of prompts to elicit some further data from the respondent.

Semi-structured interviewing involves starting from a list of prepared questions, but then allowing the respondent to answer in their own words. In the example above, the respondent is steered towards a number of aspects of service delivery. The technique can also be used to allow interview subjects to introduce their own themes within a given topic (see Table 16.5).

Unstructured interviewing

Unstructured data collection occurs when interviewees talk about anything they want to, without prompting from the interviewer. Although the interviewer will sometimes initiate the topic, there will be little attempt to control what the subject wants to disclose. This method, also known as in-depth interviewing, allows a

respondent to say what they really think about something. For instance, the opening of an unstructured (in-depth) interview might be:

Type of interview   In-depth research With young person

Opening prompt   Hi, how are you doing?

In this example, which is from a research study into the attitudes of young people, the researcher wants to know what is important to them, and doesn't want to be prescriptive about the topics discussed. The researcher has no pre-designed schedule, and although they might be interested in some specific topics (like drug-use, for example), the course of the interview will actually be led by the young person. The original interview may be tape-recorded, and a method known as discourse analysis then used to analyse what happened, so the interviewer can establish the key issues and concerns for the subject. Subsequently, the researcher may want to conduct further interviews which are more structured in design.

Observation

Another method of data collection is observation. Observation is often used for case studies (for example, observing aspects of service use in a mental health drop-in centre), or **ethnographic studies** (e.g. watching the interaction of a group of young children and adults). It can also be used in conjunction with the experimental method. An example of this might be when two groups are observed separately, one of which is subject to certain conditions and the other is not. The objective in this case is to see if there are noticeable behavioural differences between the two groups.

Observation can be by a participant observer (i.e. someone who takes part in the activities with the subjects of the study) or by a non-participant observer (see Table 16.6 and Bell, 1993).

An excellent example of a participant-observation study was made by Croft (1999). She wanted to study the ways in which men at a residential establishment (Esplanade) expressed their identities through speech and story. She spent a considerable amount of time in the house with them, sometimes helping them with tasks like laundry (although this was discouraged by the centre staff). Gradually, she learned how each of the residents liked to be listened to, and became accepted by them. As a result, she elicited a number of conversations and stories which she later recorded and used as the basis of her study.

However, one of the problems with the participant method of observation is that subjects will often modify their behaviour, simply because of the presence of a stranger (the researcher) (see sources of error and bias in Section 2).

When using the observational method, it is extremely important to decide exactly what you are measuring or recording. Bell notes that the focus of observation is usually one or more of the following (1993):

* content (i.e. what happens)

* process (i.e. the way in which something happened)

* interaction (how participants respond or react to each other)

* the way in which participants contribute to what is going on

* specific aspects of behaviour (e.g. violence, concentration span etc).

OBSERVER	TECHNIQUES USED
Participant	– researcher works/lives alongside the subjects of the study – data collection is often unstructured – the researcher records significant behaviour, situations and events
Non-participant	– researcher watches events whilst remaining as unobtrusive as possible – may use grids or charts to record what goes on (e.g. interaction between individuals in a group) – the process may be video-recorded or tape-recorded

TABLE 16.6 *Observational research methods*

SPECIMEN: OBSERVATION SHEET

Observing social interaction in service users in a day unit for people with a learning disability.

Group ....

Number in group ....

Date ....

Time from: .... To ....

Aim:

Activity during observation

Are there any 'friendship groups' evident within the group as a whole?

Are there any individuals who appear not to get involved with the activity?

Are there any obvious group leaders?

Are there any individuals who seek more attention from the session tutor than the others?

Do people share equipment with each other?

Do people help each other?

Are there any individuals who appear to be actively avoiding interaction with the others?

Candidate's Signature ....

Supervisor's Signature ....

Notes:

FIGURE 16.7 *Specimen observation sheet*

NB **When conducting interviews or observations, it is essential to work with supervision.** In practice, this means having a professional worker such as a care worker or manager present while you are interviewing a service user. This is in your interests, and those of your subject. Such a person might also advise you on questionnaire design, and how best to conduct an interview or an observation. Always take such advice when it is given, and observe any house rules or regulations when conducting your research.

There are some very sophisticated classification systems for describing behaviour which are too complex for inclusion here but are discussed and documented in Bell (1993). The sociogram as a method of presenting relationships between people in a group is explained on page 312. However, successful observation of behaviour requires a high level of skill and specialist knowledge.

Think about your research

Unless you are very confident and experienced in this kind of work, it is a good idea to avoid aiming to produce a very detailed analysis of interactions and behaviours.

Experiments

Experiments involve setting up specific situations to test the validity of particular theories or hypotheses. They are often concerned with establishing causal relationships, for example, that music therapy helps control post-operative pain. In principle, the researcher controls all the variables and parameters within an experiment, which should provide quantitative data for analysis. A good experiment is capable of *replication*, that is, it can be repeated using exactly the same conditions to compare several sets of results. If results are similar over a number of experiments, firm conclusions may be made from the data.

Some experiments are relatively straightforward to design and control, such as the testing of pharmaceutical products. A sampling frame will be set up according to pre-defined criteria (e.g. age,

medical condition) and a population selected at random from this sampling frame. This group will receive the new drug. A second or control group (which satisfies the same criteria as the first group) will either receive no treatment, a placebo, or the existing standard treatment. This method is very common in clinical trials (see page 278). Experiments can also compare and contrast the impact of different kinds of treatment on people with the same medical condition.

This type of experiment often takes the form of a **longitudinal study** (so called because it lasts for a significant period of time). Researchers can avoid prejudicing the outcome of an experiment by not telling subjects which group they belong to. This eliminates any possible psychological bias. This is considered to be even more effective when researchers themselves do not know which group subjects have been allocated to. This is known as a double-blind trial, and is often used when the control group receives a placebo rather than another pharmaceutical product.

Key concept

Longitudinal study: a research study that lasts for a significant period of time, allowing the impact of a number of variables to be taken into account.

Experiments to measure or predict human behaviour are harder to set up and control. Nevertheless, researchers, especially psychologists, do use the experimental method to investigate aspects of human behaviour. They often combine an experimental situation with aspects of the observational method. An example of such an experiment is described below (see Section 2).

Action research

Action research is a method that focuses on a particular task or problem. The project is conducted by an individual or a group (often a group of colleagues) who regularly review and monitor aspects of an issue in order to make decisions about how it should be tackled.

The term 'action research' derives from the fact that the actions of practitioners are the focus of study; it is categorised as research because whatever happens during a project is recorded just as systematically as for an observation or an experiment. The practitioner-researcher involved will also reflect on their own practice, in order to evaluate what happens, to draw conclusions, and to make recommendations for the benefit of other practitioners.

An example might be a group of health staff, who want to make improvements in the way that patients are assessed and then admitted to a treatment programme. Staff keep diaries of what is going on, interview patients and also analyse service data. They also analyse their own responses and reactions to situations as they develop. Over time, they will introduce changes to the system and monitor the impact of those changes. In a sense, therefore, the practitioner engaging in action research is both the agent of the research and the subject of the study. This method also provides a means by which a health or social care professional can further their own professional development.

Think it over

As this method usually involves the collaboration of a group of people over time, and in the context of an ongoing work situation, it is unlikely to be relevant to a small-scale project. However, the findings of other action research projects may provide useful secondary information.

Case studies

Case studies involve the in-depth observation, description and analysis of a particular situation. A case study might involve just one person, or a group of people in a given situation, such as a therapy group or an early years class.

The case study method will involve several techniques, and might combine observation with, for example, interviews, surveys, the keeping of logs and diaries and, in particular, the recording of 'critical incidents' which may have a bearing on what is being studied.

SCENARIO
Critical details

Researchers want to assess the usefulness of a new piece of equipment designed to assist people with disabilities to move between the bed and a chair.

They ask care assistants in a residential unit to test the equipment when appropriate, keeping diaries of what they do. In particular, they want care assistants to note any difficulties, and also to record any specific incidents – good or bad – relating to the new device.

They also ask the people who have been assisted to move in this way to keep similar diaries.

After six weeks, researchers study the diaries and accounts of the critical incidents. They also interview care assistants and residents to obtain further qualitative data. The number of occasions on which difficulties were experienced (and the types of difficulty encountered) can be expressed quantitatively.

1. Can you see any potential difficulties with the diary technique of data collection?

2. How objective might such data be? Does this matter?

Think it over

You might want to combine the use of questionnaires with one or more of the other techniques in this section, depending on your topic.

Using secondary research methods

It is important to do some secondary research at the start of your project. This will enable you to set your own work into context (in relation to what is going on elsewhere), and may give you some strong leads about how to organise your own study, or the questions you might seek to answer.

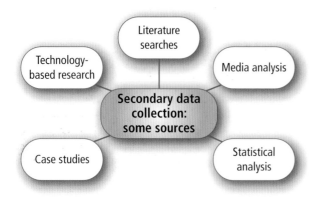

FIGURE 16.8 *Sources of secondary data*

The scenario below describes how one student used secondary research to start her own project.

Making a literature search involves checking books, and academic and professional journals, for studies that are relevant to your proposed research. Internet search-engines provide a technology-based medium for finding relevant information (some of which may have originated in printed sources). Media analysis involves identifying relevant material from TV programmes and the press. Published case studies of people or groups similar to your target population can be extremely helpful, providing comparisons and sometimes ideas about methodology. Finally, existing statistical analyses such as the National Census can provide extremely useful background information.

Natalie uses the secondary data she collects to put her research into context. She discovers other places where new ways of empowering people with learning disabilities are being tried. These methods include advocacy, self-advocacy, mentoring and facilitation. One of these projects has actually been evaluated, so she decides to adapt one of the questionnaires for use in her own project. She cites this research in her own report, giving a full acknowledgement.

Key concept

Citation: the act of making reference to another piece of research. This term is often used in research reports.

SCENARIO
Research in context

For her research project, Natalie is going to describe a new initiative in communicating with people who have learning disabilities. She is studying group sessions in one of the day units run by her local authority, where staff are using special techniques to help people with learning disabilities to express themselves. She is also going to investigate how effective these techniques are.

She needs to find out about similar projects elsewhere, to provide background information and points of comparison. To find this information she starts with the Valuing People website. Here, she finds some of the information she needs, together with links to the websites of other helpful organisations, and references to other published secondary sources.

1. Who else might Natalie involve in her collection of secondary data?

2. How should such information be stored for use later on in the project?

Summary

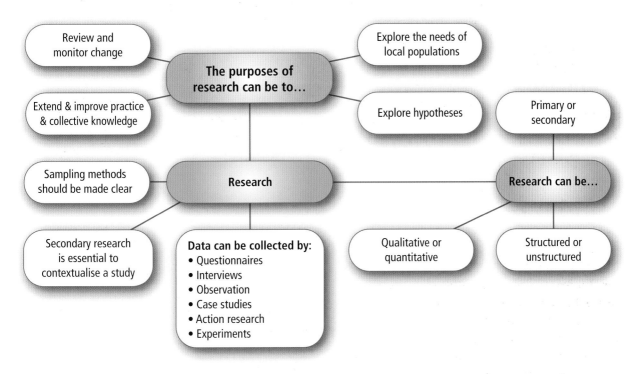

An investigation into how growing older can sometimes have an impact on a person's mental health has shown how physical, social and biological factors can be interrelated.

1. What would you say was the main purpose of this study (using the categories set out in the summary above)? Remember that there may have been more than one aim for this piece of work.

2. How might the findings be of practical use?

3. Which of the following professionals might be interested to learn more about these findings: GP, Health Visitor, Social Worker, Care Worker, Home Care Worker, Social Services Manager, Health Service Planning Manager. Describe briefly how each professional might put the research findings into use in their own work.

Section 2: Ethical issues, sources of error and bias in research

Ethics in research

Ethical practice is critical in all aspects of research methodology, and the discussion in this section considers some of the issues in depth.

Considering the participants' rights

The British Psychological Society (BPS) Code of Ethical Principles sets out guidelines for conducting research with people to guide psychologists. These principles are set out below. The BPS code is intended for chartered psychologists, but it represents good practice for all researchers and provides a point of reference for the ethics of interview (and other) research. Over time, a number of principles of good practice

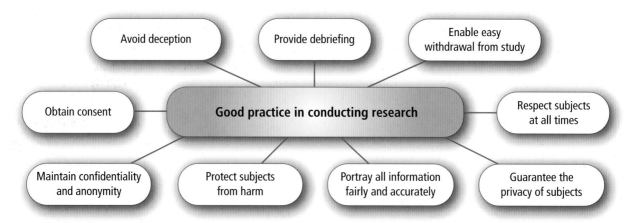

FIGURE 16.9 *Good practice in research*

have developed, in addition to the original BPS code.

The BPS code was developed to spread good practice and ensure high standards in research. Before the development of professional ethical codes like this one, some psychological studies were conducted in ways that led to unfortunate results. The following scenario describes a controversial controlled observational study conducted in the 1960s by Professor Stanley Milgram of Yale University (Milgram, 1963).

SCENARIO

How far will they go?

In Milgram's study, the subjects were ordered to administer electric shocks to 'victims' who were in fact in collusion with the researchers. The ostensible purpose of the study was to test the impact of 'punishment' on memory and learning. In actual fact, the true aim was to see how far people were prepared to obey authority, even if it involved doing something against their better judgement or moral principles.

Subjects had volunteered to take part in the study, which had been advertised (in the press) as a study about memory and learning. They were paid a nominal amount to take part. The subjects were led to believe that both they and the 'victims' were all volunteers, and that they had been randomly allocated to their respective roles. Considerable care was taken when setting up the study to convince the volunteers that this was the case. Forty males, aged 20 to 50 years, took part in the study.

The subjects were ordered (by an authority figure) to administer 'electric shocks' on command to the victims who had been instructed to react according to the 'voltage' delivered. In reality, no electric shocks were given, but the real subjects had initially been given small electric shocks to convince them that the situation was real.

Milgram discovered that 65 per cent of the subjects were prepared to keep giving shocks of up to 450 volts (at which point the victims might have died had the experiment been real). Despite the agonised cries of the victims, on being told 'the experiment requires you to continue', or 'you have no choice, you must go on', it was not until shock levels reached

continued on next page

300 volts that volunteers began to refuse to continue. Twenty-six of the volunteers continued to give shocks up to the maximum 450 volts.

Whilst the volunteers were pressurised to continue, many showed signs of extreme nervousness and discomfort, and one suffered a convulsive fit as a result of the stress.

All of the volunteers were debriefed afterwards, and told that they had not harmed anyone. A year later, they were sent questionnaires to check for any longer-term emotional damage.

A more detailed description of Milgram's study can be found in Gross, 2003.

What do you think?

✱ Does the deception involved in Milgram's experiment breach ethical principles, or could it be acceptable?

✱ What does this scenario tell us about the importance of people taking part in any study being fully informed about what is going on?

✱ How might such information affect people's behaviour during the course of the study?

✱ Is deception ever justified as part of a research project?

Milgram's findings about people's willingness to conform to authority are quite shocking. However, his work is probably now more famous for the ethical issues it raises, including whether or not it is right for researchers to place subjects into a potentially damaging situation.

As a researcher, you should check the ethical issues inherent in any study you design. The ethical aspects of using interviews, questionnaires and observation are considered here.

Issues relating to the nature and type of research

Ethics and interviews

Valuing the person

If you choose to collect data by interviewing your subjects (either face-to-face or by telephone) there are a number of specific considerations. The people you are interviewing are not simply sources of data for your project, but are unique individuals. Each has a right to be treated with respect.

You will need to have the right attitude if an interview is to be a success. You will be asking a number of people some very personal questions, and/or to give you personal (and maybe difficult) details about themselves. Because you are asking for their help, you must get their consent to take part in your research project; you must therefore explain the nature of your project, and how you will use any information that you get.

Your questions and checklists should be prepared well in advance, and preferably piloted before the 'real' interviews. Check with your tutor, or another relevant professional who knows your subjects, how you intend to conduct your interviews. Be sure that your questions will not threaten your subjects or cause offence. The single most important consideration when interviewing people is to respect and value their personal identity.

You must guarantee that you will not use real names or any details (such as addresses, details of relatives or photographs) that could identify your subjects. In other words, you must provide a guarantee of anonymity. It is also crucial to make sure that you only use the data you have gathered for the specific purpose for which the participants have given permission. Subjects should be given access to the results of the study, and even given the chance to comment before the findings are published.

Interviewing people with learning disabilities

If your research requires you to interview people with learning disabilities, you will need to take expert advice about the best way of structuring both the interview itself and the way you collect data. There are a number of specialised ways of empowering people with learning disabilities to express themselves, including using an advocate, self-advocacy and facilitated sessions, to make it easy for people to choose between options or to express their views. Information about empowering people with learning disabilities is available on the Valuing People website.

Ethics and people completing questionnaires

When designing questionnaires, many of the same considerations apply as for interviews. The purpose of the research must be relevant to the study. Asking unnecessary questions is both intrusive and time-consuming for the respondent.

You should give your respondents the option of anonymity unless it is absolutely critical for the research that you can identify each person. If anonymity is not possible, then confidentiality should be guaranteed. All completed questionnaires should be stored securely before analysis, after which they should be destroyed.

these comments are quite illuminating, and they may improve the conclusions from the project. It also gives respondents the chance to check that their contributions have been fairly and accurately portrayed.

Ethics and people being observed

The two types of observational research method (participant and non-participant) were described in Section 1 above. It was noted that the participant-observation technique can result in a phenomenon known as the 'observer's paradox', because subjects are likely to adapt their behaviour in response to the presence of the observer. Withholding the true identity of the observer (in order to encourage subjects to behave more naturally) raises ethical issues, as this is arguably deceitful. Furthermore, recording and publishing details of people's behaviour without their permission is arguably bad practice. However,

SCENARIO

Confidential but not anonymous

A team of researchers is looking at the effects of a particular drug on patients with osteoarthritis. It is important that all members of the team are familiar with each patient for the purposes of discussion within the research unit. During the course of the study, therefore, the forms on which data is recorded bear the names of each person taking part.

However, no one outside the team has the right to know this personal information. When the report is prepared, patients are designated by letters to keep their details confidential.

Think it over

Kit wants to find out about the importance of art sessions in a day unit for people with learning disabilities. She plans to attend a session to see what they do, and decides she will take part by doing some painting herself.

On her first visit, the instructor introduces her to the group, and they are so interested in Kit that they crowd around her, asking lots of questions. The session takes longer to get going than normal, and even then people sometimes stop what they are doing to go and talk to or watch Kit. One young woman becomes very jealous of the attention the others are paying to Kit, and there is a brief disagreement between her and another group member.

Kit's presence in the group has thus affected their normal behaviours and, to some extent, their relationships.

1. What can be done to minimise the impact of the observer's paradox?

2. How does this need to be built into your research plan?

3. How might the presence of an observer affect the validity of data?

You should give all respondents feedback on the results of the survey, and the option to comment on the outcomes. You may find that

it should be possible to gain permission before engaging in an observation exercise. Spending time with a group to allow them to become accustomed to your presence before data collection starts is not only courteous to the subjects, but also increases the chances of natural behaviours being observed.

One way to avoid observer's paradox is to observe subjects from a distance, as the following scenario demonstrates.

Researchers can use one-way observation glass panels to observe how children interact when no adults are present

SCENARIO
Keeping a distance
Researchers want to observe the response of young children watching TV programmes, in particular to establish whether boys react differently from girls.

The children watch TV in a room which has a one-way glass observation panel fitted in one wall. Observers note how long the children concentrate when watching different kinds of programme, and how they interact.

They record their observations on specially prepared forms. They also video-record the children's behaviour for further analysis.

1. How should children be protected during the course of a research project?

2. Are there any specific ethical considerations where children are concerned?

3. How much should be explained to children beforehand?

4. How should parents be involved in a project of this kind?

In this example, the researchers are particularly keen to know how the children react with each other. The presence of an adult would interfere with this process.

The importance of confidentiality and anonymity

The importance of maintaining the privacy, confidentiality and anonymity of those taking part in research cannot be overestimated. Sometimes, breaches of confidentiality can happen unexpectedly, as the following example demonstrates.

Consider this

Fancy seeing you here…
Mandy is taking part in a national survey of women's health. This study has been designed by a large teaching hospital, and there are a number of sites to which respondents are invited to have medical tests, and to be interviewed by researchers. All respondents have been given a guarantee of confidentiality.

Mandy attends the first appointment, which also includes a video to explain the study in some detail. To view the video, subjects are allocated to a small group. To Mandy's embarrassment, on entering the video room she discovers that her next-door-neighbour is in the same group as herself.

1. How has this situation breached some of the basic ethical principles of conducting research?

2. How do you think this situation arose?

3. What could have been done to prevent this from happening?

When designing and implementing a research project, it is important to be aware of the need to maintain the privacy, anonymity and confidentiality of all subjects at all times.

There are many reasons for this. Someone who feels uncomfortable, embarrassed or insecure about a research situation may not necessarily provide accurate or useful information. Misuse of information or the betrayal of someone's identity might put him or her in a difficult situation with others, particularly if respondents are giving information about a workplace-based situation. Even worse, a person's sense of identity or self-worth might be damaged if they perceive that their trust has been betrayed by misuse or careless handling of personal information.

It is important to note that all research subjects have the right to withdraw from a project at any time. This should be stated explicitly when the terms of the research are explained, and agreement to participation is sought from potential subjects. The Data Protection Act (1998) sets out key principles concerning the collection and storage of personal data (where this is identifiable to a specific individual). Key principles of data protection are:

* obtain data fairly and legally
* obtain permission
* data must be adequate, relevant and not excessive
* store data only for as long as is necessary
* allow individual access to own personal data
* keep data secure
* only pass data to people who have the right or the need to know it
* record data accurately.

Sources of error and bias

The basic methods of data collection – questionnaire, interview and observation – each have disadvantages with respect to error and bias. However, all three methods also have positive aspects, and it is important to select a method keeping both advantages and disadvantages in mind. By doing this, you can utilise one or more methods to the best advantage, whilst avoiding the potential for error and/or bias inherent in each method. For instance, the semi-structured interview combines the advantages of both the structured and unstructured interviews. Tables 16.7–11 summarise the advantages and disadvantages of all three methods.

Some things to consider

ADVANTAGES	DISADVANTAGES
Relatively cheap. Can include a large number of participants. Some respondents may prefer this to being interviewed. No danger that interviewer can influence the answers.	Questions may be misunderstood. Respondents may collude in answering the questions. Some questionnaires may not be returned (especially if being sent by post). Some questions may be left unanswered. Some responses may be hard to understand. Questions may be wrongly completed (e.g. two boxes ticked instead of one).

TABLE 16.7 *Self-completion questionnaires*

Some things to consider	
ADVANTAGES	**DISADVANTAGES**
All questions will be answered.	Requires more researcher time (and therefore usually involves a smaller sample).
All questionnaires will be completed.	
Interviewer can ask extra questions (via probes).	Respondents may be hard to contact/convenient times hard to arrange.
Data will be uniform if researcher uses same format each time.	Respondent may give answers they think the researcher wants (bias).
Interviewer may also collect extra (unstructured) data.	Respondent may take a dislike to the interviewer (bias).
	Questionnaire format may restrict responses.

TABLE 16.8 *Using questionnaires in structured interviews*

Some key points	
ADVANTAGES	**DISADVANTAGES**
Much qualitative data will be collected.	Very time consuming, so sample may need to be smaller.
Respondents can say exactly what they think and feel.	Interviewer needs very good communication skills.
Interviewer can probe/follow through on any topic of interest.	Potential for bias, because of personality of interviewer.
Useful at the planning stages of a research project.	Applicability of results may be limited.
	Very hard to produce quantitative data.
	Findings may be limited to sample group.

TABLE 16.9 *Unstructured interviews*

ADVANTAGES	DISADVANTAGES
Observer can watch subjects in their own environment.	Some ethical problems – especially if the observation is secret.
Observer may see behaviours that subjects are not aware of.	Observer may misinterpret behaviour.
Useful for non-literate subjects, e.g. young children.	Some behaviours may be missed if note-taking is recording method.
Both interpersonal interactions and group behaviours can be observed.	What happens may not be relevant to the aim of the research.
May be recorded to view again.	Behaviours may be affected if the observer is visible to the group.

TABLE 16.10 *Non-participant observation*

ADVANTAGES	DISADVANTAGES
Observer gains in-depth and accurate knowledge of group behaviours.	Presence of observer will inevitably affect behaviours to some extent ('observer's paradox').
Valid data is produced.	Ethical problems if observer does not disclose true identity.
Can give access to hard-to-reach or closed groups, e.g. homeless people.	Time consuming.
	Advanced social skills needed.
	Observer may lose sense of objectivity.
	Non-acceptance by group may limit value of data.

TABLE 16.11 *Participant observation*

Summary

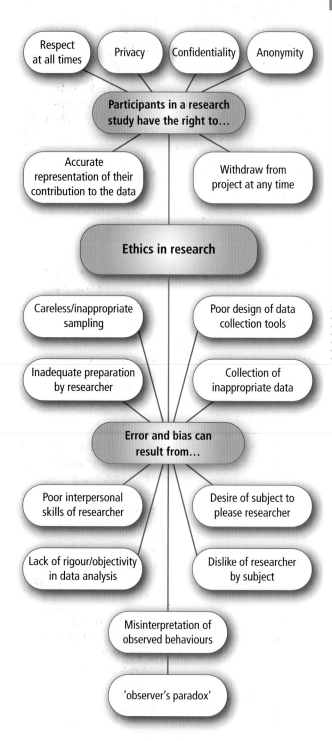

Participants in a research study have the right to...
- Respect at all times
- Privacy
- Confidentiality
- Anonymity
- Accurate representation of their contribution to the data
- Withdraw from project at any time

Ethics in research

Error and bias can result from...
- Careless/inappropriate sampling
- Poor design of data collection tools
- Inadequate preparation by researcher
- Collection of inappropriate data
- Poor interpersonal skills of researcher
- Desire of subject to please researcher
- Lack of rigour/objectivity in data analysis
- Dislike of researcher by subject
- Misinterpretation of observed behaviours
- 'observer's paradox'

Consider this

In Section 1 you were asked to consider some research on the impact of a new community centre at an estate where there are a number of high-rise blocks.

Take your thoughts a little further on this by considering the following questions:

1. How might Jon's proposal to tape-record group discussions compromise his subjects' right to anonymity and confidentiality?

2. What else might Jon do to minimise this danger? What other ways are there of recording data from group consultations?

3. Why might anonymity be important to people taking part in Jon's study?

4. What alternative methods of data collection might Jon use at this early stage?

5. Why is it important for Jon to represent people's views accurately?

Section 3: Planning, presenting and analysing findings from research

This section deals with the process of planning and implementing research, together with the analysis and presentation of the findings.

Planning the project

It is essential to begin a research study from a clearly defined task with explicit objectives. Research might involve:

* testing a hypothesis (e.g. that smoking can cause lung cancer)

* investigating a research question (e.g. where is the best place to locate a new GP surgery?).

In health and social care, topics might relate to:

* care-related situations and problems

* testing or review of existing knowledge, treatments and practices

* explaining relationships between factors affecting health and well-being

* evaluating service interventions and policies.

Some of the scenarios in this unit describe projects which might be suitable for a small-scale study. Andrea, for example, is studying transport use by service users attending a day unit for people with physical and sensory disabilities (page 289) to test a hypothesis about attendance patterns there. Natalie is investigating a research question – she is looking at the impact of a new technique for helping people with learning disabilities to express themselves. In both cases, the target population is easily defined, and the studies are manageable because of the relatively low numbers of people involved.

Following the steps in Checklist 16.2 will help to ensure that the project is adequately planned. Doing some background reading can be useful for gathering ideas on the potential aims of the study, and also on methodology. Asking advice at this early stage will help to assess how feasible the proposal is. It's no good working up a plan to study a group of under-fives, for example, if you do not have access to a group of young children, with adequate supervision. Piloting any data collection tools you devise may eliminate any errors or misleading questions, and will help you to assess how much time the main data collection exercise is likely to take.

Once you have done the preliminary work, you can then produce a research proposal. A good research proposal will include:

* aims

* rationale for the study

* methodology to be used

* details of any piloting or preliminary activity

* explanation of ethical considerations, and how these will be addressed

* specimen data collection tools

* time scale for the project.

Aims must be very clear. Examples might be:

* to establish levels of satisfaction amongst users of a specific service (e.g. of a council day care facility)

ACTION	NOTES
1. Select a topic	
2. Define the hypothesis or question to be investigated.	Are the objectives clear? Is the project manageable in the time and with the resources available?
3. Do some background reading into the topic (secondary research).	Has a similar topic been studied elsewhere? If so, is the methodology helpful?
4. Produce a research proposal, including identification of potential ethical issues.	A good research proposal will include the points set out above.
5. Identify the sample population.	Will some kind of sampling method be needed, or will this be an opportunity sample?
6. Decide on the data collection method.	Is this to be by survey, interview, observation, etc., or a combination of several methods? If time, consider some limited unstructured data collection to give you some ideas.
7. Design the data collection tools.	Questionnaires, interview schedules, observation checklists etc.
8. Pilot the data collection tools and adjust as necessary.	Unstructured interviewing might be useful at this stage, if not before.

CHECKLIST 16.2 *Planning a research project*

* to test the hypothesis that girls have better social skills than boys in a group of 7-year-olds

* to describe the characteristics of a local population using census data.

The rationale for a study sets out the reasons for choosing this particular topic and methodology, and may refer to secondary research. The importance of piloting and initial testing of feasibility has already been discussed. Production of a timescale is vital, as it is a way of working out whether or not the proposal is feasible in the time available.

Conducting the research project

Checklist 16.3 highlights key stages in conducting a research project.

You must follow ethical principles and observe the basic rules of courtesy towards everyone you approach. You are dependent on the good will and interest of everyone concerned, and it is vital to keep all parties informed of what is going on. Be sure to ask permission to proceed, both from the subject population (where personal data will be collected), and from managers and/or staff (if the study is to take place in a health or social care facility).

Make sure that you will be adequately supervised during the course of the project, particularly if and when you are engaged in working directly with a service user (for example, when conducting an interview).

Data must be recorded as accurately as possible and stored securely. Anonymity

TASK	NOTES
1. Give advanced notification of the study.	Notify everyone concerned, giving full information about the nature of the study and what is involved. A good research proposal might be used at this stage to give information to key individuals.
2. Ask permission where appropriate.	Permission will be needed from the subjects population (if personal information is sought). Managers and/or staff in health or social services facilities should also give their assent.
3. Give assurances of confidentiality and anonymity.	Consider yourself bound by the BPS Code of Ethics as much as any professional researcher.
4. Keep appointments, be punctual and courteous.	
5. Collect data using the tools as designed.	Make sure that a supervisor is present, particularly if working with children or people in a social services or health care facility.
6. Record data carefully onto questionnaires, observation sheets etc. Use video or tape-recording as appropriate.	Anonymise your notes and questionnaires. Store all data securely.
7. Analyse quantitative data selecting appropriate techniques.	Consider whether mean, median or mode are significant. Compare and contrast relationship of different variables.
8. Analyse qualitative data systematically.	Do any themes emerge? Does it throw light on the quantitative data collected?

CHECKLIST 16.3 *Conducting a research project*

and confidentiality must be preserved at all times. Names should be deleted from any case notes or records that you are allowed to see, and you should not record information in a way that is traceable to specific individuals. You should not disclose personal information to anyone else, except to people who have a right and/or need to know it. Usually, personal information can only be disclosed to others if you are given permission to do so by the subject of that information. Data in a survey is always reported anonymously, it should not be possible to identify specific individuals in the report. If a study concerns individuals, a researcher will usually give new names to these people, or simply refer to them as Mrs X, Mr Y, etc.

As the data is analysed and manipulated, ask questions constantly about the significance of what has been collected. For example, does there seem to be a relationship between certain variables? Perhaps everybody above a certain age dislikes a particular food, or the women in the sample are opting out of a certain activity. Are there any themes emerging? Perhaps, in open questioning, a significant number of people mention the fact that they feel better after having their hair done. Are there any comparisons to be made between the findings of your study, and those of any secondary research that has been consulted? Perhaps another researcher, in a different location but with a similar population, has produced similar findings to yours. This adds weight to your conclusions.

Asking many questions may lead to some surprising inferences, and some interesting comparisons.

Analysing and presenting data from research

How good is your data?

In research methodology, there are two concepts that relate to the quality of the data collected, and consequently to the significance of the conclusions reached. These are **reliability** and **validity.**

> ### SCENARIO
> ### What seems to be the problem?
> Researchers are investigating satisfaction levels of patients attending the A&E department of a local hospital. They have produced a structured questionnaire to record people's views, and have anticipated that most people will be concerned with issues such as lengthy waiting times.
>
> In fact, it turns out that patients say they understand that they may have to wait. They are more concerned about the lack of information, and also the unfriendly attitude of staff who are dealing with them. They say that if reasons for the long wait were given, together with reassurances that they haven't been forgotten and will be attended to within a specified timescale, they would be more satisfied with the service.

Reliability

Reliability relates to the extent to which a set of results can be replicated by repeating a piece of research. When researchers do systematic reviews of randomised clinical controlled trials, for example, they are looking to see (among other things) how far test results have been repeated under similar conditions. If the same results are found repeatedly, then the findings may be said to be reliable.

> **Key concept**
>
> *Reliability:* the extent to which a set of results can be replicated by repetition of a test, experiment or survey.

The reliability of survey data can be assessed by asking how far similar answers might have been given to interviewers on different occasions. It is important always to be alert to the possibility that answers to questions may be influenced by external factors. It may sometimes be necessary to repeat a study, if it is felt that these external factors have somehow skewed the data.

Key concept

Aggregate: to combine information collected at different times, and possibly from different sources.

Think it over

For a small-scale research study, it shouldn't be necessary to apply scientific tests of reliability. However, it will be important to demonstrate an awareness of the ways in which the reliability of data may be affected by the circumstances under which they were collected, and to build this into any conclusions or inferences made at the end of the project.

Validity

Data is valid if it accurately measures what it is supposed to measure. This means that the methods of data collection must be designed

to collect exactly what is needed to answer the question which the study poses. For example, it is of little use to ask extensively about the use of leisure time, if the real focus of a piece of research is personal mobility.

Key concept

Validity: relates to the quality of research results. Data is valid if it accurately measures what it is supposed to measure.

SCENARIO
How reliable is valid?

Sam has three pairs of scales, all of which show a different weight when he stands on them. However, if he puts on two pounds, all three show readings that increase by approximately that amount. Each set of scales is, therefore, reliable, in that its readings are consistent.

The problem is, Sam cannot tell which (if any) is his true weight. In other words, he cannot tell which of the three readings is valid. To establish his true weight, he must make another measure using an accurate measuring instrument. In fact, validity is always a matter of degree. Electronic scales may give a weight to the nearest ounce or milligram, whilst simpler measuring instruments may not give such precise weights.

Think it over

In a small-scale study, it isn't usually necessary to spend a great deal of time on the measurement of validity. However, it is important to make sure that you focus on your objectives, and design data collection tools to do the task in hand.

What does the data show?

Bell advises that in working through data, you should be 'constantly looking for similarities and differences, for groupings, patterns and items of particular significance' (1993). It is advisable to query the data in as many ways as possible. Are there, for example, differences between men and women in the sample? Are there differences between people of different ages? Is there anything particularly significant about one group of people (e.g. those who have been using a service for a long time, or who have a particular disability)? The different categories that can be distinguished within data sets are referred to as **variables.**

A variable might be social class (e.g. in census data), use of a particular drug (in medical research) or a type of mental health problem (e.g. in a piece of social research). The concern of researchers is often to establish whether one particular variable has a causal relationship to another. For example, they might be seeking to establish whether or not people of a certain social class or group tend to have fewer qualifications than people from a different group. Researchers may also be looking for variables that suggest further lines of enquiry. For example, people of a certain ethnic background might be under-represented in a group of service-users. Researchers would want to find out why by designing further studies.

In some cases, researchers may say that the data allows them to establish a correlation between data sets, or between certain variables. If a pattern is distinguished, e.g. a high proportion of people who smoke also experience early ageing of the skin, researchers can say there is a **correlation** between these two variables. In some cases, the data may be strong enough for a causal inference to be made. In the Chief Medical Officer's Report from 2003, a **causal inference** has been made between smoking and facial ageing, based on a relatively high number of separate studies. It is important to remember, however, that correlation of two variables does not *necessarily* imply causality. Data has to be substantiated from a number of studies, and the potential impact of other variables must be taken into account before a causal inference can be made.

Key concepts

Correlation: a link between two data sets, or two (or more) variables within a data set. Correlation does not necessarily imply causality.

Causal inference: a strong suggestion that one particular variable has a specified effect upon another.

Think it over

In small-scale studies, conclusions will often be expressed in terms of inference or suggestion, particularly since the sample size is small.

Other key concepts in the expression of findings are **relatability** and **generalisation.**

Key concepts

Relatability: the extent to which research findings may be applicable to other, similar population samples (e.g. two groups of smokers).

Generalisation: the extent to which the findings of a study are applicable to a wider population (e.g. the smokers in a study and all smokers in the wider population).

Presenting quantitative data

It is essential to express data as clearly as possible so that readers can firstly understand the points being made, and secondly form their own opinions as to how the data might be interpreted.

Suppose 50 people aged over 50 have taken part in a survey about transport use. Among other things, they have been asked if they use a travel pass. A simple way of expressing this is as a table on which both numerical values and percentages may be shown at the same time (see Table 16.12).

A good table will always show the total number of people in the sample, and should

Transport survey Sample size = 50		
	NUMBER	**PERCENTAGE**
Travel pass user Non-travel pass user	40 10	80% 20%
Total	50	100%

TABLE 16.12 *Travel pass usage*

be self-explanatory. Tables must always add up correctly. In this case, the total in the 'Number' column must add up to 50, and the percentage column must add up to 100. It is important to remember that (particularly in small-scale studies) it is not advisable to give percentages alone in a table. A small sample size, in particular, does not necessarily give conclusive results, and percentages by themselves can give a misleading impression that data is more conclusive than it really is. A figure of 80 per cent is impressive, until it is revealed that this represents eight out of only ten respondents. The data in Table 16.12 could also be expressed visually as a bar chart (see Figure 16.10).

Travel pass usage: pictograph
Sample size = 50

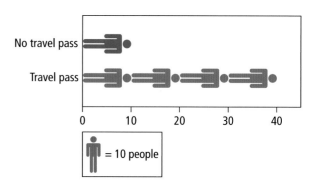

FIGURE 16.11 *Pictograph of travel pass usage*

picture or symbol to represent the quantities or values being expressed in a data set. A pictograph representing the data from Table 16.12 is shown in Figure 16.11. The way to make a pictograph is to choose a symbol representing what you would like to show; then to allocate a value to each symbol (e.g. 10 people, 10 travel passes, etc.); then plot a chart allocating the relevant number of symbols to each bar.

A pie chart is also a good way of expressing data visually (see Figure 16.12).

Travel pass usage: bar chart
Sample size = 50

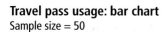
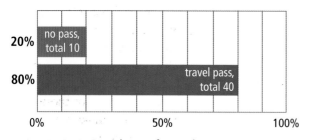

FIGURE 16.10 *Bar chart of travel pass usage*

In this case, the bars represent the percentage values of each group (i.e. travel pass users, non-travel pass users). It would be equally informative to give each bar the numerical value of each group. Visual presentation in this way can be quite striking, particularly if there is a significant point to be made about a particular variable.

A pictograph is another way of expressing data visually. Similar to a bar chart, it uses a

Travel pass usage: pie chart
Sample size = 50

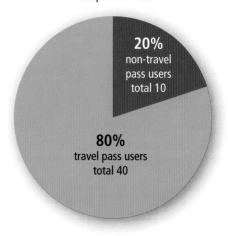

FIGURE 16.12 *Pie chart of travel pass usage*

A Venn diagram (Figure 16.13) is another effective means of displaying data visually, in particular the relationship between two or more key variables. In the following example, the researcher wants to show the relationship between

Travel pass usage: Venn diagram
Sample size = 50

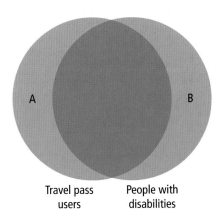

FIGURE 16.13 *Travel pass survey: people with disabilities (Venn diagram)*

people with travel passes (Circle A), and people with disabilities (Circle B).

The Venn diagram shows the relationship between two sets of people, and the intersection of the two circles shows that some of these people have things in common, in this case the ownership of a travel pass. Figure 16.13 shows that the majority of disabled people in the sample (75 per cent) use travel passes. This is expressed by the degree of overlap of the two circles, which is said to represent the co-variance between the two parameters.

Key concept

Co-variance: the degree to which two variables coincide (or overlap).

Another visual technique, which is similar to the bar chart, is the histogram (Figure 16.14). In a histogram, the bars touch each other, to indicate that the variable is continuous. Suppose, for example, the ages of people using travel passes are to be expressed visually. Age has been recorded (on the data collection form) into four categories: 50–54 years, 55–59 years, 60–64 years and over 65 years. These are now coded as Groups A–D.

Using the histogram for this example emphasises the gradual increase in travel pass

Travel pass users by age
Sample = 40

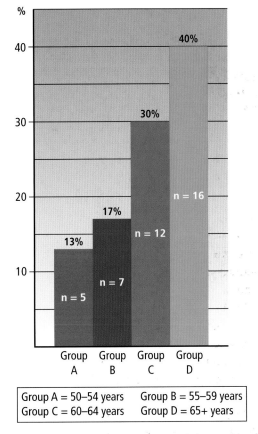

| Group A = 50–54 years | Group B = 55–59 years |
| Group C = 60–64 years | Group D = 65+ years |

FIGURE 16.14 *Travel pass users by age: histogram*

usage with age. The key retirement ages of 60 (for women) and 65 (for men) are retained as potential milestones with respect to travel pass usage. Although retirement ages are changing, there are still a considerable number of individuals for whom these ages have significance. In doing the arithmetic for these figures, the researcher has had to make some decisions with respect to the percentages. Table 16.13 shows the same data expressed in table form.

Arithmetically, 5 is 12.5 per cent of 40, whilst 7 is 17.5 per cent. Fractions are usually not considered acceptable when expressing data of this kind (in contrast to some complex scientific experimental data, where differences lower than whole numbers may be of significance). Therefore, the percentages involving less than whole numbers have to be rounded upwards

| Transport survey | | | |
| Total = 40 | | | |
AGE (YEARS)	NUMBER	PERCENTAGE (UNROUNDED)	PERCENTAGE (ROUNDED)
50–54	5	12.5	13
55–59	7	17.5	17
60–64	12	30	30
65+	16	40	40
Total	40	100	100

TABLE 16.13 *Travel pass users by age*

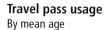

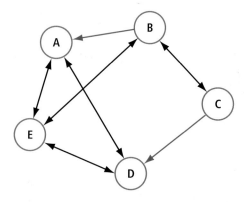

group A = 50 - 54 years
group B = 55 - 59 years
group C = 60 - 64 years
group D = 65 years +

FIGURE 16.15 *Travel pass usage by mean age*

or downwards. One convention is to round downwards any fraction that is less than 0.5, and to round upwards figures of 0.5 and above. In this case, rounding up the two age categories in question would give new whole figures of 13 and 18, which would in turn give a percentage total of 101 per cent. This is not good practice, and a decision has to be made to produce a total of 100 per cent. In this case, the 50–54 year age group has been rounded up (to 13 per cent), and that for the 55–59 year group has been rounded down (to 17 per cent). Because this is a slightly larger number to start with, rounding down will have less impact. However, on sample sizes this small, any conclusions drawn from percentages will have to be treated carefully.

Graphs are also useful to show continuous variables, and can be used to compare trends in more than one set of figures at the same time.

The graph in Figure 16.15 compares the mean ages of travel pass users and non-travel pass users in each of the four age groups, A–D. From this it can be seen easily that in this population, the non-users of travel passes tend to be younger than the people who do use passes.

The concept of the mean is a very useful one for interpreting data. This, along with a number of other mathematical and statistical concepts, will be considered in the next section. Before this, one more visual means of representing data needs to be mentioned. This is the sociogram, which is less useful for expressing the results from the travel pass survey. Sociograms are used to depict relationships between people within groups.

Sociogram of family A

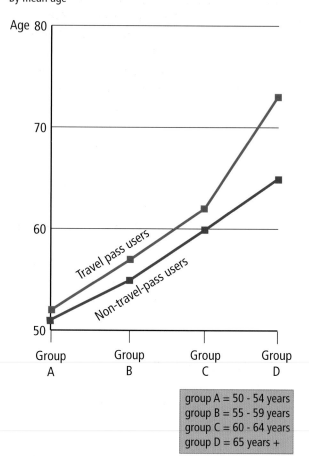

Black lines show that the two linked people 'like' each other.
Red lines show that one person does 'not like' another.

FIGURE 16.16 *A family sociogram*

Sociograms are constructed by asking group members, in this case a family, to say which other group members they like and don't like. Other factors, such as respect, or good communication, can also be established. These relationships are then plotted as a diagram, showing the relation patterns within the group. For a small group such as a family, this may be easy to do manually; however, for larger groups computer programmes are often used to map out the relationships.

Conclusions from quantitative data

This is not a textbook on statistics (see the References section for some useful further reading), but if meaningful inferences are to be made from quantitative data, a few basic mathematical concepts can be helpful. These are the **mean,** the **median,** and the **mode.** The statistical concept of probability is also useful, but you are not required to calculate probability to pass this unit.

Mean, median and mode

The mean has already been used in Figure 16.15, and is very similar to what is referred to as the 'average' in simple arithmetic. Basically, all score values are added, and then divided by the total number of scores. Table 16.14 shows how this was done for the 'non-travel pass users' in Figure 16.15.

Sometimes, two different groups may give the same arithmetical mean even if the actual values in each group are very different. In such cases,

CALCULATING MEDIAN AND MEAN SCORES PER AGE GROUP

Sample size: n = 40

Group A 50–54 years n = 5	Group B 55–59 years n = 7	Group C 60–64 years n = 12	Group D 65 + years n = 16
50	55	60	65
50	56	60	65
= 53	57	60	65
Median	= 57	61	65
54	Median	62	67
54	59	63	71
	59	Median	71
	59	= 63	73
		63	Median
		63	= 73
		64	73
		64	73
		64	75
		64	75
			75
			81
			81
			85
Mean = 261 divided by 5 = 52	Mean = 402 divided by 7 = 57	Mean = 748 divided by 12 = 62	Mean = 1160 divided by 16 = 73

TABLE 16.15 *Travel pass users by age*

another way of finding an average is needed. The median, or middle value, can be useful here. Table 16.15 shows how to deduce the median scores for the ages of travel pass users in this example.

With an odd number of scores (e.g. Groups A and B), the middle value is the median (53 and 57 for these groups). With an even number of scores, the median is the average of the two middle scores (Group C = 63, Group D = 73). In this case, median and mean are very similar for all four age groups.

The mode is the most frequently occurring score in any group, but this method is not often used in small-scale studies. In the case of the analysis by age, it is unlikely to be very useful, but it might answer another question. Suppose respondents

CALCULATION OF MEAN AGES

Group A 50–54 years n = 5	Group B 55–59 years n = 3	Group C 60–64 years n = 1	Group D 65+ years n = 1
50	55	60	65
50	55		
50	55		
50			
53			
253	55	60	65
Divided by 5 = 51	Divided by 3 = 55	Divided by 1 = 60	Divided by 1 = 65

TABLE 16.14 *Non-travel pass users*

were asked how many times a week they used their passes. Table 16.16 shows the answers to this question by people aged 60–64 years. In this example, using the mean score would indicate that most people in this age group used their travel pass to make an average of seven journeys per week. In fact, the high usage by just three users has pushed up the mean score. If the mode is taken, it can be seen that most users in this category make just four journeys (seven respondents) or less (two respondents). In this instance, the mode gives a more meaningful picture of travel pass usage.

How significant are the results?

There are statistical methods for testing whether figures have **statistical significance**, or whether they show nothing unusual.

It was noted above that some of the people in the sample have a disability (see page 311).

Key concept

Statistical significance: when figures satisfy certain statistical tests, they have statistical significance.

CALCULATION OF MODAL SCORE

Sample size: n = 12

Responses to question:
How many journeys per week do you make using your travel pass?
Number of journeys per week
2
2
4
4
4
4
4
4
4
4
10
20
20

Modal score = 4
Arithmetical mean = 7

TABLE 16.16 *Travel pass users aged 60–64 years*

Travel pass usage by disabling condition

	DISABLING CONDITION	NO DISABLING CONDITION	TOTAL
Travel pass	10	2	12
No travel pass	1	7	8
Total	11	9	20

TABLE 16.17 *People aged 50–59 years*

Table 16.17 shows that below the age of 60 (the old retirement age for women) with a few exceptions, those who use a travel pass also have a disabling condition. This is a striking correlation and looks to have significance.

Harris (1986) gives a helpful way of understanding this concept of significance, using the illustration of tennis balls and a large black plastic bag. Suppose 20 tennis balls are put into the bag, 10 have been marked 'Travel pass' and the other 10 marked 'No travel pass'. They are shaken up, and then drawn out, the first ten being allocated to the category 'disabling condition' and the second set of ten to the 'no disabling condition' category. How likely is it that scores similar to Table 16.17 would result? In other words, do the figures have statistical significance (i.e. that travel pass users under the age of 60 are more likely to have a disabling condition), or are the figures nothing out of the ordinary?

There are mathematical ways of testing what can be inferred from the data. One of these is the chi-square test, which looks for an association between two variables. Chi-square measures the **probability** of any given set of data occurring. A data set with a probability of 1 is inevitable; that with a probability of 0 is impossible. The understanding and application of chi-square test is not a requirement of this unit, but a number of items listed in the references section will provide further reading on this.

Unless you feel exceptionally confident, it is probably not advisable to attempt complex statistical techniques as part of your study. However, an awareness of these techniques and how they are applied may help in the evaluation of any secondary research used.

Writing the report

As part of the analytical process, you will need to manipulate quantitative data into visual form (e.g. tables, graphs, etc.) to decide on its significance. For the final report, choose the graphics that demonstrate the key findings. If the findings are inconclusive, this is itself worth reporting.

A professional research report always begins with an abstract, which is a very short summary of the project and its key findings. The introduction sets out the aims and rationale of the study, and may also be the place for any interesting secondary research used to inform the project. In the methodology section, an explanation of how the study was conducted is given, including a description of how the population sample was chosen, the size of the study, how long it lasted and the data collection methods and tools used.

Actual specimens of data collection tools can go in the appendix. The presentation and analysis sections of the report should be as succinct as possible. Quantitative data should always be expressed visually (e.g. tables, bar charts, etc.) as well as in words.

The conclusion should make the findings and inferences clear. Often, a researcher will describe how the findings might relate to other similar situations, or if inferences may be made to a wider population. There will usually be limited scope for this in a small-scale study.

It is essential to evaluate the study after it is finished. Evaluation is considered in more detail in the following section. Finally, it might be possible to see how the study could be followed up. Suppose, for example, in a small study of a reminiscence session, eight out of ten people were found to have trouble getting to the venue. This is an important finding, and would be worth following up with another piece of research (see Checklist 16.4).

ELEMENT	CONTENTS
1. Abstract	Summary of study, with key findings
2. Introduction	Aims, rationale; may include relevant secondary research/ background information
3. Methodology	Details of research methods and tools; sampling, sample size etc.; process followed
4. Presentation of data	Tables, bar charts, diagrams, graphs, pie charts, pictographs, Venn diagrams, sociographs, as appropriate, to enhance presentation
5. Analysis of results	Any significant trends or relationship between variables highlighted and explained
6. Conclusion	Possible causal inferences, relatability to other populations set out; inconclusive data also highlighted
7. Evaluation	Critical reflection on the study; strengths, weaknesses; how things might be done differently next time
8. Recommendations for future research	Lines of enquiry suggested by findings
9. Appendices	Specimen data collection tools; data from other sources, if relevant

CHECKLIST 16.4 *Research reports: key elements*

Making an oral presentation about your research findings

You may choose to give an oral presentation of part of your results. The following observations and checklist may help you in planning to give a talk about your research (see Checklist 16.5). There is a saying about giving a good talk. First of all, tell the audience what you are going to tell them (the introduction); then tell them (the main body of your talk); then tell them what you've just told them (the summary and conclusion at the end).

You may choose to make an oral presentation of your findings

> THE STRUCTURE OF A TALK
>
> TELL THEM what you are going to tell them
>
> TELL THEM
>
> TELL THEM what you've just told them

This is a tried and tested approach used by public speakers, whether they are politicians, salespeople, or entertainers. Good teachers and lecturers also use this structure. What is important is that it uses the principle of repetition, which is also a central aspect of teaching and learning.

If you set out what your talk will be about in a clear and memorable introduction, you have created an expectation in your audience about what they will hear. The central body of your talk should then elaborate on these points, using only information or material that is relevant. A summary and conclusion will remind the audience about what they have just heard, and make it more likely that they will remember the key aspects of the talk. People who are taking notes at a talk always appreciate a speaker who keeps to the point, and follows a structure as laid out in the introduction.

The key points of a talk will be designed to achieve the aims and objectives that have already been decided. There is no point is telling your audience to expect a talk on communicating with children, and then digress to include a mass of anecdotes about working with older people.

The same is true of any supplementary material that you decide to use. Visual material should enhance the points you are making. This might be carefully chosen photographs, or projected images showing the points you are making in bullet-point form. It is a mistake to show too much printed or written material on an overhead – it will be too much for your audience to take in, and can detract from what you are actually saying.

If you are using audio-visual aids such as a video, DVD or CD recording, make sure you can operate the equipment available to you on the day. For a short talk, it is advisable to keep the use of such supplementary material to a minimum. If there is too much material for ten minutes, but you feel it's vital to tell the audience, handouts can give additional information. They can also be used to reinforce the key points of the talk.

You might like to consider using an abbreviated form of notes for the actual presentation. Some people use prompt cards, on which are written the main points. They then speak naturally when elaborating on these key items. Other people write out the key points onto a sheet of paper. You will be required to produce some written material to support your presentation, and your tutor will advise you on this.

Managing your material: some tips

ELEMENT	COMMENTS
Structure your talk	* Introduction * Body of talk * Summary/conclusion
Link your talk to your aims & objectives	* Choose relevant material that supports your case
Visual aids	* Should be clear and concise * Should enhance the talk, not detract from what you are saying
Audiovisual material	* Keep to a minimum for a short talk * Make sure you can use the equipment
Aides memoires	Options include: * Reading from full text (but this may result in a stilted delivery) * Prompt cards * Notes on sheets of paper
Visual aids	* Should be clear and concise * Use white space to effect (don't clutter your overheads with too many words) * Should enhance (not detract from) your talk
Supplementary material	* You can use handouts to give extra material
Rehearse your talk	* Always have at least one run-through before the actual event * Make sure you keep to time * Allocate time to each item

CHECKLIST 16.5 *Planning a presentation*

Consider this

Shashi is about to make a study of a group of six children in an early years centre. Staff have introduced some new musical activities (involving percussion instruments and whistles), and Shashi is going to observe the children's reactions to these.

She is especially keen to test the hypothesis that music may help shy children to participate more in a group. She will be watching one child in particular, Stacey, who is currently very withdrawn, and who does not appear to have made any special friendships amongst the other children.

1. What decisions will Shashi have to make about how she collects her data?

2. What data collection tools and techniques might she use?

3. Which visual modes of presentation might be especially helpful in presenting the data?

4. How important will it be for Shashi to be supervised, and who should do this?

Summary

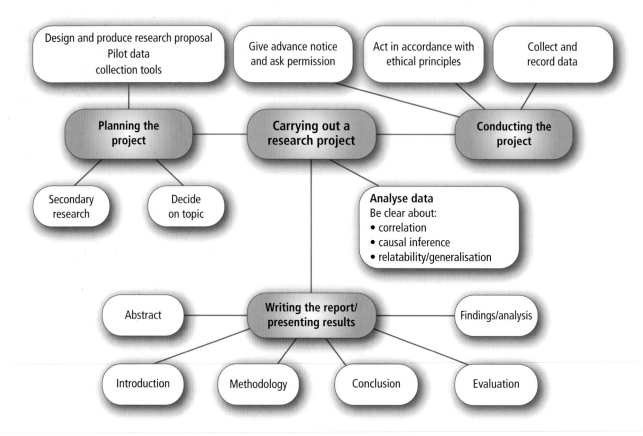

Section 4: Evaluating findings from research

Making an objective assessment

Evaluation is the process of looking back at something, to review it and assess its value. This should be done critically and objectively. This means concentrating on the facts as far as possible, leaving personal feelings aside.

Key concepts

Evaluation: to assess something, in particular its worth, value or importance.

Objectivity: a state of mind in which facts are assessed in a neutral, non-emotional way.

The following scenario illustrates how emotions can sometimes get in the way of objective thinking.

Once Rav recovered from having a difficult interview, he met with the care manager to evaluate the situation – not only the incident itself, but also the project as a whole. The care manager explained that Mrs Da Silva has rather painful arthritis, which sometimes makes her irritable. Also, the day of the interview was the anniversary of her husband's death. Her behaviour was due to a combination of physical and emotional factors, and nothing to do with Rav's interviewing skills. Rav also realised, by discussing his work with his tutor, that he had collected plenty of meaningful information in the 20 self-completion questionnaires, which gave him plenty of quantitative data. The five semi-structured interviews also resulted in some good anecdotal information, which will add a qualitative dimension to his conclusions.

Making an objective evaluation has helped Rav to overcome the negative feelings he experienced during and after the difficult interview, and also to appreciate the value of the rest of his work.

Questions to ask

Even if there have been no obvious incidents or upsets during the course of a research study, it is still important to be as critical as possible when reflecting on your project and its outcomes. The following checklists may help when going through this process. It is important to involve another person in the evaluative process. This might be your tutor, or someone who supervised you during the data collection process. These checklists might be the starting point for ordering your thoughts before meeting whoever is helping you with the evaluation.

SCENARIO
Keeping things in perspective

Rav has been assessing the effects of the introduction of a music therapy session in a day unit for older people. He collected data from 20 people, using self-completion questionnaires.

He then interviewed some of the older people individually, using a semi-structured approach. Five of the six interviewees were very positive about the music therapy, and appeared to enjoy talking to Rav. However the sixth person, Mrs Da Silva, became angry and abusive during the interview. Her care manager had to intervene, and the interview was terminated. Rav was very upset, and began to feel that the whole project had been a bad idea.

1. Why is it important for Rav to sit back and evaluate what has happened objectively?

2. What reasons might there be for Mrs Da Silva's behaviour?

ASK YOURSELF	
1. Were the aims and objectives of the project clear?	
2. Was the data reliable and valid?	
3. How representative was the target population?	
4. Was the sampling method appropriate?	
5. Were the data collection methods appropriate to the objectives?	
6. Did you observe ethical principles in choosing and applying data collection methods?	
6. How effective were the chosen data collection methods?	
7. Were the aims and objectives of the project met?	
8. Were there any unexpected outcomes of the research?	

CHECKLIST 16.6 *Evaluating research methodology*

ASK YOURSELF	
1. How thorough was the planning process?	
2. How thorough/useful was the secondary research?	
3. If you piloted the data collection tools, how helpful was this?	
4. What can be learned from the process of implementing the research?	
5. How well did you observe ethical principles when implementing your research?	
6. How well were the principles of confidentiality and anonymity observed?	
7. Were there any unexpected events or surprises as a result of conducting the research?	

CHECKLIST 16.7 *Evaluating the research process*

1. Does the report contain all the components set out in Checklist 16.4?
2. Are the conclusions clear?
3. Is the language used in the report clear and concise?
4. Do charts, diagrams and tables etc enhance the findings of the research?

CHECKLIST 16.8 *Evaluating the research report*

Summary

Evaluation helps a researcher to remain objective

Evaluation involves reviewing both the process & the outcome of research

Evaluating the findings of your research

Self-reflection is an essential part of professional practice

Use the checklists in Section 4 to evaluate your own research

Consider this

Steve has made a postal survey of people with disabilities in his locality. The aim was to find out whether there was any need for a local respite care facility in this area.

He sent out 300 questionnaires, but only received back 100 responses, and some of these were not fully completed.

1. What might Steve have done wrong in designing and implementing this project? (Some of the questions in Checklists 6–8 may help with this.)

2. How could he have improved the response rate?

3. How important should secondary research be to this project, and what form should this have taken?

4. How might a pilot stage have improved Steve's chances of success?

5. What kind of sampling technique might Steve have used?

UNIT ASSESSMENT

How you will be assessed

To be successful in this unit you must design and carry out a small-scale research project related to an appropriate health, social care or early years setting.

You will be assessed on your portfolio, which will include a report on the research project. This work must provide evidence of:

* a knowledge and understanding of three research methods, as applied to your project

* an understanding of the ethical issues inherent in conducting research

* knowledge of potential sources of error and bias in research

* a justification of the choice of the three research methods

* an ability to conduct research, using three different sources of information

* an ability to analyse and present the data collected

* an ability to evaluate the research undertaken.

Assessment guidance

You will need to produce evidence as set out in the assessment objectives (AOs).

AO1: the purposes of research; description of research methods; rationale for the research topic

The rationale behind your choice of subject should be absolutely clear, together with the purpose and aims of the study.

Good marks will be obtained for:

* a clear statement of purpose and aims

* an explanation of the rationale for the study

* clear reasons for the choice of methodologies and data collection tools

* clarity about how and why the target population has been chosen

* setting a realistic timescale

* use of key concepts including:

  * qualitative data

  * quantitative data

  * primary and secondary research

  * sampling

  * population

  * research styles, e.g. case study, survey etc.

Higher marks will be obtained for demonstrating all of the above, plus:

* awareness of the issues associated with the chosen methodology (or methodologies), including the advantages and disadvantages

* good reasons for the choice of research style and data collection tools

* an awareness of the context in which the study is being conducted

* good use of secondary research as part of the rationale and background to the study (including awareness of sampling techniques and methodologies used in secondary research cited)

* excellent planning skills, including keeping everyone informed, seeking consent, observing ethical principles etc.

AO2: ethical issues; sources of error and bias

Even when conducting a small-scale study, observation of ethical principles is essential.

Good marks will be obtained for:

* paying due regard to ethical considerations at the design stage of the project

* sensitive application of data collection tools, having regard to the needs of each individual involved in the study

* observation of the principles of anonymity and confidentiality in recording and storing data.

Higher marks will be obtained for all of the above, plus:

* a positive response to any problems or issues (for individuals) that arise during the course of the study

* demonstration of the appropriateness of the data collection tools for this particular research context

* sensitive use of questioning, prompts and probes (as appropriate) if using the interview method

* good interpersonal skills if using interview or participant-observer method.

There is always potential for error and bias in research, and a competent researcher will be constantly aware of these pitfalls, at every stage in the process.

Good marks will be obtained for:

* choice of data collection methods that are appropriate to the research context

* demonstrating an awareness of both the advantages and disadvantages of the methods chosen.

Higher marks will be obtained for both of the above, plus:

* demonstrating an awareness of the potential for bias in data collection

* demonstrating an awareness of the limitations of small-scale studies

* the use of key concepts (as appropriate), including:

    * reliability

    * validity

    * bias

    * observer's paradox

* an awareness of the ways in which data can be manipulated statistically (e.g. concept of probability).

AO3: conduct research; analyse and present the findings

Checklists 16.1, 16.2, and 16.3 may be helpful when planning and implementing a research project. The research should include data from three different sources of information.

Sources might include:

* service users

* carers and/or friends of service users

* professional staff (e.g. social workers, health visitors etc.)

* other staff

* secondary sources (e.g. literature search, media or Internet search, statistical data etc.).

When designing and implementing research, good marks will be obtained for:

* systematic and thorough planning prior to data collection

* awareness of the strengths and limitations of the data collection tools and methods chosen

* obtaining sufficient appropriate data for analysis

* application of key concepts (as appropriate):

    * primary/secondary data

    * structured/unstructured data

    * variable

    * sampling

* population

* pilot study.

Higher marks will be obtained for:

* demonstration of independent thinking in the design and use of data collection tools

* flexibility when designing and administering data collection tools (this may include piloting such tools and responding appropriately to feedback)

* a positive response to any problems or issues that arise during the course of the study

* demonstration of the appropriateness of the data collection tools to the research situation

* maintaining objectivity throughout the planning and implementation process.

Objectivity should also be maintained when analysing and presenting data. Checklists 16.6 and 16.7 may be helpful here.

When analysing data, good marks will be obtained by:

* analysis that makes clear and coherent links between the data and the original purpose and aims of the study

* making valid and justifiable conclusions from the data

* good use of key concepts such as:

    * variable

    * relatability

    * generalisation

    * aggregation

    * correlation

* clear presentation of data in appropriate visual form (e.g. tables, bar charts, graphs etc.)

* a well-structured research report.

Higher marks will be obtained for all of the above, plus:

* demonstration of awareness of the potential for bias in data

* a thorough exploration of all the data collected to establish its significance

* awareness of the limitations of small-scale studies

* use (or awareness of) of key concepts such as:

    * reliability

    * validity

    * bias

    * observer's paradox (if appropriate)

    * causal inference

    * statistical significance

    * mean, median, mode

* awareness of the ways in which data can be manipulated statistically (e.g. concept of probability)

* conclusions that contextualise the outcome of the study, and may make reference to secondary research.

AO4: evaluation of research

The discussion of the advantages and disadvantages of different research methods and data collection tools (pages 302–3) may be helpful in completing this part of the research report.

Good marks will be obtained by:

* explaining the strengths and weakness of the study

* evaluating how far the purposes and aims of the study were met

* suggesting how improvements might be made were the study to be repeated

* awareness of how research contributes to developments in health and social care

* awareness of possible implications of key concepts including:

  * bias

  * reliability and validity

  * observer's paradox (if appropriate)

  * representative nature of target population.

Higher marks will be obtained by all of the above, plus:

* a high level of analytical thinking

* critical self-awareness at every stage, including planning, choice of methods/tools, implementation and analysis

* awareness of having made choices, and the reasons for those choices

* critical awareness of the context for and purposes of research in the health, social care and early years fields.

References and further reading

Bell, J. (1993) *Doing Your Research Project* second ed. Buckingham: Open University Press

Cohen, S. et al (1991) 'Psychological stress and susceptibility to the common cold', *New England Journal of Medicine,* 325, 606

Cohen, S., Tyrrell, D.A. and Smith, A.P. (1993) 'Negative life events, perceived stress, negative affect and susceptibility to the common cold', *Journal of Personality and Social Psychology,* 64 (1), 131–140

Coles, A. and Cox, A. (2002), 'Does early treatment of multiple sclerosis prevent the progression of disability later on?', *Way Ahead,* 6 (1): 4–5

Croft, S.E. (1999), 'Creating locales through storytelling: an ethnography of a group home for men with mental retardation', *Western Journal of Communication,* 63 (3): 329–345

Department of Health (2004) *On the state of the public health: Annual Report of the Chief Medical Officer 2003* (accessed via Department of Health website)

Gross, R. (2003) *Key Studies in Psychology* fourth ed. Abingdon: Hodder and Stoughton

Halliday, S. (2001) 'Death and Miasma in Victorian London: an obstinate belief', *British Medical Journal,* 323: 1469–1471

Haney, C., Banks, C. and Zimbardo, P. (1973), 'A study of prisoners and guards in a simulated prison', *Naval Research Reviews,* 30 (9): 4–17

Harris, P. (1986) *Designing and Reporting Experiments* Buckingham: Open University Press

Martin. P. (1997) *The Sickening Mind* London: Harper Collins

Milgram, S. (1963), 'Behavioural study of obedience', *Journal of Abnormal and Social Psychology,* 67: 371–378

Slesnik, N. and Prestopnik, J.L. (2005) 'Ecologically based family therapy outcome with substance abusing adolescents', *Journal of Adolescence,* 28 (2), 277–298

Snow, J. (1855) *On the Mode of Communication of Cholera* London: John Churchill (accessed via www.ph.ucla.edu/epi/snow/showbook_a2.html)

Wakefield, A. J. (et al) (1998), 'Ileal-lymphoid-nodular hyperplasia, non-specific colitis and pervasive developmental disorder in children', *The Lancet,* 351: 637–641

Useful websites

Carers UK
    www.carersuk.org
Census data (local)
    www.neighbourhood.statistics.gov.uk
Cochrane Collaboration
    www.cochrane.org
Department of Health
    www.dh.gov.uk
Institute for Public Policy and Research (IPPR)
    www.ippr.org.uk
NHS Gateway
    www.nhs.uk

Joseph Rowntree Foundation
    www.jrf.org.uk/housingandcare/hartriggoaks/default.asp
Medical Research Council
    www.mrc.ac.uk
National Centre for Social Research
    www.natcen.ac.uk
National Institute for Health and Clinical Excellence (NICE)
    www.nice.org.uk
National Statistics Online
    www.statistics.gov.uk (National Census data)
Prince's Foundation for Integrated Health
    www.fihed.org.uk
Research Council for Complementary Medicine
    www.rccm.org.uk
Sociological Research Online
    www.socresonline.org.uk
Stationery Office
    www.parliament.the-stationery-office.co.uk (access to government publications)
Valuing People
    www.valuingpeople.gov.uk
What Doctors Don't Tell You (WDDTY)
    www.wddty.co.uk

Answers to assessment questions

UNIT 11

1

Age range	Name of stage	Key characteristics
Birth to 1.5–2 years of age	Sensorimotor	Learning to co-ordinate senses and muscles. Inability to conserve objects (understand that things still exist when not sensed)
1.5–2 to 7 years of age	Pre-operational	Pre-logical thinking inability to conserve number, weight and volume
7 to 11 years of age	Concrete operational	Concrete logic, limited reasoning and understanding
11 years and older	Formal operational	Thinking using abstract concepts and formal logic. Adult thinking.

2. Environmental, socio-economic, psychological including self-concept.
3. Any four from:
   * adults contribute to intellectual, social and emotional development
   * a setting where people develop a sense of belonging and self-esteem
   * a setting to meet physical needs, the social group to provide socialisation
   * financial support; emotional support
   * practical help and advice
   * a potential source of stress if there are tensions between individuals.
4. Environmental factors:
   * Mitesh may be at risk of increased noise from neighbours
   * there may be a risk of increased air pollution from traffic or nearby industry.
   Socio-economic factors:
   * risk of increased crime
   * risk of increased vandalism and graffiti
   * risk of increased congestion and difficulty with travel
   * overcrowding.
5. The understanding that we have of ourselves. Self-concept is a learned idea of how we are distinct from other people. Self-concept may be understood as including an image of self and also the degree to which we value what we are – self-esteem. Liam is able to take control of his life by developing positive self-esteem and self-image. The ability to construct an idea of self can be used to override past influences.
6. In Freudian theory the id is unconscious and represents animal instincts. The ego is the decision-making 'self' that enables a person to cope with external reality. The ego has both conscious and unconscious aspects. The superego represents the internalised value system of one's opposite-sex parent.

7. Adolescents have to develop a clear identity or sense of self that will enable them to be successful in adult relationships and work.

8. Ego defence mechanisms are ways in which people distort their understanding and memory in order to protect their ego. Harriet may be using denial to protect herself from the implications of the diagnosis. There may also be a degree of reaction formation in that fear might have been converted into a complacent attitude.

9. Tom would appear to be addressing his need for self-actualisation. His interest in making wooden furniture may suggest that he has engaged the aesthetic and cognitive aspects of self-actualisation. The four deficit needs of physical, safety, belonging and self-esteem all have to be successfully met in a person's development before becoming needs associated with self-actualisation can be addressed. Maslow's later work suggested that cognitive and aesthetic needs were potential steps in the process of self-actualisation. The actualising tendency is an inner biological force in Rogers' theory – quite different from Maslow's principal of self-actualisation. Rogers believed that everyone was capable of accessing the actualising tendency. Conditions of worth represent other people's demands on an individual. An individual is only worthwhile if he or she meets the demands that others – especially parents – make of them. People who access their own actualising tendency can free themselves from feeling emotionally dependent on the opinions of others.

10. Ross is receiving a better outcome (reinforcement) for getting out of his seat than he would if he concentrated on his work. A classroom assistant might try to provide attention and other forms of social reinforcement when Ross has been concentrating on his work. The classroom assistant would try to ensure that 'concentrating' behaviours achieved more reinforcement than disruptive behaviours.

11. Concrete logical thought operations mean that children can only make logical sense of issues when they can directly experience, or tangibly see or touch what is being talked about. Children cannot usually reason using abstract ideas. Internalisation involves making (or constructing) your own understanding of an issue. Internalisation is quite different from simply memorising or repeating information. Internalised learning involves a deeper level of understanding. Discussing personal experiences may help Sheveta to construct her own internalised understanding. Simply supplying Sheveta with information would not achieve this. The zone of proximal development is the range of understanding that Sheveta can work within. Discussion of personal experiences might enable her to develop a more advanced understanding of the issue. Abstract theories of power and economics would be beyond her zone of development.

12. Traits are inbuilt tendencies to react to people and events in certain generalised ways. Zoë might be described as displaying a personality trait of extraversion, whilst Poppy might be described as displaying the personality trait of introversion.

13. Bandura's research suggests that children can learn just by watching events. People can therefore learn from other people's experiences. Bandura's research suggests that people are more likely to imitate behaviour that they have witnessed if they perceive the behaviour to have been rewarded. Mark may have copied the behaviour because of reward, but it is more likely that Mark perceived the characters as being like himself. Sarah may not have copied the behaviour because of gender differences.

14. Biological: An inbuilt, perhaps inherited, tendency to become obsessional. A biologically-based tendency to respond to stress with constant checking behaviours.

Behavioural: Learned behaviour resulting from conditioning or from the reinforcement of checking behaviours.

Psychodynamic: An outcome of inner conflicts in the unconscious mind. Obsessions may relate to regression to the anal stage of development or to the use of ego defence mechanisms.

Humanistic: The humanistic perspective would stress the importance of exploring the significance of this behaviour with Joe. Joe's self-esteem of self-concept needs may not be being met and his behaviour may be a consequence – even if this is not obvious to an observer.

Social learning: Joe may have learned to imitate or model his behaviour on other people that he has witnessed behaving this way.

UNIT 12

1.

Name of part of digestive system	Function of part of digestive system
Mouth	Teeth and tongue aid in mechanical digestion, breaking the food up into small portions and mixing with saliva until small balls of food are formed ready for swallowing. Salivary amylase in saliva begins the digestion of carbohydrates.
Oesophagus	Muscular contractions known as peristalsis and gravity promote the passage of the food bolus formed in the mouth down to the stomach.
Stomach	Churns the food into a paste called chyme and allows this to pass in small spurts into the small intestine through the pyloric sphincter muscle. Hydrochloric acid, as well as killing bacteria in raw food, activates pepsin to begin digesting protein foods. Also acts as a reservoir for food and stimulates feelings of hunger when empty.
Small intestine a) duodenum	Receives chyme from the stomach in small spurts, bile from the liver and pancreatic juice from the pancreas. Protein and carbohydrate digestion continues in an alkaline medium caused by the salts in the juices delivered here. Fat/lipid digestion begins here. This is the main area for digestion by enzymes.
Small intestine b) ileum	This is the main area for absorption of the simple sugars (from carbohydrates), amino acids from proteins and fatty acids and glycerol from fats. Specially adapted by length, folds and villi.
Large intestine a) colon	Forms semi-solid faeces by reabsorbing the water poured onto food in the form of digestive juices.
Large intestine b) rectum	Exerts muscular contractions to eliminate faeces at intervals.
Anus	Sphincter controlling the exit of faeces.

2. A colostomy is when part of the colon is brought to an artificial opening in the abdominal wall so that the faeces are caught in a colostomy bag attached to the opening. An ileostomy is similar but uses a part of the ileum to exit waste material. The waste from an ileostomy is more fluid than a colostomy as the colon that absorbs water is by-passed completely.

3. (a) Enzymes are biological catalysts that are proteins. They are both pH and temperature-sensitive and only a few molecules of enzymes are required to break down a large number of molecules of protein, fat or carbohydrate. Enzymes are largely unchanged by the job that they do.

   (b) Proteins are first broken down in the stomach by pepsin which is secreted in gastric juice as an inactive substance. Hydrochloric acid from the gastric glands activates the pepsin and provides the acid medium for optimum efficiency.

4. (a) Renal failure exists when kidneys are unable to eliminate wastes from the body, control acid-base balance or blood pressure.

   (b) Hypertension is constantly raised blood pressure. It is said to exist when BP is over 160/95 mm Hg.

   (c) i. Haemodialysis means being attached to a kidney machine for several hours about three times each week. A shunt between an artery and a vein is constructed, usually in one arm for the needle to be placed in to connect to the machine. Layers of special membrane in the machine and dialysing fluid enable the waste materials and excess water and salts to be eliminated fom the blood. CAPD is continuous ambulatory (walking around) peritoneal dialysis when a special tap is constructed in the abdominal wall and dialysing fluid is introduced for several hours and then replaced by fresh fluid. The inner linings of the abdominal cavity, called the peritoneum is the membrane through which waste materials are removed. This usually is carried out twice a day. Both types of dialysis require restricted diet and fluids.

    ii. Dialysis could be stopped if Karen had a renal transplant.

5. X-rays are used to detect osteoporosis.

Ultrasound scanning is used to show a foetus in pregnancy.

X-rays with radio-opaque injections into arteries are used to demonstrate narrowed or obstructed vessels such as those in coronary heart disease.

6. A gastroscope is an endoscope used to examine the stomach and upper duodenum. It might be used to investigate the possibility of a gastric ulcer. A colonoscope is used to pass through the anus to examine the colon and rectum. It might be used to diagnose irritable bowel syndrome.

7. Ectopic pregnancy occurs when an embryo is implanted anywhere outside the uterus. It might be caused by abnormal or blocked Fallopian tubes.

8. Treatment would be by in vitro fertilisation of the woman's ovum with a sample of semen from the man. When fertilisation has taken place, embryos are reinserted into the woman's uterus.

9. The incidence of coronary heart disease is increased if the individual consumes a diet rich in fat and sugar, is overweight or obese, smokes and drinks more alcohol than recommended. A stressful lifestyle also predisposes an individual to heart disease.

10. Misha is at risk because of the genetic influence. She must take long, brisk walks (about 5 km) several times each week and ensure that she consumes a diet with adequate protein and calcium.

UNIT 15

1. (a) 59.1 million

(b) England

(c) 55.9 million to 59.1 million (or 3.2 million)

(d) Stable at 5.2 million during 1971/1981 than falling to 5.1 million during 1991 and 2001

(e) Two from:

* a prediction/estimate

* based on observable trends /measurable data

(f) Two from:

* based on reliable data

* identified trends

* large sample

* government figures.

(g)

* there may be sudden changes

* difficult to take all factors into account

* difficult to predict more than 5 years ahead.

(h) birth rate, death rate, (including infant mortality rate) migration rates – immigration and emigration

(i) the data could be unreliable because:

* it relies on the reliable collection of statistics from a range of sources

* it may not include people who overstay their visas

* it may not include asylum seekers, refugees and people who have entered the country illegally

* it may not include homeless people and other groups who are not officially registered for work, in housing, etc.

2. (a) Ways it could be used:

* develop graphs and percentages using the data

* make comparisons between different areas of the PCT

* to identify trends.

How it could help:

* to help predict future demand for services

* to identify gaps in the services

* to identify problems experienced by older people

* to identify possible changes to service provision and providers

* to help planning of services

* to decide on funding of services.

(b) Staff hand the questionnaire to them personally and sit with them while they complete it and are on hand to answer questions. Method of return of the questionnaire clearly stated. Stamped addressed envelope included. Perhaps a raffle if each questionnaire has a number or a store voucher given for completed questionnaires.

(c) Reliability would be affected as you would not get a true representative sample of the older population. Only those who have a specific reason for completing the form will take part so the results will be skewed.

* use of interpreters or forms in other languages

* confidentiality policy explained – no personal details used that can identify people

* have a short questionnaire that covers the key points – preferably no more than 20 questions

* pilot the questionnaire and rephrase questions that are unclear

* have a mixture of closed and open ended questions

* keep to a simple format throughout

* use large font – especially for older people who may have eyesight problems.

3. (a) 2.9 people

   (b) 24.1 million

   (c) 23.8 x 2.4 = 57.12 million

   (d) 17 + 8 + 6 = 31 per cent in 1971 14 + 5 + 2 = 21 per cent in 2004 (must be per cent)

   (e) Divorce is increasing, more people are living alone, fewer children in families, smaller housing units, fewer extended families living together, more single parent families, effective contraception.

4. In order to achieve a high grade in this question, candidates will be able to compare the two different household types and discuss factors that have led to these patterns.

   The overall pattern shows a rise of one-person households under state pension age from 6 per cent to 14 per cent in the period. The pattern of one-person households over state pension age shows a similar increase over the same period, from 12 per cent to 15 per cent of all households.

   The rise in one-person households under pensionable age can be attributed to the some of the following factors:

   * increase in divorce and family breakdown

   * higher numbers of students

   * increased mobility for education and employment

   * people marrying later in life.

   The rise in one-person households over pensionable age can be attributed to some of the following factors:

   * increase life expectancy for both men and women

   * women are more likely to become widows and live alone

   * better health

   * local health and social care policy that encourages people to live independently in their own homes as long as possible.

5. Role of women as seen in the past:

   * wife, mother, carer

   * subservient to husband

   * dependent on husband financially

* position in society determined by husband's job/class

* fewer jobs for women

* less independent

* seen as weaker, fragile

* often restricted education

* little contraception.

Role of women today:

* wage earner, equal partners in relationships

* more independent

* better education available

* less defined as solely wife/mother/carer

* more likely to share domestic responsibilities with partner

* seen as able to do most jobs

* more likely to seek divorce

* better contraception

* later pregnancy/fewer children

* more career orientated

* higher expectations.

However, better students should also recognise that the status of women today is still affected by their social class, ethnicity, occupation and age and not all women fit the stereotype of the 'modern woman'.

6. (a) Pattern shows the changes that have occurred between 1971 and 2001 and the predicted changes until 2021 of the under 16s and the 65s and over in the UK. By 2021 it is predicted that there will be more people aged 65 and over than those who are under 16.

(b) If the predictions are correct there will be implications for:

* the family: with less children being born, the family as a whole, will become older. The family will contain increasing numbers of older people who will need to be cared for, for longer periods of time

* the workforce: there will be less younger people joining the workforce so there may be more choice for young people looking for work. Older people will be recruited into work and they would be encouraged to continue to work rather than retire. There may be a labour shortage and so there could be recruitment of workers from other countries. New technology may be developed that will need less skilled workers to operate

* early years services: with less younger children there may be unemployment for those with child care qualifications. Training places for teachers may be reduced. Services for early years may be reduced, but it could be that with less demand for these services more children will be able to access them – especially specialist services such as mental health and speech and language therapy

* services for older people: if the population is becoming older and represents a larger proportion of the population as a whole, services will have to meet the increased demand. The use of the voluntary sector will increase. There may be a shortage of specialist services for older people including orthopaedics, diabetic services, hearing and visual services. Demand for equipment to allow people to remain independently in their own home will increase and a more flexible approach to care of older people may be developed – sheltered housing, respite care, extra care.

* government policy: if the population is becoming older and less children are being born the government might consider increasing child benefits to encourage women to have children. With less economically active people in the population contributing taxes and national insurance, the government will have to think of other ways to raise revenue. State pension changes may occur with those who have occupational pensions being means tested so that state pensions are only provided for the most needy.

Glossary

A

accommodation process which happens when existing knowledge is changed to fit with new learning.

action research a research style that focuses on a particular task or problem. A group of people works together to solve the problem, reviewing and monitoring their own actions as they proceed. This can also be done by an individual, who proceeds by regular reflection and evaluation on a particular problem or issue.

adrenaline a hormone produced by the adrenal glands which boosts the heart rate and strength of the heart beat.

advocacy when someone speaks on the behalf of someone else who is unable to voice their views because of learning difficulties, mental health problems or other reasons. The advocate can be a professional, a volunteer or a relative.

ageing population a population in which the proportion of people over the age of 65 is increasing.

ageism negative feelings towards and discriminatory behaviour against a person on the basis of their age.

aggregation to combine information collected at different times, and possibly from different sources.

anabolism using simple molecules to build up complex molecules.

angina pectoris chest pain indicative of coronary heart disease.

antibody a protein in the blood that counteracts an antigen.

antigen a foreign substance or toxin, that produces an immune response in the body.

assessment a formal method of identifying the health and social care needs of a person in order to set up a care plan.

assimilation changing our understanding of an issue in the light of new knowledge

asthma a respiratory complaint characterised by breathlessness, wheezing and tightness of the chest.

atherosclerosis narrowing and hardening of the arteries.

attachment the emotional process that results in a loving relationship between people. John Bowlby emphasised the importance of attachment during the early years of a child's development.

attitude a mental pattern or posture which can influence thinking, emotions or behaviour.

autism a mental condition of complete self-absorption and reduced ability to communicate with the outside world.

autonomic nervous system consists of sympathetic and parasympathetic branches serving internal organs and glands. There is no conscious control over this system.

B

behavioural approach the approach taken by health and care practitioners to try to influence people to change their behaviour.

bias distortion of the results of a piece of research, caused by the undue influence of a specific factor.

biopsy removal of a small sample of tissue for investigation.

birth rate the number of live births per 1,000 of the population.

bolus masticated ball of food ready for swallowing.

bonding the emotional tie between an infant and his or her mother.

bradycardia slower heart rate than normal.

bronchitis inflammation of the bronchi.

C

CAPD continuous ambulatory peritoneal dialysis for renal failure.

cardiac output volume of blood pumped by the heart in one minute.

care plan the plan of treatment and care decided upon in partnership between the service user and the named nurse or key worker.

case conference formal meeting of professional, service users and family to plan future action.

case report a detailed descriptive study of one particular case. This could be an individual patient or service user.

catabolism breaking down of complex molecules to provide simpler molecules.

causal inference a strong suggestion that one particular variable has a specified effect upon another (e.g. that smoking causes lung cancer).

census full scale national survey undertaken every 10 years since 1801 (apart from 1941). Statistics from the census form the basis for planning social policy and welfare services.

cerebral palsy a medical condition caused by damage or injury to the developing brain. This may occur during pregnancy, birth or in the early post-natal stages.

charities non-profit making organisations set up to support different groups, and they may also lobby on behalf of certain groups.

Charter Mark a national standard of customer service excellence that is awarded by the Cabinet Office.

chemoreceptors Specialised receptors that respond to changes in chemistry.

Child Support Agency Established 1993 by the Conservative Government to reduce the cost to the taxpayer of financial support to one-parent families. Absent parents (usually the father) are traced by the CSA and required to pay an appropriate amount of support.

citation the act of making reference to another piece of research.

Clinical Governance action taken by NHS Trusts to ensure that clinical standards are maintained in hospitals and in the community.

Clinical Nurse Specialist a trained nurse who has had additional training in a specific area asthma or dermatology so that she/he can take responsibility for caring for patients.

clinical trial *see* Randomised Clinical Controlled Trial

clinician any health professional who is directly involved in the treatment and care of patients – e.g. doctor, midwife.

closed question the kind of question that has a fixed set of answers. These questions are often used to arrive at quantitative data. Closed questions can also be answered 'yes' or 'no'.

Code of Conduct professional code of behaviour and practice drawn up by a professional body in order to set standards e.g. General Medical Council, the Nursing and Midwifery Council.

cognition a term which covers the mental processes involved in understanding and knowing.

cohabitation when a woman and a man live together as man and wife but they are not legally married. This term could be extended to partners of the same sex under the changing legislation.

cohort study a systematic study of a specific group of people.

Commission for Social Care Inspection (CSCI) a statutory body set up in 2004 to register and inspect all social care organisations.

Complementary and Alternative Medicines (CAMs) a term used to refer to treatments and therapies not encompassed by conventional medicine.

concrete operations the third stage of intellectual development in Piaget's theory. At this stage, individuals can solve logical problems, provided they can see or sense the objects with which they are working. At this stage, children cannot cope with abstract problems.

conditional positive regard valuing a person only when they conform to your expectations. Conditional positive regard is a form of social control identified by Carl Rogers who worked within the Humanistic perspective.

conditioned learning learning by association. Classical conditioning was described by Pavlov, Operant conditioning where a behaviour is strengthened by reinforcement was described by Skinner. Conditioned learning forms an important part of the behaviourist perspective.

conjugal roles the roles played by husband and wife within a marriage. Because of the increase in cohabitation, sociologists tend to refer instead to the division of labour.

conservation the ability to understand the logical principles involved in the way number, volume, mass and objects work.

constructivist learning theory the theory that each person builds their own system of thinking in order to be able to understand and cope with life. Constructivist learning theory belongs within the cognitive perspective of psychology.

corpus luteum the glandular body produced by the ruptured follicle after ovulation.

correlation a link between two data sets, or two (or more) variables within a data set. Correlation does not necessarily imply causality.

council housing homes built for, and rented out by, the local council as a low cost alternative to buying. Public housing stocks have reduced following the selling of council homes to tenants. In new housing developments built by private agencies a percentage of homes have to be 'social housing ' and these are managed by housing associations.

counselling a form of therapy which is based on an in-depth understanding of at least one psychological perspective together with advanced interpersonal communication skills.

culture the collection of values, norms, customs and behaviours that make one group of people distinct from others. A person's culture will influence the development of their self concept.

cystic fibrosis an inherited condition of thickened mucus that predisposes to infection.

D

death rate the crude death rate is expressed as the number of deaths per 1,000 of the live population.

deep-stored stored at low temperatures in special conditions.

defence mechanisms in Freudian theory ego defence mechanisms are ways in which people distort their understanding and memory in order to protect their ego.

deficit needs these are the physiological needs, safety needs, belonging needs and self-esteem needs that represent the four deficit needs described in Maslow's hierarchy of need.

demography the study of a population, with particular reference to its size and structure, and how and why it changes over time, through changes in birth and death rates, marriage rates, patterns of migration and other factors.

diastole relaxation of the heart chambers.

diffusion transport of molecules from a region of high concentration to one of low concentration.

direct payment system system by which payments can be made directly to the service user in order for them to purchase care.

direct taxation taxes income tax or inheritance tax directly levied on a person's income or wealth.

disproportionate random sampling a technique to make sure that small groups within a target population are adequately represented in the sample, where this is felt to be important.

district nurse a qualified nurse who works closely with the GP and is employed by the PCT.

domiciliary services health and social care services that take place in the service user's home.

Down's syndrome a genetic condition caused by the presence of an extra chromosome.

dual-worker families families in which both the male and female partners work.

E

ECG electrocardiography, a system for monitoring the electrical activity of the heart.

eclectic an approach which draws on a range of perspectives or theories. An eclectic approach to counselling would involve combining ideas from different perspectives and authors.

Ecologically Based Family Therapy a method of working with an individual, taking all aspects of his or her life into account.

ego a term used in psychodynamic theory to describe the decision-making component of the mind. Ego has some similarity with the notion of 'self' used in other perspectives.

emphysema a condition resulting from the breakdown of alveolar walls in the lungs.

empowerment supporting people to become active participants in their care.

endoscopy using a long, thin flexible fibre-optic tube for investigation of internal organs.

enzymes biological catalysts of chemical change.

epidemiology study of the geographical incidence of disease in order to demonstrate potential causes (and cures).

equilibration creating a balance between theory and experience, to make sense of observations.

equilibrium an equalling up of concentrations resulting in no overall loss or gain.

erythrocytes red blood cells.

ethnographic study study of aspects of human behaviour in a specified situation. This usually concerns large groups of people.

experiential learning learning from experiences. The 'Kolb Learning Cycle' is an example of one theory which explains how experience might provide a focus for the development of understanding.

experiment a research style involving the comparison of two groups (in social research) or of the behaviour of a specific substance under different conditions.

F

family credit a social benefit in the UK which tops up the income of low-paid workers with children.

feminism the ideological perspective that examines society and events within society from the viewpoint of women.

fixation in Freudian theory fixation is when life energy (called libido) remains attached to an early stage of development. Life energy can also become fixated on objects and people in a person's life.

formal operations the forth stage in Piaget's theory of intellectual development. People with formal logical operations have the ability to solve abstract problems.

FSH follicle stimulating hormone from the pituitary gland causing ovarian follicles to grow.

G

gamete a cell that cannot develop further unless united with a gamete of the opposite sex.

generalisation the extent to which the findings of a study are applicable to a wider population.

genetic code a set to of instructions passed on from one generation to another for building a living organism.

glycosuria abnormal glucose in urine.

goblet cells mucus producing cells.

governance the way organisations in health and care ensure the quality and safety of the services they provide.

granulocyte the most common type of white blood cell.

H

haemodialysis use of a kidney machine to purify the blood in kidney failure.

haemoglobin the iron carrying protein in blood, important in transporting oxygen around the body.

Health Care Assistant a health worker who is not a registered nurse but has achieved Level 3 NVQ award. HCAs work in a variety of settings in hospital and in the community.

Health Care Commission an organisation set up in 2004 to encourage and monitor improvement in public health and health care in England and Wales.

health visitor a registered nurse with additional training who works in the community with children under 8 years old.

Healthy Living Centres centres offering a range of activities and support for people in deprived communities. They were part of the government's regeneration policy.

His, bundle of a strand of conducting tissue that bridges the fibrous ring between the atria and ventricles.

holistic approach to care this approach takes account of the 'whole' person, not just their clinical condition. Assessment will include their emotional and social needs.

home care services community team which provides social care for clients in their own home.

homeostasis maintenance of the constant internal environment around cells.

I

id a term used in psychodynamic theory to describe the 'powerhouse' of drive energy that motivates the behaviour. Instinctive drives develop from the id.

identity the understanding of self which an individual needs to develop in order to cope with life in modern society.

ideology a systematic set of beliefs which explain society and its policies.

imitation learning learning to imitate or copy the behaviour of others.

income money that an individual or household gets from work, investments or other sources.

Income Support a means tested benefit for unemployed people, single parents and disabled people whose income has been assessed as inadequate.

Independent Complaints Advocacy Service ICAS this is a statutory service offering free, impartial and independent support to people who wish to complain about their hospital care or treatment. They are situated in all areas of the UK.

independent sector agencies that provide health and social care independently from statutory providers. They could be private or voluntary agencies.

indirect taxation taxes that are levied on goods and services (VAT). This form of taxation takes a greater proportion of the income of poorer groups.

infant mortality rate the number of deaths of infants under one year old per 1,000 live births An indicator of general prosperity.

informal care care (usually unpaid) that is given by friends, family or neighbours.

in-group a social group which an individual identifies with. A group that individual is 'in with'.

intermediate care services designed to assist the patient in their discharge from hospital towards independence or to prevent admission to hospital. These services can be provided locally in rehabilitation beds in a range of settings including private nursing homes or in the patient's own home.

internalisation internalised learning is deeply understood learning which is likely to be remembered for a long time and which an individual can use to solve problems. The importance of internalisation was stressed by Vygotsky.

Investors in People a type of award that rewards good practice.

ion an atom or molecule that has lost or gained one or more electrons, e.g. hydrogen ions (H^+ or H^-).

J

joint commissioning where the NHS and social services co-ordinate services and share costs.

K

key worker/lead professional a named person who ensures that the care plan is followed and care is given to the user. In health care this would be a named nurse.

L

leucocytes white blood cells.

LH luteinising hormone from the pituitary gland causes ovulation and corpus luteum formation.

life expectancy the average number of years a new born baby can expect to live.

local authorities political bodies that control towns, cities and rural areas as distinct from national government.

local development plan a plan for the development of health and social care services in the local community that is drawn up and agreed by all partnership members.

longitudinal study a piece of research conducted over a significant period of time, allowing the impact of a number of variables to be taken into account.

lymphocytes white blood cells that produce antibodies.

M

mean a figure arrived at by dividing all score values, and then dividing this by the total number of scores.

means tested benefits social benefits which are delivered only when the claimant is able to show need. Many older people in need tend not to apply for these benefits.

means testing assessing the income of a person and deciding how much they will pay for a service provided by social services.

median the middle value in a set of figures.

meta-analysis a comparison of all research into a specific topic.

metabolism all the chemical reactions in the body = anabolism and catabolism.

mixed economy of care the public, private and voluntary sector provide goods and services for service users e.g. day centres, nursing homes.

mode the most frequently occurring score in any group.

modelling people often imitate or copy others without direct reinforcement or conditioned association taking place. Albert Bandura argues that it is enough to see other people being rewarded for us to choose to copy the behaviour that seems to be rewarded.

monocytes large white blood cells skilled in engulfing bacteria and foreign material.

MS multiple sclerosis, a disease of the nervous system where plaques of white matter deteriorate.

multi-disciplinary teams teams of professionals who are qualified in different disciplines who work together in the community or in hospital.

myogenic muscle capable of contraction without a nerve supply.

N

National Patients Survey annual surveys that take place every year to monitor patients satisfaction with the services they receive.

National Service Frameworks (NSFs) National Standards in certain conditions or focussing on particular age groups that have been set by government in order to improve standards.

needs based assessment an approach to assessment focussing on the needs of the person, rather than the resources available in the service.

negative reinforcement an outcome which strengthens or reinforces behaviour. Negative reinforcement means that a bad situation improves or gets better and this improvement strengthens the behaviour associated with it.

NHS Direct a 24-hour telephone service staffed by nurses.

NHS trusts hospitals and PCTs which are independent bodies and employ staff to deliver health care.

NICE the National Institute for Clinical Excellence. This body issues guidance about clinical care including drugs and procedures.

norms patterns of behaviour that are expected to be followed by the members of a particular society or group.

O

object permanence the understanding that objects exist whether they can be seen or not.

occupational therapist a therapist working in health or social care who assists people to be more independent through the use of aids and appliances.

oestrogen female sex hormone produced by the ovary and placenta.

official statistics statistical data provided by central and local government and government agencies unemployment rates, crime rates, etc.

OFSTED (the Office for Standards in Education) a statutory body set up in 1993 to monitor all educational provision. It also monitors child minding and out of school provision for children up to the age of eight.

open question a question to which the respondent replies in his or her own words. Such questions cannot usually be answered by a simple 'yes' or 'no'.

operant conditioning conditioning caused by reinforcing outcomes which cause a behaviour to become strengthened.

opportunity sampling the use, by the researcher, of those people who are available and/or willing to take part in a study.

osteoporosis condition where the protein background of bone degenerates.

out-group a social group which is the opposite of an 'in-group'. A group which an individual is not a member of; and the individual may feel hostile towards.

Overview and Scrutiny Committees (OSCs) committees of local councils who have social service responsibilities who monitor and scrutinise the planning, provision and operation of NHS services in their area.

P

pacemaker artificial device for controlling the heart rate.

PALS Patient Advice and Liaison Service. These are departments within every NHS Trust that advise patients on the services, and they may deal with queries and complaints.

parasympathetic nervous system a branch of the autonomic nervous system active in peace and contentment.

Parkinson's disease a neurological disorder caused by degeneration of part of the brain.

patriarchy term used by feminists to describe society as organised by men for the benefit of men and the oppression of women.

PCTs Primary Care Trusts set up after 1999 to commission services from hospitals and other agencies to deliver care.

peak-flow monitoring used in asthmatic conditions to measure the maximum speed that air can be forced out from the lungs.

pH a measure of the hydrogen ion concentration of a substance, showing its acidity or alkalinity.

pharmacist qualified professional dispensing prescriptions and giving advice to patients.

phobia an irrational or unreasonable fear which influences an individual's behaviour

physiotherapist a professional who supports people after illness, accidents or surgery to get back to health and fitness through exercise and other techniques.

pilot study a 'dry run' to test out a new data collection tool; doing this allows for modifications and improvements to be made before the actual study begins.

pituitary gland endocrine gland at the base of the brain.

placebo something that looks like a medical intervention, but which in fact does not contain any active treatment at all.

plasma proteins special proteins that circulate in blood.

pleura membranes covering the lungs and inner chest wall.

polydipsia excessive thirst as occurs in untreated diabetes.

polyuria large volumes of urine produced.

population as well as meaning the people who live in a particular area or country, this term is used in research methodology to indicate the total number of people who are being studied.

positivist approach an approach to research which is based in scientific principles of testing theories and reaching generalisations through the use of quantifiable evidence.

poverty a lack of sufficient resources to achieve a standard of living considered to be acceptable in that particular society. Benefit system in UK is based on the idea of an absolute poverty line if the person's income falls below that line they are said to be in poverty. In the European Union, the poverty line is usually drawn at 60 per cent of the average income in that particular society.

PPI Forums these are Patient and Public Involvement forums which replaced CHCs (Community Health Councils) in 2004. They are made up of patients and members of the public who have a special interest in the NHS. They are attached to PCTs and hospital trusts and they monitor services and represent the public.

pre-operational the second stage of Piaget's theory of intellectual development. A pre-logical period when children cannot reason logically.

primary care health care that takes place in the community.

primary data the information collected by a researcher during the course of a study.

primary health care team members of the health care team that are usually based at a health centre or surgery and include practice nurses, health visitors and GPs.

primary prevention prevention of illness and disease through immunisation or by adopting a healthy life style.

privatisation government policy in which the public sector is reduced and services are transferred to private agencies, e.g. gas, water, electricity.

probability in statistics, this term refers to the likelihood of a set of data being obtained. A data set with a probability of 1 is inevitable; that with a probability of 0 is impossible.

progressive taxation direct taxation which increases dependent on the amount of income received. This measure is to achieve a greater equality of distribution of income and wealth in a society.

proportionate stratified sampling a technique to make sure that the subjects chosen for research represent the characteristics of the target population; thus, if 70 per cent of the target population is female, the gender split of subjects in the actual sample must be 70 per cent female, 30 per cent male.

psychodynamic a psychological perspective which interprets human behaviour in terms of a theory of the dynamics of the mind.

psychoneuroimmunology (PNI) a scientific discipline that specifically explores the relationships between the mind and the various systems within the body, in particular the immune system and hormonal systems.

Purkinje fibres modified muscle fibres forming the conducting tissue of the heart.

Q

qualitative data data that cannot usually be expressed simply in terms of numbers. It is often concerned with people's values, attitudes and/or opinions. It is usually collected through interviews but it also may be collected through diaries, life history accounts, focus groups.

quantitative data can be expressed in numerical form. It can also be presented in tables, bar charts, pie charts, graphs, etc.

quota sampling the selection of a specified number of subjects, who satisfy a number of predetermined criteria; often used by market researchers when stopping potential subjects in the street.

R

racism ideas about race are translated into negative feelings and discriminatory action against a particular racial group.

random sampling selection of subjects at random from the sampling frame.

randomisation allocation of a group of selected subjects to either a treatment group or a control group. This can be done manually, or by computer.

randomised clinical controlled trial (RCCT) a research method involving more than one sample group. One group receives a specified treatment, the other doesn't (it either receives another treatment, a placebo or no treatment at all) and the results are compared.

recession deteriorating economic conditions when unemployment increases and productivity declines.

reconstituted families families in which one or both partners have been previously married or cohabiting and children are living with a step-parent and step-brothers or step-sisters. This type of family is becoming increasingly common.

redistribution in which income and wealth are taken from the rich by progressive taxation and given to the poor in the form of benefits.

registration the process through which the CSCI, OFSTED and other bodies assesses whether institutions offering services are suitable to do so.

regression when children under stress revert to a younger way of behaving.

relatability the extent to which research findings may be applicable to other, similar population samples.

reliability the extent to which a set of results can be replicated by repetition of a test, experiment or survey.

research this term is used to refer to a systematic enquiry that is designed to add to existing knowledge and/or to solve a particular problem.

respondent a person who takes part in a survey, and who 'responds' to the questions (either by self-completion of a questionnaire, or during an interview).

risk assessment procedure that assesses the risks in the environment to the service user (unsafe homes). It can also be applied to people with mental health problems when a doctor will decide whether they are a risk to themselves or to others.

rounding an adjustment made to a quantity so that it is expressed as a whole number (rather than as a fraction or as a decimal).

S

S–A node sino-atrial node that is the natural pacemaker in the heart.

sampling the selection of a representative cross-section of the population being studied.

sampling frame a comprehensive list of the potential subjects for a study.

schema an organised pattern of thought.

school nurse registered nurses who visit schools and advise on health issues. They may also be attached to family planning clinic for young people.

secondary data data collected by people other than the researcher of a given project, and found in other published or Internet sources.

secondary health services health services that take place in hospitals.

secondary prevention preventing serious illness and disease by identifying the presence of disease at an early stage through screening.

self-actualisation an important need identified by Maslow which explains that individuals need to fulfil their potential. Most people spend their life focused on deficit needs and do not achieve self actualisation.

self-actualising tendency a natural tendency to develop and grow identified by Carl Rogers. According to Rogers everyone is capable of responding to their inner self-actualising tendency.

self-advocacy the service user is encouraged to speak on their own behalf about the services they need.

semi-structured data information collected about specific topics, but expressed in the respondents' own words.

sensorimotor the first stage in Piaget's theory of intellectual development. Infant's learn to co-ordinate their muscle or motor movements in this stage.

social class the status given to different types of occupation or work.

social exclusion being excluded from opportunity people with fewer life chances to become economically prosperous than the majority of people.

Social Fund budget made available under the Department of Work and Pensions to provide loans to the recipients of social security benefits.

social impact theory we respond to the 'social impact' of the people that surround us. Our behaviour is strongly influenced by our perception of others. We go with the crowd and seek to fit in with the social norms of others.

social role a set of expectations which guide an individual's behaviour in specific circumstances.

Social Security the system of welfare support provided by the state for its citizens.

Social Trends annual digest of statistics produced by the Central Statistical Office.

socialisation the process by which we learn the norms, values and behaviour that makes us a member of a particular group.

speech and language therapist a professional who helps adults and children with communication problems and also with swallowing difficulties.

sphygmomanometer device for measuring blood pressure.

stakeholders a term used by national and local government to cover every agency and individual who has an interest in the way health and care services are organised.

statementing the legal process undertaken by the education authority to identify the individual needs of a child and to decide the level of support available.

statistical significance when figures satisfy certain statistical tests, they are said to have statistical significance.

statutory sector services provided by the state either directly or indirectly. The statutory sector includes services provided by the NHS and by the local council.

strategic health authorities 24 health authorities that are responsible for assessing needs in their area, delivering services through the PCTs and trusts, and monitoring quality of service.

stratified random sampling selection of subjects in proportion to the numbers of a group from a sampling data.

structured data data collected in a standardised way; such data can usually be quantified.

subject as well as meaning a 'topic' (e.g. English, Social Care), the term subject(s) is used in research methodology to indicate the person or people being studied.

Sure Start Centres a programme set up by national government to improve life chances for children and families in deprived areas.

survey a descriptive study which has a very broad scope. It involves the systematic collation and analysis of data from a target population.

sympathetic nervous system branch of the autonomic nervous system that is active in stressful conditions of fright, flight and fight.

systematic review a thorough and systematic comparison of RCCTs to produce convincing evidence for the effectiveness (or otherwise) of a particular drug or treatment.

systole contraction of heart chambers.

T

tachycardia abnormally fast heart rate.

thrombocytes a blood platelet.

tissue typing the composition of the recipient individual's antigenic make-up is determined from blood tests and matched to a donor's make-up so that they are as closely matched as possible to prevent rejection.

trait a stable quality within an individual's personality which may influence their behaviour.

triangulation the comparison of data from different sources on the same subject.

U

unconscious mind within psychodynamic theory the unconscious mind contains drives and memories that influence our behaviour. An individual is not conscious of these influences on his or her behaviour.

unstructured data data that is not tightly controlled by the interviewer, or by the questionnaire being completed. Such data is expressed in the respondents' own words.

V

validity relates to the quality of research results. Data is valid if it accurately measures what it is supposed to measure.

variable something that can occur in different forms, i.e. it can vary in its characteristics.

voluntary services services that are independent of the statutory sector and provide a range of services commissioned by local councils, PCTs and health trusts. They also represent the interests of certain sections of the community and lobby government on their behalf (e.g. Age Concern, Mencap, National Children's Home).

Z

zone of proximal development the limits of development which apply to a particular area of understanding within any individual. The concept of a zone of proximal development might focus teachers on the way they should seek to explain an idea.

Index